Jewish Girls Coming of Age in America, 1860–1920

Jewish Girls Coming of Age in America, 1860–1920

Melissa R. Klapper

NEW YORK UNIVERSITY PRESS
New York and London

NEW YORK UNIVERSITY PRESS
New York and London
www.nyupress.org

Library of Congress Cataloging-in-Publication Data
Klapper, Melissa R.
Jewish girls coming of age in America, 1860–1920 /
Melissa R. Klapper.
p. cm.
1. Any other girls in this whole world like myself: Jewish girls and
adolescence in America— 2. Unless I got more education: Jewish
girls and the problem of education in turn-of-the-century America—
3. Education in the broadest Sense: alternative forms of education
for working class girls— 4. A perfect Jew and a perfect American:
The religious education of Jewish girls— 5. Such a world of pleasure: adolescent Jewish girls and American youth culture.
Includes bibliographical references and index.
ISBN 0–8147–4780–9 (cloth : alk. paper)
1. Jewish girls—United States—Social conditions—19th century.
2. Jewish girls—United States—Social conditions—20th century.
3. Jewish girls—Education—United States. 4. Jewish girls—
United States—Social life and customs—19th century. 5. Jewish
girls—United States—Social life and customs—20th century.
6. Jewish religious education of girls—United States. 7. Jewish
teenagers—United States—Social life and customs—19th century.
8. Jewish teenagers—United States—Social life and customs—
20th century. I. Title.
E184.36.S65K53   2004
305.242'2'089924073—dc22   2004015012

New York University Press books are printed on acid-free paper,
and their binding materials are chosen for strength and durability.

Manufactured in the United States of America

10 9 8 7 6 5 4 3 2 1

Dedicated with love to my parents,
Ferne and Mitchell Klapper,
and my sister, Jennie Klapper Fine,
for giving me an American Jewish girlhood
I will always treasure.

Contents

Acknowledgments

I have incurred many debts, both professional and personal, while writing *Jewish Girls Coming of Age in America, 1860–1920*. As a significant revision of my Rutgers University dissertation, this book has lived through many incarnations. Without the support of numerous teachers and friends, archivists and librarians, grant agencies and academic organizations, none of the work would have been possible.

Let me first express my deep appreciation for the fellowship support provided along the way by the Department of History at Rutgers University; the Feinstein Center for American Jewish History at Temple University; the Bildner Center for the Study of Jewish Life at Rutgers University; the National Women's Studies Association; the Jacob Rader Marcus Center of the American Jewish Archives; the Hadassah-Brandeis Institute at Brandeis University; the National Foundation for Jewish Culture; the College of Liberal Arts and Sciences at Rowan University; and the Lucius N. Littauer Foundation.

While doing the research for this study, I traveled to archives in many cities. I would like to acknowledge the always professional, courteous, and helpful staffs at the Jacob Rader Marcus Center of the American Jewish Archives, the American Jewish Historical Society, the Center for Judaic Studies at the University of Pennsylvania, the Chicago Historical Society, the Chicago Jewish Archives, the Jewish Museum of Maryland, the Jewish Theological Seminary, the Maryland Historical Society, the Special Collections Division of the New York Public Library, the Philadelphia Jewish Archives Center, the Special Collections Division of the Rutgers University Libraries, and the 92nd Street Young Men's/Women's Hebrew Association Archives. The interlibrary loan librarians at Rutgers University and Rowan University were also enormously helpful, as were all the librarians at Baltimore Hebrew University. It would be remiss of me not to mention by name Eric Greenberg, Joy Kingsolver, the late Lily

Schwartz, Steve Siegel, and Erin Titter for their extra efforts on my behalf. I would also like to give special thanks to Kevin Proffitt and his staff at the American Jewish Archives Center in Cincinnati, which was the single facility where I spent the most time. All these research trips were made possible and pleasant in large part by the friends and relatives who opened their homes to me. I am grateful to Beattie Broide, Rachel Meyers and David Berstein, Miriam and David Meyers, Stephen and Cheryl Karesh, and especially my good friends Shira and Boruch Leff and Elky and Reuven Pelberg.

It gives me great pleasure to thank my many mentors. I have been extraordinarily fortunate all my life in my teachers. There is no adequate way to express my gratitude toward Alice Kessler-Harris, who as my graduate advisor and dissertation chair, was and remains an ideal mentor. She has consistently pushed me to new levels of analysis and insight and demanded the highest of standards with an always caring, "tough love" approach. She read more drafts of each chapter during the dissertation phase than I dare to recall, and she has always been committed to me, as to all her students, as a whole person. Gerald Grob, Dee Garrison, Jenna Weissman Joselit, Pamela Nadell, Jonathan Sarna, and Yael Zerubavel generously gave of their time and expertise and offered valuable comments. My undergraduate mentors at Goucher College, especially Peter Bardaglio, Julie Jeffrey, and Laurie Kaplan, were important role models of commitment to both exciting teaching and innovative scholarship. It is an honor to be their colleague now. Many fellow graduate students, particularly Kim Brodkin, Jennie Brier, Idana Goldberg, Jane Rothstein, and Serena Zabin, encouraged me to think "bigger" about my arguments and the implications of my work. My colleagues make the Department of History at Rowan University a remarkably pleasant environment in which to work.

My "nonacademic" friends also played a very important role by keeping me grounded in reality as well as footnotes. Thanks to Devorah Taitelbaum, Rivkah Fischman and family, Malka Miriam Mandel, Ilana and Ammiel Bachrach, Sarah and Bonnie Gersten and family, Stephanie and Moshe Sherman, Mike and Marsha Wasserman, Chevi and Adam Aronson, Judith and Barry Levitt, and Janet and Danny Eisenberg. Most important, as the dedication to this book illustrates, my parents, Ferne and Mitchell Klapper, and my brother-in-law and sister, Josh and Jennie Klapper Fine, have been consistently supportive and loving. I could not have done this work without them.

Introduction

Monday, January 4, 1864
In the evening we sat up in the nursery. Aunt Rachel told us several things that happened to her when she was young. She showed us a Journal that she wrote when she was engaged to get married. . . . I made up my mind that night to write one of the next year. I wonder if I will have patience to continue writing it. It takes but a very few minutes every day. I am sure I waste twice as much time as it would take me to write. . . . A friend of mind says I will go on writing for a month or two and will then stop but this book will speak for itself.

Monday, April 13, 1864
What an Idiot I was to write a Diary.

When Rachel Rosalie Phillips began keeping a diary during her prolonged stay in Washington, D.C., with her uncle and aunt, she took her commitment seriously. She wrote about the dresses she wore to synagogue services, the books she read, the Hebrew she learned from her uncle, the sewing projects she completed with her cousins, and the letters she wrote to her family in New York. Despite the skepticism of her unnamed friend, she did in fact make regular entries in the diary for more than a month or two. Her pleasure in attending social functions, her distaste for working in her uncle's store, and her dismissal of the proposal of marriage from a non-Jewish Union military officer all tell the story of one individual's experiences as an American Jewish girl during the Civil War.[1]

And then the story ends. It ends not with marriage or death, two of the life cycle passages that most typically disrupted the keeping of a diary, but with a cryptic self-denunciation followed only by a few brief entries in

April 1864 and December 1866 and a list of books read in 1866 and 1867. The modern reader can only take Rachel Rosalie Phillips's word for what prompted her to start keeping a diary and can never really know what led her to condemn herself as an idiot and stop writing shortly thereafter. Yet it is in flashes from the past such as these that history is preserved. This is true on a personal or individual level, as is evident from the fact that at some point in her later life Rachel apparently presided over a transcription of her girlhood diary and annotated it in her own handwriting. It is also true on a social or collective level, as the voices of the girls and boys, the young women and young men who lived through, were part of, and contributed to history live on through their own words and deeds.

Jewish Girls Coming of Age in America, 1860–1920 is first and foremost a history of girls. This book places adolescent girls, broadly defined as girls between the ages of twelve and twenty, at the center and explores the late nineteenth- and early twentieth-century development of adolescence from their perspective. Other historians have done similar work, and this book owes an intellectual debt to Joan Jacobs Brumberg, Jane Hunter, and others who have not neglected girls when writing about girlhood.[2] My goal is to explore the multidimensional experiences of girls by focusing on a particular group: adolescent Jewish girls in America during the latter part of the nineteenth century and first decades of the twentieth century. This book therefore also makes a contribution by looking beyond the urban, middle-class, northeastern Protestant girls, who have most often been the subjects of the history of American girls and girlhood. The tripartite identities of adolescent Jewish girls in the United States—female, Jewish, American—all had to be learned within the context of a time period when each of those identities was in flux. Their education, social lives, and religious experiences formed the basis of adolescent lives that Jewish girls believed were of great significance. Standing at the intersection of age, gender, class, ethnicity, and religion, adolescent Jewish girls in America struggled with their identities and their place in history.

As adolescents, girls, Jews, and Americans, they deserve a place in history because of the ways their lives contribute to the story of profoundly gendered encounters between tradition and modernity. While the choices rarely seemed so stark to them, Jewish girls had the delicate task of managing their affinities for both Jewish and American identities while also negotiating the liminal state of adolescence. In their diaries, letters, memoirs, scrapbooks, and other personal papers, they considered the need to balance the various elements of their lives. Both by inclination and communal ascription, they viewed themselves as arbiters of identity and culture brokers. Within their communities, they functioned—sometimes consciously—as both keepers of tradition and agents of acculturation. As a result, Jewish girls invested their adolescence with both familial and communal meaning beyond their own coming of age. In that sense, this book is also about the role gender played in acculturation for a group of adolescents who represented and transmitted elements of modernization to their families and communities. They found modernization neither inevitable nor necessarily positive, often acknowledging that there would be gains and losses within all cultural exchanges. But adolescent Jewish girls also both recognized and were recognized for the role they played in maintaining a particular ethnic identity and religious culture while still aiming for integration into American society at large. Their story is an important part of the fundamental development of ideas about becoming American in a pluralist society.

The encounter between tradition and modernity in America was experienced not only along gender lines but also along lines of class, ethnicity, and race. For the Jewish case, scholars such as Riv-Ellen Prell have concentrated on intraethnic clashes over class and gender, in particular.[3] Prell's exploration of gendered representations common within American Jewish history is a good example of how prescriptive literature could affect people's real lives. Jewish girls were not immune to the images surrounding them, and they made life choices in reaction to cultural productions. Those choices were additionally shaped by the fact that there was never a monolithic or unitary Jewish community in America, and tensions ran high during the turn-of-the-century period of mass migration. Adolescent Jewish girls stand as an example of the critical processes at work in the acculturation experiences of all turn-of-the-century immigrants to America. However, even historians such as Sydney Stahl Weinberg and Susan A. Glenn, who have written about young Jewish women, as opposed to Jewish womanhood, have primarily focused on the iconic American Jewish "sweatshop girls."[4] An additional goal of this book is to pay close attention to the Jewish community in America *prior* to mass migration and especially to the third, fourth, or even fifth generation American-born Jewish girls of the late nineteenth and early twentieth centuries. There were important differences but also important similarities among Jewish girls of all backgrounds during this period.

The issue of similarity and difference is what makes a study of the experiences of lived adolescence among Jewish girls such an important part of the history of youth in America. Exploring the lives of Jewish girls illustrates how a particular cohort learned, played, prayed, and related to their families and communities. It is also the case, however, that charting their history contributes to a coherent vision of turn-of-the-century adolescence that to some degree transcended ethnicity and even class, though never gender. When adolescent experiences rather than immigration or religious experiences are foregrounded, it becomes apparent that Jewish girls participated in an American girl culture of great significance. This girl culture's significance was not least due to the fact that it was capacious enough to accommodate a diverse population of girls and provide them with similar experiences despite their striking differences. Jewish girls had many goals, ambitions, interests, and desires during the period between 1860 and 1920. Some, related to religion and ethnicity, may have been different from those of other girls in America, but most, relating to gender and education, were the same. What makes Jewish girls so valuable as historical subjects is the intersection of their differences with the preponderance of their similarities.

The history of youth is a curious thing. Full of insight into the development of childhood and adolescence in a wide variety of times and places, it provides analysis of multiple topics: toys, clothing, juvenile literature, education, play, delinquency, parenting techniques, and courtship practices, among others. Yet children and adolescents themselves are oddly absent from much of this literature, which tends to be grounded in cultural studies and to focus more on the construction of images and discourses of youth than on the lived experiences of youth. The problem is particularly evident in the study of girls, a field for which the nickname of "girl culture" clearly demonstrates the methodological approach of culture and gender studies. There are exceptions, naturally, and there are also good reasons for why the historiography has developed in this direction. Prescriptive sources for the history of childhood and youth are far more accessible than descriptive sources left by children themselves. Even this book about American Jewish girls, with its explicit goal of analyzing lived experience, still must rely on prescriptive sources to some extent. It is neither possible nor desirable to draw impenetrable lines of demarcation between the culture of youth and the lived experiences of youth. The most rewarding history may lie in the intriguing spaces between representation and lived experience. However, with rich studies of historical representations of childhood and adolescence in place, it is important to begin to shift the center of attention back to the children and adolescents who lived history. No matter how tantalizing the trail of past representations of childhood and adolescence, it would be a mistake to erase the identity, experience, and agency of children and adolescents themselves.

With the goal of capturing both Jewish girls' specific experiences and the broader adolescent world in which they lived, the first chapter of this book provides the necessary context of the history of adolescence, the history of Jews in America, and the history of gender roles at the turn of the century. The shared concerns of Jewish girls regardless of background and historical moment yield a solid foundation for the construction of a collective history. The second chapter explores the variety of Jewish girls' experiences with formal education, which was an issue of critical importance to most of them. The growth of secondary education was one of the most significant factors in the development of adolescence in America, and Jewish girls participated in that process, with all its promise and pitfalls. Working-class Jewish girls, many of whom were immigrants or the daughters of immigrants, had considerably less access to formal education and relied instead on multiple forms of broadly defined alternative education for their learning experiences. The third chapter analyzes the variety of communal institutions that served as providers of alternative education to Jewish girls. The fourth chapter focuses on the development of religious education within the Jewish community and concentrates on the role gender always played in that development. The various Jewish educational systems were microcosms of the issues of acculturation and tradition that continuously confronted Jews in America. Adolescent Jewish girls found that their social lives also continuously confronted them with decisions about how to prioritize their interests and identity. The fifth and final chapter considers the ways in which they were engaged in contemporary youth culture within the limits of Jewish identity.

Sources

The sources for this study of Jewish girls in America are rich and varied but, like experience itself, fragmented into kaleidoscopic patterns. The source of light illuminating the patterns of any particular girl's adolescence could change—now religion, now gender, now class—but turning the kaleidoscope of experience made it possible for her to create a coherent identity and for the careful observer to perceive the design emerging from the fragments of the historical record. The word "identity" hovers around the edges of the kaleidoscopic patterns and appears only rarely in the material on which this study is based. Yet it lights up the past and provides a framework for the fragments of late nineteenth- and early twentieth-century Jewish girls' experience still available today. Re-creating the patterns of adolescent Jewish girls' lives not only restores an overlooked group to the pattern but also illuminates some of the shadows cast by neglect on the larger designs of gender, religion, and acculturation in turn-of-the-century American history.

The kaleidoscopic materials on which this study are based comprise three major categories of sources: personal papers, including diaries, memoirs, correspondence, and other manuscript material; institutional papers, including school records, published conference proceedings, organizational reports, and social service and philanthropic records; and American Jewish periodical literature, including children's publications, women's periodicals, and local and national Jewish newspapers. In addition to these major categories of evidence, numerous documents drawn from contemporary educational, social, and cultural writings as well as religious texts and general audience periodicals provide evidence for the contexts in which Jewish girls experienced their adolescence. Less traditional sources such as tattered report cards, painstakingly preserved scrapbooks, dog-eared confirmation programs, and randomly saved event tickets provide rich texture for their collective story.

The bulk of source material drawn upon here has languished unread and unappreciated. Located in archives large and small, the nearly one hundred and fifty memoirs and two dozen or so diaries whose authors are at the heart of this book amply represent a group of people whose gender, youth, and religious background have relegated them to the sidelines. American women's history has marginalized Jewish women; American Jewish history has marginalized women; Jewish women's history has marginalized nineteenth-century middle-class Jewish women; American social history has marginalized adolescents. The very existence of these turn-of-the-century diaries and memoirs demonstrates that Jewish girls valued their individuality and subjectivity in ways that demand historical consideration. While personal narratives have long been key documents in social and women's history, the Jewish girls whose lives have so much to offer history have never before been viewed as windows into the development of the American Jewish community and the emergence of American girlhood more generally.

Private expressions of identity appear in the diaries, memoirs, and correspondence of Jewish girls, who kept valuable records of their longings, loves, and lives. Religion, education, and socialization were virtually always a central part of recorded experience and memory. Most Jewish girls, grounded in both American and Jewish value systems that promoted family and marriage, envisioned a future as wives and mothers. Many of them, however, buoyed by individual inclinations toward education, jobs, religiosity, and social activism, were not content to imagine themselves as purely domestic beings. In some cases they hoped merely to stay in school a little longer or exercise greater control over courtship or spend more time out of the house than their mothers. Only a very few asserted their autonomy by turning away from all that their mothers' lives represented. They reacted to the new opportunities opening to women without necessarily rejecting more traditional life patterns.

While the content and form of personal papers varies depending on the historical setting of each girl's life, identity forms an important thematic link among young Jewish women of very different circumstances. These personal papers are windows into the lives of individuals who juggled conflicting expectations and available opportunities while trying to assert their own desires and needs. The struggles between society, community, family, and individual for the power to shape the futures of Jewish girls are reflected in their perceptions of their own experiences. Some of these sources reflect consciously on the effect of American and Jewish identity on the authors' lives. Others are less reflexive but still valuable indications of the centrality of being and becoming American to American Jewish women's history. The central tension between domesticity and opportunity that is so evident on the structural level in institutional and organizational records and on the communal level in the American Jewish press appears most poignantly in the papers of the young Jewish women themselves.

The institutional records of schools and organizations' activities reveal a great deal about the priorities and agendas of segments of the American Jewish community at various times. In a frenzy of anxiety to do the correct thing, many philanthropic, educational, and social service agencies kept copious records of their activities, successes, and failures. The preservation of committee and board meeting minutes, published annual reports, student and client lists, budgets, and correspondence allows a detailed look into the goals and rationales for a variety of institutions. School records, in particular, testify to the not uncommon presence of deep social and cultural divides between educators and students.

The contemporary American Jewish press offered a constant stream of observations on issues relating to women, education, and the process of adapting to America. Depending on the orientation of the periodical, editors and journalists reflected the range of opinions on issues affecting the community. Beginning in the 1860s, the proliferation of English, German, and Yiddish periodicals in the urban centers home to large concentrations of Jews enjoyed a fairly wide circulation that created a public sense of identity for American Jewish communities. All these periodicals addressed themselves to the full range of problems that faced their Jewish constituencies, including concerns with education, religious training, women's status and activities, and family issues. All employed women as regular contributors. Annual reports from communally supported homes and schools for girls, symposia on the appropriate education of women, coverage of Jewish women of note, and discussions of women and work all demonstrated the vital interest in Jewish women, as well as indicating sizeable female audiences. The American Jewish community prided itself on its high level of literacy, and the popularity of these periodicals makes them important sources for gauging the preferences and problems of their readers.

Taken all together, these sources allow for the re-creation of the American Jewish lives many girls led during the late nineteenth and early twentieth centuries. Because the bulk of the archival research was purposely done in places other than New York City, this study also illuminates Jewish communal life outside New York, an important corrective to the historiography's continuing reliance on New York as the model for all American Jewish development. While New York was indeed home to the largest concentration of Jews during this time period, there were other significant centers of Jewish life. Baltimore, Boston, Chicago, Cincinnati, Philadelphia, and San Francisco, among other cities, all boasted Jewish populations in their own right. They were also home to significant numbers of middle-class Jews, many of western or central European descent, whose ancestors had emigrated during the first half of the nineteenth century. The earlier Jewish migrants settled all over the interior of the United States as well as urban centers, resulting in small Jewish communities with very different kinds of histories. Girls growing up in these smaller communities sometimes faced different issues than their urban counterparts, although they shared concerns as well. While this study intentionally focuses on an understudied group—adolescent girls—who lived in understudied places—Jewish communities outside New York—the combination of local and national source material allows for some powerful conclusions about American Jewish girls, in general, and the processes of cultural adaptation and social integration for American Jewry as a whole.

The fact that this study analyzes archival material previously untapped and examines the voices of girls previously unheard does not mask some of the methodological problems attendant on all primary sources. American Jewish periodicals had highly variable circulation rates and may not have reached as wide an audience as they claimed. Many of the most popular periodicals originated in New York, reinforcing New York's place as the self-proclaimed center of American Jewish life. Their format, following that of most other contemporary American periodicals, also presents some difficulties, as they frequently reprinted whole news stories, fiction, and didactic material from other publications without attribution. Institutional papers offer a different set of challenges. In many cases Jewish organizations were so caught up in the turn-of-the-century concern with rationalization and professionalization that the form of the reports and records obscures the people involved by highlighting procedure instead. The condescension with which many, though not all, middle-class communal activists treated recent immigrants suffuses the papers of institutions set up to promote acculturation. The self-help organizations immigrants created for themselves were similarly shadowed by a pervasive negativity toward already Americanized Jews. With the important exceptions of institutions founded expressly for, and sometimes by, girls and women, gender conventions limited women's participation in Jewish communal life throughout much of this period, leaving the activities of girls difficult to trace in even the most voluminous papers.

Personal papers, the richest and most meaningful sources, must be used with care as well. The published and unpublished autobiographies and memoirs housed in archives and on library shelves yield a wealth of information and fascinating details about Jewish girls' experiences. Yet the memory of girlhood is inherently complex. Lapses of memory haunt the memoirs and other testimony of older women recalling their lives of long ago. For questions of identity and sensibility, the emotional accuracy of firsthand accounts may be just as important as "the facts," but the interpretive twist girls grown into women give their own narratives still needs to be taken into account. Even the most acute memoirist or autobiographer writes from a set of psychological and emotional distances that complicate the life records.[5]

Even more than memoirs, diaries allow immediate glimpses into Jewish girls' experiences as they lived through them. However, diaries are also constructed narratives and as such notoriously difficult sources. Despite the appeal of the guided tour through experience they provide, diaries are inherently limited sources. Many diaries surviving in the archives represent only one installment of a multivolume personal guidebook. No key to abbreviations, no glossary, and no introduction to characters appear at the front or back of the often small and crumbling books. The diarists wrote for any number of purposes. Some maintained brief records of daily activities, some kept spiritual journals, some reflected at length on their aspirations and ambitions, and some complained about their families and disappointments. Most never intended to lead a tour through their lives, and their directions are limited to areas they were willing to chart by committing experience to paper and thus to a potential—if usually unimagined—readership. Explorers who map experience through diaries discover signposts of individuality in addition to well-traveled roads of collective experience.

While the methodological issues are real, the sources for this study nonetheless allow for a detailed collective portrait of adolescent Jewish girls in America between 1860 and 1920. The research design provides for many different kinds of evidence to corroborate each other. Focusing on adolescent girls provides a fresh approach to institutional records and Jewish periodicals and identifies as important previously overlooked materials of this nature. Most of the letters, personal papers, and memoirs—and virtually all of the diaries—used to capture their experiences have never been used before. They are previously untapped veins of rich historical ore that, once mined, reveal the multifaceted lives of a significant group of people. Jewish girls spoke for themselves in the past, and a major goal of this study is not only to let them speak for themselves again but also to illuminate the ways in which their words and deeds reflect their engagement with the important issues of their historical moments.

Girls and Diaries

Diaries are among the key sources for a more subjective history of adolescent Jewish girls and as such require special consideration. Like countless other girls, the majority of them middle-class daughters with time and space enough to keep regular records of their lives. Jewish girls, too, filled pages and pages, ranging from terse summaries of each day's events to long passages of passionate introspection.[6] Keeping diaries was one of the ways in which Jewish girls' habits resembled those of their non-Jewish counterparts. Adolescent girls who kept diaries were balancing the individual expression prized by modernity with the conventional form of female writing most accepted by tradition.

Because diary keeping was so widespread a practice, a number of standardized versions appeared. Jennie Franklin's 1890 diary was typical. A leather-bound book with a flap that fastened in front, Jennie's *American Diary* was mass-produced by Case, Lockwood, & Brainard Company and included not only a calendar at the front but also charts of postage rates, astronomical calculations, moon phases, and weights and measures, among other features.[7] Some girls used five-year diaries that provided a page for each date divided into five small sections so that one book could be used over a period of five years. Other girls used blank school notebooks.

Physical format notwithstanding, the diarists made their records very personal. All kinds of material went into Jewish girls' diaries. Rachel Rosalie Phillips immodestly wrote, "I do not think I ever looked better" than in the white tarlatan dress and pink flowers she wore to an 1864 party in Washington, D.C. Jennie Franklin preceded each day's entry with a literary quote and attribution and also kept track of her cash accounts in her diary. Rachel Phillips in the 1860s, Amelia Allen in the 1870s, Ann Green in the 1920s, and others kept lists of the books they had read in the backs of their diaries. Marie Syrkin copied the poems she wrote into the plain notebook she used as a diary. Emily Frankenstein pasted photographs, swatches of fabric, and even a dried pressed rose into her diary. Mathilde Kohn, far away from her friends after immigrating in 1866, and Ann Green, temporarily separated from her college classmates during winter break in 1922, both used their diaries to keep track of letters received and sent. The form of the diaries may have been standardized, but the content was highly individual.[8]

As the most direct, though still problematic, sources for Jewish girls' personal experiences, diaries provide unique access into adolescence. Like the concept of youth itself, keeping a diary was hardly new to the end of the nineteenth century. Women, in particular, had long been associated with the kind of intensely private writing that characterized the diaries of

Tuesday June 11, 1918

A little before noon, Jerry came over. He brought me his golf clubs to use while he's gone. We were going downtown for lunch and afterward Jerry had some things to do. Before we left, I sewed a sergeant ensignia on his sleeve. He is expecting to be made a sergeant any day and had his old one with him.

We went to Grant Dewey's first and had our picture taken together. It was a notion — but we were happy — and it was only for ourselves. Mr. Dewey teased us though.

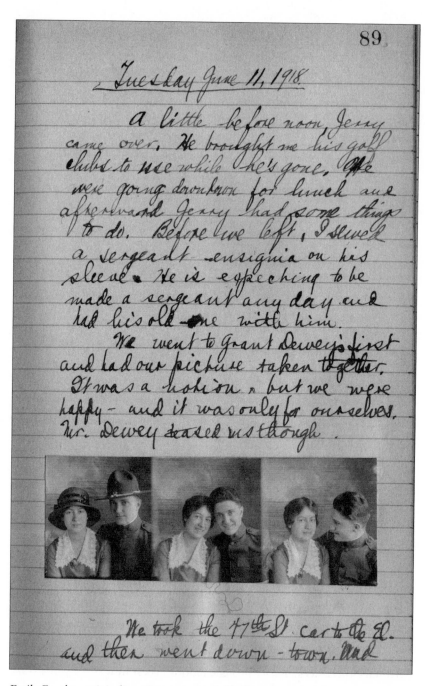

We took the 47th St car to the El. and then went down-town. And

Emily Frankenstein's diary, June 11, 1918. Emily, age 18, is pictured in Chicago with her boyfriend Jerry, who is wearing his World War I army uniform.
Courtesy of the Chicago Historical Society.

adolescent girls.[9] Frequently barred from public expression by constraints of gender, women turned to diaries as outlets for their creative impulses. Even when the serial form of women's diaries paralleled that of men's diaries, the topics and attitudes often differed as one expression of the internal differences resulting from external gender distinctions. Women often treated their diaries as emotional confidantes, confessing their inner feelings through writing when no person was available or seemed an appropriate recipient of such confidences. Even when women's diaries appeared to be a collection of matter-of-fact entries about the weather, housework, and routine activities, the very act of recording such information reflected the value diarists saw in even their mundane lives.[10] Some theorists have suggested that women were particularly drawn to keeping diaries as a way to assert their identities in the face of their limited opportunities for self-definition. Others have explained that the flexibility of the form of diaries appealed to women whose time was not necessarily their own to manage at will. Still others point out that as a literary tradition of female writing, diaries fulfilled women's desires to establish themselves within a history that all too often overlooked the female experience.[11]

It is highly unlikely that any of the adolescent Jewish girls who kept diaries devoted much thought to these abstract concerns. Yet many of them did reflect on the act of keeping a diary. One of the most common conventions of keeping a diary was to dismiss its importance and question its necessity. The opening entry in Eliza Moses's diary, which she started just after the Civil War broke out, was typical of the combined sense of purpose and self-deprecation found in girls' diaries.

> I begin tonight what I have long wished to begin, but something which I have never thought myself competent to do. Nor do I feel competent enough to do so now, but have at least common-sense enough to write simple facts and such things in general as I feel like writing. I will not pledge myself to write any stated time or length, but have made up my mind to write when and how I feel inclined, as I am not going to let any, or at least very few persons see this nonsense: for such it must be if I write it.[12]

Eliza, along with many of her contemporaries, was uneasy about asserting that her life was significant enough to justify placing herself at the center of a personal narrative. In 1862, nineteen-year-old Bertha Wehle wondered, "Can I, in the monotony of my daily life, find enough of interest to write in a journal?"[13] Thirteen years later in Philadelphia, Fannie Allen was eager to keep a diary but worried that "so little happens in a week that it will scarcely require a ream of paper to meet the demands of my ready pencil." She experienced some trouble finding something to say every day, as "my life is so monotonous that the daily routine is not worth writing down." A year later she complained that "nothing startling ever occurs to break the treadmill of daily existence except in books."[14] Two generations after Fannie, Marie Syrkin wrote in the same vein that her commitment to keeping a diary was confounded by the "meaningless and wearying tale of futile aspirations and desires" that characterized her days.[15] Whether they began to keep diaries during the 1860s or the 1910s, most girls exhibited a need to disparage their personal writing before proceeding to explore their satisfaction or discontent with their current lives, express their hopes for the future, and consider their relationships to family, friends, and God.

Despite their reservations about "the daily round of littles that large life compound[s]," most of these girls turned to their diaries regularly.[16] Bella Weretnikow made daily entries even when she had to stay up after a late night of studying to do so.[17] Seventeen-year-old Rosa Feinberg used her diary as a confidante, writing in 1868

> I have everything that I need . . . a good home a kind mother & a good Sister but still I am dissatisfied and why? oh this longing, this longing, if only I knew what would fill the void in my heart, or if only I had a friend to whom I could speak but in this world there is no such thing as friend but one consolation I have & that is I can at least confide to you dear book my thoughts and longings.[18]

Sometimes special events prompted girls to become regular diarists. Though she did not quite live up to her decision "to write down all my experiences of my trip right away," Mathilde Kohn began a diary when she and her mother and sister emigrated from Prague to the United States in 1866.[19] Lacking such an obvious event to inspire her, Marie Syrkin found it easier to keep a diary when she was in a bad mood or troubled about something. Without the stimulus of real or imagined turmoil, she had "no desire to write now, but methinks this diary would be a doleful collection if I only recorded my frenzies of grief and morbid fantasies.

And yet I truly know not what to say!"[20] Nevertheless, she was a fairly faithful diarist who made regular entries.

Family members generally supported the practice of keeping a diary. They did not see the individual expression of diary writing as a threat to family cohesion. Though he gently derided the amount of time his daughters spent "filling up those books with nonsense," Clara and Alice Solomon's father went to a great deal of trouble during the Civil War to provide them with appropriate books in occupied New Orleans. It was difficult for him to keep up with his daughters' prolific writing, however. Clara, who addressed her diary as "Philomen," commented in 1861, "Alice and I are 'booking' it. . . . And indeed we do devote a lot of time to you. Many a leisure moment would we have did we not consider the duty we owe to you. . . . Alice has just been writing in her beautiful book, but two weeks and it is one half through."[21] Emily Frankenstein's father also gave her the books she used as diaries, and she promised him to "try to fill them with lively interesting and pleasant accounts of happenings and also with my loveliest nicest thoughts."[22] Though she did not write every day, she usually updated her diary if she had let anything important pass unremarked.

Support from family members and others did not entitle them to read the diaries they encouraged girls to write. Unlike the Christian spiritual accountings or diaries kept explicitly for parents and teachers by middle-class Protestant girls, Jewish girls' diaries seem to have been private affairs.[23] Emily's father may have given her a blank diary, but he certainly was not the intended audience for her description of her clandestine relationship with her boyfriend Jerry. In her diary Bella Weretnikow respectfully but repeatedly rejected her mother's life, secure in the knowledge that her immigrant mother could not even read the English in which the diary was written. Marie Syrkin confessed that she was "afraid to write frankly even in this sanctuary" because she worried about deceiving herself, not because she feared someone else had access to her diary.[24] Private, individual expression was an acceptable part of these girls' adolescent experiences that in no way threatened their roles as family members.

With few exceptions, the diarists were not rushing toward modern independence, particularly if that independence implied disconnection. They were tightly bound to family, religious culture, and tradition, and for the most part were content to be so bound. Although many things changed in girls' lives between 1860 and 1920, there are remarkable thematic consistencies in their diaries. Even a cursory reading makes it clear that Jewish girls' senses of self were a product of their effort to resolve the tensions of blending particular family culture and religious and educational experiences within the context of the options available to adolescents. All the diarists contended with similar concerns and problems while they came of age as young women, Jews, and Americans, although few seemed to realize that their private struggles were shared by many of their contemporaries. The recurrent themes that appeared in the diaries allow them to serve as effective and reliable historical sources for Jewish girls' lives despite all the major changes of the period. Friendship, marital prospects, educational opportunity, religious sentiment and observance, nationalism, and social life were important to girls across the span of these decades. If in 1896 Bella Weretnikow had read Fannie Allen's 1876 diary, she would have recognized her own patriotic appreciation of the United States. Ann Green, whose social life in 1922 was constrained by the paucity of available Jewish men in Maine, would have sympathized with Eliza Moses's similar problem in the rural South during the Civil War. In 1890, Jennie Franklin might have been less anxious about choosing between social and educational activities if she had known of Bertha Wehle's comparable dilemma thirty years earlier. It is easy to imagine these girls recognizing themselves in each other despite widely varying personalities and backgrounds. They experienced adolescence over a long and complicated time period, yet there is striking similarity in themes, topics, and personal expression found in their diaries.

The strengths of the shared experiences captured in the diaries outweigh the limitations, but limitations there are. The conventions of diary keeping among middle-class women and girls seems to have filtered out the potentially abrasive nature of the girls' adolescence, even when family, school, or religious conflict is evident. With the exception of the twentieth-century diarists like Marie Syrkin and Emily Frankenstein, sexuality was erased from adolescent Jewish girls' diaries in ways unlikely to reflect the realities of at least some of their lives. In general, little dissension appears in the diaries, which may signal the reluctance to pull away from their families that most of the diarists felt. In the cases of Eliza Moses, who lamented the death of her sweetheart in a Civil War battle, and Amelia and Fannie Allen, who bemoaned their apparent inability to find husbands in 1876, conflict was the result of difficulty in staying within or replicating the family circle rather than rejecting it. While it would be anachronistic to assume that continuous strife was a natural part of adolescence, its absence in Jewish girls' diaries does raise the question of what was omitted. However, the greater presence of conflict in the diaries of girls born after 1895 suggests that the pull of youth culture and adolescent autonomy accelerated with the twentieth century.

It is worth pointing out that the girls whose diaries are still extant as many as 140 years later were probably not "average" American Jewish girls, although their collective experiences do illuminate the average American Jewish girl's experience. In many, though certainly not all, cases, women's diaries are preserved as records of lives outstanding. Adolescent diaries are no exception. Jennie Franklin, for instance, became a prominent clubwoman and activist in the Chicago reform community of the turn of the century. Another adolescent diarist, Marie Syrkin, emerged as a leading American Zionist and intellectual during the 1930s. In spite of the later accomplishments that mark at least some of the diarists as anything but typical, their diaries were individual accounts without necessarily being accounts of turning away from a sense of community. Like "average" Jewish girls, the diarists relied on an interlocking set of family, religious, social, and educational experiences to counteract the uncertainty they felt as individuals.

Two concluding remarks about sources are in order. It should be noted that virtually all the personal papers this study draws upon were only serendipitously saved from the literal dustbin of history. As such, they do not and cannot provide a full accounting of any one individual's life. With the exception of the few adolescent Jewish girls who grew up to become famous women, there is virtually no way to track an otherwise "ordinary" Jewish girl of the late nineteenth or early twentieth century who kept a diary or scrapbook as an adolescent. Not even later fame necessarily contributes to a fuller record of someone's early life. In all cases, presumption of later marriage (a near inevitability for Jewish women during this period) further complicates the issue of tracking these girls through life, as not even basic census records would be useful without knowledge of the girls' later married names. As a result, it is virtually impossible to follow girls past the arbitrarily rescued records of their own lives. Even in those happy cases where family members eventually donated personal papers to an archive and thus provided some clues as to the girls' later lives, the paper and photographic trail is limited at best. In fact, in several instances where family members did donate their grandmothers' diaries or memoirs, they often provided only heavily edited versions of them. The "purest" sources are thus often the ones with the least amount of accompanying material. This is the case even for memoirs written by adult women recalling their adolescence, since many of the memoirs used as sources in this book were written for family members and not for some unimagined public audience.

Finally, it should also be noted that the purpose of this study is to explore the experiences of adolescent girls, not the women they would later become. As a discipline, the history of childhood and youth strives to focus on children and adolescents *during their childhood and adolescence* and not to cast the long shadow of their adulthood over their youth. It is important to learn about Jewish girls from diaries, letters, and other personal papers that take seriously the concerns of youth because they were the products of youth. The value of these sources is severely undermined by projecting their authors into their future before they arrived there, even on the rare occasion when that is possible. Therefore, the first time any girl about whom there is more information appears in the text, a brief biographical sketch is attached to the relevant endnote. However, only rarely will references to any girl's future life be found in the book itself.

1

"Any Other Girls in This Whole World Like Myself"

Jewish Girls and Adolescence in America

During the winter of 1889–1890, the editors of the nationally circulated weekly *Jewish Messenger* decided to sponsor a written symposium on the topic of "The American Jewess." In a publication that had always run numerous articles by, about, and for women, this idea was not particularly surprising. Other Jewish periodicals had carried out similar projects, and during the 1860s, *Jewish Messenger* itself had run a series of articles on "The Religious Education of Our Females."[1] The editors contacted a number of Jewish women and asked them to comment on the status of the American Jewess. As the introduction to the published symposium explained, "the question was thus worded so as to elicit the opinions as to her education from every point of view—the religious, intellectual, social, and economic." The introduction went on to explain that *Jewish Messenger*'s motive for organizing this discussion was a firm belief in "the desirability of the Jewess taking a more active part in the American synagogue."[2] A consideration of American Jewish women's status would provide ample evidence that women were ready, willing, and able to take their place in American Judaism—indeed, that they had already done so to a considerable degree. The symposium ran for four consecutive weeks in March 1890.

The women who contributed to the *Jewish Messenger* symposium were a varied lot. Some, such as educational administrator and communal activist Julia Richman and playwright Martha Morton, were nationally prominent.[3] Others, such as public school principal Ella Jacobs and Young Women's Union founder Fanny Binswanger, were highly visible in their local or regional Jewish communities.[4] Some lived in cities with large Jewish communities and some did not. Some of the contributors were married and some were not. Some were traditionally observant and some supported radical reform in Judaism. What they shared was a devotion to the Jewish community and a conviction that women should not only have a prominent place in that community but in fact were essential to building and shaping it. For all the writers, the key to present and future success in this vital endeavor was the next generation of American Jewish women. Jewish girls, they argued, were the most important members of the American Jewish community. Girls bore the responsibility and the privilege of shaping the future. The original topic about the American Jewess was interpreted by virtually every symposium contributor as a question about Jewish girls in America. The writers invested Jewish girls' broadly defined education with significance beyond their own coming of age. The girls' personal and collective struggles to define an identity reflected the struggle of the American Jewish community as a whole to maintain a particular ethnic identity and religious culture while still aiming for integration into American society at large. As they had already been for at least thirty years, Jewish girls in America would serve as both guardians of tradition and agents of acculturation.

The contributors to the symposium drew on a variety of approaches to these weighty matters. As Richman explained, "The American Jewess must be regarded as a triangular unit, which requires development in three directions lest the harmony of the whole be destroyed." Any American Jewish girl must necessarily deal with nationality, religion, and gender simultaneously.[5] Like Richman, most of the symposium contributors wrote not only out of their professional or social expertise but also out of their own past experiences as Jewish girls in America.

A few of the writers believed gender was the fundamental consideration and stressed preparation for womanhood above all else. Annie Nathan Meyer, who had the previous year been among the founders of Barnard College, stated baldly, "I do not know that I advise any particular training for Jewish young ladies beyond the best that can be had for all young ladies."[6] Others, including Richman, agreed that the American Jewess was "first, a woman," but argued that as womanhood itself was undergoing such dramatic change, all American girls would grow up into a world greatly enlarged for women as the century drew to a close. Writing from Richmond, Virginia, Binswanger believed "the American Jewess stands in the same relation to the changing conditions of our time as do her sisters of other faiths." For Binswanger as for others, girls' comprehensive education in matters intellectual, moral, and domestic should serve as the foundation for Jewish womanhood as it would for American womanhood.[7]

Another group of symposium participants disagreed with the idea that Jewish girls' primary identity was female. Judaism was the vital center as far as they were concerned. Belle Minzesheimer of New York wrote, "I consider, above all things, the Jewess of to-day should be imbued with a more decided faith in her religion." For these authors, it was neither possible nor desirable to separate womanhood and Judaism, since Jewish girls would presumably become Jewish mothers in due time. Therefore, wrote one author, "the training of girls is far more important than that of boys, because in their hands again rests the education of the next generation." Helen K. Weil of Kansas City agreed, urging attention to religious feeling and learning among girls because "they are the future mothers of its Hebrew citizens, and upon them depends what the coming Jew will be." Just as the authors arguing for primacy of womanhood had to deal with major changes, so did the authors focusing on religion. American Judaism was undergoing its own period of dramatic shifts and realignments. The writers acknowledged this issue but neatly sidestepped it with a show of nondenominationalism that belied the religious tensions of the times. Jacobs, for example, explained that every Jewish girl "must necessarily be trained in Judaism, be it orthodoxy or reform, it matters not; but she must be taught consistency, unwavering devotion to those great principles of our faith which none can deny." In this view, Judaism was too critical, too basic to the experiences of Jewish girls to be weakened by petty denominationalism.[8]

A minority of the writers argued that American identity should come first for American Jewish girls, even while admitting the difficulties. As Minnie D. Louis, an educator and civil servant, carefully elaborated, "An American is an American whether professing Catholicism, Protestantism, Judaism, or Atheism, and the consideration of a special training for the American Jewess is suggestive of a separateness that should be avoided."[9] Another author emphasized that environment, especially national environment, "is a more powerful agent than any that can be evoked by specific acts of training." "In our land," she continued, "the entire atmosphere is changed," and American influence would inevitably be the most important factor in any girls' coming of age. Yet any author writing in 1890 could not help but be aware of the beginnings of a massive wave of immigration that would probably spark transformations in American identity parallel to those occurring in Judaism and notions of womanhood.[10]

As the symposium both consciously and unconsciously made clear, identity for American Jewish girls was no simple thing to explain or examine, let alone prioritize. Elements of national, religious, and gender identity necessarily interacted with one another. Many of the contributors recognized this reality and addressed it, most often in discussing motherhood and morality in a changing world. Rachel Menken, for instance, staunchly believed that "motherhood and wifehood are her noblest destiny" but encouraged every American girl to "take her place in the onward march of progress" by availing herself of new opportunities in education and work. Menken hoped each girl, equipped with new knowledge, skills, and legal status, would in her role as mother eventually "cooperate in the changing conditions of her time, that the problems of civilization may be helped by her moral force." Several of the other writers agreed with these sentiments but challenged the premise that all American Jewish girls would automatically become wives and mothers. They pointed out that traditional understandings of destined motherhood and domesticity could and should not be taken for granted. "Girls, we cannot all be wives; the supply is greater than the demand," wrote Richman, herself an unmarried professional woman. "J" commented on the "gradual, but accepted and acknowledged fact that woman can no longer look to married life as the *positive means* of making her future a busy and happy one." The world, these authors agreed, was a rapidly changing place.[11]

What, then, to do in this changing environment? According to the thoughtful prescriptions freely dispensed in the symposium, American Jewish girls stood at the threshold of a modernizing world. Their decisions about which opportunities to embrace or reject, which traditions to affirm or deny, which points of their triangulated identity to emphasize or ignore, would not only affect their own individual lives but also their families and communities. During this stage between childhood and adulthood, just beginning to be known as adolescence, Jewish girls faced both tremendous freedom to choose and serious constraints on their choices. Jewish tradition and gender norms could not lightly be cast aside, even in a land of apparent freedom or a time of apparent change. The 1890 *Jewish Messenger* symposium provided a valuable communal forum for taking stock of these issues.

Jewish girls themselves, individually and collectively, were engaged in their own forms of taking stock both before and after these communal moments. One of the Jewish girls considering on her own many of the same concerns addressed in the symposium was Jennie Franklin. Sixteen going on seventeen in 1890, Jennie lived in Chicago's middle-class Jewish community. Her father, Henry, had immigrated from Germany in 1867, and her mother, Hannah Mayer, was the Chicago-born daughter of German immigrants. She had three brothers and one sister. Throughout her adolescence (and much of her later life), Jennie wrote briefly in her diary almost daily. There is no evidence in the diary Jennie kept so faithfully that she read the *Jewish Messenger* symposium. As staunch Reform Jews, the Franklins would have been more likely to subscribe to *American Hebrew* or *American Israelite,* both known for more liberal religious outlooks than *Jewish Messenger.* Yet her diary entries for 1890 touch on all the issues raised in the symposium: education, religion, social life, and the anxiety-inducing struggle to find an identity as an American Jewish girl on the cusp of womanhood. Jennie's individual narrative of identity formation as constructed in her diary both reinforces and personalizes the discussion in the *Jewish Messenger* symposium.[12]

Education, broadly defined, was public high school junior Jennie's primary concern. She completed her school work before doing anything else. During particularly busy times, this commitment meant that her diary entries might consist of the single word "studied" each day for a week at a time. As well as high school, extracurricular activities such as lectures, reading, and literary clubs formed an important part of Jennie's education. Among the lecturers she heard speak in 1890 were Felix Adler, founder of the Ethical Culture Society, speaking about children's religious education, and Emil Hirsch, rabbi of the Franklins' synagogue, speaking about Jewish history. Jennie was an avid reader who generally preferred serious literature that would enhance her knowledge. After finishing a historical novel in April, she wrote, "Very much pleased; think I learned some history and will remember it longer than if I had studied it." She also attended Chicago's Hebrew Literary Society meetings on Friday nights and often served as the appointed "critic" for the papers presented by the members, even running for vice-presidency of the group. Although Jennie usually enjoyed Hebrew Literary Society debates on such serious matters as woman suffrage, capital punishment, and racial theory, at times she "wish[ed] I could get into a society where some are better informed than I."[13]

For Jennie the desire to become an educated person became a con-suming passion. She centered her adolescence around education to such an extent that school experiences affected her mood and entire outlook. Jennie's senior year of high school, which she had eagerly looked forward to, was threatened by what she perceived as her disappointing academic performance. She fretted:

> Am having a terrible time at school; expected to enjoy my Senior year so much; well, as far as the class is concerned I am doing so since Hunter, who sits in front of me, and I have great times whispering or writing notes about the society. But in as much as I have stood pretty high so far, I hate to take such a tumble in the last year; and yet it is not my fault for I study as hard as ever and my Latin is tormenting me fearfully; why I do not know, but I sincerely wish it would get better.

Two months later she was at the head of her class but still worried that "I meet with no real success anywhere and once in a while become quite dis-heartened." Jennie was well aware that her last year of high school might well be her last year of formal education, and she feared that unsatisfac-tory academic achievement might threaten her as-yet undecided future.[14]

In addition to education, religion also played a key role in shaping Jen-nie's coming of age. She was confirmed in May 1890 and decided to seek guidance about her future from her rabbi, as she was sure "he probably would give me a start on the road I wish to travel." Noting Rosh Hashanah in September, she included the new Jewish calendar year of 5651 in her diary and wrote about the sermon she heard at synagogue services, which she referred to as "church." She and her family were in "church all day" on Yom Kippur as well.[15]

That she took music lessons on Saturdays and wrote in her diary on the Sabbath and holidays, both activities forbidden by traditional Jewish law, did not weaken Jennie's devotion to her faith. Her allegiance to the Reform Judaism practiced by her family was thoughtful. After visiting a cemetery in September, probably to visit the graves of her relatives before the High Holidays, she reflected on the relationship between God and in-dividuals. "Everytime I visit such a place it recalls to me the blessedness of being a firm advocate of religion," she wrote, continuing, "If man does his duty and knows that he does it, why should he fear; the Almighty can-not desire us to waste our lives in blind worship and prayer." She understood Judaism as a living and valuable spiritual force, even when divorced from more traditional ritual and observance.[16]

Judaism provided Jennie with a social context as well as a religious framework. Though she certainly spent time with many non-Jewish peers at school, her social life as seen through her diary was primarily within the Jewish community. The Hebrew Literary Society provided one such social forum, and the list of entertainments, picnics, and parties at the back of the 1890 diary is dominated by Jewish names. It was not that Jennie never socialized with her high school friends; it is probably safe to assume that the classmates with whom she went to a football game in November were a "mixed" group. However, the friends whose names appear repeatedly and whom she commented on in the diary were Jewish.[17]

During the summer between her junior and senior years of high school, Jennie paid an extended visit to her aunt's home on the Missouri River, a train ride away from Chicago. Among her companions there were Jules Rosenberger, whom she told her diary "is certainly a very bright boy," Jac Lowry, another "very bright young man," and Arthur, "a very good natured and an admirable character." Jennie never wrote Arthur's last name in her diary, but it is clear from other comments that he, too, was Jewish. She liked him so much that she even gave some thought to his future potential as husband material. She concluded, "Must say that I enjoy his company as well as that of any other young man; he is very easily managed by a girl though and if he remains so his wife will have an easy time of it." While this was hardly a damning indictment, she also described him as "not very man-ny." Manly or not, as a presentable Jewish young man, Arthur was within the circle of potential mates for Jennie. As she went horseback riding, learned to shoot a rifle, attended her first baseball game, tramped around the countryside, and went swimming and dancing, Jennie participated in the leisure activities of any other adventurous middle-class girl. However, the "very nice boys" and other girls she spent the summer with were a particular group of Jewish peers, a smaller group than her high school acquaintances. As she grew older and moved toward the serious decisions she would soon have to make, Jennie's social circle became increasingly Jewish.[18]

Although Jennie enjoyed her summer of fun, she was also aware that social pleasures were a temptation to be fought as well as enjoyed. After returning to Chicago, she wrote, "My trip will ever remain a pleasant dream in my memory; I will ever regard this summer as one of the happiest of my life, true it has influenced me some, but not enough to shake my principles or desires in life." She took those principles and desires very seriously. She dutifully recorded in her diary the opera glasses, handkerchiefs, portfolios, gloves, and books she received for her seventeenth birthday. But on August 23 she also noted her birthday by marking her diary "sour 17" in small letters and writing discontentedly, "Another year of life gone by though I do not believe in making myself old— *far from it,* yet am beginning to feel that it is high time for me to definitely shape my career and awaken to the duties of a woman." Two months later she continued to worry, "I do not know what is the matter. I would like to know whether there are any other girls in this whole world like myself."[19]

Jennie's uncertainty about her age, accomplishments, and aspirations typified the anxieties that adolescent girls faced during their transition from childhood to adulthood. Like other middle-class girls in turn-of-the-century America, she was unsure what was expected of her and concerned about her place in the world. Her individual coming-of-age experience was deeply influenced by her Jewish identity, just as the *Jewish Messenger* symposium had suggested was the case for girls of all backgrounds within the Jewish community. Religious values reinforced an orientation toward tradition that comforted and strengthened Jennie as she struggled to reconcile the various pressures of family, school, community, and personal desire. Though Jennie and her Jewish peers discussed by the symposium contributors resembled other American girls in many ways, the role that Jewish tradition and religious culture played in their lives set their adolescence apart. This was true for Jewish girls of almost all backgrounds during the last decades of the nineteenth century and the first decades of the twentieth century. Even as they moved warily into an adolescence framed by a period of modernization, they continued to cling to some tradition. Jewish identity provided girls special rewards and satisfactions through spirituality, family closeness, and community involvement that shaped their experiences with both adolescence and modernity.

The history of adolescent Jewish girls is a window into a central theme of American history, the question of how individuals from traditional groups navigate between the twin shoals of cultural retention and cultural adaptation. The issue of how to adapt to modern conditions by constructing culture was critically important to immigrant groups of all kinds who made a new home in America. In the case of Jewish girls, participating in an emerging adolescent culture while retaining older family values was complicated by ethnicity and religion. Studying the power of ethnic and religious culture on adolescent girls across class boundaries not only injects ethnicity into adolescence as a factor to be considered but also demonstrates how inaccurate it is to associate ethnicity with the poor or with immigrants alone. Ethnic values particularized experience in partnership with class. For Jewish girls, the self-involvement typically associated with adolescence was common but limited by the emphasis placed on family by religious and ethnic culture.

Despite the obvious problems these tensions could have caused Jewish girls, the majority of them apparently remained oblivious to the stresses of their situation. Adolescence might have been in crisis at the turn of the century, but few American Jewish girls seemed to be in anything remotely resembling crisis. While some had educational or social or religious difficulties of one sort or another, their diaries, memoirs, and personal papers reveal a remarkable absence of conflict in their lives. This absence is the more remarkable because it existed in both the direction of tradition and the direction of modernity. Jewish girls, particularly those from middle-class families, generally enjoyed the opportunities for modernization that their non-Jewish peers did, but they often chose to prioritize tradition instead. They believed that a sense of community and religious identity, if not ritual observance, were valuable and worth preserving, even at the cost of constraining their participation in the modernization occurring all around them. The decades between 1860 and 1920 were hardly static, and some change in perspective did occur over time, particularly with the increase of the impact of sexuality and work on women's lives. For the most part, however, modernization affected the context of Jewish girls' lives without necessarily affecting the essence.

Jewish girls did not simply turn away from the promises of modernity. They expressed personal ambition even while they followed tradition. They took advantage of many educational opportunities and participated in American youth culture with enthusiasm, but also with restraint. Ironically, part of their roles in their families was to embrace the innovative in order to strengthen the traditional. Given the acculturation project in which virtually every Jewish family in America was engaged on some level, individual girls' processes of coming to grips with personal identity had ramifications for their families. Most Jewish families offered their children to the larger American society both as proof of their willingness and ability to integrate and as testimony to their refusal to abandon all distinctiveness as Jews. Girls stood at the vanguard of Jewish families and ultimately Jewish communities' ventures into their brave new American world. Jewish adolescents in peer environments like schools and clubs were well placed to test and consider social limits, both as individuals and as family representatives. Coming of age was a gradual process for adolescents that took place over a number of years, just as acculturation was a gradual process for Jews in America that took place over a number of generations. Yet unlike American Jewry as a whole, which rarely retreated from acculturation, Jewish girls who moved through the charged period of adolescence often gravitated toward tradition, even as modernization continued apace around them.

Young, Jewish, and Female in America

During the period between 1860 and 1920, adolescence and modernization emerged as parallel phenomena in American society and culture. Both involved the process of individuation, of pulling away from a broadly defined communal orientation, and both identified with the future rather than the past. Many young people began to value their youth and reject tradition just as the dynamic of modernity began to prize freedom and innovation. At its birth as an acknowledged stage of life, adolescence was plunged immediately into the crisis of modernity, posing special problems to adolescents. Although the concept of youth was certainly not new, the idea that adolescents were an identifiable social group defined by shared activities, responsibilities, characteristics, and expectations that superseded family or community interests became institutionalized. Dramatic growth in the number of students attending American secondary schools, patterns of consumption, expanding opportunities for mobility, and the emergence of leisure pursuits all contributed to the development of adolescence as a distinct social category. These factors were also features of a modernization process that tended to separate individuals from their former reliance on continuity for stability. The tensions arising from both adolescence and modernity were heightened in the case of Jewish girls, who were strongly attracted to tradition as reinforced by religious family culture but also felt the appeal of the new autonomy promised by modern adolescence. The pull of individuation was especially strong for girls from immigrant backgrounds, who often identified modernity with acculturation.

The development of adolescence as an acknowledged part of the life cycle occurred gradually as the nature of the transition from childhood to adulthood changed during the second half of the nineteenth century. Gender was key to this process. Because the emerging category of adolescence was always related in some fashion to both biological and social maturity, the differences between women and men exerted a great influence on the coming-of-age experiences of girls and boys. Growing anxiety over female sexuality and independence combined with nineteenth-century biological models meant that in some ways girls set the standard of adolescence. For girls, puberty brought physical, social, and psychological danger. For boys, puberty merely brought manhood. Once adolescence began to be conceptualized in social and cultural terms rather than just biological terms, a late nineteenth-century development, the focus shifted to a more masculinized model that extended the norms of white, middle-class boyhood across ethnic and class lines but obscured girlhood. With the beginning of the twentieth century and the 1904 publication of G. Stanley Hall's seminal book, *Adolescence: Its Psychology and Its Relations to Physiology, Anthropology, Sociology, Sex, Crime, Religion and Education,* came a new understanding of adolescence as a time for individuals to grapple with emotional, intellectual, economic, and sexual independence in a modern world. As the destiny of women destabilized in that modern world, girls' adolescent years of preparation for womanhood became a critically important but perilous period for both defenders and attackers of traditional gender roles and opportunities.[20]

The historical treatment of adolescents has generally followed the same trajectory as the development of social scientific thought about adolescence. Early studies explicitly centered on the social experiences of boyhood as shaped by cultural understandings of manhood and masculinity.[21] Historians interested in girls most often dealt with "the girl problem" of the late nineteenth and early twentieth centuries, working to uncover conceptualizations of the problem of female juvenile delinquency.[22] Only recently have histories of childhood and adolescence begun to grapple with the social and cultural ramifications of the transformation of adolescence into a stage of life focused on individuation. They explore the effect of the ways in which the relationship between self and society was thrown into crisis at the turn of the century. The apparently impersonal forces of industrialization, urbanization, migration, and secularization in fact exerted a great deal of power on the lives of adolescents struggling to balance mass culture's promises of personal pleasure with the risk of alienation.[23] Taken as a whole, the growing body of literature on adolescence and youth represents a significant contribution to the understanding of the social, cultural, and economic dimensions of modernity in turn-of-the-century America.[24]

Just as adolescence in America during the period between 1860 and 1920 was undergoing significant development and transformation, so, too, was Judaism in America. The changes over this period were many. The Jewish population of the United States grew from approximately 150,000 in 1860 to more than three and a half million in 1920, by which date American Jewry made up nearly 25 percent of world Jewry (but less than 4 percent of the U.S. population).[25] American Jews became more urbanized over time and tended to concentrate in fewer areas by the early twentieth century than they had during the nineteenth century. As Jewish communities further established themselves, the network of communal and religious institutions grew rapidly. During the nineteenth century, even small towns with small Jewish populations typically could point to the presence of Jewish fraternal groups like B'nai B'rith, Jewish religious institutions such as synagogues and cemeteries, and Jewish charitable organizations like women's sewing societies and benevolent groups. By the turn of the century, large cities home to expanding Jewish populations boasted major communal institutions like federations of Jewish charities and thriving networks of organizations devoted to providing Jews in America with religious, social, and even economic opportunities. While some of this massive organizational effort was defensive, a response to the increasing polite and impolite anti-Semitism in America, much of it was also a tribute to the collective strategies used to retain Jewish identity in an American context, where Jewish cultural, ethnic, and religious continuity required active maintenance. The propensity of Jews in America to build institutions and participate in explicitly Jewish activities should also be seen in the context of both Jewish traditions of *tzedakah*, righteous charity, and American traditions of community organizing.[26]

The major issue affecting the shape of and shift in Jewish community relations—both internal and external—at the turn of the century was immigration. As the population figures indicate, the relatively small Jewish immigration of the mid- to late 1800s was dramatically expanded at the turn of the century by mass migration. The contours of this shift are well known. Following the patterns of general immigration to the United

States during this period, much of the pre-1880 Jewish migration to America was from central and western Europe, while much of the post-1880 Jewish migration to America was from eastern Europe. By 1860 and certainly by 1880, some of these Jewish families had already lived in the United States for two generations or more. After 1880, increasing violence and persecution pushed burgeoning numbers of eastern European Jews into emigration. The daughters of these families, some of whom had themselves immigrated, were apt to be less secure in their places in America. The basic historical narrative does support this interpretation to some extent. However, it is no longer historiographically acceptable to divide "German" and "Russian" (serious misnomers) Jewish experiences in America in quite this way. Historians now view the period between 1820 and 1920 as one of continuous Jewish immigration to the United States.[27]

There was significant continuity in experiences of Jewish immigrants over the century of immigration. Important differences in reference to class and religiosity must be addressed, but the similarities in the process of adaptation over time were also striking. These similarities are particularly relevant to a history of adolescent Jewish girls, whose relationships with their families bore remarkable resemblance to each other regardless of decade or circumstance. In addition, this book does not focus on the poorest working-class Jewish population. Most of the girls in this book were middle class or upwardly mobile working class. Because so many of their activities, goals, and experiences were the same, it would be a mistake to treat them as separate entities.

None of this discussion of similarity should or could elide all difference. The lives of Jewish girls in America were undoubtedly and importantly marked by class, religious observance, education, and family character, among other factors. However, even some of these factors were shaped into difference by structural similarities. Gender, for instance, was central to all Jewish girls' experiences. Paula Hyman has eloquently made the case for the vital role gender played in Jews' process of adapting to America. The divergent gender norms of western and eastern Europe shaped Jewish responses to the social conditions and pressures for Americanization on the other side of the Atlantic. Jews from western Europe were typically already accustomed to the "Victorian" gender roles operative in mainstream American society, particularly in the economic realm, which assigned the domestic sphere to women and the public sphere to men. Although innumerable Jewish women from western Europe worked to help consolidate family businesses, it was a sign of family success when these women could retire to their "rightful" places in the home and educate their daughters not to have to work. Jews from eastern Europe were used to a completely different system of gender roles in which the ideal was a scholarly husband who absented himself from the marketplace and a wife whose economic activity supported the family. This cultural ideal was rarely achieved but still resulted in widespread acceptance of women as public, economic actors. Adaptation to America was therefore doubly difficult for eastern European women, whose success typically rested on an inversion of traditional gender roles and the potential loss of their public status. For these immigrant families, too, educating a daughter not to work was a luxury but one that marked family success in both economic and cultural adaptation. While the schematic division of gender roles and Americanization did not work so neatly in the actual lives of all Jewish families in America, it is clear that gender roles and expectations were critical factors in the experiences of Jewish girls, whose opportunities were both contained and expanded by this framework.[28]

Parallel to the role of gender in the economic and family life of Jews in America was the role of gender in their religious lives. As Jonathan Sarna has pointed out, the transformation in American Judaism began well before mass migration. A growing emphasis on Jewish nationhood, a reconsideration of universalist principles that had for a while seemed to be at the heart of all American forms of religion, and a turn away from the most radical reform back to some elements of tradition all marked what Sarna calls the "Jewish Awakening."[29] An additional factor in the "Jewish Awakening" was the role of women in Jewish life in America. Karla Goldman has argued that American Judaism underwent a process of feminization similar to that occurring within American Protestantism, resulting in Jewish women's dramatically increased presence in synagogues and participation in Jewish public life. The general move toward mixed seating at synagogue services, confirmation ceremonies that included both girls and boys, and significant Jewish women's groups, such as synagogue sisterhoods and the National Council of Jewish Women, supports Goldman's claim that Jewish women played a pivotal part in the development of an explicitly American Judaism.[30] It is less clear that women's movement into Jewish public life resulted in abandonment of Jewish home life. In any case, adolescent Jewish girls, particularly those whose families, regardless of national origin, had been in the United States for several generations, grew up in an environment where they could choose to be active participants in their religious community.

The growth of Reform Judaism in America contributed greatly to this environment. Reform Judaism's conception of personal spirituality, reflecting a developing modern emphasis on the individual, to some extent detached Judaism from the accumulated weight of centuries of observance. Lacking anything approaching a comprehensive Jewish education about ritual and tradition, and, more important, eager to modernize their religious lives, many Jews in America embraced Reform Judaism.[31] Jews who did have a more thorough religious education and understanding were also drawn to a modern form of an ancient religion that seemed to offer, as Alan Silverstein has phrased it, "alternatives to assimilation."[32] With its emphasis on a new spirit of Judaism and a place for women, Reform appealed to Jewish women in America who found in it yet another way to become more like their mainstream Protestant neighbors while still maintaining their particular religious heritage. The religious education systems that developed in response to Reform Judaism, both to support it and to challenge it, had an important effect on the religious lives of adolescent Jewish girls, who for the first time had organized, collective access to Jewish education.

Not all Jews in America were Reform, and more traditional families' religious practices and affiliations obviously had a great impact on many girls' relationships to Judaism. However, denominationalism as it is currently understood did not exist during the late nineteenth century and even into the twentieth century, with the important exception of Reform. Almost no one construed "Orthodoxy" as an oppositional, institutionalized denomination until well into the twentieth century. The Conservative movement was born during these years, usually dated from the reorganization of the Jewish Theological Seminary in New York and the arrival of Solomon Schechter in America in 1902–1903. The terminology for the spectrum of religious belief and observance then in use was "traditional" and "observant," "liberal" and "modern." Few Jewish girls at the time thought in terms of denominations, although many did think often about Jewish practice and heritage and placed themselves somewhere along the spectrum. Jewish education for girls, embraced by both the Reform movement and traditional segments of American Jewry, played a role in girls' self-identification as Jews.

"Americanness" also played a role in Jewish girls' religious identities. As one example, it was undoubtedly the case that some eastern European immigrant girls' mothers read Yiddish *tekhines,* a form of private devotional literature. *Tekhines* had also been published in the United States, first in German and then in English, since the mid-nineteenth century.[33] However, hardly ever did even the most traditionally pious Jewish girl read *tekhines* as a form of prayer. In all probability, the middle-class Jewish girls whose families had been in America for at least one or two generations (and often more) by the 1870s found the German versions incomprehensible and the English versions incompatible with their visions of themselves as American girls. Girls who immigrated from eastern Europe, or who were the daughters of immigrants, might have been rooted in Yiddish culture at home but more often than not were also encouraged by teachers, parents, and even religious institutions to adopt a more American form of Judaism that had little room for "old fashioned" women's prayers. Jewish girls' religious lives were thus shaped by conventions of both gender and Judaism within the context of American Jewish history.

Shared Concerns across the Decades

Reading diaries kept in 1864 or 1918, letters composed in 1881 or 1913, memoirs written in 1914 or 1939, or oral histories transcribed in 1965 or 1979, it becomes quickly apparent that adolescent Jewish girls across the decades shared a set of primary concerns. For example, diaries and memoirs both testify to adolescent Jewish girls' drive to stand out. As a consequence of both their individuality and gradual changes in roles for women, many girls expressed fervent desires to be unique and do extraordinary things. They harbored desires to become special, better, or at least different from the models of religious domesticity with which they were so familiar. They believed that finding themselves should entail finding something wondrous within that would assure them of rich and interesting internal and exterior identities.

Jewish girls' longing to travel down roads less taken took many forms. Growing up in St. Louis during the early 1900s, Fannie Hurst craved recognition as extraordinary. She found it "intolerable from the beginning that the teachers paid me little or no heed," since she "wanted them to regard me as the most interesting girl in the school" and was determined to "excel somehow, some way." Fannie felt "a tormenting sense of being trapped into mediocrity" and strove to rise above her surroundings.[34] Sixteen-year-old Marie Syrkin was also typical for her oft-expressed desire to be extraordinary. She fretted to her diary in 1915 that "I am becoming common place, ordinary, the very thought of it maddens me. To relapse into mediocrity, to feed, to sleep, to gossip, and to be *content*. To become sluggish, to let the soul stagnate, ah God, this is not life." "I shudder when I consider how trivial, how absolutely bourgeois I have grown in my sentiments," she wrote a few days later. "All the time there is continually forcing itself more clearly upon my consciousness the terrible truth that I am absolutely 'ordinary.' Ordinary, what dismal pictures the word conveys."[35]

While perhaps less dramatic than Fannie or Marie, other girls shared their fierce desire to become extraordinary and agonized over goals that seemed incompatible with traditional paths. Bertha Wehle was concerned about her own aspirations, asking her diary in 1862, "Why is it that we have hopes and aspirations which can never be fulfilled? Ambition is often a source of great happiness; but often, too often of much misery and wretchedness."[36] In Seattle a generation later, Bella Weretnikow also worried about how best to direct her ambitions, writing, "O! That problem of what I am going to be, how it does haunt me. The fear of choosing the wrong thing is continually present." Bella's stepfather's belief that traditional homemaking was the only conceivable destiny for a girl exacerbated the anxiety and even guilt she felt about being attracted toward another goal.[37] The burning question for these girls was how best to achieve the extraordinary selves and lives they so ardently desired without forsaking what they valued of tradition.

The benefits of maintaining a traditional focus ultimately exerted the strongest pull in most cases. There were limits on how extraordinary even the most resistant Jewish girls wanted to be. As a rebellious teenager in New York, Kate Simon was determined to do something unconventional with her life, but even she rejected the idea of becoming a music critic as "too remote for a girl who had it dinned into her that Jewish goals had to be modest and those of a Jewish woman more modest still."[38] Conventions of tradition shaped the boundaries of her ambitions. The possible ramifications of conspicuous difference also affected girls' desires to be extraordinary. During the 1870s, Maud Nathan found that her family culture and religious observance made her different enough without adding the extra factor of personal ambition.

I can well remember how irksome at the time seemed these religious observances. The long walk back and forth from synagogue, instead of riding, the being debarred from social functions other than family gatherings on Friday nights and Saturdays; the insistence upon the rigidity of certain dietary laws, all seemed to me, at the time, so unnecessary. I longed to live the same life as my playmates.

Although Maud eventually came to appreciate the ways in which Jewishness "forged the background of my spiritual life," as a child and adolescent she resented her difference from her peers.[39]

Another primary concern shared across the decades was religion. For Jewish girls in America, religion had the potential to be a site for extremes of both modernization and tradition. The conflict between traditionalists and modernizers, which typically, if not exclusively, also included class and ethnic differences, contained a gender dimension with consequences for the religious experiences of young Jewish women.[40] The level of ritual observance per se was not usually the major religious issue confronting Jewish girls. Patterns of development in America Judaism left the method of observance fairly open, even within single families, while still valuing religious tradition. Judaism functioned as a constant link to the past that most American Jews valued but did not let prevent them from moving forward into the future. For most Jewish girls, religion was a means of preserving continuity without being defined solely by it. Their Jewish identities provided a solid, reassuring anchor as they coped with the demands of becoming modern American girls.

Because of the stability of Jewish tradition, if not ritual observance, Jewish girls frequently relied on religion as a fundamental answer to their adolescent searches for identity. They developed not only ties to their ethnic and religious community but also individual relationships to God and to Judaism that heightened their sense of self and invested their lives with meaning. Girls made decisions about the character of these relationships and decided how to position themselves as individuals in relation to Judaism and Jewishness. In these ways religion offered Jewish girls a number of possibilities. They embraced or rejected ritual observances. They believed in the constant presence or direct intervention of God in their lives. They emulated their parents' ideas about Judaism or developed their own. Girls both tapped into preexisting communities and shaped themselves as individuals. As a set of both private beliefs and public practices, religion had the potential to encourage both individuation and communal affiliation, a combination extraordinarily appealing to girls working out the relationship between individuals and community in the modern world.

Judaism was not merely functional; many Jewish girls were sincerely religious. Clara Lowenburg "was very religious and took the time of getting confirmed very seriously." In Mississippi during the 1870s, she learned how to read and translate Hebrew and to recite daily prayers from the rabbi.[41] Birdie Stein wrote continuously of her religious faith and belief in God. While preparing for a journey in 1882, Birdie wrote of leaving her home in Baltimore, "It is then that we find how thankful we should be to our Heavenly Father who every day protects and takes care of us." Birdie's observations of the world around her reflected her constant refraction of experience through a prism of piety. Describing a magnificent sunset at sea, she asked her diary, "Who when beholding such a scene, if he need be convinced of the existence of God, could fail to recognize His might, power, and wisdom?"[42] The joyous spiritual tone of Birdie's entire diary revealed the significance of religion to her life and worldview.

Although the spiritual expressions found in their diaries and memoirs were anything but instrumental, religion did serve both communal and individual functions for Jewish girls. Girls asked God for help, turned to God for comfort, compared Judaism to other religions, praised Judaism for the blessings it brought to their lives, and expressed their doubts about the efficacy of ritual and prayer. Their attitudes toward God, Judaism, and devotion in general had less to do with when they lived than where and with whom. Both the pettiness and the grandeur of their adolescence seemed to require thinking seriously about religion, especially when their identification as Jews did mark them as different from their mainstream adolescent contemporaries.

Many girls felt God as a constant presence and comfort in their lives. During the Civil War, Eliza Moses relied on faith in God to see her through the hard times. Crushed by the death of her cousin and erstwhile sweetheart Albert, she affirmed resolutely that "God, who knows and does all things for the best, has seen fit to deprive me of my greatest treasure, so I must bow in submission to his will."[43] Fannie Allen addressed God frequently in her diary. After learning that her uncle was about to die and leave behind orphaned children, she sympathized with their plight, having seen the impact of her own father's early death on her family. "O God!" she wrote, "Give me patience to bear this wearing poverty and its consequent evils, with a heart at peace with my fellow creatures." Some months later, returning to Philadelphia from an unsuccessful husband hunting jaunt to New York, she beseeched, "God help me to be independent."

More than any aspect of her life, her unmarried state prompted Fannie to turn to prayer. On New Year's Eve, 1875, she wrote, "I pray God that it may not be my lot to love and be unloved." Her sense of God's presence in her life was palpable, and she used these diary entries to reaffirm her faith. Fannie reminded herself, "in a book you can see the end, but we have to live the life of uncertainty and it is at times that we can catch glimpses of God's mercy." Her religious tendencies led her to greater belief in God, even when her prayers seemed unanswered. She relied on faith to see her through what seemed to be years of disappointment as she struggled to establish herself as a Jewish wife and mother.[44]

Fannie's sister Amelia, a student and then a teacher in the Sunday School system organized in Philadelphia by Rebecca Gratz, took religion even more seriously and espoused a stricter observance of Jewish law and custom than many of her contemporaries.[45] She carefully observed the Sabbath and reproached herself for transgressions such as visiting the Centennial Exposition grounds on a Saturday in 1876. Clinging to traditional observance may have been her way of dealing with her own difficulties in marrying and establishing a conventional Jewish household. She found religion a source of strength and serenity, especially while she waited "for the companionship of some one congenial person." She tried to comfort herself with the knowledge that she was hardly the first young Jewish woman who faced breaking tradition by remaining unmarried and believed her troubles would "purify me for the world to come." Noting the Jewish holidays, Amelia wrote with good humor of Passover, "I am not at all tired of matzas though they seem tired of me for they feel just now as if they were all sticking in a lump in my throat." Her stricter observance influenced her family as well. All the Allens, not just Amelia, stayed home from the most exciting day at the Centennial in Philadelphia because it was Yom Kippur and they belonged in synagogue.[46] They ultimately agreed with Amelia that their traditional religious identities would take precedence over their other interests.

The powerful appeal of religious tradition was apparent even within families whose members opted for the most radical forms of American Judaism. In New York during the early 1860s, for example, the Wehle family observed the Sabbath on Sunday, but observe the Sabbath they did. Bertha Wehle's father took his role as religious educator and inculcator very seriously. Every week "he would talk to us of the goodness and greatness of God, as seen in all His works, and read to us from the Bible in his clear expressive voice."[47] This weekly ritual of collective religiosity drew on centuries of traditions about religious time as family time, despite the modernized version of the Jewish calendar the Wehle family adopted. Tradition prevailed in families whose members did not all preserve the same religious rituals as well. Though not ritually observant herself, Hilda Satt respected her mother's piety so much that she went to great lengths not to write on the Sabbath or otherwise transgress the holy day.[48]

Because family typically played a critical role in the formation of girls' Jewish identity, religion generally reinforced family relationships that might have been under stress from other sources. Even parents far less attuned to some aspects of tradition than Bertha's father or Hilda's mother made some effort to maintain Jewish households. Marion Rosenwald, daughter of Sears-Roebuck tycoon Julius Rosenwald, would not say that

> our household was overly Jewish-oriented, but it certainly was a Jewish household. My father always went to Temple on Rosh Hashanah, on Yom Kippur, and on most Sundays—the day the Reform prayer service was held. We girls did not. But we were imbued with the feeling that Jewish families are known for their closeness, for respecting each other, and for family loyalty.[49]

Alice and Florine Haas, who grew up in the 1890s in a heavily assimilated segment of the San Francisco Jewish community, celebrated Christmas and Easter with their families but also learned from their parents to attend High Holiday services and participate in Jewish philanthropy in order to affirm their Jewish identities.[50]

Like Alice and Florine, many girls associated their Jewish identity with the holiday celebrations that brought families closer. Holidays were important affirmations of Jewish identity, no matter how acculturated families were. Helen Arnstein, who grew up in the same San Francisco community as the Haas sisters, experienced Judaism more as an ethical code than a religion, yet she and her siblings still observed Jewish holidays by staying home from school "so as not to offend other Jews."[51] Even in such an assimilated household, a Jewish as well as a secular calendar had an effect on identity. For Sara Liebenstein in Chicago during the 1880s, "the Jewish holidays meant two things: a festive dinner and new clothes." Every year she and her sister looked forward to the Jewish New Year and Passover as a time to replenish their wardrobes.[52] While their anticipation was hardly spiritual in nature, the association of holidays with pleasure still underlined the role the rhythm of Jewish time played in their lives. Edna Ferber's family was also not particularly devoted in the sense of ritual observance, but her parents closed their store on the High Holidays, her mother put on her best dress, they attended synagogue, and they invited any Jewish visitors in town to festive dinners after Rosh Hashanah services.[53] Judaism provided a sense of community and practice of tradition that comprised an undeniable part of these girls' multifaceted identities as Jews, Americans, and young women.

For many Jewish girls in America, religious holidays carried more meaning and pleasure than merely a vacation from school or new clothes. During the 1870s in Chicago, Jennie Rosenfeld experienced holiday observances as the bedrock of her Jewish identity. Resting on the Sabbath helped American-born Jennie "understand dimly, the spirit of the old ghetto, when the people lived humbly, despised and persecuted, but somehow, rose to spiritual heights with the sinking of the sun on Friday." By participating in similar, if altered rituals, she felt connected to Jewish history, even if no prayers were uttered or no Hebrew understood in her own home. Passover preparations implied not only spring cleaning and unusual foods but also an adherence to the Jewish lunar calendar. Jennie found Rosh Hashanah the most meaningful holiday of all. To attend synagogue services, to gather with her family, to enjoy a festive meal was "to catch a little of the feeling of belonging." The holidays, Jennie believed, "brought something very precious and inspiring into the home."[54] The religious calendar, with its set holidays and festive seasons, acted as a counterweight to the more amorphous rhythms of modern time that beckoned to Jewish girls outside their families and religious communities.

In Chicago during World War I, Emily Frankenstein's family typified Reform Jews who belonged to a synagogue and observed major Jewish holidays. Until she was confronted with her Jewish beau's interest in Christian Science, however, Emily accepted her Jewishness but gave relatively little thought to the traditional ritual observance her family had gradually forsaken. Emily's religiosity consisted of a conscious effort to draw meaning from the world around her. She found spirituality "in literature, my school work, reading and thinking for myself and seeing . . . things in a new or different light because of the experiences I have—and because my mind, is developing and growing as the years advance."[55] She viewed education and learning as one of the best means to improve herself and read widely to satisfy a hunger she considered spiritual as much as intellectual. Though formal Jewish religious observance played little part in Emily's daily life, she followed her parents' example and sought spirituality in other aspects of her life. Both her parents encouraged her to become more involved with Jewish social and cultural groups as a way to maintain a connection to the Jewish community they valued but did not associate exclusively or even primarily with traditional religious forms.

Emily was surprised at the extent of her discomfort with her suitor Jerry's growing devotion to a religion other than his own. Comparing her response to Jerry's apparent defection from his Jewish roots to nonbelievers who found themselves praying under stress, she wrote that people "who have scoffed at prayer, have been known to pray when deeply moved or in distress. Whatever their walk in life, their belief, their faith, their sayings and doings, somehow people put a trust in God and pray."[56] Emily herself occasionally addressed prayers to God in her diary, usually asking for help in convincing a mistaken Jerry of his religious errors. She and her family may not have been traditionally observant, but they valued their religious and cultural heritage too much to overlook an external threat in the form of an alternate faith. After visiting a Christian Science reading room to educate herself, Emily conceded that a person of Jerry's nervous disposition might be helped by Christian Science's tenets of faith but insisted that "one can find the same truths in Judaism."[57] She found Jerry's break with their shared religious tradition deeply disturbing.

If modernization implied a loosening of the bonds of traditional affiliations that preserved the integrity of the Jewish community, then even the most self-identified modern girls were unwilling to embrace it completely. Like Emily, many Jewish girls reacted to such threats by moving closer to tradition rather than further away from it. They valued the freedom and independence modernity promised them but used that freedom and independence to preserve a sense of continuity. Religious observance per se was not the major factor. Girls across a wide spectrum of ritual observance found that Jewishness shaped their experiences and inner lives and added a unique dimension to their identities. Cultural and religious heritage provided an automatic link to centuries of tradition that Jewish adolescents treasured, despite the pull away from family and community that external social and cultural change exerted on them.

Education was another primary focus of Jewish girls across the decades. The centrality of education in their lives is readily apparent from the recurrence of schooling as a theme in their personal writings. Educational achievements became important milestones for girls struggling to define themselves. Four years after her high school graduation, Amelia Allen continued to mark the date in her diary.[58] In 1875, her sister Fannie remarked in her diary, "I ought to give a sigh that I am out of my teens, but really I don't feel a bit older; on the contrary I feel younger than at fifteen, for then the sudden leaving of schooldays aged me and made me older in feeling."[59] Fannie was less affected by her twentieth birthday than she had been by leaving school, which she considered a more important landmark. Sophie Ruskay associated the beginning of her adulthood with her matriculation at the Normal College in New York, despite the fact that she was still a teenager. Carefree youth behind her, she "was a little taller, my skirts a little longer and my hair turned up, tied with a ribbon at the nape of my neck as befitted a freshman."[60] Though education was only one factor in self-definition, it played an important part in the way Jewish girls perceived themselves.

Because of the premium Jewish tradition placed on all kinds of learning, many Jewish girls did not equate education with formal schooling. They combined their individual interests in learning with communal interests and continued to seek education once their school years were behind them, synthesizing personal goals with traditional values. Nineteen-year-old Bertha Wehle, a teacher in New York, took private French lessons, read serious literature, and went to classes at Cooper Union to continue her education. She especially enjoyed the chemistry classes she attended with her brother, telling her diary, "I am glad that I joined the class for I think that it will afford me a great deal of pleasure." Bertha justified her educational activities to her skeptical parents both by asserting her right to seek personal pleasure and reassuring them—and possibly herself—that the classes would make her a better teacher. Her brother, a peer as well as a family member, needed no such convincing that continuing education was an appropriate activity for his sister.[61]

Not all Jewish girls were enthusiastic seekers of knowledge like Bertha. When education did not seem compatible with a traditional sense of what the future would bring, some girls were disinterested in it. Sixteen-year-old Clara Solomon was not averse to learning, in general. Her goals for the summer of 1861 included sewing and plans to "improve ourselves wonderfully." Throughout her diary, however, she continuously attributed her low spirits to her dislike of the Louisiana Normal School she attended. In October 1861 she wrote, "It is said that a person is never affected with the 'blues,' unless there is some cause, and that too is my opinion. Well, my principal cause is that I don't like to go to Normal School."

Clara claimed that the work was too hard and grumbled constantly about her lessons in grammar, rhetoric, arithmetic, history, geography, singing, elocution, and dictation. More important, she had no intention of following in her sister Alice's footsteps and becoming a teacher. She saw little connection between becoming "familiar with the maps of Mexico and Central America, with the English discoveries in America, with the nature and properties of verbs" and preparing for future domestic responsibilities. Much preferring to spend time with her mother at home, she was not cheered even by her impending graduation. Clara assured her diary that graduation was "hailed with no delight, for I am sure I will kill myself studying. And for what?" With no discernible connection to a conventional domestic future, secondary schooling was at best an inconvenience for girls like Clara, who had no desire to pull away from the most traditional values, even when their families freely offered them the opportunity to do so.[62]

At the opposite end of the spectrum from Clara were girls who viewed education as key to their future selves, whether or not they took the traditional paths toward adult womanhood, and they judged themselves in terms of education. Bella Weretnikow depended on education to help her move from adolescence to adulthood. For Bella, who emigrated from eastern Europe during the 1880s when she was a toddler, education was potentially a more disruptive force within her working-class family than for American-born or middle-class Jewish girls. Sixteen-year-old Bella's privately expressed questions, "What occupation shall I choose to make my life a success? Where can I find the answers?" demonstrated the extent to which she looked outside her family and traditional values for direction. Deciding early on that succeeding in school was the key to controlling her life, she made education the focus of her adolescence. She preferred studying and reading to almost all other activities. In 1896, during what turned out to be her last semester in high school, she told her diary, "Work is real hard this term, but I hope resistance will bring out my better powers, if there are any." She was disappointed with less than perfect grades, expressing annoyance at a 93 percent on a history paper, and she worried a bit about the effects on her health of staying up so late to study every night. She was frustrated by her troubles in geometry, writing that she "would give anything to be able to see into originals as some students do, but they must be gifted or something." Like other diarists, Bella exaggerated her deficiencies; she earned a grade of more than 90 percent for the term's work in geometry.[63]

Bella tried to spend time learning for the sake of knowledge alone and attempted to carry this attitude to school with her. She hoped she would "always employ the same amount of time in pursuit of knowledge, that my school life may not be the end of my life education." She attended a special lecture on photography, took drawing classes, and reminded herself that a history grade she thought unfair should not dim her enthusiasm. "After all," she scolded herself, "tis not the grade I get but the amount I learn." Although she enjoyed shopping, celebrating the Jewish holidays, and visiting her father, who was divorced from her mother, she was determined not to lose sight of her priorities. By the end of the school year, Bella had decided to turn away from the more conventional options available to her. She refused to resign herself to a life working at her parents' store and was not ready to think about marriage yet. She sent away for a catalog from the University of Washington and decided to leave her Seattle high school before graduating in order to begin college at once. Although her decision to skip a year required a difficult summer of preparation, she was sure the price was worth paying. After the first day of classes, she wrote with satisfaction, "Got my books, enrolled in classes and am beginning to feel at home in the University although it is so very different here from the High School. One is so entirely independent." Her whole adolescence had been directed toward the independence education could assure her.[64]

Although schools provided very different environments for some girls and became natural sites of adolescent identity formation for others, discomfort rather than outright alienation was generally the result. As a high school student in St. Louis during the early 1900s, Fannie Hurst felt like two entirely different people depending on whether she was at home or at school. At school, she was stimulated and interested in studying but also under self-induced pressure to excel. At home, she was the indulged daughter who received attention merely by virtue of her status as an only child. Fannie "liked both my worlds" and felt that "coming home from school . . . was like walking into open arms," but she was increasingly drawn to her "growing intellectual interests outside" and eventually identified herself as a writer who needed to have experiences far from home. The break was neither abrupt nor easy. After a scouting trip to the University of Missouri in Columbia, Fannie gratefully acceded to her mother's tearful pleas to stay at home with her parents and go to college in St. Louis. By the time she graduated from Washington University, however, she had resolved to make a life for herself outside her parents' cushioning but smothering world. Though her parents remained bemused all their lives by Fannie's decisions, her mother's middle-class aspirations and her father's admiration for learning helped the family cope with her gradual process of pulling away.[65]

In families like the Hursts, the congruence of a daughter's ambitions with at least some family values meant that individual goals did not cause permanent rifts between parents and adolescents. For many other Jewish families, the premium traditionally placed on men's religious learning was transfigured into an appreciation of all education. Some girls saw education as an avenue toward maintaining the focus of their families' primary values. Adolescent schooling provided them with a way to sustain tradition rather than disrupt it. Marie Syrkin, for instance, clearly understood education, and particularly literature, as a means of connecting to her cultured parents by sharing their interests. She and her parents agreed that the focus of her adolescence should be her schooling, and much of her diary was concerned with her academic performance.

Sixteen-year-old Marie wrote in her diary with a dramatic flair that begged to be read aloud. Unlike some other diarists, she appears to have written for an audience, and she may have occasionally shared her diary with her parents. Of her troubles at her New York school—troubles belied by her high grades—she wrote in 1915, "My life is a tragedy, ay a tragedy worthy of being enacted in the most exalted scenes. I have but one despairing thought haunting me now, that is my failure to make good in school." She populated her diary with the "exalted scenes" she so fiercely desired, describing her "demoniacal Latin teacher, Mr. C——" as "such a slimy reptile" and complaining that "my worthy chemistry teacher publicly held me up as an example to the class of all that is obnoxious and despicable in a pupil." The excellent report she received later that month sent her into a rapture difficult to perceive as private, as she seemed to urge an expectant audience to "Rejoice! The Gods are with me! Oh yes, indeed I marvel at my miraculous good fortune! How my honorable pedagogues were deluded enough to give unto me the marks they did is a mystery to me!"[66] Mining her emotions and experiences, Marie used rhetorical flourishes to portray herself as the heroine of her own adolescence, the central figure in an educational dramaturgy scripted in part by her parents.

Marie acknowledged her volatile nature and confessed that her parents worried about its effect on her future. She admitted in her diary that her sudden spring passion for a classmate was affecting her concentration, sighing ruefully, "I would to heaven it were over as I stand excellent chances of flunking all my mids because of my temperamental nature." One of the greatest demands she placed upon herself was "to attain at least a fair portion of the world's knowledge" by reading such disparate authors as Marx and Dostoyevsky. The thirst for passion that pervaded her diary and later her professional career as a literary critic and author was evident even at sixteen, when she wrote with acuity of Milton's *Prometheus Bound,* "a truly majestic work," that "there is something soul satisfying in the sonorous flow of language of the ancients that I find entirely lacking in modern literature." Her innate talent for reading emotion into life shaped her school experiences into the stuff of drama.[67] Not coincidentally, setting out on a program of classical reading was a sure way to grow closer to her intellectual parents as well as to improve her own mind.

The possibilities that schooling held for those who took advantage of extended education in America brought parents and children together in common aspirations for the future. In San Francisco Harriet Lane and her father shared a special closeness when

> on the first day of each month I flourished my high school report before his eyes. I pretended that the marks were low, and Father, troubled, fitted his glasses. When he read for himself the unbroken line of "A's," we laughed together at my deception, because I was still number one in my class. He was happy in giving me the education which, to him, was an incantation commanding the powers of light and darkness.[68]

During the 1910s, the Frankensteins also took an active interest in their daughter's education. The exclusive private school for girls Emily attended in Chicago for her last few years of high school offered a fairly rigorous academic curriculum. Emily appreciated the quality of her schooling but found studying tiresome and was often the least enthusiastic family participant in her education. Her parents frequently expressed their dismay that Jerry, her favorite suitor, was a diversion from her studies. After receiving letters from Jerry, who was stationed as a quartermaster in Tennessee during World War I, she wrote, "O—yes, I am happy tonight and I would feign go on and tell just how happy, but I have to study about Civics . . . and cramm for a test on the first Romantic Poets, Wordsworth, Coleridge, Southy, Scott, and know something of their poetry." Emily won honors at graduation in French and art history despite

the distraction of Jerry's letters.[69] Ultimately, she agreed with her parents
that her primary duty as a high school student was to do well in school.

Like religion, education was not only a major concern for adolescent
Jewish girls but also a fairly safe one because it was usually a family concern as well, even when not all family members agreed how to approach
it. Even for working-class immigrant Jewish families, there was generally
agreement that education at least to the extent of learning English was an
important goal for the entire family. This process of adaptation worked
in much the same way for the mid-nineteenth-century Jewish immigrants
as it did for the late nineteenth- and early twentieth-century Jewish immigrants. Schooling played a vital role throughout the broad period of
Jewish migration to the United States. Early Jewish immigrants made use
of their children's education to smooth their own transition to their new
home, as did their counterparts at the turn of the century. Though family
and education did not always reinforce each other, for the most part adolescent Jewish girls did not have to choose one over the other.

Adolescent Role Models and Tradition

As Jewish girls, consciously or unconsciously, grappled with the central
tension between the communal orientation of tradition and the individu-
alistic orientation of modernization, they often turned to a variety of role
models for help in becoming the kind of young women they wanted to
be. These role models, ranging from real-life figures to prescriptive images, at times preserved tradition by elevating religious domesticity above
all other values and at times disrupted tradition by encouraging personal
ambition. For the most part, the family members, teachers, and friends
whom Jewish girls took as role models were somewhat more likely to
support individual opportunity, though they often expressed their doubts
about the value of independence and difference. Role models found
within prescriptive literature such as American Jewish periodicals tended
to bolster more traditional views of women. The importance of various
kinds of role models in girls' conception of themselves reflected the social, cultural, religious, and familial contexts of their lives. As those contexts changed over time, the interplay of the competing attractions of
modernization and tradition became more complex. Despite this increasing complexity and the growing opportunities for girls to choose their
own paths, the most popular role models were usually those who, like

American Jewish girls themselves, claimed some of the benefits of modernization without relinquishing a strong connection to tradition.

Family members were the most common role models for girls, many of whom looked no further than home for examples of how to reconcile the competing forces in their lives. Most Jewish girls admired their parents and wanted to earn their respect by emulating them. Nineteen-year-old Bertha Wehle considered her father "the very model and perfection of mankind" and thought of him as "one of those very few who may be called nature's own noblemen." She confided to her diary that she was afraid her father did not love her as much as some of his other children. Still, she felt "that I worship my dear father more than any being in the whole world."[70] In New York during the 1920s, Gertrude Edelstein appreciated the difficulties of her mother's divided life.

> When I learned in school that Gaul was divided into three parts, I remember thinking of my mother. My mother was divided into three parts. Or, even worse, she was three people—a wife, a worker, and a mother.[71]

Gertrude understood this complicated identity as a pattern she might well have to follow and looked at her mother as an example of how to reconcile competing identities gracefully.

Even when family members represented a kind of life to which Jewish girls did not aspire, family rifts did not automatically result. In Seattle during the 1890s, Bella Weretnikow was determined not to replicate her immigrant mother's illiteracy and simple domesticity. She respected her mother's household skills but decided not to follow in her footsteps. "One thing it has taught me," she wrote in her diary after a day of what she considered domestic drudgery, "that wherever I intend to look for happiness, not to seek among those who have to do house work and to do my best to keep off that role." Rejection of her mother's daily life notwithstanding, Bella still took her mother as a role model. She admired her mother's fortitude and determination to improve her life.[72] In some cases parents hoped that their daughters would not follow in their footsteps. Proud of the fact that she and her husband had achieved such financial success, Augusta Rosenwald purposely did not teach her younger daughters to cook and sew, skills she hoped they would never need. Ironically, her youngest daughter Marion envied the domestic training time her older sisters Adele and Edith had spent with their mother and regretted the opportunity lost to emulate her mother's own girlhood occupations.[73]

Teachers were also inspirational figures to many Jewish girls, encouraging many of them to develop their full potential regardless of convention. While attending South Division High School in Chicago during the 1880s, Sara Liebenstein met a woman who had a great influence on her and was a role model for years to come. Helen Doty Compton was Sara's rhetoric and English teacher.

> She was one of those unusual pedagogues who can make their pupils outdo themselves. She taught not merely the parts of speech and the elements of grammar; she made us think about the words we set down and about the thoughts we tried to express. A tall stout, handsome woman, with a stately figure, she had dark blue eyes and soft brown hair. She always dressed in black.

Sara was so taken with Mrs. Compton that she frequently bought her flowers and went to her home for biweekly private English lessons from the time of her graduation until her marriage.[74]

Immigrant girls who felt this kind of attachment to teachers were often especially grateful for their help in learning to become American. Teachers seemed to offer the best tools for breaking away from the past and heading toward the future. Polly Adler, who came to the United States by herself as a thirteen-year-old girl in 1913, loved her teacher Mrs. O'Sullivan, who was "kind and patient and took extra time to help me catch on to American ways." Polly was particularly appreciative of this assistance, as the family with whom she boarded did little to aid her adjustment.[75] Regina Katz's sixth-grade teacher, Charlotte G. Eckel,

> had a great deal of influence on my embracing this wonderful land. She was a unique human being, teacher, and friend. Before going to high school I spent a year in her class. . . . She fostered my cultural development right from the start. I was full of Europe and she was the epitome of American culture.[76]

Teachers taught these immigrant girls far more than school subjects. They served as models of what women could be and do. They taught valuable and lifelong lessons about what it meant to act, feel, and look American, lessons that immigrant family members often could not provide.

Adolescent Jewish girls also found a range of real-life models in the American Jewish press, which vacillated between showcasing extraordinary Jewish women and highlighting the accomplishments of traditional Jewish women. An 1896 *American Jewess* article profiled three Jewish female doctors in San Francisco: Amelia Levinson, Natalie Seeling, and Adele Solomons. Solomons, a graduate of Hahnemann Medical College in Philadelphia, gave weekly lectures on physical fitness to groups of young women, who presumably would benefit from exposure to new ideas.[77] Prominent Jewish figures like educator and clubwoman Rebekah Kohut were also held up as exemplars for Jewish girls. While acknowledging that the "peculiar character of *the* American Jewess is exceedingly difficult to define," an article in *Opinion* suggested that all American Jewish girls might do well to emulate a woman who had

> won the respect and admiration of the community at large by giving it an opportunity to see an American Jewess at work in bringing men and women of all religions and classes together in a common understanding of what needs to be done and what can be done for suffering and aspiring mankind.[78]

While these exceptional women stood as real-life role models, the attainable goals of more average Jewish girls were also important. *American Israelite* and other major American Jewish periodicals routinely listed girls who graduated from high school, holding them in high esteem. *Sabbath Visitor,* a Jewish youth periodical, even provided details of their commencements, reporting solemnly in 1891 that at the graduation exercises of the Girls' High School in San Francisco, Lilian V. Cohn and Wanda Shirek read essays on "History of My Study of Mathematics" and "Whistling Girls and Crowing Hens," respectively.[79] At the same time as the accomplishments of these real-life girls and women seemed to demonstrate the opportunities available to Jewish girls who stepped away from tradition, however, the communal emphasis remained on the religious domesticity that had been associated with Jewish women for so long.

In addition to the family members, teachers, and real-life role models, an array of historical, cultural, literary, and religious images were also important in Jewish girls' search for identity. These images were almost uniformly, though not simplemindedly, on the side of preserving rather than disrupting tradition. *Sabbath-School Visitor* regularly published pieces about significant Jewish women in history, although the purpose was

Henrietta Szold, age 17, 1877. Henrietta is wearing the Peabody Medal awarded for academic excellence by Baltimore's Western Female High School. *Courtesy of the Jewish Museum of Maryland, JMM 1989.79.9a.*

clearly to elevate religious domesticity above all other merits. An 1874 sketch on "Beruria, the Wife of Rabbi Meir," did refer to "her great learning, her talents, and other excellent qualities of mind and heart" but concluded with a peroration to "the noble woman, the faithful wife, the excellent mother."[80] When A. S. Isaacs, editor of *Jewish Messenger,* suggested to nineteen-year-old Henrietta Szold in 1879 that she might like to write about Sara Coppia Sullam, an exceptionally learned Jewish woman of Renaissance Italy, he recommended focusing on her womanly traits as well as her intellectual ability. He told Henrietta that this subject was especially "worthy of your powers," as who better to write about such a figure than another young Jewish woman who could appreciate her importance as a role model.[81]

These figures were positive role models, to be sure, and they were widely accepted. The importance of having such Jewish women as role models was apparent. Over a period of decades, though, the thrust of the presentation remained oriented toward religious domesticity. In 1912, one woman suggested that studying the Biblical narratives about women

> should help the Jewish girl to put a greater value on her inheritance, and to have a deeper reverence for her religion and a higher regard for her greatest responsibility—that of being some day the Jewish mother of the coming man and woman.

"A little of the society of Hannah, Deborah, Ruth and Esther of old," she wrote in *American Hebrew*, should stimulate "our Hannahs, Deborahs, and Esthers of today."[82] Renowned educator Rebekah Kohut, participating in a 1916 symposium on "Women in the Synagogue," led a long tour through the history of great Jewish women in order to justify American Jewish women's growing presence and activity in synagogues. Her article, which made the somewhat daring suggestion that women as board members and congregation presidents could "guide the destinies of the synagogue as successfully as men," still relied on rhetoric about "the mother in Israel" to argue that "woman is a vital factor in the religious life of the Jewish community."[83]

The popular Jewish press abounded with these images of Jewish women, designed to present Jewish girls with their ideal futures. In January 1898, an *American Jewess* editorial reminded the middle-class readership that "marriage is the foremost aim of the American Jewess as it was for her mother and grandmother."[84] The Jewish girls who read this kind of material over and over again were left to wonder what place their individual desires or characteristics might have in the welter of communal expectations about their roles. In response to such mixed messages, Jennie Franklin pasted a clipping of an article called "When a Man Wants a Wife" into her 1890 diary. The article assured her that "men do not always marry the style of woman they admire," a sentiment which may have comforted Jennie, who believed she was socially awkward and clumsy.[85] For girls like Jennie, who treasured education and religious expression, the available images of Jewish women seemed limited, even when they were capacious enough to acknowledge the importance of individuality.

The tension between upholding traditional ideas about women's roles and supporting innovative ideas about women's roles was apparent in American Jewish periodicals no less than in Jewish girls' lives. Rosa Sonneschein, editor of *American Jewess,* supported the expansion of Jewish girls' education and even job opportunities, but the monthly periodical lost few opportunities to highlight the satisfactions of enlightened religious domesticity.[86] She published a lengthy discourse by Rabbi David Philipson entitled "The Ideal Jewess" that encapsulated *American Jewess*'s usual position on the importance of maintaining womanliness in a new age of expanding options for women. Philipson explained:

> As far as external rights go, let woman have them all as long as they do not endanger her womanliness; let her have all the advantages of education, of developing mind and heart; let her have a directing hand in all the institutions of our modern life, but let her be shielded from all the influences that shall make her merely like man and less than woman.[87]

For Philipson, Sonneschein, and most contributors to the American Jewish press, Jewish women's identification with religious and moral superiority granted them recognition as autonomous individuals but also underlined the importance of their maintenance of Jewish homes and families.

Communal as well as individual ideas about the model American Jewish girl changed over time. The changes were supported by developments in American women's status and American Judaism more generally. For example, in 1898, Hebrew Technical School for Girls founder Minnie D. Louis wrote in *American Hebrew* with little fear of contradiction that religious education for the Jewish girl was vital because "she is the ordained home-maker, hence the character-maker, hence the citizen-maker, hence the society-maker; and as the *girl* is moulded, so will she crystallize into the woman." By 1919, however, contributors to a symposium in the same periodical on "The New America, and American Jewish Women" emphasized "Americanness" rather than "Jewishness."[88] In the aftermath of World War I, Federation of Temple Sisterhoods president Carrie Simon wrote that the American Jewish Woman in a large sense is stirred by same impulses which react on her Catholic and Protestant sisters. She, too, has enjoyed the freedom of the American atmosphere, the opportunities of education, the training through clubs and organizations, the experiences and vexations of our industrial problems.

Carrie Simon also believed that "the most valuable contribution which the Jewess in our land can bring to the cause of Judaism is a religious enthusiasm . . . and an unquenchable insistence on the sanctity of the home."[89] Though their place as women, Jews, and Americans had all shifted during the period from the Civil War to World War I, Jewish women were still responsible for religious hearth and home. The question of useful role models for Jewish girls remained vexing as long as there seemed to be a central contradiction between preparing for a future that would resemble the past and making ready for a future that would take into account the present.

Continuity and Context

Though the role models most available reflected and shaped the ways in which tradition was highlighted by Jewish girls' social, cultural, religious, and familial contexts, the emphasis on continuity was neither entirely pervasive nor entirely linear. The context of girls' lives changed over time and so did their choices. When in 1861 Clara Solomon rejected secondary education as disconnected to her dreams of domesticity, she could not have imagined Jennie Franklin's fight to attend business college in 1891 despite failing family finances, let alone the Syrkin family's strong support for Marie's matriculation at Cornell in 1918. Amelia Allen's adherence to traditional observance during the 1870s was as far removed from Helen Arnstein's casual acceptance of religious holidays as ethnic celebrations during the 1890s as both were removed from Emily Frankenstein's attempts to counteract the appeal of Christian Science to her beau after World War I. Family expectations, so important to the paths Jewish girls chose, also shifted as the relationships among family, tradition, acculturation, and individualization were transfigured by the larger forces of modernization.

The power of Jewish girls' adolescent experiences to both free them of some family ties and bind them to their families explains a great deal. It explains why most Jewish parents supported education, even when it threw up a barrier of knowledge and worldliness between them and their children. It explains how highly educated daughters could and often did remain close to their parents' sensibilities. It explains the important roles both family and peer socialization played in Jewish girls' adolescence and provided the underlying, perhaps unconscious, rationale for the Jewish context of much of that socialization. It explains why transformations in American Judaism rarely caused a break between generations, even when girls' spirituality and observance led in different directions than their parents. Declining ritual observance eased the process of acculturation into American society and culture. Though few Jews in America, whatever their origins or length of residence, desired complete rejection of their past traditions, fewer still desired complete rejection of their new future in America.

As a result, it is too simplistic to categorize Jewish girls as more like or unlike their non-Jewish adolescent counterparts. In important ways Jewish girls' adolescence was shaped by their Judaism and Jewishness, but in other ways their adolescent experiences resembled those of countless other girls and boys coming of age in America at the turn of the century. The combination of factors that determined to what extent a Jewish girl's adolescence paralleled or intersected the mainstream was as individual as the girl herself. For instance, immigrant Jewish girls, or the daughters of immigrant parents, generally shared a widely based experience of initial financial struggles that often resolved themselves into a family economy that required their labor. From 1880 forward, most immigrant Jewish girls lived in an urban environment of ethnic enclaves that held fast to some Old World traditions but embraced some American values as well. The push and pull between tradition and acculturation was felt by immigrants of virtually every age, religion, and place or origin, including Jewish girls. Like other immigrant youth, Jewish girls made use of resources such as role model teachers, popular culture, and reading to move closer to what they perceived as the American model of girlhood.

In other ways, however, immigrant Jewish girls' experiences were quite different. Many enjoyed somewhat greater access to education than other immigrant girls, an extension of the traditional Jewish esteem of learning. Eastern European Jewish families brought different gender models with them, and greater acceptance of women's public and economic role, though contested and challenged in America, influenced adolescent Jewish girls' opportunities. As one extension, Jewish girls were typically freer to move about on the streets than many of their non-Jewish immigrant counterparts. Mobility led in turn to participation in peer-centered youth cultures that relied on untraditional spaces outside the homes that represented tradition for so many.

Middle-class Jewish girls, usually at least second and sometimes third or fourth generation Americans, appeared on the surface to resemble their non-Jewish counterparts even more closely than did immigrant girls. Their educational patterns, which increasingly over the last decades of the nineteenth century took high school graduation for granted, ran along the same track as American girls' education, in general. They participated in school and extracurricular activities among heterogeneous groups that often brought together girls and boys from any number of ethnic and religious backgrounds. Middle-class gender models that positioned men as workers and money-earners and women as domestic caretakers reinforced the family patterns many mid-nineteenth-century central and western European Jewish immigrants had been accustomed to in Europe and continued to promote in America. A middle-class Jewish girl was likely to spend her leisure time in much the same way as any of her other middle-class friends.

Yet acculturated Jewish girls' lives were still differentiated by religion, and the Jewish element of their identities had important implications. For example, religious difference carried implications for social interactions, especially courtship and dating. Some indiscriminate youthful socializing might have been acceptable, but there was also pressure on girls to associate with other Jewish youth and ultimately to choose one of their own kind as a husband. The rare occurrence of exogamy among middle-class Jewish families through the early twentieth century testifies to the sense of difference and importance of heritage Jewish girls themselves felt. The expansion of religious education to include far more girls than had ever had access to Jewish education before also made religious identity a point of distinction for Jewish girls, even when the format of that education closely resembled non-Jewish religious instruction.

As the social landscape of American adolescence was transformed during the period between 1860 and 1920, Jewish girls embraced many of the changes that would aid their desires to pull away from their families and tradition and move toward their peers and modernity. Yet the process was never simple or linear, particularly because of the ambitions for acculturation so many American Jewish families shared with their daughters. The process was complicated further by the refusal of nearly all Jewish girls to reject their Jewishness. Their attachment to religious tradition, regardless of the form that tradition took for each of them, meant that they continued to be set apart from their non-Jewish peers. Choosing to sustain the distinction of Jewishness required focusing on identities other than adolescent, no matter how appealing the individuation promised by both adolescence and modernity.

Their resemblances to and differences from their non-Jewish adolescent peers made Jewish girls effective bridges between worlds. Their adolescent experiences benefited their parents and siblings as well as themselves. Jewish girls' education had social and economic consequences for themselves and for their families. Their work made economic contributions to the family finances. Their religiosity helped set the spiritual tone of the household no matter what the level of observance. Their socialization patterns created a comfort zone from which to deal with their Jewish and American communities. Guardians of tradition and agents of acculturation, Jewish girls' adolescence developed within this context of dual heritage and double roles. Continuity was as important as discontinuity. Jewish girls' desire for autonomy, invested with meaning for their families as well as themselves, rarely became a drive for alienated independence. In finding themselves as adolescent Jewish girls, they also helped define what it meant to be Jews in America.

2

"Unless I Got More Education"

Jewish Girls and the Problem of Education in Turn-of-the-Century America

During the spring of 1872, thirteen-year-old Jennie Rosenfeld ventured out with trepidation to take the entrance examination for the public high school in Chicago. Though her mother was afraid to let Jennie go downtown alone, she felt that the possibility of extending her daughter's education outweighed other considerations. After the examination, Jennie waited while her tests were marked. She returned home that evening enrolled for the fall, one of a limited number of Chicago adolescents to become a high school student. She felt much less afraid of the long journey home than she had of the journey there. Before she even began classes, high school had already opened up a new geographic world to her. She looked forward to the new educational and social worlds awaiting her. Jennie's widowed mother was as pleased as her daughter. Like other Jewish parents of the period, she was proud of her daughter's educational opportunity and unworried about any possible effects on family relationships or ties to the community. She was also well aware that only her own hard work and extended family support made it financially possible for Jennie to enjoy secondary education of any kind.[1]

Jennie and other Jewish girls who aspired to be high school students were aided by the relationship of the American Jewish community to education. They benefited from both the greater likelihood of American parents to keep girls, rather than boys, in high school and the high value Jewish tradition placed on education. By the beginning of the twentieth century, all but the very poorest or most rural white children in the United States at least attended elementary school, no matter what their parents' level of education had been. Formal secondary education remained a great wall over which only the few could climb, but the wall was lowered every year.[2] As a result, Jewish girls from middle-class families, and eventually working-class families as well, began to take secondary schooling for granted. They understood that education provided cultural capital for upward mobility and was a crucial marker of class. Working-class families used education as a means of increasing the return on work, while middle-class families relied on the profits of work to finance prolonged education. In both cases, gender was central to perceived success. Because work and education were such central parts of nearly all Jewish girls' lives in one form or another, traditional values exerted a strong influence on their opportunities.

American education's theoretical emphasis on individual opportunity and personal identity had the potential to move adolescents away from their families and communities. In practice, however, institutionalized education was so closely tied to conventional ideas about class, gender, and race that high schools often preserved rather than disrupted traditional values. Though the expansion of secondary education did break down some barriers by offering growing numbers of students similarly structured high school experiences, it often conserved traditional social values at the expense of helping all students fulfill their individual potential.[3] Because of this basic conservatism in what purported to be the most modern of institutions, Jewish high school students pursued educational opportunity, participated in the construction of American youth culture, and developed as individuals while still maintaining close ties to their families and communities.

In the public schools most Jewish adolescents attended by the end of the 1800s, there was a diverse enough population that the students' family traditions were not directly threatened by school experiences. Still, as they walked the same high school halls, girls and boys shared educational and social experiences that set them apart as a distinct and privileged group in American society. These shared experiences led many adolescents toward identifying more with each other than with their families or religious groups or ethnic communities.[4] However, only on very rare occasions did Jewish girls' peer identification outweigh family and community identification. As a result, college education, which tended to take girls away from home, was much more problematic than high school for Jewish girls. Their ties to traditional values might be more threatened if they left their family and communal settings to go to college.

By attending secondary schools, whether public or private, academic or finishing, for two years or four, Jewish girls participated in the educational experiences emerging as a cornerstone of American adolescence without negating their other priorities.[5] The combination of traditional social stratification and modern individual opportunity made high schools a particularly fitting environment for Jewish girls, who wished to assert themselves as individuals while maintaining strong links to traditions of family and religious or ethnic community. The content of their educational experiences may have changed over time, but the context did not. For instance, Jewish girls during the 1860s probably faced decisions about whether to attend high school while Jewish girls during the 1910s may have faced decisions about whether to attend college, but their decisions in most cases were based on a shared set of values that prioritized connection to family and community.

Connection to community, and particularly to family, shaped working-class Jewish girls' educational opportunity as well, but within the context of the family economy. The economics of education, underlined by the gendered structures of both education and work, meant that only financially secure families could afford their daughters the protected adolescence that allowed for extended schooling. Working-class Jewish girls had to contribute to the family economy directly by working for or within the family circle.[6] Only when prolonged education served the family economy was it a possibility for most working-class and immigrant Jewish girls. The economic constraints on these girls' education reinforced the difficulty many of them had in asserting their individual needs and desires outside their families' goals.

Demands of class and ideas of gender combined to limit immigrant and working-class Jewish girls' access to secondary education. While there were more girls than boys graduating from American high schools by 1900, this pattern did not always hold true for Jewish adolescents. The Jewish community, which traditionally held education in the highest esteem, tended to be willing to sacrifice instant financial gratification by investing in their children's schooling. As extended education was increasingly linked to greater earning potential, this investment generally had a good return. But because that return was larger for boys, whose opportunities for work were significantly greater than for girls, it made sense to many working-class Jewish families that boys, rather than girls, should be the ones to stay in school. This strategy was not always possible to put into action, of course. The gendered labor market meant that even without education boys could earn higher wages than girls. Some

Jewish families found it was impossible to forego boys' wages while it might be possible to forego girls' wages.

The tightening connection between education and work at the turn of the century also affected working-class Jewish girls' educational opportunity relative to the labor market.[7] The deskilling of craft work shattered the possibility of upward mobility through on-the-job training. This development, combined with new hiring procedures that relied on prior credentialing, accorded education a new importance and relevance among the working class. The managerial revolution and rapid expansion of office work required workers with skills best learned in schools, linking a whole new category of employment to education. As education became tied more closely to work, limits on women's work translated to limits on working-class girls' education.[8] Each adolescent Jewish girl's educational opportunity was thus shaped by a combination of traditional values, developments in the labor market, and her individual family's needs.

During the period between 1860 and 1920, Jewish girls' educational opportunity was limited by both internal and external considerations. Internal factors of personal, family, and community expectations generally approved of education, unless it removed girls from their family circles and traditional values. External factors of class generally held education as a positive value as long as it served the family economy. Linking the experience of confronting all these factors for both middle-class and working-class Jewish girls was gender. Ideas about appropriate gender roles suffused secondary education and actually grew more influential as more American adolescents began to attend high school. Traditional Jewish notions of gender led some American Jewish families to view extended education for girls warily. Gender divisions in the workplace were reflected in classrooms and schoolyards. Adolescent Jewish girls experienced a wide array of educational forms and made many of their own decisions about the kind of schooling they wanted for themselves. Their educational opportunity, however, was always constrained by the ways in which gender affected both family or community expectations and economic realities.

Jewish Girls' Education and Family Relationships

The centrality of the family to American Jewish life during the last decades of the nineteenth century and first decades of the twentieth century made the connection between girls' education and family relationships an important one. While parental support for daughters' schooling was not uncommon, neither was parental opposition. Rarely was either attitude merely the result of blind prejudices on the part of parents, who typically did the best they could for their daughters, given their own social and economic circumstances. Additional circumstances beyond anyone's control, such as birth order or numbers of siblings in a family, were also contributing factors to educational opportunity. Jewish girls themselves were highly sensitive to both the positive and negative possible consequences of their education for their families and sometimes made their own decisions accordingly.

Both working- and middle-class Jewish families generally valued education. Immigrant parents attempted to support their daughters' aspirations by balancing the cost of losing their immediate economic contributions with the benefit of increased economic opportunity gained through prolonged education. Marie Grunfeld, one of innumerable Jewish girls attending New York City public schools at the turn of the century, grew up in an environment where "all dreams and hopes drew their inspiration from the promise of the free educational system." Her immigrant parents defined success as "anything that had to do with books" and encouraged Marie's schooling as a way to "rise above . . . their own uneducated fate."[9] Their concern with their daughters' education led working-class and middle-class Jewish parents alike to make sacrifices. Anna Moscowitz, who did not attend her elementary school graduation because she could not afford a dress, was only able to go to Wadleigh High School in New York when her father gave up smoking so that Anna could use the cigarette money for carfare.[10] On the other end of the economic spectrum, Emily Frankenstein's mother sold a necklace to pay for Emily's tuition at an expensive Chicago private school that she believed would bring her daughter the best advantages.[11] Emily's mother probably viewed the education offered by an exclusive private school as external support of the values the Frankenstein family cherished as self-consciously cultured members of the Jewish middle class.

Another sacrifice some Jewish parents made was household peace and harmony. Not all parents agreed about the best options for their daughters' education in America. Emma Beckerman's father insisted that she go to work after graduating from a New York elementary school in 1912, but her mother refused to take her to get working papers. Instead, Emma's mother pawned a ring to get enough money to send her to business school so that when she did go to work, she could find employment in an office and not in a factory.[12] One parent's attempt to change another parent's attitude often resulted in a series of uneasy compromises. Although Brenda Weisberg's teacher and mother together persuaded her father to allow her to attend high school, not even her evident academic talent or her mother's interference could convince her father to permit her to move on to college. As her father insisted, sixteen-year-old Brenda reluctantly turned down a college scholarship and began to teach in her rural Ohio neighborhood after a summer session at a normal school following her 1916 high school graduation. Her mother sympathized, but she was unwilling to contradict her husband again.[13]

Mothers were just as likely as fathers to impose limits on their daughters' education. When Anna Moscowitz won a scholarship to attend law school at night, her mother objected because she feared that studying law would make it difficult for Anna to find a husband. "Anyhow," she added, "Who ever heard of a woman being a lawyer?"[14] Many mothers who struggled themselves to reconcile the demands of domesticity and economic need shared a lack of faith in a "daughter's ability to earn her own livelihood," as one girl put it, and had still "less faith in the power of a[n] . . . education to enhance her matrimonial chances."[15] As long as marriage was collectively considered the ultimate goal of all girls, shifting social opinion about the intrinsic value of girls' education met with mixed reactions.

Even when parents did encourage their daughters' schooling, gendered ideas about education could limit their support. For example, ambivalence about nursing as a respectable women's profession affected Jewish girls across the country. Contact with the bodies of strangers did not meet the requirements of proper work for Jewish girls of any class and threatened family respectability. As a teenager in Omaha, Fannie found her plans to go to nursing school rejected by her mother because "she didn't think it was the right thing for a girl."[16] Some parents would allow prolonged education only if it led to a specific set of job options and refused to countenance any less acceptable ambitions. Kate Simon "begged to be allowed to go to a general high school, where they taught biology, history, and writing book reports," but her father demanded that she take a commercial course. Once at the commercial school, Kate found supportive teachers to help her convince her father that she belonged in an academic course, but only the widely accepted authority of American-born teachers over immigrant parents helped her get her way.[17] Kate Simon's father's ideas about his daughter's future were limited by gendered notions of acceptable women's work. He also held a widely shared conception of the family economy that conceived of education as a means to improve earning capability. Because most Jewish girls from immigrant families could realistically aim no higher than office work, their parents often believed that their daughters should use the privilege of their education to prepare for commercial employment that would benefit the family.

Everything considered by parents when making decisions about their daughters' education was also considered by daughters themselves. Many had some control over their schooling, and some demonstrated this control by curtailing their education even before their parents or circumstances demanded it. A few refused to carry out their parents' plans for their futures and chose to leave school rather than follow a prescribed path. In 1881, Florentine Scholle left high school before graduating, against her parents' wishes, and enrolled in a training course for kindergarten teachers.[18] May Weisser, denied her dream of becoming a lawyer by parents who feared that a legal career would virtually guarantee spinsterhood, declined to become a teacher as her parents wished and instead refused to go to high school at all.[19]

Most Jewish girls who chose to leave school did so for more practical reasons. Desire to help their families or protect their parents from working too hard was a major motivation. Gertrude Mandelbaum chose the commercial course at John Marshall High School in Chicago, much to her mother's disappointment, so that she could find employment immediately after graduating and her mother could stop working.[20] In 1916, Minnie Seltzer finished her second year of high school in Camden, New Jersey, but "could not endure my parents' struggle for existence. I decided to leave school and go to work since I already knew the basics of bookkeeping and some office work. My parents were rather distressed over the situation since education was important to them." They compromised, and Minnie continued her education at night school.[21]

The poverty experienced by very recent immigrant families did not always allow even for the kinds of educational choices Minnie and Gertrude made. Sophie Ruskay's mother, who immigrated to New York during the 1870s, was compelled to leave school almost immediately when her mother became so sick that she could no longer carry out even the simplest household duties. Though she tried to study her brothers' books at night, the burden of running a household was too much for the adolescent, and her chance for formal education slipped away. Whether

Minnie Seltzer, age 5, 1905. Minnie's family had come to Philadelphia from Russia two years earlier. The photograph shows Hyman Seltzer with daughter Clara, Lena Seltzer with daughter Pearl, Dora Muchnik with granddaughter Minnie, and (standing from left to right) Dora's unidentified son and Dora's daughter Rose Muchnik. *Courtesy of the Philadelphia Jewish Archives Center.*

rejecting parental proscription and prescriptions like Florentine and May, choosing to work to help their families like Minnie and Gertrude, or replacing parents incapacitated in some way like Sophie Ruskay's mother, these girls and others like them determined their own relationships to education and work.

Jewish girls' experiences with education and work in America were also shaped by their places in the family. Because immigrant girls were generally socialized to think of others first, older daughters usually had more responsibility than their brothers or younger siblings.[22] An annual report of Chicago's Scholarship Association for Jewish Children described the recipients as "a most self respecting group, ambitious not only for themselves but for their brothers and sisters."[23] Many of the teenagers helped by the organization were the oldest children in their families and felt a keen responsibility to secure their siblings' future, sacrificing their own educational opportunities when necessary.

As Sydney Stahl Weinberg has shown, younger siblings' education was likely to be supported by older siblings' economic contributions.[24] Sarah Jackson, youngest of six children, was able to graduate from the Manual Training High School in Brooklyn and then to earn a degree at the Brooklyn Public Library Training School because her siblings' collective earnings allowed her to focus on education rather than work. The case of the Jackson family also proved that strengthening the family economy, no matter how accomplished, was the ultimate goal. While youngest sister Sarah benefited from most of her older siblings' work, her older sister Betty also stayed in school. Frail but bright, Betty graduated from high school when her sister Edith left school after finishing eighth grade and went to work, but in this case Edith was the younger sister. The Jackson family collectively decided that Edith, who was physically strong, could immediately contribute more to the family than Betty could and proceeded accordingly. Betty graduated from high school in 1901 and became a teacher after a one-year course at a normal school in Brooklyn. Her status as a teacher was higher than it would have been as a factory worker, so the Jackson family strategy succeeded in the long run.[25]

Girls like Sarah and Betty Jackson who benefited from their siblings' labor sometimes felt guilty about their debt. Mary Antin, whose family emigrated when she was thirteen, regretted the circumstances that allowed her to attend school while her older sister went to work.

> It was understood, even before we reached Boston, that she would go to work and I to school. In view of the family prejudices it was the inevitable course. No injustice was intended. My father . . . was compelled to make his children self-supporting as fast as it was practicable. There was no choosing possible; Frieda was the oldest, the strongest, the best prepared, and the only one who was of legal age to be put to work.[26]

Rose Gollup felt especially guilty when her poor health forced her younger sister to leave school for work. For Rose, the only saving grace was that her sister, "like the rest of us, did not look upon 'free schooling in America' in a matter-of-fact way. She, a little Jewish girl from an out-of-the way Russian village of which no one had ever heard, was receiving an education! It seemed a wonderful privilege."[27] Coming from places where extended schooling was accessible to only the elite or very lucky, most immigrant families focused more on the positive side of living in a country where education was available to those who could take advantage of it and less on the negative side of the formidable, often unfair, limitations on that availability.

Jewish communal leaders recognized the problems presented by the frequently inequitable division of labor and economic responsibility within families but were unsure how to effect positive change. When considering in 1910 whether or not to open a trade school for girls at the Educational Alliance in New York, Education Director Allan Davis concluded that "we should not introduce any trades into the Alliance that would take the girls away from their home." He did, however, also acknowledge that "if there is a family of many girls and one or two of those girls can do the cooking and make the dresses and hats for the other members of the family, it would be wasteful for all the girls to become housewives." He conceded that the customary household and economic responsibilities of the oldest daughter in a family might free younger daughters for other kinds of opportunities but pointed out that no matter what a girl's position in the worlds of family, education, and work, "it cannot be questioned that any girl might well be taught the principles of household science."[28]

As Davis's conclusions about what kinds of classes would be appropriate for girls make clear, not only birth order but also gender played a role in family decisions about education. Ideas about who needed which type of education meant that boys' education was sometimes underwritten by their sisters' work. In 1908, Leo Carlin's fifteen-year-old sister Sara began to work full time as a cashier at a local Chicago nickelodeon while Leo went to high school and college. Sara's contributions to the family economy allowed Leo and another brother, Tom, the time and space they needed to graduate from law school, although she never finished high school herself.[29] This practice of sisters facilitating brothers' education was widespread in the American Jewish community. That the privilege of education, especially among working-class and immigrant families, was determined by gender, age, and birth order was an uncomfortable but accepted part of the American Jewish experience during the late nineteenth and early twentieth centuries.

Education within the Family Circle

While family relationships clearly affected basic access to education for immigrant and working-class Jewish girls, they also affected the form and content of education for middle-class Jewish girls. Particularly during the period prior to 1900, a great deal of middle-class girls' education took place at home, within the family circle. Jewish girls schooled at home faced the fewest of the challenges education sometimes posed to students by pulling them toward institutions and socialization outside the family. As had been the case prior to the Civil War, some families considered education a family duty rather than a public responsibility. Within this framework, economic and social status made all the difference to adolescent education, as only families with financial resources could afford to provide their older children with an extended education that both kept them in the family circle and depended on their removal from a family economy.

Engaging a governess or other tutors to give private lessons was one form of education that took place in the home rather than in a school. Middle- and upper-class Jewish parents used this kind of education to strengthen their daughters' communal affiliations as well as cultivate their individual abilities. However, although engaging a governess for young children or adolescent girls was not unusual among the upper middle class and wealthy during the late 1800s, Jewish families in America could only do so warily if their goal was to keep their children safely within the community. Jewish periodicals inveighed against the practice of bringing strange women to live in Jewish households and warned of the dangers non-Jewish governesses might represent to susceptible Jewish children. When the Solis family of Philadelphia hired Margaret Quandril Clark in 1864 to teach their twelve-year-old daughter and nine- and seven-year-old sons, they requested that the new governess steer clear of all religious subjects. Their fears were not unfounded. Margaret agreed to abide by their terms but found her desire to help the Solis children see the light a constant temptation. She confided to her diary:

> They are Jews, but I have become accustomed to that, at first I could scarcely bear to think I dare not speak to them of our dear Saviour . . . I honor the Jews, I would not by a word add one finger's weight to the burden they already bear, to the curse laid upon them, but it is a bitter

thing to me day by day, to feel that these children know not their re-
deemer.[30]

Margaret's strong missionizing impulses made the Solis parents' concern particularly apropos, but the pitfalls of hiring non-Jewish governesses were apparent to many Jewish families. Because very few young
Jewish women took up such work, however, parents were left with few
other options if they wanted to employ governesses. Despite these widely
shared concerns, parents sometimes hired governesses for particular tasks
that essentially required non-Jewish women. They put their class interests
above their fears of religious contamination by outside forces.

Many financially comfortable Jewish girls were educated with a combination of lessons at school and at home. The rounds of school and private lessons made for busy schedules. Frieda Schiff, daughter of highly
influential and wealthy Jacob and Therese Loeb Schiff, spent her full days
devoted to the educational pursuits her parents chose for her. One of the
first Jewish girls to go to the exclusive Brearley School in New York, she
attended school every day until 1:10 p.m. and then spoke French with the
governess who escorted her home. On Monday and Thursday afternoons
she took riding lessons, on Tuesday and Friday piano lessons, and on
Wednesday Bible lessons. She completed her homework after these private classes and practiced piano at least half an hour a day. While some
evenings after dinner she relaxed by bowling with her father in the basement of their Fifth Avenue mansion, on other nights she had fencing and
dancing lessons to contend with as well. The Schiffs further encouraged
Frieda's education by requiring her to speak English to her mother and
German to her father.[31] This exhausting routine, designed to mold her
into an accomplished young woman but not one with career aspirations,
was an extreme but still representative example of the schooling proffered
the daughters of families who were proud to employ governesses and private tutors. Frieda's education and accomplishments reflected class status,
and her Biblical instruction reflected the Jewish identity her parents saw
as intrinsic to her development.

National as well as Jewish identity was also important to nineteenth-
century middle- and upper-class Jewish parents. Though most of them
valued their American identity, they wanted their children to feel an attachment to their ethnic traditions as well. As a result, American Jewish
girls were not infrequently sent to the parts of Europe from which their
families had originally come. In Cincinnati, for instance, a group of Jew-

ish parents that had emigrated from Frankfurt in the 1840s sent their daughters to young ladies' seminaries there.[32] By spending time in their ancestral homelands, these girls developed ties to their foreign relatives and to their family histories. For Clara Lowenburg, who at sixteen years old went to the Valentinisher Institute in Germany, remaining in her hometown of Natchez, Mississippi, for her final years of formal education was never an option. Going away to school was necessary for educational reasons, as there was no real secondary school in Natchez, and for social reasons, as the circle of Jewish peers at home was very small. Clara's exposure to German culture also fulfilled her expatriate father's dream of "sending me to school in his beloved Germany."[33]

Making the most of the autonomy their American adolescence supposedly granted them, girls did have some say in where or whether they studied abroad. Parents generally treated their daughters as individuals, and sisters did not always make the same educational choices. Favoring math over foreign languages, Hannah Greenebaum chose to go to high school in Chicago rather than the Jewish boarding school in Germany that her three older sisters had attended.[34] Fannie Bloomfield, a committed student of music, actually moved to Europe with her mother to study for a professional career as a pianist.[35] Fannie persuaded her parents that her individual needs would best be met in Europe. Though she did not study abroad primarily to satisfy her parents' loyalty to family tradition, she ended up meeting numerous relatives and learning about her European heritage.

Jewish girls attended all kinds of school in Europe, from finishing schools to academic institutes. A European education signified culture and refinement, regardless of the quality of the foreign school. Sixteen-year-old Clara Lowenburg and the two cousins who entered the Valentinisher Institute with her were the first Americans to attend the "very select school for English and German girls," and they found it quite different from the gentle tutelage of the school in Natchez they had gone to earlier.

School was very strictly run and the economics were very strange and new to us. The teachers were the best in Frankfort. Special professors from the Gymnasium came certain days to teach us history, art, architecture, and geography. Learning the German language was our most difficult task and to use it in our studies, and I lived with my nose glued to the dictionary. However, the German girls were wonderfully kind and helpful; we had to walk with one of them and speak German except on Fridays when we had to speak English for their sakes.

By the time Clara returned to the United States, she was "a very worldly young woman of seventeen and felt myself a superior and travelled young woman speaking German and French with Papa and his friends as well as taking a glass of wine or beer at table." Her adolescent school experiences abroad drew her closer to her father and affected the rest of her life, as she consciously set out to re-create a sense of European culture and refinement in her own home.[36]

The practice of sending daughters abroad decreased over time, but the girls who did go to school in Europe continued to connect to their family heritage. In 1913, soon after Beatrice Joseph arrived at the home of relatives in Paris, she began a correspondence with her father that strengthened her relationship with her family. Writing frequent letters from Buffalo to his seventeen-year-old daughter, Jacob Joseph dispensed equal measures of practical advice, money, family news, moral lessons, and expressions of love to his dear "Beaches." Beatrice, who anxiously awaited every letter from home, relied on her father as her chief correspondent and readily agreed to preserve their letters as a record of her time away. Her father encouraged her not to be homesick and to take advantage of her opportunities. "Education, dear Beach," he wrote

> is something that no one can take away from you. Misfortune may come to us all, but education remains. . . . Remember, one respectable person is as good as another, no better no worse, do not go around with a chip on your shoulder, looking for trouble, if you do, you'll have no trouble finding it, but again do not allow any one to impose on you, you have rights as well as others. Respect the rights of others and you will find they will respect yours.

Jacob Joseph concluded this riff on Polonius's advice to Laertes by assuring Beatrice, "I have full confidence, full confidence in your ability." Signing his letters, "Love lots of love, kisses lots of kisses, hugs lots of hugs from Father," he was proud of his ability to provide such an enriching educational experience for his daughter and delighted by her growing pleasure in learning in a different environment.[37] Beatrice's parents and younger sister joined her in Europe in May 1914 to travel as a family, although the impending war cut their trip short.

Family travel such as the Josephs planned was another intimate connection between education and family solidarity. Traveling itself was widely viewed as a broadening experience. The Arnstein family left San Francisco in the late 1890s for a long trip to Europe, during which Helen and her siblings were tutored in the language of each country they visited. After they returned home, the Arnstein children achieved great popularity because of the many stories they had to tell of their family's peregrinations.[38] As Helen alternated between home-based education and school-based education, family played a major role in her learning experiences. Far from viewing education and family as opposing forces, the middle- and upper-class Jewish girls whose schooling revolved around governesses, tutors, study in ancestral homelands, or family travel found that the interaction of family and education bolstered both their individual and communal identities.

The Expansion of Institutional Secondary Education

Though some middle- and upper-class Jewish families continued to rely on education within the family circle, between 1860 and 1920 most secondary education steadily moved out of homes and into schools. Despite the obvious limitations of secondary schooling that reached only a fraction of adolescents until well into the twentieth century, Americans took great pride in the idea of education as a critical component of American meritocracy. As Henrietta Szold stated in an oration on "Our Public Schools" at her graduation from Baltimore's Western Female High School in 1877, "the democratic belief that every boy and girl has a right to as much education as he can take" had joined other heartfelt convictions as the bedrock of American democracy.[39] The character and even the purpose of education changed over time, but the development of secondary education as part of a democratic ethos perceived as unique did not. There is no question that the expansion of institutional secondary education increased opportunities for women, immigrants, minorities, and upwardly mobile families.[40] However, few Americans were willing to criticize or even acknowledge the inequities in schools that privileged boys over girls, whites over African-Americans, and middle-class students over working-class students. Jewish families, like other American families, both appreciated the meritocratic elements of expanding, institutionally based secondary education and tried to cope with the gender, race, and class inequities endemic to private and public education.

The expansion of institutional secondary schooling reflected great popular support for education. During the course of her 1893 visit to the United States to investigate American girls' secondary education, British educator Sara Burstall found herself presented at every turn with "the extraordinary enthusiasm for education shown by nearly all classes and sections of the community." Respect for teachers and schools, large community expenditures, and frequent discussion of educational issues in the press led Burstall to conclude that there was enormous public interest in schooling. She judged that Americans attached such importance to education for a number of reasons. Common education, Americans assumed, created good citizens and helped meld them into a worthy, unified citizenship. Education reinforced the importance of ideas in a heavily materialistic society. Schooling was a critical means of absorbing immigrants into American society and culture.[41]

High schools offered both academic and practical education to a wide constituent base of students in an effort to deal with the difficulties resulting from moving extended education out of the province of very different families into unified schooling environments. This tactic worked to a great extent in terms of increasing the base of student population. Whereas in 1890, 1 out of every 210 adolescents went to high school, by 1915, that number had risen to 1 out of every 73 adolescents.[42] Jewish girls participated in this growing trend. By 1905, when a number of prominent Jewish communal workers were profiled in *The American Jewish Year Book,* virtually every one of the 90 women included in the capsule biographies had enjoyed at least some secondary education. Of the 61 women who had both graduated from high school and been educated in the United States, 39 had attended public high schools, 14 had attended private high schools, and 8 had attended some combination of public and private high schools.[43]

As the number of schools and students increased, education came more and more to be considered a great leveler, the institutional embodiment of the democratic promise of America. Large urban centers like Boston, Cincinnati, San Francisco, Chicago, and St. Louis all had secondary education firmly in place by the mid- to late nineteenth century, but at the end of the century, new high schools appeared as if overnight. By one count, the number of public high schools raced from 110 in 1880, to 203 in 1890, to 519 in 1900, to 915 in 1910, to 2,200 in 1920.[44] While economic and other social structures complicated that promise throughout the period between 1860 and 1920, there was no doubt that high schools played an important, prominent, and very real role in both shaping American society and in reflecting social change.[45]

Institutional education became the norm as the nineteenth century came to a close, but the kind of schools Jewish girls attended depended largely on class and location. For much of the late nineteenth and early twentieth centuries, middle- and upper-class Jewish girls were regular students at private schools. In addition to marking class status, this propensity also reflected the long-standing tradition of private secondary education for girls in a national context of developing public secondary education.[46] By one estimate, in 1890 there were still 47,397 female students in private high schools compared to 116,351 female students in public high schools. Private education continued to provide an important school setting for girls.[47] Despite socioeconomic differences among the student bodies of private and public schools, Sara Burstall was surprised to note a marked—and growing—degree of similarity of curriculum and standards in all secondary schools.[48] This development was due in part to the slowly but steadily growing numbers of girls who expected their secondary schools to prepare them for going to colleges and universities.

There was great variety in the nature of private school education. Some of the better-known private schools for girls prided themselves on their academic character and were attended by girls from all over the east coast. Other academies and seminaries, particularly after public secondary education began to spread following the Civil War, symbolized social exclusivity more than academic rigor. Jewish girls attended private secondary schools ranging from glorified finishing schools to intensive college preparatory schools to Jewish boarding schools that set themselves apart by offering religious education. As secondary education became more and more acceptable and then expected for middle-class girls in America, Jewish girls' private school experiences changed as ideas about girls' education evolved. The competition mustered by rising educational standards that accompanied the spread of public secondary education eventually prompted most private schools to standardize and improve their own curricula. Other private schools purposely set out to surpass public schools by demanding more of their students than their public counterparts.

Around the country, private schools offered varying degrees of hospitality to Jewish students. For instance, Fannie Hurst found Harperly Hall in St. Louis less than welcoming of her Jewish self. At Fannie's initial interview both she and her mother sensed the headmistress's prejudices.

> The headmistress, a large woman with a wide shelf of a bosom, and salt-and-pepper hair which she wore in a high stern pile, received us. She had my application and school grades before her. Mr. Hurst's occupation? Age. Grandparents, maternal and paternal, names and places of birth. And here it came! Religion? Jewish, replied Mama, as if she were biting off a thread. The headmistress's pen paused an almost imperceptible second and so did my breathing, then both proceeded. What else could Mama have said! But, punily, I would have given anything not to have had her say that word to this lady whose professional graciousness seemed to curdle for the instant and then turn back into cream.[49]

Though she was accepted to Harperly Hall and began the school year there, Fannie felt very isolated and transferred to St. Louis's public high school after three months of private school misery.

As a result of the mixed reception of Jewish girls at private institutions, certain schools in cities around the country became known for welcoming large numbers of Jewish students. Generations of Jewish girls attended Madame Ziska and Miss Murison's schools in San Francisco. The Benjamin Dean school in New York drew Jewish girls from all over the country. Mildred Blum's parents sent their seventeen-year-old to the Benjamin Dean School from Chicago for her senior year, hoping the school would introduce her to museums, opera, and classical music.[50] Hosmer Hall in St. Louis and Miss Hildebrand's school in Cincinnati were two of the private boarding schools that attracted Jewish girls in the Midwest. Hosmer Hall had so many Jewish students that a regular chaperone was assigned to escort the girls to synagogue services.[51]

The academic standards at these private schools were mixed. Miss Murison in San Francisco was known for demanding a great deal of her students and never bothered to have her school accredited, as she felt confident that anyone she educated would pass college boards.[52] The emphasis during Helen Arnstein's years there was placed on English literature, rhetoric, Latin, and French, with some attention to geography and science.[53] Madame Ziska's San Francisco school had a shakier record. Amy Steinhart viewed the school more as a training ground for social leadership than an academic institution.

My two older sisters graduated from Madame Ziska's. There was an article in the *Argonaut* newspaper which in describing this school said that
there was better training in the social graces than in the three R's. The
Argonaut wrote that many alumni learned to count on their fingers, and
I remember going to visit my sister in Chicago and here she was, count-
ing on her fingers![54]

Madame Ziska's did raise its standards over time. Latin was added to the
curriculum the year Amy started high school, and when the school was
turned over to a Miss Lake a few years later, academic concerns moved
to the center of the curriculum. When she was in high school, Alice B.
Toklas was much happier with the curriculum at Miss Lake's than she
had been at her previous school.[55]

Even within a particular private school, standards might be different
for various groups of students. Clara Lowenburg thought her brothers
received a better education than she did during the 1870s in the girls' department of the Campbells' school in Natchez. Though both Mr. and
Mrs. Campbell "were considered fine teachers and a very dignified and
intellectual couple," Clara resented the fact that Mr. Campbell seemed to
think education was less important for girls than for boys.[56] Her education was clearly limited by gender, which played a role in determining the
curriculum at most private schools. Twenty years later, Gertrude Hess
also experienced schooling shaped by gender. She received "the education of a young lady at that time," as defined by her headmistress, Miss
Brackett.

> Miss Brackett's idea of education was to give "young ladies" a polite ed-
> ucation. We had some Latin, French history and literature in French,
> German literature and history in German, a great deal of American and
> English literature, a great deal of Art through pictures of what was in the
> museums all over the world, a smattering of Science—zoology, physiol-
> ogy, botany—and mathematics going a short way into geometry.[57]

Gertrude's education was aimed more at her ability to fit into her class
status than at her intellectual capacity.

The fact that the proprietors of private schools exercised a great deal
of personal discretion over the curriculum also affected the nature of the
education available there. When sixteen-year-old Leonora Levy attended

Miss Rust's school in Richmond during the 1860s, students submitted daily essays on improving themes to their headmistress, who concerned herself with their moral development as well as intellectual growth.[58] Julius Sachs, proprietor of a school in New York, was known for both an explosive temper and a demanding curriculum of French, history, German, literature, and mathematics, although the school remained popular as one of the few run exclusively for Jewish girls.[59] While the curriculum wars being waged in public education had some effect on private education as well, the range of courses available at private schools depended heavily on the predilections of principals and teachers.

At both private and public schools, educators shared the goal of developing secondary education as "a phase of education lying between the earliest period of family-nurture, which is still a concomitant and powerful auxiliary, on the one hand, and the necessary initiation into the specialties of a vocation" on the other hand.[60] Andrew Kerr, principal of Baltimore's Western Female High School, was concerned to "exercise the critical and reasoning faculties" with a course of study that would produce "the best mental discipline," a mental discipline educators believed unlikely to develop outside the institutional setting of schools.[61] Another educator asserted in 1890 that high schools had become the producers of educated men and women by using rationalized methods that families could not effectively provide in industrial society, no matter what their social class or character.[62]

The path toward universal secondary education implied as a desideratum by these educators was rarely smooth. With her British perspective, Sara Burstall pointed out that by setting out to serve the average youth, public schools deprived the exceptionally talented students of opportunities to excel. The democratic ideals of American schooling might, in fact, be robbing especially gifted students of the chance to reach their potential.[63] Other educators fretted that the rhetoric about universal schooling willfully overlooked the large cohort of adolescents whose class status and likely social and occupational futures made high school education not only difficult to attain but also impractical preparation for life. They worried that for all the hand-wringing over the gap between secondary and higher education, the much bigger problem was the relationship of secondary education to the practical necessities of American adolescents and their families.[64] For all its democratic promise, the United States was still a highly stratified society, and the successful expansion of secondary education exposed the different desires, needs, and practical ambitions of various strata.

Through the end of the nineteenth century and into the twentieth century, most high schools remained highly traditional educational spaces. In Alice Marks's classrooms in New York during the 1880s, the teachers sat at special desks on raised platforms at the front and spent most of their time hearing recitations during a school day that lasted from 9 a.m. to 2 p.m.[65] A decade later this kind of passive, teacher-centered education still prevailed. At Central High School in St. Louis, Fannie Hurst found little enthusiasm for either learning or teaching. Although Fannie thrived on the challenge of making herself noticed amid the "overcrowded school of mass education, mass evaluation, and mass graduation," other girls' appreciation of school was dictated in part by the relationships they did or did not establish with teachers.[66] By the mid-1910s, educators had become more attentive to the importance of personal relationships. Brenda Weisberg's rural high school superintendent, for example, invited whole classes to his home for parties that bridged the gap between teachers and students.[67]

As the public high schools expanded and began to serve a growing immigrant population in urban areas, school officials tried to keep track of who their students were and what educational paths they chose. In an effort to analyze student body information, for instance, McKinley High School in Chicago kept careful records of its entering students' personal backgrounds. A typical registration entry recorded that Dora Friedman, enrolled at fifteen years old in 1899, was born in Chicago and was the daughter of Julius, a jeweler, or that Gertrude Cohn, enrolled at fifteen years in 1899, was born in Russia and was the daughter of Mrs. B. Cohn, no occupation listed. Entering students ranged in age from thirteen to sixteen, an indication of still erratic patterns of secondary school attendance.[68] One of the main concerns of high schools like McKinley was the low retention rate of the Dora Friedmans, Gertrude Cohns, and others. Of the 515 girls and 170 boys who entered McKinley in 1892, only 206 girls and 45 boys received diplomas four years later.[69] In St. Paul and Minneapolis, 87 percent of the Jewish girls in immigrant neighborhoods stayed in school until age fifteen in 1910, but nearly the same percentage went to work at age sixteen without graduating from high school.[70] These numbers were typical of urban high schools with large immigrant and working-class populations.

While retention rates rose steadily from 1870 to 1930 and then were ironically given a significant boost by the Depression, relatively few students went to high school and even fewer graduated for much of this period. During the early 1890s, after learning that close to 50 percent of eligible students attended grammar school and less than 10 percent of eligible students attended high school, Brookline, Massachusetts, school administrators decided to increase the number of secondary teachers to reduce student/teacher ratios and try to improve attendance rates.[71] These kinds of measures gradually succeeded. After setting thirteen as the minimum age for admission in 1870, Baltimore's Western Female High School saw first a slight dip in student population but then a steady rise. A school that had no more than 454 students between 1864 and 1873 enrolled closer to 1,000 yearly between 1894 and 1903 and well over 2,000 between 1914 and 1923. As the number of pupils rose, so did the percentage of Jewish students. Henrietta Szold was the only Jewish girl in her Western graduating class in 1877, but subsequent classes enrolled significantly more Jewish students.[72] When Gertrude Mandelbaum attended Chicago's Marshall High School, the student body was more than 90 percent Jewish, just as it had been in her neighborhood elementary school.[73] In the context of such concentrated Jewish populations, institutional secondary education was even less likely to pose a threat to the traditional values shared by an American Jewish community concerned about social integration without loss of Jewish identity.

Secondary Education and the Conservation of Traditional Values

Despite the growing number of teenagers going to high school during the late nineteenth and early twentieth centuries, the privileges of secondary education remained dependent on economic and social status. As one educator pointed out in 1922, "Secondary education is not education for adolescence, as elementary education is education for childhood, but rather education for a selected group of adolescents."[74] The link between family means and schooling not only limited some working-class Jewish girls' educational opportunity but also perpetuated a class division among American Jews that was exacerbated by the freedom from work enjoyed by some but not by others.

Fortunately, for working-class and immigrant Jewish girls who longed for extended schooling, education and work were not mutually exclusive.

Anna Moscowitz worked in a New York button factory every Sunday while she was in high school and taught English to recently arrived immigrants for twenty-five cents a lesson.[75] In Omaha, Lena Meyerson convinced her employer to let her go to Central High in the mornings and work in the afternoons.[76] These girls and many others like them combined work and education to the greatest possible advantage to themselves and their families. Indeed, working-class Jewish girls' education could have a profound effect on their families. By increasing their earning potential, girls could make a significant contribution to the family economy. Through exposure in school to accepted social norms and cultural themes, immigrant girls could assist their families' acculturation process and even facilitate upward mobility by bringing "American" values into their homes. Members of the more established Jewish community who worked with immigrants recognized that daughters shared their parents' dream that with a steady job and a decent salary, a working girl might become "the fairy godmother, who transplants the family from the odious tenement house to the inviting apartment of some pure-odored locality."[77] To that end, individual interest was subordinate to family advantage.

In fact, many eastern European Jewish immigrants were long accustomed to valuing girls and women as sources of income. The working-class immigrant community, whose decisions were driven by need as well as by tradition, saw little to decry in the contribution of daughters to family economies.[78] As Leah Dvorah Orenstein found out firsthand, immigrant families often registered their children in school as two years older than they actually were so that they would be able to leave school and legally begin work earlier. Although her family eventually decided that their collective interest would best be served if she took a business course after elementary school and Leah Dvorah thus did spend two years at a Philadelphia secondary school, neither she nor her family questioned the inevitability of her eventual role as one of many wage earners working on behalf of the family.[79]

Most immigrant Jewish families believed that poverty and ignorance were inextricably linked. As Rose Gollup noted, "We were all ashamed of showing our ignorance. A girl who could not read and write would do anything to hide it. We were as much ashamed of it as we were of our poverty. Indeed, to show one was to show the other. They seemed inseparable."[80] The consequences of decisions about children's education were immediate and dire. "A child that came to this country and began to go to school had taken the first step into the New World," Gollup explained.

"But the child that was put into the shop remained in the old environment with the old people, held back by the old traditions, held back by illiteracy."[81] Immigrant Jewish girls like Polly Adler saw a direct connection between education and brighter prospects for the future. Unhappy with her factory job, sixteen-year-old Polly "felt strongly that it would always be like this for me unless I got more education."[82]

As education became tied more tightly to vocation in turn-of-the-century America, girls increasingly saw schooling as the necessary preparation for a range of new jobs opening to them. Working-class girls found that education would not only improve their opportunities even within traditional women's industrial wage labor but also open up new occupations in office and clerical work or retail and commerce. Middle-class girls' access to new women's professions like social work and librarianship depended on specialized education. While all these types of work operated within a gendered dimension of labor that continued to ascribe certain kinds of work to women, the effects of expanded education for girls on the labor force were undeniable.[83]

Different segments of American Jewry had varying perspectives on the relationships among education, work, and female adolescence. Some Jewish educators deployed middle-class women's leisure as a trope to promote educational segregation along class lines. In 1898, educational administrator Julia Richman asked:

> What matter if the future wife of the workingman fail in her attempt to draw type-solids in groups from the object; fail to recall the bewildering rules and exceptions in technical grammar; fail to extract the cube root of a number . . . what matter? But how grave a matter if she fail to make and keep a home for her young husband; fail, when expending his hard-earned wages, to purchase with prudence and judgment; fail to prepare for him a wholesome and inexpensive meal; fail to rear their children with proper care for their physical and moral welfare! . . . The girls reared in the real homes where comfort and cleanliness rule are fully entitled to the higher education that brings in its train literature, philosophy, languages, and abstract mathematics; but for those who must forego these with other luxuries, special training must be provided that shall enable them to handle the difficulties of housekeeping.[84]

For Richman there was little to no belief that class lines could blur or be crossed, nor did she seem to recognize that gender created barriers to work and education as surely as class did. Richman's blindness to these issues reflected debates of the day, as even the most thoughtful of educational critics typically overlooked the ways in which class and gender limited the ostensibly democratic nature of American education.

Richman represented an influential group of prominent educators, who believed that in no sense should immigrant Jewish girls' schooling enable them to aspire to or achieve more than their social status dictated. This widely shared inability to recognize Jewish immigrant parents and daughters' hopes for and expectations of education led even the most involved communal workers to denounce "the misguided ambition of parents whose only conception of education is that it transforms their daughters into teachers or at least book-keepers."[85] Many established American Jews had worked so hard to distance themselves from the immigrant Jewish families that they could not conceive of sharing similar ambitions for their daughters or even of sharing the value of education beyond its importance as direct job training.

Whether unpaid household work or waged labor, most American Jewish girls understood work as an inevitable part of life. However, the economic differences within the Jewish community expressed themselves within the different roles work played for working-class and middle-class girls. The immigrant girls living at the Jewish agricultural school in Woodbine, New Jersey, during the 1890s attended to all the housework of the school in addition to their class work. They were expected to help prepare meals and wash dishes, to serve at the tables, to iron and mend clothes, and to do general cleaning.[86] Household work of this kind also dominated Celia Kamins's adolescence in rural North Dakota, where she moved with her mother and stepfather in 1912. Making time for school amid the demands of farm life was very difficult for Celia, who was

> almost a dropout in school because there were only certain days that I could go to school. I couldn't go on Monday because I had to help my mother wash clothes. I couldn't go on Tuesday because we had to iron and bake. I would go Wednesday and Thursday, but Friday I had to stay out because we had to clean house and bake for the weekend.[87]

Whether helping their mothers with chores or performing continual, time-consuming domestic duties, working-class Jewish girls grew up with work as a constant companion.

Middle-class Jewish mothers also often required their daughters to do some household work, as a signifier of their domestic destinies, if not their essential contributions to homes that required their labor. Among the families of Jewish girls attending Baltimore's Western Female High School during the 1890s, mothers "made few demands on our time though quite a number did dutifully enlist our services in cleaning or baking . . . and perhaps even required a few daily chores."[88] For upwardly mobile families, daughters' household work was a tricky business. While girls' leisure signified class status, many Jewish families never felt quite secure and worried about what might happen to unprepared girls should there be a reversal of fortune. The American Jewish press warned parents not to relieve their daughters of all responsibility for just this reason. Writing in 1890, playwright Martha Morton urged middle-class Jewish parents to remember that "because of the hazard of fortune, shifting with the times, every individual member of a family should be educated to the means of self-support."[89]

The upper crust of American Jewish society felt free to ignore this pessimistic advice. The wealthy Kahn family excused daughter Carmen from all household tasks and sent her to a boarding school in St. Louis where her peers were from equally privileged backgrounds. At Hosmer Hall, Carmen and her friends "were spoiled by having maids come to wash our dishes, pots, and pans, after cooking classes! It was assumed—and rightly so—that none of us had ever washed dishes in our homes."[90] The fact that these wealthy girls took cooking classes, despite assumptions that they would never have to cook for themselves, illustrates the centrality of domesticity in educational practices shaped by gender as much as class.

Although ideas about girlhood and womanhood were very much in transition at the end of the nineteenth and beginning of the twentieth century, at no point were they removed from the educational opportunities of Jewish girls. Conventions of gender had everything to do with the ways in which immigrant Jewish families acculturated into American society, as adapting to widely accepted gender roles, even as they shifted, was a prime means of demonstrating successful Americanization. The connection between girls' education and women's independence, much discussed in the American Jewish press, provided another bridge toward integration into American society. This bridge was undergirded in part by normative, middle-class gender models, despite the fact that the actual social conditions of women were changing. The changes did not go unrecognized, but they were continually linked to widely shared assumptions about women's essential domesticity. Girls' education was thus addressed simultaneously by both continuity and change in gender roles.

At the turn of the century, Americans of virtually all backgrounds viewed education as a key to independence, whether economic or personal or some combination thereof. For immigrant girls, in particular, any sustained education might well propel them into an entirely different social or cultural arena and thereby support independence, even if they continued to live at home. In modernizing American Jewish society, marriage became an increasingly questionable solution to girls' presumed economic dependence. Education offered a different kind of solution to problems of independence and social roles. While most American Jewish girls still married eventually, there was a growing communal concern with ensuring that girls of all classes prepare for lives as individuals, not just as wives and mothers, whose identity would be determined by their relationship to others.

Contributors to the American Jewish press expressed repeated interest in the notion of fostering independence in Jewish girls. Among poorer Jewish families, one writer pointed out in 1903, the "adequate education of women follows by consequence" the state of affairs in which "the economic no less than the spiritual survival of the family depends upon the exertions of its women as well as its men."[91] Another writer addressed better-off Jewish families on the same theme, writing that the wealthy mother would do well, "equally with those forced to do it, if she would thoroughly educate her daughters in one of those trades or vocations, thus devoting worthily the time and money uselessly spent on accomplishments which accomplish naught but annoyance to friends and neighbors."[92] Julia Richman agreed, speaking broadly to Jewish girls when she wrote in 1890 that the central contradiction for all Jewish girls, no matter what their class background, was the problem of training "our girls for wifehood without making it seem the chief aim in life."[93]

The rhetoric and logic of these writers echoed a broader cultural debate over "the girl question" and the "girl of the period."[94] Women's rights activists had long deplored female dependence as a major factor contributing to the great gender divide in Western industrial society. By the 1880s, education was widely touted not only as a means of increasing the quality and quantity of experiences shared by young men and women but also as a means of rehabilitating women's perceived mental and physical inferiority. As activist Mary Livermore said:

As the theory that "all men support all women" does not fit the facts, it is time for us to reform our theory as well as our practice. I would give to all girls equal intellectual and industrial training with boys. I would not give them the same training unless they were fitting for the same work, business, or profession; but I would, in all cases, give to them equal advantages. . . . Self-support would then be possible to her, and she would not float on the current of life, a part of its useless driftwood, borne hither and thither by its troubled waters. There would then be fewer heavily taxed fathers and brothers, toiling like galley-slaves to support healthy and vigorous human beings in stagnating idleness—idle for no earthly reason than that God has made them women.[95]

The growing currency of this kind of progressive attitude toward girls' education had a powerful impact on conceptions of the gendered relationship between education and productivity. The great challenge was to build an educational system that would respond to the modern concerns of this relationship.

Class, Curriculum, and Coeducation

The benefits of education were real, especially for middle-class families whose daughters' secondary schooling confirmed their class status and for working-class families whose daughters' extended education strengthened their economic situation. However, the content and form of secondary education was deeply rooted in conventions of class and gender that compromised girls' independence. Just as Jewish girls' educational opportunity was limited by these conventions, so were their educational experiences even when they did attend secondary schools. Ironically, social roles and norms exerted more, not less, of an influence on American secondary education as greater numbers of adolescents attended high school. As the public high schools that most Jewish girls attended by the end of the nineteenth century grew in size, they were better able to separate students into groups to be educated according to their class and gender identities.

Educational historian Lawrence Cremin has called the comprehensive high schools "one of the most significant innovations of American schooling," praising them for affording more students a wider array of school opportunities.[96] Yet Cremin, no less than turn-of-the-century educators, recognized the influence of family needs and desires on the education of daughters and sons. The Cardinal Principles of Secondary Education, formulated in 1918, reflected these concerns, stating that "secondary education should be determined by the needs of the society to be served, the character of the individuals to be educated, and the knowledge of educational theory and practice available."[97] The heated debates over curricula and educational content that dominated the turn-of-the-century educational scene reflected the basic tension between the democratizing promise of liberal education and the economic need of many, if not most, students for practical schooling if extended education were to be justifiable.

While few would have disagreed with Progressive Era educator Ross Finney that the development of the modern high school was a landmark "development of American education because it signifies that a liberal instead of a meager education is to be furnished to everybody," the contested definitions of "liberal" and "meager" education affected every high school student, parent, teacher, administrator, and theorist of the period.[98] Students may not have been aware of all the theoretical debates, but they recognized the ways in which the resulting options affected their own educational choices. Grand ideas about education were not necessarily the rationales behind the choices Jewish girls made, however. In San Francisco, Sylvia Hirsch preferred Lowell High School to Girls High School because she was afraid that at the latter school she would have to take sewing and cooking, subjects which held no interest for her.[99] Before her family moved away from Philadelphia, Minnie Seltzer was unsure whether she should attend William Penn High School for the commercial course or Girls High School for the academic course. She wanted to do what would be best for family finances in the long run.[100] Though these girls made individual decisions, they did so within the context of gender and class imperatives that structured their choices. Sylvia rejected the gender conventions she feared would shape her education at a sex-segregated school, while Minnie used her class status to determine the education best for her family.

The decades during which the population base of public secondary education expanded saw frequent changes in basic curricula, many of which reinforced rather than broke down gender and class structures. Trying to respond to the varying demands of a wide range of students, educational theorists, college administrators, and employers, high school officials tinkered endlessly with the kinds of courses available in high schools. Though there was little formal standardization from school to school, except in the largest, most well-organized city systems, some broad trends

Setty Swartz, age 13, 1881. The Swartz family was in Westwood, Ohio, not far from Setty's Cincinnati home. The photograph shows her extended family, including Deborah Stix, Caroline Swartz, Mrs. J. J. Wertheimer, Louis J. Wertheimer, Louis J. Friedman, Harry L. Swartz, Charles Stix, Christopher Schrommel, and Sol L. Leowitz. Setty is the figure reading with a hat on her lap. *Courtesy of the Jacob Rader Marcus Center of the American Jewish Archives.*

were observable. Until 1910 or so, the high school curriculum characteristically featured foreign languages, English literature, mathematics, science, and some history. Setty Swartz's education at Hughes High School in Cincinnati was typical. Before graduating in 1886, she took four years of Latin and French, three years of composition, two years of English, two years of history, one year each of algebra and geometry, one year each of zoology, natural philosophy, and chemistry, and one year of elocution.[101] After 1910, the percentage of students studying Latin, German, mathematics, and some sciences declined, while the percentage studying French, English literature, and history held steady or rose. The number of students taking the newer subjects of general science, manual training, home economics, and commercial subjects increased rapidly.[102]

The formation of various curricula within the schools reflected, in part, the pressure high schools exerted on colleges to broaden the basis of admission. As David E. Weglein, principal of Baltimore's Western High School from 1906 to 1921, explained:

> In a modern high school, pupils should be permitted to select one of a number of suitable curricula, and should not be allowed to select subjects at random. Each of the curricula should provide all the elements that go to make adequate high school education, so that no matter which curriculum a pupil may select, an adequate secondary education may be observed.[103]

Schools across the country, especially in the urban areas where most Jewish students lived, operated on these principles. Connecticut's Bridgeport High School, for instance, offered six curricula: a college preparatory course, a scientific preparatory course, a general course, a normal course, a commercial course, and an industrial arts course. All were coeducational, except the normal course, which was for girls, and the industrial arts course, which was for boys. Suburban schools had similar options even when the student body was smaller. At Mt. Vernon High School in New York's Westchester County in 1921, girls could choose from the classical, scientific, general, commercial, or household arts tracks. The wide range of options meant that parents and students exercised considerable control over the high school experience, although their decisions were always shaped by economics and other external factors.[104]

Western Female High School, which enrolled ever-increasing numbers of Jewish students as the fortunes of the Baltimore Jewish community rose, exemplified these curricular changes. While in 1876 there was still a one-year course in English, history, physical geography, physics, and bookkeeping available for students who only wanted or could only afford a single year of secondary education, this program was phased out in order to better serve the regular—and growing—student body. History, which had sporadically been in the curriculum since the 1850s, became a requirement for all students from the time of a curricular organization that departmentalized teachers in 1901. Freshmen took ancient history, sophomores medieval and modern history, juniors English history, and seniors American history and civics. An early mathematics offering focused on algebra and arithmetic. After 1901, freshmen took algebra, sophomores took plane geometry, and juniors and seniors had electives in solid geometry and trigonometry. Starting from 1892, four years of Latin were offered so that girls at Western would have the same opportunities as the boys at Baltimore City College, Western's male counterpart. French was featured in Western's curriculum from the school's early days. German was taught for all four years by 1885, but in 1893, students began to choose either French or German as electives while also taking Latin. From 1903, all students chose either French or German or Latin as their foreign language, until in 1917 German was discontinued due to World War I anti-German sentiment and Spanish replaced it for commercial students. Science remained a constant part of the curriculum, but there were no experiments or lab work in freshman botany or physiology, sophomore zoology or biology, junior chemistry, and senior astronomy or mental philosophy until 1910.[105]

Perhaps the most telling curricular changes at Western were the addition of stenography in 1902 and a complete commercial course of bookkeeping, commercial arithmetic, and typewriting from 1904. Home economics classes began in 1912.[106] These additions reflected a movement toward diversified high school curricula and the elective system that permanently altered the landscape of secondary education in America.[107] Instead of providing a reasonably common experience for all high school students, secondary schools gradually began to offer curricular tracks of varying intensities focused on different student needs and requirements. The elective system took hold, and separate courses within the same school became commonplace. Most pervasive were the vocational courses added to virtually every high school's classes. In some cities separate vocational high schools were established to serve the large numbers of high school students who wished secondary education to have more of a practical purpose than traditional academic preparation.[108] As a result of the shift toward vocationally oriented education, girls and boys' school experiences differed more than they had previously. The courses in shop, architectural drawing, woodwork, and mechanics offered to boys at Chicago's English High and Manual Training School for Boys were nowhere to be seen amid the sewing, cooking, and home economics classes at the Lucy Flower Technical High School for Girls.[109] As high schools increasingly became preparation venues for adolescents' future rather than sites of primarily academic learning, the differentials of gendered social futures exerted retroactive pressure on secondary education and ensured the divided school experiences of boys and girls.[110]

The advantages of vocational education that encouraged both individual and family advancement were apparent to parents and children involved with a range of schools. Commercial education was popular at all high schools, not just explicitly vocational institutions.[111] In Boston, 9 out of the 11 high schools open to girls offered commercial classes by the beginning of the twentieth century. By 1913, over 67 percent of the girls enrolled in Boston high schools studied at least one commercial subject, with the percentages the greatest where economic pressure was the heaviest.[112] Of 145 Jewish girls attending the high school in Bridgeport, Connecticut, in 1920, 55 percent enrolled in the commercial course as opposed to 23 percent in the college course, 21 percent in the normal course, and 1 percent in the general course.[113]

Despite the popularity of vocational education, which included domestic science and industrial arts as well as commercial training, there was sustained opposition from some educators, students, and parents to what they saw as an unfortunate move away from liberal education.[114] Chicago schools superintendent George Howland believed that vocational education in public schools would lead to schooling stratified by class. "In the high school I never found crocheting a special help toward mental or moral culture," he wrote in 1888, during the earliest stages of vocationalism's growing influence.

> Our schools are to educate not servants but citizens; and whenever the darning and the frying, the starching and the stewing become important parts of the school work, the wealthier classes will send their children to private schools and the public school to which we look for the preparation of our children for responsible places in our business and social life, will become but an industrial school for cooks and second girls, instead of intelligent men and women ready to act well their parts in whatever pursuits their inclinations or necessities may lead them to engage.[115]

Concern about the effect of vocational education became an issue in the American Jewish community as well. Commenting on "Some Tendencies of Modern Education" at the Jewish Chautauqua Society some twenty years later, Henry Leipziger pointed out:

> We have now reached that stage of the conflict in which it has become generally apparent to the thoughtful that while practical studies are a

primary necessity to insure to a youth a place of usefulness and a compe-
tence, that is but a narrow, one sided, perverse training which looks only
to the skill of the hand, accuracy of the eye, alertness of the mind and
omits the development of taste and of the faculty for enjoyment in the
realms of literature, art, music, aesthetics and all the other refinements
of the education of culture.

Urging Jewish educators to participate in "the spiritualizing of knowledge," he argued that ignorance led to lack of religion and that it had always been the role of Jews to lead the world toward "the pathways of
progress." Leipziger believed firmly in the separation of church and state
but was also convinced that the presence of innumerable Jewish students
in public schools that had lost their way required a distinctly Jewish response.[116]

No significant response was forthcoming, perhaps due to the fact that
the vocationalism Howland and Leipziger feared was denuding all liberal
education was not entirely doing so. The development of the elective system and the creation of differentiated curricula within comprehensive
high schools still offered most high school students and their families
some choices about education that they were responsible for making.
Bertha Markowitz opted for traditional classes in English, history, Latin,
German, and mathematics at Edmonds High School in Burlington, Vermont, during the mid-1910s, despite the wide range of commercial subjects offered at the school.[117] Rose Zetzer, who took stenography and
home economics and other vocationally oriented classes at Eastern High
School in Baltimore, still listed English and history as her favorite subjects
in her scrapbook.[118] Just as few girls perceived education as a force that
alienated them from their collective family goals, few considered the
boundaries between vocational training and liberal education as an impermeable one.

Vocational education and liberal education may have coexisted to
some degree, but the trend toward practical education did have consequences for the role of gender in schools. The rise of vocational education
led to a kind of regression in the spread of coeducational secondary education. Once progressive educators situated schooling as a practical
process, designed to prepare students for their future roles in society, the
undeniable differences between socialized gender roles seemed to call for
different, and necessarily separate, education for girls and boys. To some
extent this development countered the rapidity with which high schools

had become coeducational in the first place. During the 1891–1892 school year, only fifteen cities maintained separate high schools for girls and boys. While some of these cities, such as Baltimore, Boston, and Philadelphia, were large and influential in the educational world, they were clearly bucking a growing trend. In some of those same cities that continued to support separate boys' and girls' schools, new high schools built there were coeducational alternatives. As a result, by 1900, only 72 out of 6,005 American high schools were sex-segregated; in 1910, 60 out of 10,213 were sex-segregated; and in 1920, 78 out of 14,326 were sex-segregated. The large growth in high school facilities across the nation is evident in these statistics. The fact that in absolute terms there were more sex-segregated schools in 1920 than in 1910 may be explained by the building of separate vocational schools that were more likely to be for girls or boys only.[119]

The positive aspects of coeducation, which was still promoted as natural, impartial, economical, convenient, and beneficial for girls and boys alike, were emphasized by college-level educators and women's advocates, who wished to strengthen the case for coeducational colleges and women's higher education more generally. In smaller towns, expense also precluded the possibility of supporting separate girls' and boys' schools during the high school building boom of the second half of the nineteenth century. When Maud Nathan's family moved to Green Bay, Wisconsin, in 1875, she found going to the same school as her brother a novel experience but a pleasant change from the private girls' school she had attended in New York.

Maud thought that going to a coeducational school affected the content of her education as well as her adolescent social interactions. She was sure that her New York school would never have bothered to teach the Constitution to a group of girls who would not become full citizens.[120] Maud and other girls also enjoyed the social side benefits of coeducation. Sara Liebenstein "had no special interest in boys" but found them highly congenial study partners less easily distracted than her female classmates.[121] Maud took pleasure in the more casual relations between boys and girls fostered by coeducation.

One feature of co-education appealed very strongly to me; this was the freedom that resulted in regard to social relationship. When school was over, the boys took the girls home in their sleighs—perhaps taking them for a sleigh ride first—or they walked home with them, chivalrously carrying their books for them. These girls and boys, having been brought up together from babyhood, naturally called each other by their Christian names. My parents were shocked to find that I was sharing in this familiarity. They thought that the boys ought to call me "Miss Maud," and that I should address them by their surnames.

Maud did no such thing and relished the educational and social opportunities that resulted from her coeducational experiences.[122] The customs of her peers mattered more to her than the traditions of her parents in this regard.

The peer culture that followed from coeducational schools was one of the ways in which secondary education did disrupt traditions that kept the sexes segregated. Because of the social conventions that had kept boys and girls apart for so long, not everyone accepted coeducation with equanimity. School administrator Ross Finney's casual remark in 1921 that "there never was any dispute about the equal status of girls in the public high schools" obscured a more complicated history of coeducation.[123] When Jennie Franklin read her graduation essay on the subject in 1891, she was countering arguments that coeducation flew in the face of propriety, ignored boys' and girls' unequal capacities, led to overlarge schools, reversed traditional social segregation of the sexes, and exposed girls to the vicious influence of boys.[124] Influential social theorist G. Stanley Hall believed firmly that adolescence was precisely when the sexes should diverge in civilized society and that coeducation discouraged girls from embracing the domestic tasks for which they should be trained.[125] Coeducation seemed to threaten the very social traditions that institutionalized education generally supported.

Even teachers who applauded coeducation in theory expressed their doubts about its practicality, given observable differences in girls' and boys' behavior. One experienced teacher explained that

> when the girls enter the High School, they are more mature, more honest in work, with greater powers of concentration, and are more apt in acquiring information. This lasts for a year or two; then the boys develop, and become at 16 thinking beings. Boys excel in mathematics, economics, and civics; girls hold their own in languages and history, and many do well in science. Girls always do rote work better than their brothers.[126]

In 1905, the principal of Englewood High School in Chicago, committed to the idea that woman had "the right to an equal opportunity with man for intellectual and social freedom," nonetheless arranged an experiment in separating boys and girls into different classes within the coeducational school. Concluding that the separation benefited both girls, who could better be drawn out in segregated classes, and boys, who could better be disciplined in separated classes, he successfully petitioned the Chicago Board of Education to broaden the practice in his school.[127]

The perception that coeducational schools served girls and boys differently was widespread. The school superintendent in Baltimore, concerned that schools did less for girls than boys, reported in 1907:

> In the secondary schools a boy may get the training that will fit him quite well to enter at once, upon graduation, into remunerative employment in any one of a number of occupations; the girl, in our High School course, finds open to her only one vocational department—that of stenography and typewriting.[128]

In fact, the superintendent omitted that other type of girls' vocational education, domestic science, which would have reinforced his point still further. Ironically, progressive education, with its focus on social efficiency, was so rooted in gendered ideas about social functions that it led to a regression in the same coeducation that was supposed to ensure healthy interactions between the sexes.[129] Social rather than academic school activities became the locus of the benefits of coeducation.

As the debate over coeducation makes clear, healthy social interactions between the sexes at school did not necessarily translate into similar educational experiences. However, regardless of the strictures of gender and class present in their education, most students at the turn of the century appreciated their opportunities and continued to regard their high school experiences as important parts of their lives. Graduates of Chicago's West Division High School held yearly reunions with entertainment to commemorate the privileges of their secondary school days. In 1895, the class of 1885, which had been comprised of 64 girls and 22 boys, issued a special booklet marking their tenth-year anniversary. The *History and Records of the Class of 1885, Chicago West Division High School* included entries offering informative updates on each graduate. Classmates could learn that Esther Friend had married Harry Falkenau, a book dealer, and still lived in Chicago, or that Carrie Hershman had married Isaac Guthmann, a merchant, and lived in La Salle, Illinois, with her husband and son Elias.[130]

At her reunion in 1902, Lizzie Black Kander, historian of the Milwaukee High School class of 1878, recalled her classmates' first day at school. Comparing the raw freshmen they had been with "a group of immigrants just landed," she went on to describe their school experiences and explained how influential they had been in so many lives.[131] Despite all the grand ambitions their education fostered in the graduates they had been, almost all the girls had settled into traditional lives as wives and mothers. This did not necessarily mean abandoning all earlier interests. Lizzie herself, heavily involved in settlement work, retained her adolescent sense of justice and obligation. Even the few girl graduates who did not join their classmates in matrimony and motherhood, however, followed one of the few prescribed paths for women. Like Lizzie's high school friend Bertha Kahn, most were teachers.

As a result of a continuous set of traditional expectations for women, gender shaped American secondary education for both middle-class and working-class girls, regardless of the kinds of secondary schooling they experienced. Jewish girls were particularly bound by these conventions because the Jewish community was reluctant to let go of girls, whose gender roles within the community made them too important to experiment with. This trend was most evident in Jewish girls' post-secondary educational opportunities or lack thereof. Although there was change over time, the discrepancy between numbers of Jewish girls who attended high school and those who attended college reveals the limits on their educational opportunities enforced by a combination of American and Jewish traditions.

Post-Secondary Education and the
Limits on Jewish Girls' Opportunity

As the female graduates at Lizzie Black Kander's high school reunion demonstrated, teaching represented one of the few paths toward post-secondary education for adolescent girls at the turn of the century. Because teaching was increasingly associated with women, the normal school training that qualified many young women as teachers during the late nineteenth century did not threaten gender conventions any more than secondary education did. In fact, many girls' high schools had originally been founded as teacher training institutions. In some cities, separate public normal schools at the secondary level were especially popular with girls. The 1870s and 1880s were the heyday of normal schools at the high school level. When Anna Allen and Ella Jacobs went to normal school in Philadelphia in 1876, they only attended classes every other day due to overenrollment.[132] By the 1890s, however, pedagogy was being phased out of high school course work because purely professional training in separate normal schools was preferred.[133] Post-secondary education became the preferred option for girls who wished to teach as well as those who had other goals in mind.

Jewish girls who wanted to attend college during the late nineteenth and early twentieth centuries were likely to face some obstacles. Parental opposition played a large role in the decisions of girls not to prolong their education—and their adolescence—by going to college. Maud Nathan never even entertained the idea of going to college. She was aware of her mother's strong opinions about colleges and girls. Maud's mother, reflecting the late nineteenth-century belief in the inviolate mother-daughter bond, believed that "when a girl was sent to college . . . it was a sure sign that the girl's mother had lost control over her and had felt it necessary for her daughter to be disciplined by college life." When her mother died shortly after Maud's high school graduation, she still gave little thought to college. She continued piano and sewing lessons and read history, literature, and French, but continuing education and formal higher education were not synonymous to her.[134]

Parents who opposed college education for their daughters were not benighted or cruel. They worried about the effects of flouting convention, or sincerely believed that higher education was unnecessary, or had other ideas about what their daughters should do. Helen Arnstein was interested in going to college after finishing high school in San Francisco, but her mother, an inveterate reader and active clubwoman, preferred Helen to stay home.[135] Anticipating resistance, Frieda Fligelman began her college campaign early. At fifteen, she tried to find a job so that she could finance her own upcoming college career over the united opposition of her parents, who wanted to send Frieda and her sister Belle to finishing school like their neighbors' daughters.

All the other girls that we knew in Helena went to finishing school. And were they finished! They came back knowing how to be Ladies. They could play the piano and they knew how to sit down without crossing their knees. They made Ladies out of the crudest of us. And our parents were very anxious that we should go, too. A finishing school was attended after high school and instead of college. No Lady would go to college. That was a little crude.

The Fligelmans believed that finishing school would confer untold advantages upon their daughters and wanted them to have every opportunity, but Frieda had other ideas. Though she did not find a job, her strong feelings eventually convinced her parents to send her to college against their better judgment.[136]

The small number of Jewish girls who attended college reflected the reality that most middle-class families, Jewish or not, simply did not perceive college education as necessary or desirable for girls and may also have worried about the observably low marriage rate of female college graduates. Working-class families that favored girls' education were still struggling to provide their daughters with high school diplomas. College seemed a distant dream to most working-class girls, even in cities like New York, where free tuition was available at some institutions of higher education.[137]

The desire of some Jewish girls to go to college faced the vexed relationship between American high schools and colleges.[138] Only a small number of adolescents graduated from high school, and an even smaller percentage of these high school graduates went on to college. In the academic year 1889–1890, for example, 295,733 students attended public and private high schools. Of these pupils, only 55,517 were enrolled in college preparatory courses and fewer still actually matriculated at colleges and universities.[139] Jewish girls' college attendance lagged even further behind. As late as 1916, only 2.2 American boys and 1.1 American girls went to college out of every 1,000 people. The comparable numbers were 3.6 Jewish boys and .4 Jewish girls per 1,000 people. A 1920 study of 106 major colleges and universities found that among non-Jewish students, the ratio of female to male students was one to three. Among Jewish students, however, the ratio of female to male students was one to five.[140]

The high standards of many of the colleges that did accept women made it difficult for most girls who did not attend explicitly college preparatory institutions. When Bertha Szold graduated from Baltimore's Western Female High School in 1888, she had to attend the Misses

Adams's school for two years before going to college because she was not yet prepared for Bryn Mawr, which prided itself on especially rigorous admission standards. Despite graduating from a highly regarded high school, only after receiving an additional certificate of proficiency in English, mathematics, and foreign languages and passing another entrance exam could Bertha matriculate at Bryn Mawr.[141] Recognizing the still uneven, if slowly improving, standardization of secondary education, Barnard for a long time admitted students who were unprepared as "two-year specials." Iphigene Ochs was one of these students who was not prepared for the regular college course, and after initially beginning in the special program, she started the difficult preparation for the four-year course entrance exams. Not until her junior year did Iphigene pass all the requirements and become a regular Barnard student. She graduated in 1914 with a major in economics and history.[142] The difficulty these girls had in gaining access to college education reflected not only parental ambivalence and communal indifference but also institutionalized weaknesses in girls' secondary education.

When the National Education Association's Committee of Ten issued its landmark report on college admission requirements in 1893, the report stated as fact that

> the secondary schools of the United States, taken as a whole, do not exist for the purpose of preparing boys and girls for colleges. Only an insignificant percentage of the graduates of these schools go to colleges or scientific schools.

While supporting the independence of high schools by suggesting greater curricular flexibility, the Committee of Ten deplored this situation and tried to align secondary and higher education more closely. The report continued, "The colleges and scientific schools should be accessible to all boys or girls who have completed creditably the secondary school course" and urged colleges to accept "the attainments of any youth who has passed creditably through a good secondary school course, no matter what group of subjects he may have mainly devoted himself in the secondary school."[143] This recommendation, gradually put into place by American secondary schools, had important consequences. It allowed students to make decisions about college at any point during their high school years, replacing the earlier necessity of deciding right away which kind of secondary education to pursue. The ancillary, though ultimately even more important, effect on secondary education was the subsequent need to teach all subjects the same way to all pupils, college-bound or not. As the suggestions of the Committee of Ten gradually took effect, preparatory departments became less common and less necessary as college admission standards broadened and high school education standardized. However, the process was a contentious one that took a long time to succeed.

Dubious attitudes toward higher education for women were even slower to dissipate.[144] In an address delivered at the oratorical exercises of the University of Cincinnati in 1891, nineteen-year-old Jennie Mannheimer regretfully acknowledged that "in this so-called intellectual age there is still found a goodly number of people, who claiming to be abreast of the times, nonetheless look upon a higher or college education as superfluous for women." She supported both coeducational and women's colleges, commenting mildly that each had its place in American educational life. Jennie pointed out that Jewish girls, in particular, could draw on a rich tradition of "Hebrew ancestors," who elevated women and insisted on their learning. Directly addressing the problem of parental, particularly maternal, opposition, she informed her audience at the coeducational University of Cincinnati that

> few mothers now keep their daughters away from college through fear that their heads may be so filled with the classics and the ologies and osophies that there will be no room left for the knowledge of managing a household. They recognize more and more that the methodical habits acquired at college make themselves felt in every work to which their hands may turn.[145]

In 1891, such debates about women's higher education raged throughout the country. As the cohort of college women increased in size and religious and ethnic inclusivity, going to college became more and more acceptable a goal for girls.

In Jewish families, like other American families, changing attitudes toward girls' higher education were visible across the generations.[146] College never presented itself as a possibility to Lizzie Spiegel Barbe, who did not even complete high school, but during the late 1890s her daughters Ella Rachel and Myrtle Agnes continued their education at the University of Chicago and the Armour Institute of Technology, respectively.[147] One of the first actions taken in 1899 by the newly formed Western Female

Jennie Mannheimer, age 18, 1888. The photograph shows Jennie's graduating class at Hughes High School in Cincinnati. The girls clearly outnumbered the boys at the coeducational high school. *Courtesy of the Jacob Rader Marcus Center of the American Jewish Archives.*

High School Alumni Association, headed by Henrietta Szold, was to sponsor a scholarship for Western graduates who wished to attend the Woman's College of Baltimore. This group of women, who by generation and circumstance had largely been unable to attend college, wished to ensure that "the higher education for women in this city [will] receive an impetus that promises to carry it forward swiftly and surely" for the rising generation of high school graduates.[148]

Not even support from their mothers' generation could prevent the old prejudices exposed by Jewish girls' new opportunities. Though to some degree Jewish girls' college experiences resembled those of such fictional characters as Ruth Fielding and other "college girl" heroines, in many cases their Jewishness presented something of a social barrier.[149] Proponents of college education for Jewish girls uneasily tried to dismiss this apparent difficulty. Writing about "What the American College Means to the Jewess" in 1914, an alumna carefully explained:

If a Jewess is seldom elected to the more desirable and honor-bearing offices such as president of the class or of the undergraduate body, this is only natural because the Jewish girls are, after all, in the minority and the majority prefer a president who is just as capable and perhaps closer to them.

She acknowledged that sororities were likely to be closed to Jewish girls on any campus but was quick to point out that this disadvantage left Jewish students with more time to excel at their studies.[150] Sylvia Hirsch knew that her acceptance into the University of California at Berkeley's Torch and Shield honor society was unusual for a Jewish girl. At the time she matriculated in 1919, there were Jewish community concerns about campus discrimination.

> I was rushed to a few sororities, but not seriously, because most of them didn't take Jews, and I was so consciously Jewish, although I had a lot of friends from high school that weren't Jewish. I went to several rush things, but I told them I was Jewish and I didn't think I belonged. . . . It was unusual that I got into Torch and Shield, because there were very few Jewish girls who did it. There was an article about me published in the *Emanu-El*, the Jewish newspaper. It was titled "One Jewish Girl." There were many accusations of anti-Semitism on the campus, that Jewish women couldn't get any high offices. . . . A lot of Jewish girls weren't interested in campus activities, but I loved it.[151]

Social barriers notwithstanding, Sylvia and most other Jewish college students reveled in their educational opportunities. However, the social prejudices that kept Jewish girls always a little apart undermined the very processes of acculturation that brought them onto campus in the first place.

Jewish Girls and Educational Boundaries

The conventions that kept Jewish girls a little apart on campus also kept them a little apart within the Jewish community. By the time Sylvia graduated from the University of California at Berkeley, a small number of Jewish girls attended colleges and universities all over the country. Like Sylvia, they found college an exciting mix of academic and social life that resembled their high school experiences. Yet they also found that there was a price to be paid within their own communities for going so far beyond traditional expectations for women. One group of Jewish girls with college degrees, still a remarkable achievement in 1920, discovered that their unusual accomplishments hindered their marital prospects. In a letter to Chicago's *Sunday Jewish Courier,* they lamented:

> We consider that it would be a waste of all our training and hard work at school to choose as our associates young men who have not had as good a training as ours; yet it is practically impossible for us to meet the kind of man with whom we should like to associate . . . are our young Jewish doctors, lawyers, and other professionals too busy to enjoy the company of girls who are not only pretty but also intelligent?[152]

The same young men who had in many cases been their college classmates and shared their experiences were now looking for wives among the less adventurous and less modernized Jewish girls. The reluctance of so many Jewish parents to allow their daughters to go to college reflected in large part the reality that the Jewish community as a whole was unprepared to support girls' education once it became more directly threatening to religious and social traditions. Resistance to girls' education increased as the intellectual growth and sometimes physical separation from home and community implicit in higher education seemed to pose an unacceptable threat to the centrality of the family.

In general, the educational experiences of adolescent Jewish girls reflected the steady expansion of secondary education throughout America between 1865 and 1920. Jewish girls' education moved out of the home and into the school. As the number of public high schools exploded in cities and towns all over the country, the population of high school students widened to include both middle-class students who might previously have attended private schools and working-class students whose family finances allowed them to stay in school. The development of a variety of curricular options within any given institution made secondary schooling even more appealing to a wider base of families who looked to schools to teach useful skills and strengthen commonly shared ideas. As the American Jewish community became increasingly committed to acculturation, high schools seemed to offer Jewish girls and boys the ideal spaces to integrate into their peer group and develop their abilities without seriously challenging core communal values. Jewish parents were far more ambivalent about post-secondary education for girls, which they identified as a possible threat to family unity and traditional goals.

As long as education was perceived as encouraging individual development without endangering allegiance to home and family, most Jews embraced the opportunities for schooling that America provided, even for the daughters who had traditionally been excluded from many forms of institutionalized education. American high schools, structured in so many ways to bolster rather than undermine widely shared assumptions about gender and class, seemed to provide ample space to sustain tradition while still exposing students to the individual benefits of modernization. For the sake of intellectual growth, economic advancement, and family acculturation, Jewish girls and their families took full advantage of the rapid expansion of American secondary education. Family and communal identity remained a critical factor in their educational experiences at the same time as going to and graduating from high school drew Jewish girls into the wider world of turn-of-the-century American youth culture.

3

"Education in the Broadest Sense"

Alternative Forms of Education for Working-Class Girls

In 1892, when Rose Gollup was twelve years old, she and her unmarried aunt left their Belarus village to travel to America and join her father in New York. Though she went to work right away, even as a child she recognized that her opportunities in her new country were likely to be limited by illiteracy and ignorance unless she took action. Once her mother and other siblings arrived a year later, Rose tried to use the time she had previously devoted to keeping house for her father to attending evening classes in English. She had to skip dinner and hurry from the shop to the school, as the doors were locked once class began. She had trouble staying awake long enough to learn anything.

> When I came into the class, the lights, the warmth to which I was not used, and the girls reading in a slow monotonous tone, one after another would soon put me to sleep. Before I dropped off the first night I learned one word, "Sometimes." It was the longest word on the page and stood out among the rest.

In her exhaustion, she soon dropped out of the class. A few years later, accompanied by her sister this time, Rose tried again. She could "not bear to stay away. I had a feeling that the world was going on and I was being left behind. This feeling drove me on and I went to the class and learned painfully a word or two at a time." Steeling herself against the humiliation of learning more slowly and reading aloud more awkwardly than all her classmates, including her younger sister, Rose stayed in the class until she achieved reasonable literacy.[1]

Rose's determination not to be left behind and to go to night school despite the obstacles exemplified not only her own determination to adapt to her new country but also an attraction toward Americanization widespread throughout American Jewry. Although historians have increasingly denounced the turn-of-the-century Americanization movement aimed at immigrants as the worst kind of social control, the experiences of Jewish girls in America suggest a considerably more complex situation. It was undoubtedly the case that the established Jewish community expressed near panic at the prospect of hundreds of thousands of new Jewish immigrants pouring into the United States without much idea of how to live, let alone succeed, in their new country. The established Jewish community would have preferred the new immigrants to follow their own nineteenth-century paths of acculturation and was constantly frustrated by their apparent inability or refusal to do so.[2] However, it was also true that few turn-of-the-century Jewish immigrants arrived in the United States expecting or desiring to preserve their ways of life intact.[3] Mass migration of eastern European Jews may have been prompted in large part by persecution and intolerance, but the mythic allure of America as a land of opportunity exerted a powerful pull that was a force of Americanization in its own right. The new Jewish immigrants impressed even the wariest of their acculturated Jewish predecessors by the "avidity with which they seek betterment from every source."[4] That tension among various segments of the American Jewish community existed testified not necessarily to a difference in kind about attitudes toward becoming American but a difference in degree and pace. With very few exceptions, Jews in America wanted to live as Americans.

To many late nineteenth- and early twentieth-century Jews in America, education seemed to be the most obvious path toward acculturation. One did not have to be born with innate "Americanness." Conceiving of Americanization as a set of learned values, ways of behaving, and modes of thinking reinforced the possibilities of education for both recently arrived immigrant groups, who could integrate into American society by learning how to be American, and more established ethnic groups, whose own lifestyles proved that such integration was possible. In a country that prided itself on free public education, a solution that would combine education and Americanization seemed obvious. The best way to achieve Americanization was to target youth. Children were assumed to be more adaptable and presumably less attached to certain kinds of traditionalism. They represented the future success of any community. Since they attended school at no cost to parents, immigrant children's acculturation through American education would assure their own success and, hopefully, help their parents Americanize as well.[5]

While in theory the idea of focusing Americanization efforts on the education of immigrant youth seemed unassailable, in practice there was a fatal flaw. The family economy of most immigrants did not allow children to stay in school. If Americanization was dispersed largely through public education, the hundreds of thousands of immigrant families whose children were at work and not at school would be completely cut off from a system that would then be doomed to failure. Even among Jewish immigrants, who seemed to recognize a link between education and success more clearly than some of the other ethnic groups, it was impossible to sacrifice family economic well-being to regular education for their children.[6] This was particularly true for adolescents. While middle-class adolescence was increasingly associated with regular, formal schooling of some kind by the end of the nineteenth century, other options were critical for adolescents who had to work in order for their families to survive. Therefore, some form of alternative education was necessary to put into practice the theories about youth and Americanization.

Alternative education appeared outside a regular, graded public or private school. It took many forms, including print media, lectures, cultural activities, and a wide variety of programs at community institutions. Teacher-student interactions were not necessary, although alternative education sometimes included classroom learning that resembled regular school education but differed from it by virtue of place, time, and student population. Alternative education occurred in the family, on the street, in community centers, and in other settings outside the graded classroom. Immigrant Jews in America participated eagerly in many of these activities, viewing them as paths to acculturation. They applied a traditional respect for learning to new educational venues and supported a wide array of alternative forms of education. Young immigrant men and women were among the most likely to take advantage of these opportunities for learning. Their educational accomplishment, however achieved, reflected well not only on themselves and their families but also on their ability and willingness to embrace an important component of American life.

The large Jewish institutional base of alternative education that developed at the turn of the century was primarily a response to mass eastern

European Jewish migration. The network of philanthropic and educational institutions that sprang up throughout the country demonstrated both loyalty to traditional Jewish ideas of *tzedakah* and self-help and the established Jewish community's conviction that they owed it to themselves to help speed Jewish immigrants' process of Americanization. The idea of learning to be American, though interpreted variously by different segments of American Jewry, was especially important in the context of nativism and resurgent anti-Semitism experienced by Jews across class and denominational lines. Despite their unwillingness to accept immigrants among them without an extensive socialization process, Jews whose families had lived in America for several generations played a critical role in founding hundreds of institutions of alternative education all over the country. Alternative education was a tool to achieve the acculturation and independence so prized by American society and culture and by so doing to raise the perceived collective value of American Jewry.[7]

Jewish immigrants took full advantage of the alternative education available to them. At the same time, however, the rather undefined process of Americanization exacerbated and created tensions among American Jews. Many immigrants resented the expectation that they consider the administrators and patrons of alternative education as "benefactors." The tensions were encapsulated in the outlook of some of the largest, most successful Jewish communal institutions. For example, the teachers at the Jewish Training School of Chicago encouraged immigrant children like the Satt siblings to change their names from Hinda, Welvel, and Gutcha to Hilda, Willie, and Rose so as not to betray their immigrant origins.[8] The Philadelphia Committee of the Baron de Hirsch Fund helped maintain a school for nearly 1,500 immigrant children but was quick to add in its report that "there is also in connection with the school a system of free baths" for the presumably dirty children.[9] If recently arrived immigrant Jewish families were interested in alternative education, they initially had little choice but to accept the opportunities these institutions offered, regardless of the blatant condescension of the established American Jews who generally ran them.

The supply-and-demand relationships of alternative education were fraught with tensions over class, gender, ethnicity, and religious practice. Although not all established Jewish families in America were middle class and not all immigrant Jewish families in America were working class, the culture of the American Jewish community typically divided along those lines. Alternative education, like regular education, became a primary means of performing, exhibiting, and acquiring class status. For Jewish girls as well as their brothers or non-Jewish female counterparts, education and class were symbiotic. Because class status in industrializing America was cultural as well as economic, education was key to the performance of a class status that would signify acculturation as well as financial security. As a primary force for socialization, regular education reinforced middle-class Jewish girls' positions as individuals with a personal responsibility to improve themselves. Alternative education buttressed working-class Jewish girls' positions as members of families that worked collectively to improve their circumstances. The difference between the educational offering of community institutions serving girls from both established and immigrant families was not difficult to discern. In 1890, for instance, the Young Ladies' Auxiliary in New York boasted two branches. The "uptown" branch offered French and dancing to middle-class Jewish girls, while the "downtown" branch offered English, dressmaking, and cooking to immigrant girls.[10] The kind of education available to each group reflected both social expectations and economic imperatives.

Class differentiated the alternative education of Jewish girls and gender conventions dictated the shape of the differences. As far as most providers of alternative education were concerned, learning to be American included learning the gender roles so entrenched in middle-class American society, even if that meant rejecting parental models. If achieving middle-class status was to be the marker of success for immigrant Jewish families, then girls would have to learn how to be American middle-class women and run American middle-class households. Alternative education was not only about their own enrichment but also part of a larger family and community project of Americanization that was at once desirable and coercive. Alternative education thus linked girls to the American Jewish community in both its traditional and progressive senses while also providing the wherewithal for modern, individual achievement and advances.

The American Jewish Press as a Source of Alternative Education

One of the forms of alternative education available outside any classroom or institutional setting was that provided by the American Jewish press of the late nineteenth and early twentieth centuries. Periodicals of all kinds reached a wide range of Jews in their homes around the country. In 1884, even before mass Jewish migration had really gotten underway, the Associated Jewish Press boasted a total circulation of 114,300 among 19 periodicals published in New York, Cincinnati, Philadelphia, Boston, San Francisco, and Chicago. *American Hebrew* and *American Israelite* claimed circulations of 10,000 and 9,000, respectively, with subscribers nationwide.[11] When they read these publications, Jewish girls participated in the public culture of American Jewish life. However, that public culture was rife with the same kind of internal divisions that segmented the American Jewish community as a whole. There were distinct, easily identifiable audiences for many of the periodicals, ranging from acculturated Jewish families whose first language had been English for several generations to recently arrived Jewish immigrant families who relied on Yiddish publications for advice on how to adapt to their new country. Within the community, divisions based on level of Americanization and class status were further divisions based on gender. Periodicals aimed at middle-class Jewish women, for instance, published in German far longer than other American Jewish periodicals because of the assumption that women's home-based domesticity would delay their acquisition of English. Like other forms of alternative education, the press both reflected and shaped the ways in which class and gender operated in the American Jewish community.

Articles about Jewish and American history, coverage of politics and economics, and didactic fiction and poetry all contributed to American Jewish periodicals' function as educational materials. The syncretization of American and Jewish culture was reflected in the pages of major Jewish periodicals, a majority of which were publishing in English by 1880. Assuming an audience literate and comfortable in English, the editors of weekly newspapers like *American Hebrew* and *Jewish Messenger* offered their readers publications that stressed Americanization. The fact that learning to be American appeared as a desirable goal, even before mass migration of eastern European Jews to America began during the 1880s, indicated the long-standing importance of acculturation to American Jews still facing limits to social integration even when economically secure. For Jewish families whose presence in the United States over several generations had not resulted in middle-class status, the American Jewish periodicals suggested ways in which greater social mobility might be achieved. Once mass migration of eastern European Jews did begin, new, often Yiddish, periodicals joined the array of publications offering alternative education to Jews in America. The eastern European American Jewish press developed along a similar trajectory, with the majority of periodicals publishing in English rather than Yiddish by 1925. Like a few German-Jewish periodicals, however, there were some Yiddish periodicals that continued to appear in their original languages.[12]

Across the spectrum, many of the American Jewish periodicals included a woman's page with articles and features of special interest to women.[13] Recommendations for children's clothes and books, nutritious meals, refined dress, and cultured speech filled these pages and offered a wide-ranging education in Americanization for women. Many suggestions focused on daughters. If mothers could not, for whatever reason, successfully acculturate themselves to American life, it was their moral duty to ensure that their daughters did. In addition to praising the growing tendency of Jewish girls to graduate from high school, the woman's pages also encouraged their readers to find additional sources of education and culture.

The popularity of the woman's page in general American Jewish periodicals led to the publication of several magazines designed specifically for women. *Die Deborah, American Jewess,* and others provided Jewish women with sectarian counterparts to mass circulation magazines like *Godey's Ladies' Book* and *Ladies' Home Journal.* The religious content of these magazines was equivocal. While Jewishness was assumed to be a constant and critical part of the readers' identities, little in the way of formal religiosity or observance appeared in the pages of the periodicals. The more explicit thrust of the Jewish women's periodicals, which included items of interest to girls as well, was a push toward acculturation.

One prominent American rabbi, writing for *American Jewess* in 1897, described "The Ideal Jewess" as one who "takes an intense pride in her faith" but hastened to add that "it is scarcely necessary for me to say that by being religious I do not mean the strict observance of a great number of traditional customs in the household." His assumption that most of his audience had modernized by abandoning many home-centered religious rituals did not imply that women should abandon the home. On the contrary, he described an idealized middle-class, acculturated lifestyle for the American Jewish woman, for whom "the scene of her noblest activity is the home."[14]

Integration into middle-class American society, the publications warned, could only be accomplished through perseverance, tact, and education. Rosa Sonneschein, the editor of *American Jewess,* wrote urgently of the need for education among Jewish women in America. In her column "The Woman Who Talks," she encouraged education ranging from the study of physiology to the integration of domestic science into girls' school curricula.[15] The educational imperative she and other editors emphasized encompassed a lifetime of learning that would ideally extend far beyond school years. In much the same way that education became linked to professional and economic opportunity, especially for men, education also became closely identified with women's successful social and cultural integration. Jewish women and girls found their religiously based traditional value of learning extended to their own education through these emerging cultural applications.

In addition to the periodicals edited and designed by and for women, Jewish girls also found an educational forum in the publications produced for Jewish children. Periodicals such as *Young Israel* and *Sabbath Visitor* arrived weekly or monthly in Jewish homes across the United States, contributing to a common literature and Jewish youth culture for thousands of children.[16] For Jewish girls living outside large Jewish communities, these periodicals provided one of the most important links to American Jewish culture and society. While growing up in a Colorado mining town during the 1890s, Rose Cohn considered *Helpful Thoughts,* a Reform Jewish monthly for children, an interesting and entertaining source of information. Among her favorite departments was a "special one of Know Your *Bible.* In order to successfully win prizes, one had to know the Old Testament from cover to cover."[17] Experienced Jewish communal workers like Rebekah Kohut and Julia Richman were heavily involved in the production of the children's magazines and considered their educational purpose to be of paramount importance. By turning Bible education into a game, periodicals like *Helpful Thoughts* reached outside Sabbath school classrooms to instruct Jewish children through alternative forms. In some cases the periodicals were used in religious schools as curricular materials, but in general, they were an alternative source of religious and moral education.

A typical Jewish children's periodical contained a variety of articles, poems, and news items. The March 16, 1883, edition of *Sabbath Visitor,* one of the largest publications of the genre, included chapters from the serialization of a novel; religious and didactic poetry; excerpts from a biography of Jewish Enlightenment figure Moses Mendelssohn; Jewish historical fiction; Bible lessons; a translation of a chapter of a German history of the Jews; moral anecdotes; news items related to Jews around the world; and editorials addressed directly to the children who read the periodical.[18] The editor encouraged boys and girls to write to *Sabbath Visitor* and offered space for readers to publish their own work once it reached a certain standard. The periodical also published numerous letters from children all over the country who, like twelve-year-old Flora Rothschild, wrote to express their appreciation for "the only sign of Judaism visible to us children in the country . . . where there is no chance of attending Sabbath Schools of our own denomination, or being taught in Hebrew, by teachers, nor any chance of going to a temple."[19]

In addition to offering general educational material to Jewish children and providing Jewish girls with opportunities to publish their writing, children's periodicals also offered examples of Jewish women and Jewish womanhood to their female audience. *Sabbath Visitor* admiringly printed the names of girls who graduated from high school and also reported on the junior philanthropic and literary societies joined by adolescent Jewish girls. *Young Israel* filled its news section, "The Month," with accounts of noteworthy women's activities in and contributions to the Jewish community. The periodicals highlighted famous Jewish women in history with sketches like "Beruria, the Wife of Rabbi Meir" and used them as models of noble Jewish womanhood.[20] Over time, the Jewish children's periodicals also began to address contemporary issues of concern to young women, including education.

Immigrant girls also used the American Jewish press as a source of alternative education. Publications in both English and Yiddish offered a wealth of advice to young women and men determined to become Americans. The *Jewish Daily Forward,* which first appeared in 1897, was probably the largest Yiddish periodical in the United States. There was a woman's page from the earliest days of publication.[21] Under the editorship of Abraham Cahan, the newspaper also began a feature column known as "A Bintel Brief" in 1906 that provided a forum for letters from the readers. There was a humorous side to many of these letters, especially the often tongue-in-cheek responses that Cahan usually wrote himself. However, most of these letters dealt with the serious, often painful issues facing immigrants doing their best to succeed. In 1907, a fourteen-year-old girl whose family had been in the country for two years wrote to ask whether she should leave school and go to work to help her family, even though her parents wanted her to stay in school. Cahan advised her that her education was giving her parents more satisfaction than her wages would. Other letters presented the situation of girls who were fired from their jobs for refusing the advances of their corrupt employers or who were unsure whether they should marry men less religious than they were. The responses reflected the socialist perspective of the *Jewish Daily Forward,* as Cahan advised filing grievances through the union and suggested that "the fact that the girl is religious and the man is not can be overcome if he has enough influence on her."[22] Jewish girls who read this newspaper were educating themselves to a particular way of approaching life in America.

The success of American Jewish periodicals in reaching reasonably wide audiences led the institutions that served various segments of the American Jewish community to recognize the value of print as an educational media. The Jewish community center or local club without its own newsletter was rare. By soliciting member contributions and reprinting articles by American Jewish social and cultural leaders, the newsletters became sources of information and current events. Girls and women wrote frequently for the Philadelphia Young Men's Hebrew Association's monthly, *The Review.* The *S.E.G. News,* published by the Saturday Evening Girls, an umbrella name for a number of Jewish and Italian working girls' clubs in Boston, published an article on Zionism, a controversial issue in 1915. Sadie Guttentag, an S.E.G. club leader, wrote a piece for the *S.E.G. News* on the history of the education of women.[23] The attention paid to issues of contemporary concern by these newsletters changed them from mere program announcements to small but significant contributors to the education of the Jewish girls constituting their readership. Writing for *The Club Scroll,* the newsletter of Baltimore's Synagogue House, Pearl Frank explicitly considered the myriad sources of education available for the enrichment of young women's and men's lives.

"Education," what does this word mean to you? Does it convey a thought of broadening the moral, intellectual and physical powers? Does it convey a thought of obtaining a wiser conception of life so that its dreams may become realities, or does it merely mean the attendance of a school? Today we are living in a world full of advantages, full of opportunities, a world that offers a hand to every willing worker, and yet how many people go through life in ignorance?[24]

Club, society, and institutional newsletters not only publicized the ways in which Jewish girls could avoid lives of ignorance but also offered within their pages educational material no less valid for its extracurricular origin.

Another purpose of such newsletters was simply to publicize events and scheduled activities. In 1902, *Alliance Review*, published monthly by the Club Department of the Educational Alliance in New York, reported proudly that the cooking class had made dinner for members of the Nurses' Settlement household, with well-known communal workers Rose Sommerfeld and Belle Lindner also in attendance, and encouraged more girls to join the Clara de Hirsch Literary Society, which enjoyed both educational and social activities.[25] In Boston, the monthly *S.E.G. News* published various groups' reading lists, public exhibitions, and mission statements.[26] As the yearly report stated in 1917, "The S.E.G. are making it possible for many children to become acquainted with good literature, to learn to sing and dance, and to belong to clubs which endeavor to spread the spirit of good comradeship."[27] In presenting these activities to the public, newsletters were important sources of information about alternative forms of education available to those who wanted it.

The Institutional Setting of Working-Class Jewish Girls' Alternative Education

Using the American Jewish press as a source of alternative location was a strategy available to adolescent Jewish girls across class. Other forms of alternative education, however, were intrinsically structured by class-related opportunities. The primary difference between alternative education for the acculturated, often middle-class American Jews and for the more recently arrived Jewish immigrants was location or context. Acculturated and middle-class Jews tended to rely more on their families and individual rather than communal endeavors, while immigrants and working-class Jews tended to look to community institutions for alternative education. Because there were so many opinions about what did or did not constitute education, or what the purpose of education should be, even the most successful community institutions were centers of interethnic and interclass strain as well as ostensible Jewish unity.

As crucial socializing agents for immigrants, alternative educational institutions worked to infuse girls with gender norms inculcated by family and possibly traditional schooling within the middle class. For example, philanthropist Ida Straus generously established recreation rooms to relieve the minds and bodies of Jewish girls tired from working at home and in school. However, the working girls were not always tempted by Straus's ideas for what kind of recreation should be available—evening classes in millinery, embroidery, and cooking that would help them learn American ways of doing things.[28] The Jewish ladies of means who founded the Louisa M. Alcott Club for Boston's poor Jewish girls worked hard to provide their charges with the opportunities to learn about art and literature but also ran domestic training classes in which the object was "to qualify the girls to wait at our own tables."[29] These classes and clubs did indeed serve as important educational providers, but underlying, linked gender and class tensions between provider and students affected the experiences of Jewish girls who frequented them.

The centrality of institutions in urban Jewish areas meant that the most important providers of alternative forms of education for Jewish girls were the community centers found in every sizeable Jewish community. New York's Educational Alliance, Philadelphia's Young Women's Union, Chicago's Hebrew Institute, and many cities' Young Women's Hebrew Associations offered a range of educational activities and programs to women of all ages but focused on teenage girls and young women as a group both most easily influenced and most influential as future wives and mothers. Classes in English, literature, and citizenship; training in trade, industrial, and domestic skills; courses in art and music; physical education; access to reading rooms; all this and more was available either free of charge or for nominal fees at the educational centers cum social service offices. Some of these institutions, like the Educational Alliance, were founded as philanthropic projects to aid new immigrants. Others, like the Chicago Hebrew Institute, were started by members of the Jewish immigrant community as self-improvement agencies. Still others, like the Young Women's Union and some of the Young Women's Hebrew Associations, were originally established during the late 1800s by young Jewish women primarily interested in social centers. Eventually, as the needs of local Jewish communities grew exponentially in response to mass Jewish migration, they were transformed into educational and service centers.[30]

No matter how they began, these community centers shared the mission of educating the community. As the 1900–1901 Announcement of Courses for the Educational Alliance stated:

The Educational Alliance is an institution of education in the broadest sense of the word. The work is not confined to instruction with occasional provision for social intercourse and education. The all around development of the faculties is the goal toward which the Trustees have directed the energies of the Alliance.[31]

The range of activities offered by the Educational Alliance was impressive indeed. Classes in everything from bookkeeping to psychology, German literature to mandolin, millinery to mathematics attracted sizeable numbers of students, ranging in age from kindergartners to adults. Eager learners were almost never turned away for lack of funds. During its early years, the Educational Alliance committed itself primarily to offering classes unavailable to Jews from other educational sources, although the unending demand for certain types of courses justified some duplication of services. The academic classes given at the Educational Alliance during the 1890s were unique, however, as other alternative education programs focused almost exclusively on literacy and skills courses. At the Educational Alliance, interested adolescents and adults had the opportunity to take classes in history, political science, physics, chemistry, and art in addition to English, commercial subjects, and domestic science.

Jewish girls who lived on the Lower East Side eagerly took advantage of these local opportunities. In 1900, one young immigrant woman who had learned English at the Educational Alliance paid a visit to David Blaustein, superintendent of the Educational Alliance, to inquire about the textbooks she had kept for several years after the class ended so she could study them while tending the newsstand she ran. She was so attached to the books from which she had first learned English that she wished to buy them. Blaustein gave them to her.[32]

The place of women and girls in this institutional temple to alternative education was uneasy at times. Although many classes were either coeducational or offered to both men and women in separate sections, students' presence in the Educational Alliance building was distinctly affected by gender. During one week in 1895, only 182 women and 242 girls visited the Educational Alliance reading room in comparison to 4,308 men and 2,588 boys. At the same time, the activities designed expressly for women and girls were well attended. During that same period, 300 girls attended sewing classes, 30 girls went to cooking classes, and 40 women took physical culture training. Two women's literary societies also attracted respectable female turnout.[33] The Committee on Women's Work reported 5,500 visitors to the women's social room during 1895 and was especially gratified by the numbers of young women who attended a series of "moral talks," including Julia Richman on "Physical Training for Women," Mrs. Leopold Stern on "Culture," Dr. Gertrude B. Kelly on "How to Keep Well," and Mrs. D. P. Hays on "Who are True Women."[34] Activities designed specifically for girls expanded as the Educational Alliance grew. In 1903, Jewish girls could not only learn English and obtain religious instruction at the Educational Alliance but also visit the gymnasium, take music and art classes, join social and literary girls' clubs, participate in the Penny Provident Bank, attend evening commercial and vocational classes, and apply for a vacation at a summer home for working girls in Shrewsbury, New Jersey.[35]

Despite the attention given to girls and women by the Committee on Women's Work and sympathetic superintendents like Blaustein, the Educational Alliance remained a gendered educational space. The stated purpose of the trustees in 1902 was "to make every man a worthy citizen, every woman fit to be the mother of children to whom the destiny of the country will be committed."[36] The differentiation of the destinies of men as citizens and women as mothers led to distinctions even in a mixed-sex environment. The Roof Garden, which welcomed 403,374 visitors in 1902, provided special games and programs for young working women and monitored their activities more closely than that of their male counterparts.[37] Boys' clubs meeting at the Educational Alliance outnumbered girls' clubs two to one. The Halevy Singing Society included both young men and young women who could sight-read music, but the Rubinstein Orchestra, which required more training and time away from home, was open only to boys and young men.[38] Underlying much of the gendered nature of Educational Alliance programs was a fear of what might happen to a girl whose exposure to too wide an education might lead her into temptation and moral depravity. If such a girl should fall, warned a guest speaker at the 1902 annual meeting, "when she falls she sinks lower than her fallen brother."[39]

There was little question that the Educational Alliance provided vital services to the immigrant Jewish community. No other institution offered similar opportunities to people for whom language barriers and economic imperatives blocked access to more traditional forms of education in the regular school systems. William H. Maxwell, superintendent of the New York City public schools, praised the Educational Alliance's "genius for education" and credited it as "a constant source of inspiration and instruction" to public school educators. Yet the definite push of girls toward domesticity and morality paralleled the larger goal of the Educational Alliance to "train into self-supporting, self-respecting American citizens the dense masses of (ignorant) foreigners who herd together in large cities."[40] Educational Alliance programs were always concerned with acculturation as much as "intellectual and material progress."[41] Course offerings changed over the years to reflect this commitment to Americanization above all else. Even in 1908, after a generation of immigration had necessarily altered Jewish communal relationships, the Americanization of immigrants remained the "chief duty" of the Educational Alliance.[42] As an institutional provider of alternative education, the Educational Alliance followed Maxwell's dictum to be a

> pillar of cloud by day and a pillar of fire by night to guide the dense population of this neighborhood through the desert of dirt and sordidness and sin into the promised land of cleanliness, independence and happiness.[43]

Maxwell approved of the ways in which the philanthropists and social workers who ran the Educational Alliance sustained a self-conscious orientation toward Americanization that affected every aspect of the classes, clubs, and programs of this New York institution.

The top-down approach of the Educational Alliance ensured a reasonably solid status and professionally run institution, but it was not the only model for community centers as alternative sources of education for Jewish immigrants. In Chicago the Hebrew Institute (CHI) developed along different lines. Priding itself on its history as a "people's institute, fostered and supported in considerable measure by the people themselves," the CHI was much more of a bottom-up institution. While philanthropists and communal activists originating from the established Chicago Jewish community did play pivotal roles in founding and supporting the CHI, the Jewish immigrants who made up its constituency began to determine educational, cultural, and social programs and policy soon after its inception. Its early activities included evening classes in English, foreign languages, music and drama, domestic science, and lecture series.[44] The availability of music, art, and drama may have reflected the experiences of some of the young immigrant policymakers of the CHI at the Jewish Training School of Chicago, which emphasized arts and crafts and provided instruction in vocal and instrumental music, painting, clay modeling, and drawing.[45] The property that Sears Roebuck executive Julius Rosenwald helped the CHI acquire in 1909 included a gymnasium that became a central feature of the institution's educational activities.[46]

Like the Educational Alliance in New York, the CHI's mission was broad in scope.

> The object of the Hebrew Institute shall be education, civic training, religious, moral and physical culture; the amelioration of the condition and social advancement of the Jewish residents of the City of Chicago, Cook County, Illinois, and its vicinity, and the maintaining and constructing for that purpose of schools, libraries, laboratories, reading classes and club rooms, gymnasia, music and lecture halls, and the acquiring of such lands and erecting of such buildings as may be requisite for the accomplishment of such object; all to be conducted under Jewish auspices.[47]

Unlike the Educational Alliance, however, the CHI gradually phased out religious training and had discontinued all Jewish education by 1920, although other religious organizations continued to use the building for classes and activities.[48]

A number of features made the CHI unique among large Jewish community centers. A fee was charged for every activity regardless of age as an "indication of the self-support principle which is involved." Yiddish-speaking groups were encouraged to meet at the CHI "as a means of promoting their culture; their getting together in an Americanized Jewish institution gives them on the one hand their opportunity, and on the other is a means of helping them in the process of adjustment to conditions in this country." Most similar Jewish institutions in other communities frowned upon the speaking of Yiddish as antithetical to Americanization. Possibly because it began a little later than organizations like the Educational Alliance or YWHA, the CHI adopted a broader perspective on Americanization than the others, explaining in an annual report that "Americanization implies appreciation of the culture that foreign people bring to this country as well as the promotion of a knowledge of what America stands for among foreign-speaking people."[49] The CHI offered a much more limited program of vocational education than other Jewish community centers, focusing instead on fine arts and performance, Jewish holiday celebrations, and physical education.[50]

The success of large Jewish centers like the CHI as alternative providers of education depended on the willingness of the Jewish community to take advantage of its offerings. The interest or lack thereof in various activities was reflected by attendance records. During the 1917–1918 season, for instance, 90,340 people attended concerts and 125,835 patrons used the library; 2,920 students attended the civics class and 138 the English class; 54 children went to the CHI kindergarten and 172 to the Sabbath School run by the Maccabee Club. The CHI's emphasis on cultural and social activity rather than more formal or traditional education was also clear from enrollment records. Sixty people joined the clay class but only 15 took bookkeeping; 154 took piano lesson but only 64 enrolled in stenography.[51] The people who frequented the "people's institute" helped shape it into a different kind of organization than its institutional counterparts in other large Jewish communities.

Jewish girls who looked to the CHI for broader educational opportunities were not disappointed, although, as usual, they were somewhat underserved compared to boys. Girls joined boys in the dramatic society and orchestra but had no camp to attend as the boys did. Their playground facility was slightly smaller, but they had access to a pool the same size as the boys' pool. Folk, interpretive, and aesthetic dancing classes were open to all adolescents. A home-making department housed in models of a kitchen, dining room, bedroom, and sitting room taught girls the domestic arts, with a special emphasis during World War I on food economy. Separate classes were conducted in office work for boys and girls, but most of the other commercial classes were coeducational. Girls could take dressmaking and millinery while boys could take cutting classes, reflecting the gender division prevalent in the garment trades. In general, the "bottom-up" nature of the CHI influenced the environment and educational offerings of the institution but did not much affect girls' experiences with the CHI as a gendered alternative source of education.[52]

In addition to spending time at general Jewish community centers like the Educational Alliance and the Chicago Hebrew Institute, Jewish girls also participated in alternative forms of education designed and provided especially for women by institutions like the Young Women's Hebrew Associations (YWHA). In New York, the YWHA was a major center for Jewish women's education. Organized in 1902, the YWHA rented a building accessible to the growing Jewish neighborhood of Harlem and began to offer religious services, recreational activities, clubs, and classes. Membership in the YWHA was originally restricted to Jews above the age of twenty-one, but the age restrictions were dropped as adolescent girls became a significant constituency. Male members were allowed, but no men served on the board until 1943. After a successful fundraising campaign in 1911, the YWHA moved into a new building on 111th Street that boasted a pool, synagogue, dining room, library, gym, classrooms, and residential accommodations for 150 working girls. Through 1930, the main programs of the YWHA were commercial classes in shorthand, typing, stenography, and switchboard operation; Americanization instruction in English, elocution, and civics; an employment bureau; and religious services. The institution explicitly defined itself as an alternative provider of education, claiming that YWHA educational work aimed "to develop character, as well as to teach subject[s]" and that it offered "larger opportunities for physical, social, and religious development, than in public schools."[53] By offering extensive day and evening classes and teaching short courses in "culture subjects," the YWHA set out to provide educational opportunity to Jewish girls and women who required scheduling flexibility and variety.

One of the ways in which the YWHA achieved its goals was to integrate educational, social, and religious activities. Study circles associated with various courses combined academic and social functions, and all commercial and English students were encouraged to join at least one club in addition to attending regular classes.[54] During the summer, groups like the Civil Service Club and Stenographer's Speed Club met weekly to share job tips and experiences as well as a friendly environment of like-minded people.[55]

The YWHA also succeeded in adapting to the changing needs of its students and the times, as reflected in its location in an uptown neighborhood where it could be of most use to the upwardly mobile daughters of immigrant families who had managed to escape downtown tenement life. Quick to see the possibilities of office work for women, the YWHA developed a comprehensive program of commercial education that included switchboard operating, legal stenography, and dictaphone work at a time when most other educational institutions confined commercial education to typing, bookkeeping, and shorthand.[56] During World War I, the Class Committee considered starting a course in steel work to better prepare young women for defense industry jobs and added a class in War Emergency Cooking to the popular domestic science curriculum.[57] Commitment to Americanization, also a routine part of the YWHA's program, appeared in the emphasis placed on English, elocution, and voice culture for immigrants and their daughters.[58] The superintendent's reaction to one girl's application for a scholarship to the commercial classes was typical.

> Anna Kanofsky was recommended to us by the Amelia Relief Fund who assist the family. Anna is reported to us as an unusually bright, willing girl who should have an opportunity to find work in something higher than shop or factory.[59]

By offering classes and schedules unavailable to Jewish girls and women in other educational venues, the YWHA successfully provided alternative educational opportunity to "the ambitious young women who seek to progress" through education.[60]

Institutions that offered alternative education to girls who could not stay in school sometimes created valuable social bonds among various segments of the Jewish community. Ambitious middle-class and immigrant girls and women alike were served by female-centered environments like the YWHAs. The Young Women's Union (YWU) in Philadelphia was founded by a group of middle-class Jewish young women who hoped to benefit themselves as well as help needy immigrants.[61] In 1885, twenty-three-year-old Fanny Binswanger, whose father refused to allow her to attend college, called together a number of her friends from the established Jewish community in Philadelphia and formed the YWU. Ostensibly created to help immigrant mothers by providing day care and to facilitate immigrant children's acculturation by inculcating middle-class values, the YWU also gave its young founders a sense of purpose and involvement in something outside their own homes.[62] During its early years only unmarried Jewish women could be members and officeholders of the YWU.[63] By creating, staffing, and developing the YWU, Binswanger and other middle-class Jewish girls broadened their own education through the new method of social service as well as broadening the educational opportunities of immigrant Jews through the new institution.

Although the YWU started small with only a kindergarten designed to help working Jewish mothers find day care for their children, its programs expanded rapidly. In 1886, the YWU moved into a larger space and began a household school in addition to the kindergarten. Under Amelia Allen's guidance, ten- to thirteen-year-old girls learned household management tasks and domestic skills ranging from sewing and millinery to nutrition. Older working girls were encouraged to attend the school on Sundays. Two years later, Mary Cohen organized evening classes in

English, reading, and arithmetic for Jewish working girls, and her sister Katherine started a library the following year. In 1893, the executive board — still comprised exclusively of unmarried women — ran a Chanukah fundraising campaign and secured $800 in addition to generous donations of food and clothing. The YWU began to offer sewing classes four times weekly for immigrant girls and encouraged them to participate in a penny savings bank under Alice Jastrow's supervision. By 1898, there were 60 children in the kindergarten, 107 students in sewing classes, and 169 participants in trips to the country. When the YWU moved to a larger building the next year, Sunday afternoon clubs and an evening club for working girls were added. The new building also housed a gymnasium, where girls and women participated in calisthenics and gymnastics. The YWU bought La Grange House in 1902 as a vacation home for working girls and also started to run mothers' meetings, as some of the original girls who went to the YWU reached marriage and motherhood themselves.[64]

The passage of time changed the nature of involvement in the YWU for the founders as well, many of whom also married, and the daily operations of the YWU were increasingly left in professional hands. Soon after a head social worker was hired in 1901, 80,142 people using the YWU facilities were counted in one year. At the banquet honoring the twenty-fifth anniversary of the YWU, Ella Jacobs, one of the original founders and now a public school principal, reminded the audience of the dual purpose of the YWU.

> Twenty-five years ago, when the Union was first started, the men, the fathers and brothers, looked upon it as a play society. It was rather nice, they thought, that the young girls, their daughters and sisters, were going in for charitable work. But as they watched us grow, they had to sit up and take notice that it was no play society; it was really doing good work.[65]

By energetically and successfully involving themselves in communal work, the young women of Philadelphia's middle-class Jewish community came of age. Leaving the supposedly trivial pursuits of girlhood behind them, they proved their worth as contributing members of society by transforming a "play society" into an enterprise of evident value. Fanny Binswanger, Ella Jacobs, Amelia Allen, and their peers accomplished more than one goal in creating and administering the YWU. They im-

Young Women's Union reading room in Philadelphia, ca. 1905. *Courtesy of the Philadelphia Jewish Archives Center.*

pressed "the fathers and brothers" by demonstrating the ability of young women to do meaningful work, while also demonstrating their own conviction that the example of Jewish womanhood they provided to others was worthy of emulation. In serving the Jewish immigrant community, the middle-class Jewish girls who founded the YWU had also served themselves and proved their value to the Jewish community at large, making the YWU a vital alternative source of education for Jewish women in Philadelphia across class lines.

Evening Classes and Night School

The YWU was also notable as one of the first institutions to perceive a need for evening classes for working immigrants. Evening classes and night schools were among the most popular, though problematic, alternative sources of education for Jewish girls, who hoped that they could achieve greater economic success and social integration. Evening classes in English, citizenship, and other subjects served thousands of immigrants throughout the United States in a number of institutional settings. Private groups were the first to offer classes to working people whose only chance for education came after hours. The need for this kind of instruction for immigrants was apparent as early as 1888, when Mary Cohen drafted the daughters and sons of established middle-class Philadelphia Jewish families to teach writing, history, reading, and arithmetic on Monday and Thursday evenings to eighteen students at the YWU. The classes were popular enough with the students, who paid 25 cents for the season, that twenty more girls wanted to enroll after the summer break, but the classes were discontinued for a lack of teachers.[66] As the number of immigrants in Philadelphia grew and the demand for evening classes increased, the YWU began to offer evening classes again. In 1896, the YWU recruited Henrietta Szold, then serving as executive secretary of the Jewish Publication Society in Philadelphia, to teach an evening course in American literature.[67]

Szold's involvement in evening education had begun in her hometown of Baltimore, where she spearheaded one of the first immigrant night schools in the country. Unlike the YWU's evening classes, which suffered from continuous staffing problems, the "Russian Night School," as the Baltimore institution was called, flourished under a succession of capable supervisors until it closed after the city public schools started evening classes of their own.[68] By 1901, the city-operated night schools in Baltimore offered separate classes for adults and adolescents "so that those mature needing only the new language will be placed in separate classes from the English-speaking boys and girls, who make too much progress for them and who otherwise mortify" them. Baltimore's night schools also tried to hire teachers who knew the immigrants' native languages and would be "in sympathy with them in their struggle to be Americanized much after the manner of instruction which used to be provided in the Russian night schools provided by private subscription."[69] In Baltimore, as elsewhere, the burden of immigrant education in night schools gradually shifted to the public sector, away from private initiative. Night schools operated as city and public services obviously served immigrant populations beyond just the Jewish community. However, there was such a demand for evening classes, that both public and private night schools grew in number and size between 1890 and 1920, and many Jewish immigrants continued to attend night school within the Jewish community.

Whether or not the "sympathy" invoked as a necessary part of evening education also expanded was open to debate. Budding labor activist Rose Schneiderman, who began by attending night school four times a week, stopped going altogether when she found that the instructor wasted time and "seemed more interested in getting one-hundred-percent attendance than in giving one-hundred-percent instruction."[70] The superintendent of New York's Educational Alliance attributed the persistence of private night schools to the fact that

> the night schools of the city Board of Education do not altogether satisfy the people of the East Side, because the discipline is not understood. It must be remembered that most of these people have come from countries where there are no public schools and where tyranny has taught them to regard all public institutions as instruments of oppression.[71]

Some night school teachers exacerbated these problems by treating their students with thinly disguised disdain. Goldie Tuvin, attending night school in New York during the 1890s, was astonished by the assumption of idiocy embedded in her textbook. She already knew five other languages and was offended by a primer that offered pictures of cats, chickens, chairs, and tables and sentences like "The pretty black cat does like the white milk." She left the "stifling classroom" after one night, never to return.[72] However, even those who greatly disliked the format of night school classes continued to attend them, determined to learn as much as possible no matter how distasteful the process.

Despite the difficulty in establishing night schools deemed satisfactory by both students and instructors, evening classes remained a common feature of immigrant girls' experiences. A newspaper article about the CHI praised the large numbers of young men and women who went to night school. According to the article, these young people were securing "their first initiation into the mysteries of the English language. Here, when the day's toil is over, instead of seeking diversion in dance halls and theaters, they perseveringly master the intricacies of English."[73] Learning English was widely perceived as the crucial first step toward Americanization for immigrants such as these night school students. John Foster Carr's "Guide to the United States for the Jewish Immigrant" informed new arrivals that "you cannot be in America a single day without understanding the necessity of speaking the same language that all other men in America speak." Carr advised immigrants to listen carefully to English whenever they heard it, to buy cheap English newspapers and study them, to go to American theaters and lectures, to make friends with Americans, and, finally, to go to night school.[74]

Going to night school was actually very difficult for working girls. Teenager Goldie Prelutsky's employer, Sears, helped pay her tuition at the Lawson Evening School in Chicago, but Goldie found the daily routine of "all day long cooped up in the shop; and right after supper away to school then come home from school and do my lessons" hard to maintain.[75] Rose Turnonsky became physically ill from the strain of working every day and studying every night and eventually dropped out of night school.[76] The pressure on immigrant Jewish girls to learn English was immense for both professional and personal reasons. Fluency in English often led to better job prospects as well as greater desirability on the marriage market within an immigrant community pushing and being pushed toward rapid Americanization.

The administrators and teachers of night schools took few pains to disguise their goals of fostering Americanization through English instruction. In 1912, the Hebrew Education Society of Philadelphia reported that its principal aim was to help immigrants adjust not only their language skills but also their social opinions as swiftly as possible.

This course is exceedingly valuable, because it affords an opportunity of presenting to the foreigners attending the classes the best views on political and economic situations. This is found to be a means of correcting wrong impressions formed by the young people who come from different lands, who, because of preconceived notions, are prone to criticise conditions in America without having had an opportunity of judging conditions here, or having had any personal experience to warrant them.[77]

The content of the commonly used textbooks confirmed the ideological bent of evening instruction. *English for Foreigners* consisted of a series of simple sentences that imparted wisdom about American values. One lesson read:

This is the family in the sitting room. The family is made up of the father, the mother, and the children. That is the father who is reading. The father is the husband. That is the mother who is sewing. The mother is the wife. The father and mother are the parents. The sister is playing the piano. The brother is standing beside her. The family makes the home.[78]

Another lesson taught as much about middle-class standards of hygiene as English vocabulary and syntax.

> The woman washes her hands. She washes them with warm water. She takes the brush in her hand. She washes her fingers. She washes her finger-nails. She wipes both hands dry. She wipes them on a towel. She cleans her finger-nails. She cuts her finger-nails. She pushes back the skin from her nails. She had clean hands and nails.[79]

The class and gender implications of these language lessons were important components of the education offered to immigrants by the night schools. Immigrants were usually aware of the indoctrination into American values inherent in night school education. Some of them even welcomed it. Rose Schachter regretted the sporadic nature of her attendance at night school after arriving in Chicago in 1915, because she felt deprived of the chance to learn about socially acceptable behavior or to become socialized to American mores.[80]

The closing of city-sponsored night schools during the summer and the dislike of many immigrants of their nature meant that private Jewish institutions continued to offer evening classes. In 1916, the YWHA in New York looked for volunteers to teach more English classes at night, and the CHI also operated its night school year-round, as opposed to Chicago's Board of Education classes, which only ran for five months a year.[81] The continuing popularity of night school among Jewish immigrants was commented upon in an educational study conducted in 1922, which noted that "this indicates an unusually strong interest in an academic education . . . as well as exceptional energy and earnestness in the pursuit of educational opportunity, since voluntary attendance at evening school at best involves serious immediate, personal sacrifice."[82] The wide availability of evening classes in an array of institutional settings made night school an important and common alternative source of education for Jewish working girls.

Alternative Education and the Generation Gap

Night school was a form of alternative education accessible to women and men of all ages as well as adolescents, but a great deal of institutionally based alternative education focused on youth. The concentration of most institutional efforts on children and adolescents followed from the assumption that malleable young people would naturally find Americanization easier than their parents. In 1903, David Blaustein, superintendent of the Educational Alliance in New York, argued that four to six months at the Educational Alliance's special school were enough to teach immigrant children English, to "impress the children with the idea of patriotism and acquaint them with American customs and usages," and then to send them to public schools to complete the process of Americanization.[83] Envisioning similar progress through the Columbia Religious and Industrial School for Jewish Girls, Mathilde Schechter described the aim of the New York school to quickly produce "good, clean, moral Jewish girls," who "by keeping the Jewish ideals . . . will *naturally* become most desirable Americans." After emerging from the Columbia Religious and Industrial School, Jewish girls would go on to public schools, where "the Jew, and the Jewess more so, is quick and adaptable, and through the wonderful American school, they get at the channel of what is best in American institutions."[84]

Children and adolescents made up the majority of most classes at community centers and other Jewish institutions. However, the focus of many alternative providers of education on children and adolescents rather than adults exacerbated a generation gap that inevitably developed in Jewish families following immigration. Jewish girls' family relationships were affected by the discrepancy in educational opportunity afforded them in America. As a twelve-year-old living on the Lower East Side prior to World War I, Bella Cohen used both formal and alternative education to construct a world more closely aligned with the ideals her American education were inculcating in her. She was

> acutely conscious of the sordidness of the life about me. To escape, I hid behind my books and built up a life of my own in the public school I attended on East Broadway and at the settlement house on Madison Street. These were more real to me than any home or the street. My mother . . . did not exist for me as vividly as did Queen Guinevere or my piano teacher.[85]

The harsh realities of immigrant life rarely allowed parents the time and luxury of extended education. Their daily routines of work and home keeping did not expose them to the greater variety of educational forms available to their children. As a result, parents' labor bought their children's freedom to learn at the cost of family solidarity.

This lack of sympathy between immigrant parents and children was of great concern to Jewish communal workers. While supporting children's alternative education as a means of family acculturation, they also came to realize that there were deleterious effects of promoting Americanization by teaching children to look down on traditional customs and values. An *S.E.G. News* editorial lamented that "the tragic gap between the first and second generation is the high price of assimilation. There is no remedy."[86] The problem was bigger in many ways for girls, whose acculturation frequently called for them to reject women's traditional economic activity as a benighted feature of Old World life. Henrietta Szold warned that "in this . . . economic readjustment in the family, the relation between parents and daughters suffers a more serious disturbance than the relation between parents and sons," adding that "girls once brought to the point of rebellion are more radical than boys."[87] Though the financial circumstances of most Jewish immigrant families rarely allowed girls to abstain altogether from work in the name of American middle-class gender ideology, the social and cultural ideals learned at schools and in community institutions that promoted Americanization created family rifts between expectations and ideals on the one hand and needs and realties on the other hand.[88]

While recognizing the prevalence of a generation gap exacerbated by children's education, communal activists continued to believe that education was crucial to immigrants' success. Sadie American warned members of the National Council of Jewish Women that "we see many tragedies because there are children who show dis-respect to their parents who do not know English," but she still insisted that they should "immediately on their arrival . . . learn English, not only to benefit themselves but for the best interest of their families."[89] Sadie American and others like her acknowledged the effects on a family of children's alternative education, but they felt it was a price worth paying if the family achieved greater acculturation as a consequence.

Immigrant Jewish parents agreed. Girls who attended public lectures, took extra home economics classes, joined literary or musical societies, and learned new skills often received parental encouragement, even though their parents knew that education might widen the gap between them. In Seattle during the 1890s, for instance, Bella Weretnikow's mother was committed to making sure her daughter would live as an American girl whose future would bear no resemblance to her own life of ignorance and drudgery, despite the fact that Bella's education made it difficult for mother and daughter to relate to each other.[90] Because Jewish girls' success at Americanization became as important a factor as their economic potential when their desirability as marriage partners was determined, education outside the formal school system proved attractive to girls and their parents alike. The educated, acculturated, English-speaking American Jewish girl might distance herself from her family, but at least her parents could rest assured that they had encouraged her development toward greater opportunity.

In some immigrant Jewish households, parents and children worked together to take advantage of alternative forms of education in their shared desire to become knowledgeable and Americanized. If all the members of a family learned English or celebrated national holidays or adopted household standards presented to them as American, the learning process of acculturation could act as a unifying force between parents and children. In Chicago, Lillian Herstein's father gathered the entire family around the kitchen table to discuss current events, ensuring that from the time they were children Lillian and her siblings were "oriented in the conviction of participation in the activities of this great country."[91] Gertrude Mandelbaum's mother indulged her own love of books whenever possible, buying a complete set of the "Books of Knowledge" and reading to her children on Friday nights when she washed their hair.[92] In these families the generation gap was closed, or at least diminished, through family participation in a variety of alternative forms of education that supplemented the children's formal schooling.

Alternative Education in Specialized Institutions for Jewish Girls

Communal leaders recognized that it was much easier to promote Americanization when a family was intact. Broken families, especially households with no mother present, seemed to require the organized Jewish community to intervene with specialized institutions that could replace various family functions. The most extreme responses to Jewish family issues raised by the promotion of acculturation were residential facilities such as orphanages and homes for working girls. Like other forms of alternative education, these institutions were established with the best of intentions. They provided safe homes for many needy Jewish children and adolescents but often resulted in strained and difficult relationships between benefactors and recipients. The uncertain economic situation at the turn of the century, in combination with disease, desertion, and the perils of immigration, left many families bereft of one or both parents and unable to stay together.[93] Jewish orphanages and homes for working girls developed in response to these needs. The Jewish community valued these institutions, as it was widely considered a tragedy if a Jewish child were cut off from her community by being sent to a nonsectarian residence. Aiming "to replace as fully as possible to the child, both the parent and the home," Jewish orphanages placed the Jewish community between the needs of dependent children and the unreliable, possibly sectarian alternative institutions.[94] Homes for working girls provided a different sort of intervention on behalf of a population perceived to be at great risk if not safely ensconced in a protective environment. Prior to the state's assumption of responsibility for dependent children and minors, ethnic and religious communities took care of their own.

Obeying Biblical injunctions to protect orphans and fearful of the missionizing character of Protestant institutions, Jewish community leaders made building orphanages a priority in cities across the United States. Jewish orphanages were common long before mass Jewish migration from eastern Europe began. The Cleveland Hebrew Orphan Asylum, founded in 1868, served 162 children bereft of one or both parents by 1873. Boasting of its "charity to the individual and charity to society," the Cleveland Hebrew Orphan Asylum claimed to stand "at the head of all similar institutions of states and denomination." The content and form of education available to children in Jewish orphanages was of primary concern. As was common among orphanages prior to the 1890s, the children who lived at the Cleveland Hebrew Orphan Asylum attended school at the institution, receiving "extra instruction in penmanship, drawing, natural philosophy, music, and gymnastics," in addition to the "course of common school education." They also learned German, their native tongue in most cases, and a "complete course of Hebrew and Biblical history." The interest of the Cleveland Jewish community in the orphanage was satisfied by yearly open examinations and exhibitions in which girls and boys displayed their educational progress.[95] In orphanages as in other settings, educational rituals provided means of performing achievement. The sight of knowledgeable Jewish children was an important means of justifying communal sponsorship and encouraging further support. As institutions serving the community, Jewish orphanages were expected to be open to those whose support enabled their continued existence.

As S. M. Fleischman, superintendent of the Jewish Foster Home of Philadelphia explained in 1898, the community bore a responsibility to act as a foster parent to orphans who would become Jewish men and women and secure the preservation of Judaism. While Fleischman expressed concern "that the orphan shall not feel that it is unfortunate" and insisted that "the education of the orphan can best be gained by love for him," his major focus was on the relationship of the community to its wards, their relatives, and the state.[96] Jewish orphanages were expressions of the Jewish community's ability and willingness to care for its own without relying on external institutions or interventions. They also represented major opportunities for the patrons, administrators, and staff to transform the children into solid American citizens.[97]

Over time, ideas about the relationship between Jewish orphanages and external institutions changed, particularly in reference to education. After 1900, children living in Jewish orphanages were far more likely to attend public schools during the day. In 1916, the Chicago Home for Jewish Orphans was proud to report the number of its wards attending secondary school. With 24 teenagers at Hyde Park High School, 1 girl at the Chicago Normal School, and 1 boy at Lane Technical School, the Chicago Home for Jewish Orphans claimed to send more students to high school than any other similar institution in the city. The classrooms that had once been used for regular elementary school instruction were now used for the orphans' manual training, physical culture, and "that moral and religious education which should enable them to grow up as good Jews and good American citizens."[98] Jewish orphanages in other cities also took pride in the educational achievements of their residents. The children and adolescents who lived in Jewish orphanages may even have enjoyed greater opportunities for both formal and alternative education than their peers, who were more likely to have to leave school and go to work to help support their families.[99]

The influx of eastern European young Jewish women, who came to the United States alone or left their families' homes in America for any number of reasons, led to the development of working girls' homes as a kind of extension of the custodial care of Jewish children in orphanages, although not all of the working girls living in such homes were orphans. Ilene B., who grew up in a Jewish orphanage, was typical. With no home or family to return to after graduating from Baltimore's Western Female High School, she left the Hebrew Orphan Asylum only to take up residence at a Jewish working girls' home.[100] Like Ilene, most of the girls who lived in these homes were under twenty years old. The phenomenon of single Jewish working girls, which was related in part to the large numbers of Jewish girls who immigrated without their families, resulted in a widespread perception of need for institutional care. In some cases, the girls who lived in Jewish working girls' homes chose to leave their families or were encouraged to do so by communal workers who feared that their families exerted a negative influence on them. Hannah London, who worked as a girls' supervisor for Hecht House in Boston after graduating from Radcliffe, found her charges "a sorrowful group such as I had never met. Their parents in most cases were in bad financial plight. I visited their cold dank homes . . . the girls reflected the atmosphere they were brought up in." Hannah was convinced that these girls were better off living apart from their families in a working girls' home.[101]

By the time Hannah began working at Hecht House during the late 1910s, homes for Jewish working girls were long established as educational and residential centers. In Baltimore's Daughters in Israel home for working girls, founded during the late 1880s, only girls without parents or guardians were eligible for residence. In 1895, twenty girls lived in the home, each with her own bed, wardrobe, and table. Far more girls applied for residence than could be accepted. Board was two dollars a week and included maid service. The housekeeper established cooking and dressmaking classes for small extra fees, and the resident directress, Martha Reizenstein, offered a Bible class on Saturday afternoons. During the summer, group excursions were arranged every week, and the autonomy allotted to these quasi-independent working girls was demonstrated by the weekly social evening during which girls could entertain male as well as female friends.[102]

Homes for Jewish working girls all over the country tended to resemble each other. Of the forty girls between ages ten and eighteen who lived at Chicago's Ruth Club in 1917, about half worked and the rest went to school with scholarship assistance from the local Baron de Hirsch Women's Club. All the girls had "regular domestic duties assigned them each day and thus rapidly became good little housekeepers."[103] At the Ben Akiba Home for Jewish Working Girls in St. Louis, the residents, mostly immigrants, all worked and paid 40 percent of their wages for board, lodging, and laundry. Girls who earned enough to rent rooms in

Millinery class at the Clara de Hirsch Home for Working Girls in New York, ca. 1900. *Courtesy of the 92nd Street YM-YWHA Archives.*

good private homes were generally not accepted. The Ben Akiba Home joined its sister institutions in helping the girls find better jobs and providing special training in a safe, Jewish atmosphere.[104]

Like the Jewish orphanages, homes for Jewish working girls also changed their educational policies over time. In 1912, after consulting with Rose Sommerfeld at the Clara de Hirsch Home for Working Girls in New York, Daughters in Israel began to offer limited vocational education and instituted requirements that the girls perform "daily tasks in cooking, chamber work, and waiting, that they may become good housekeepers."[105] The daily upkeep of the home became the girls' responsibility, and in 1915, superintendent Dora Weil commented in response to tales of girls' maladjustment after leaving the home that "if we do spoil them for dirty homes with lack of all privacy and accustom them to regular homes and regular meals at a clean table, we have accomplished something."[106] Daughters in Israel also prided itself on the fact that "the Sabbaths and holidays are observed as far as possible, and as American citizens all national holidays are celebrated."[107] The effect of living in an environment dedicated to both Jewish and American life was itself designed to be educational. This institution devoted decades to giving Jewish working girls a place to live and learn and generally use their separation from their families as an opportunity to improve themselves.

As places where working girls could safely—and respectably—live until rejoining families or marrying, working girls' homes, like orphanages, were important alternative providers of education for Jewish girls. Daughters in Israel tried to be a

> home where the highest ideals of man are upheld, where the characters of young girls are molded in looking forward to honorable living, high morality, and, in a degree, to be self-dependent. Not self-dependent in the sense that each girl would be a separate unit, but where every one was a link in a strong chain of sisterhood.[108]

This emphasis on morality and character was echoed by the founders and administrators of working girls' homes across the country. Miriam K. Arnold wrote that the object of the Industrial Home for Jewish Girls in Philadelphia was to "rescue and protect Jewish girls who have been exposed to temptations and wrong through their unfortunate surroundings and lack of moral principles, fitting them for useful work and strengthening them in moral and religious rectitude."[109] A description of Chicago's Ruth Club also stated that "in the last few years the policy has been adopted of making the Ruth Club a home for adolescent girls, with the idea that it is at this formative period that the best results may be obtained, for then it is that girls need the influence and guidance of the older and wiser person."[110] These concerns with Jewish girls' morality were largely a reaction to the growing awareness of the perils faced by single females in urban areas. Threats to the safety and well-being of Jewish working girls were not imaginary; concern with white slavery may have been exaggerated but was not groundless.

In response to reports of immigrant Jewish girls' widespread—if unwilling—participation in white slavery and prostitution, a new cluster of Jewish girls' homes appeared. In 1904, the Clara de Hirsch Home for Working Girls opened a separate facility for immigrant girls that housed and aided unattended Jewish immigrant girls in New York. The new Clara de Hirsch Home for Immigrant Girls provided board at low rates for immigrant girls who had no suitable homes of their own. Supported by the Jewish Colonization Association and the Baron de Hirsch Fund, the Home for Immigrant Girls secured government recognition as a responsible agent for the thousands of Jewish girls arriving alone yearly and facing deportation without a sponsoring family member or agency. Representatives met Jewish girls at Ellis Island and brought them to the Home for Immigrant Girls, not allowing them to leave without an inspection of their prospective living quarters. The Home for Immigrant Girls helped the girls find jobs and generally assumed responsibility for their welfare, accommodating temporary and permanent boarders and preventing girls from falling into "evil ways."[111] This work with new immigrant girls was a form of alternative education designed to protect and ease their path toward integration into their new society.

The National Council of Jewish Women also worked to protect immigrant girls, recording the name of every Jewish immigrant girl in the United States and either visiting her or sending an inquiry as to her safe arrival. As Sadie American explained to the Jewish International Conference on the Suppression of the Traffic in Girls and Women in 1910, the National Council of Jewish Women coordinated correspondents in more than 250 American locales so that the safety and suitability of each immigrant girl's environs, no matter what her destination, could be ascertained. National Council of Jewish Women representatives at the docks in major ports of entry also distributed leaflets in English, German, and Yiddish containing words of welcome and warning for immigrant girls and providing emergency addresses in sixty cities.[112] Whether operating a working girls home in New York or monitoring Jewish girls throughout the country, Jewish communal workers were determined to help these girls both for their own sake and for the sake of the good name of the American Jewish community.

The popularity of homes for Jewish working girls increased as migration from eastern Europe peaked. In 1906, the New York YWHA used a new building to provide rooms for eighteen female residents. The YWHA also ran a Room Registry for Jewish Girls and Women that found suitable homes for Jewish working girls and in 1912 mounted a successful building campaign that included plans for residential accommodations for 150. For the first pool of applicants into the YWHA's new dormitory in 1914, current residents and Clara de Hirsch Home residents were given first priority. Some girls moved from institution to institution, as did Rebecca Goldberg, who had been brought up at the Hebrew Orphan Asylum and then lived at the Clara de Hirsch Home before coming to the YWHA in March 1919. At times, sisters who had no other relatives in New York came to the YWHA together, as did Rose and Annie Cohen, each of whom earned six dollars a week when they moved into the dorm in 1916. Approved as dorm applicants at the same time as the Cohen sisters were Pauline Ruderman, a twenty-year-old operator earning nine dollars a week; Clara Truberman, an eighteen-year-old dressmaker earning eight dollars a week; and Rose Wallach, an eighteen-year-old embroiderer earning ten dollars a week.[113]

Unlike some of the other Jewish girls' homes, the YWHA was exclusively for working girls and did not accept any students. Girls who earned too much money were expected to find other places to live, as did Rose Klein when her salary reached twenty-eight dollars a week. The turnover in all these girls' homes was high, as any number of reasons could prompt girls to come and go. A YWHA Dorm Committee Report in 1917 recorded a variety of reasons for girls' departures. Mollie Bronstein left to live with her family, Mary Eisenstadt went west, Molly Eisenstadt moved to the Workers' Amusement Club, Eva Siegel got married, and Ethel Pines was asked to leave.[114]

The degree of control over the residents' lives did not sit well with everyone who lived at the YWHA. When Tillie Lerner moved in right after World War I, there were 140 girls living there, mostly teenagers from broken homes. Each girl shared a room with another girl, was expected to behave decently, and was not allowed to have male visitors except in the lobby. When Tillie first arrived, there was "a certain kind of menial comfort." The girls ate in a central dining room but were waited on and "treated with some kind of human dignity." Overdue rents were overlooked if girls lost their jobs. Shortly thereafter, however, a new director instituted a number of changes.

> First, she inaugurated the cafeteria system—a new idea at that time. No more were you granted the pleasure of sitting at a table after a hard day's work and being waited upon. Henceforth, you stood on line and were dished out the amount of food she deemed sufficient. Also, if a week passed and you were behind in your rent, you were warned that within another week, you would have to pay or look for some other place to live.

When her roommate was evicted after defaulting on her rent, Tillie tried to organize the other girls to challenge the new director's authority by presenting her with a list of demands and forming a grievance committee. One hundred forty girls got up in the dining room and threatened rent strikes if their demands were not met.[115] While they were only moderately successful in achieving their goals, the rebellion of the teenage working girls at the Young Women's Hebrew Association pointed up one of the most persistent problems of alternative sources of education. Regardless of where or with whom immigrant girls lived, a tense relationship between the providers and recipients of alternative education persisted.

The Impact of Alternative Education on the American Jewish Community

Orphanages and residences for Jewish working girls embodied both the most negative and the most positive tendencies of alternative education within the turn-of-the-century American Jewish community as a whole. Despite the acrimony that often accompanied the relationships between working-class, immigrant students and middle-class, acculturated providers, institutions such as the Jewish Foster Home of Philadelphia or the Clara de Hirsch Home for Immigrant Girls in New York necessitated cross-class interaction. Students and providers alike shared the belief that Americanization was a desirable goal, and this common vision helped bridge the rifts between them. Increasing rapprochement between the two groups exerted a particularly strong influence on Jewish communal forms of alternative education. A gradual shift in the balance of power within Jewish communal institutions also appeared, as immigrant Jewish families that had achieved a certain level of security demanded more control over the alternative education provided their American daughters. Although alternative education could not and did not resolve all the issues contributing to the divisiveness of the American Jewish community, it did foster cross-class interaction, interorganizational cooperation, and a shifting balance of power that contributed to communal conciliation.

While institutions such as the Educational Alliance or the YWU served largely immigrant populations, they were initially staffed by members of the more established Jewish community. The classes for recent immigrants at Jewish community institutions that the founders and administrators deemed most appropriate gradually offered an education in the larger sense for them as well. Some established, upwardly mobile Jews found their sense of superiority confirmed by contact with poor and struggling immigrants, but many more learned from interaction and repeated encounters that the ability to "become American" provided virtually all American Jews, whenever they came to the United States, with a common experience. Notwithstanding significant distinctions in religious observance, virtually every Jew in America joined the struggle to balance Jewishness and Americanness. Using Jewish community buildings, observing the same religious holidays, and working in concert against anti-Semitism and nativism gave Jews of all origins common ground. Alternative education, particularly in its urban institutional setting, provided both physical and social space for the beginnings of a larger American Jewish culture.

One result of this feature of institutional alternative education was a remarkable amount of interorganizational cooperation. Institutions of alternative education kept track of comparative salaries and programs.[116] A variety of agencies were likely to develop close relationships with each other. The Hebrew Education Society of Philadelphia distributed the garments made by girls in the machine sewing class to other local institutions, including the Hebrew Sunday School Society, and the Home for Hebrew Orphans.[117] The Clara de Hirsch Home for Working Girls in New York accepted many residents recommended by other agencies, including the Hebrew Orphan Asylum of New York and the YWU of Philadelphia.[118] At times, groups of students at one school interacted with the students and facilities of another, as when Clara de Hirsch Home for Working Girls residents joined the YWHA's summer stenography club or the alumnae of the Columbia Religious and Industrial School gave a program at the Hebrew Technical School for Girls' impressive auditorium.[119] The set of interlocking networks of Jewish communal workers, teachers, administrators, and philanthropists shared ideas, programs, and advice in the hopes of making individual institutions strong and viable contributors to the enrichment of the American Jewish community at large.

As time passed, the balance of power within many educational institutions shifted. While the children in Jewish orphanages still had little say in their daily routines, supervisory positions and institutional boards began to be filled by social service professionals and community activists more sympathetic to problems of immigrant adjustment than previously. Girls living in Jewish working girls' homes demanded—and sometimes received—a voice in the administration and rules of their institutional homes. The large urban Jewish community centers were increasingly staffed by educated first-generation immigrants, many of whom had attended classes in similar institutions themselves, whose own experiences established a common bond with the people they served. Despite her own negative experiences with night school, for instance, Goldie Tuvin Stone came "to recognize the value of the system of public night schools" and in later years used her experiences to help "interpret that system to those immigrants whom it was my special privilege to serve."[120]

Even after the first generation of eastern European Jewish immigrants "came of age" as Americans, more immigrants continued to arrive in the United States during the 1910s and 1920s, still depending on alternative education to help them cope with difficult economic circumstances. Class status remained critical in determining the Jewish community's relationships to alternative education. However, regardless of family background and economic status, Jewish girls, particularly in urban areas, still relied on alternative education to provide and supplement their learning experiences. Gender consistently played a role in shaping the form and content of alternative education and also affected individual opportunities, whether those of rising middle-class girls or working-class girls.

The common goal of Americanization made gender a less divisive factor in Jewish community relations as time went by, although immigrant women's need to work remained troubling to some. Immigrants of all ethnic and national origins increasingly emphasized middle-class gender ideology, especially the separation of home and work, as prerequisites for acculturation. The pervasiveness of this gender ideology, however imperfectly realized, across class meant that Jewish women of many backgrounds automatically shared a bond. American Jewish identity was worked out at least in part in alternative educational spaces that fostered rapprochement among groups separated by class, gender, and religious practice.

During the mid- to late nineteenth century, Jewish girls found that their conformity to popular notions of American womanhood conferred social acceptance on them while also reinforcing their families' upward mobility. During the late nineteenth and early twentieth centuries, Jewish girls were encouraged to lift their families into higher social and cultural spheres by performing the gender identity of idealized American girls. The distinction between boys' and girls' anticipated family and communal roles affected their access to alternative forms of education throughout the entire period. In all cases, Jewish girls' behavior reflected on their families and influenced their integration into American society. Girls' education, alternative or otherwise, was key to the process of acculturation. The proliferation of Jewish community programs that offered alternative education to girls outside the graded schools indicated communal awareness of the important role girls played in their families' process of becoming American.

4

"A Perfect Jew and a Perfect American"

The Religious Education of Jewish Girls

Amelia Allen opened her 1876 diary with the hope that "God grant that the end of this year may find me in all respects a better and wiser daughter in Israel, a more affectionate sister, and a true friend." During the course of the year, she and her family participated in the local excitement of hosting the Centennial Exposition in Philadelphia. The patriotism engendered by the Centennial was tinged with religious significance for Amelia, who observed, "Thankful ought we to be both as a nation and as a religious body that we are allowed to think and act as we wish!" Her connection of civic and religious independence was rooted in the kind of religious education she had enjoyed since childhood. A student and later a teacher in the religious educational system founded in Philadelphia by Rebecca Gratz in 1838, Amelia was used to the idea that national and religious identity complemented rather than contradicted each other.[1] Her sister Fannie similarly linked Jewish and American themes. Prompted by the approach of Passover, Fannie reflected in her diary, "How glad I am that I should have been born in a Republican country," one where she was free to practice religion and patriotism alike without fear of contradiction.[2] The sisters' formal religious education provided them with a means of synthesizing the Jewish and American aspects of their identity.

The growth of religious education was in some ways unique to American Judaism.[3] For centuries, formal Jewish schooling had been the preserve of the intellectual elite. With rare exceptions, girls had never fallen into that category, although lack of formal religious instruction had not prevented generations of Jewish women from being extraordinarily devout. In the most traditional Jewish communities in nineteenth-century eastern Europe, only a very few gifted men engaged in Torah study as a full-time pursuit beyond childhood, but the strong emphasis put on such study meant that scholarly men remained the ideal. Jewish women's education tended to be informal, take place in the home, which was the center of their religious activity, and focus on the particular issues that required their knowledge and accountability, such as Sabbath observance or dietary laws. A growing number of families even in these traditional environments began to provide their daughters with more extensive Jewish education as the nineteenth century wore on, but girls' religious instruction was not seen as a communal responsibility until the twentieth century and even then was controversial. In central and western Europe, nineteenth-century Jewish communities were somewhat more likely to value the idea of girls' religious education. This was particularly true once Reform Judaism, with its emphasis on personal and private religious expression, began to spread during the 1840s. Still, few central or western Jewish communities provided extended formal instruction for all boys, much less all girls.[4]

Whether in eastern or western Europe, the concept of community was very strong among most Jews. The Jewish environment automatically provided by community meant that Jewish families could and did assume that much of their children's Jewish education would come organically through participation in the community. This attitude dovetailed nicely with general expectations that girls would inevitably learn to be women from their mothers at home. During the second half of the nineteenth century, there was growing concern that such home schooling was failing to produce knowledgeable young Jewish women, and a few schools for Jewish girls appeared in response.[5] However, most Jewish immigrants arrived in the United States accustomed to the idea that Jewish community essentially equated with Jewish education.

In America, it became quickly apparent, this neat equation would not work. Even the earliest seventeenth-century Jewish arrivals in New York had seen the need to provide religious education to their children, who were so isolated in a heavily Christian environment. By the mid-nineteenth century, anti-Semitism was less of a problem than it had been for colonial Jews, although social discrimination and missionary activity were common. But for Jews spreading out across the small towns of the American interior, formal religious education of some kind represented virtually the only chance for Jewish continuity. America was killing Jewish identity with kindness; the very possibility of easy assimilation and intermarriage meant that families had to make serious efforts if they wanted to maintain Jewish life. Even in cities with growing, concentrated Jewish populations, the temptation to succumb to the myth of the melting pot presented Jews in America with the ongoing dilemma of how to prevent the total meltdown of Judaism. For many, religious education seemed to present a viable solution, a way to preserve Jewish religious and cultural heritage in their new land.

Gender was both explicitly and implicitly part of the discussion of Jewish education in America. There were other factors involved for individuals—where a child lived, his family's mode of observance, her family's economic status. The issue that enveloped all these factors for the community was the question of how to integrate Jewish and American identity. Fear of losing a precious religious, ethnic, and cultural heritage was balanced by a desire to embrace a new national identity that, after all, most Jews in America had actively chosen. For Jewish girls during the second half of the nineteenth and early twentieth centuries, gender ideology provided common ground for women's claims to both American and Jewish identity. Fulfilling their social and religious roles as knowledgeable Jewish daughters and mothers was also a way for Jewish girls to perform their patriotic duty as American girls. Girls involved in Jewish education were taught the importance of the family as a cornerstone of both American society and traditional Jewish life. Similar notions of women's roles created a synergy between the two value systems that at least theoretically made it easy for American Jewish girls to understand their relationship to their national and religious communities. No matter what their country of origin or how long their families had lived in the United States, Jewish girls could define themselves as Americans, secure in the spiritual and moral authority accorded women by both religious and national traditions. Religious education for girls grew ever more popular as Jewish families in America recognized its double potential not only for making Judaism a meaningful part of their daughters' lives but also for adding spiritual significance to their nascent national identities.

This is not to overlook the major changes in American ideas about womanhood and gender at the turn of the century. However, at the same time as female citizenship was the subject of spoken and unspoken discussion, traditional ideas about Jewish gender roles were also undergoing transformation. Debate raged over the place of Jewish women in an emerging, distinct American Judaism that sought ways to catch up with—but never to outpace—larger trends in American society. Jewish traditions of charity and communal self-help fit neatly into the American heritage of associations and organizations that continued to develop at the turn of the century. Women's traditional involvement in these social, religious, and cultural organizations became increasingly formal participation in associational politics that required the preparation of girls for their future roles as backbones of civil institutions. Jewish girls' religious education worked in much the same way to ready them for mature participation in the American Jewish community.

Religious education located Jewish girls within a network of Jewish institutions and a local, national, and even international Jewish community. By learning ritual, history, and literature in a classroom as well as experientially at home, girls were formally connected to the past, present, and future of the Jewish people. Whether they learned more about Judaism at home or at school, the learning process made religion a significant and, ideally, meaningful part of their actions and worldview. When shared observances led to family solidarity, religious education provided a larger framework for the family. The emphasis put on the home within traditional Judaism shaped girls' relationships with their families and by extension their larger communities. Because formal religious education for girls was fairly new, it informed a new relationship of women to the Jewish community that paralleled and replicated Jewish girls' experiences with increasing opportunity in American society.

Students who shared teachers, curricula, and religious educational experience would surely share carefully defined dual commitments to Americanism and Judaism. Inculcating such loyalties, conventional wisdom would have it, was a particularly important component of girls' religious education, as "Jewish women, single and married, wielded a potent influence on the polity and piety of their country, preserving its territorial and spiritual wealth."[6] One prominent girls' educator wrote that her goal was to ensure that each student's soul "should be suffused with the fervor of a political and a spiritual patriotism; the stars in the escutcheon of her free native land and the bright luminary of the free all-reaching faith of her fathers should shine into her being with equal brilliancy."[7] The creation of patriotic, devout American Jewish women depended on the education of American Jewish girls.

The writer's hyperbolic reference to the "faith of her fathers" rather than the faith of her mothers underlined the difficulties for a Jewish girl trying to locate herself in relation to her religion or nationality. Jewish personhood, like American citizenship, was always gendered. Even when religious educators explicitly set out to address girls and boys together, the cultural, social, and political associations of citizenship and manhood overcame their best efforts. In an 1898 article on "Judaism and Americanism" in Philadelphia's *The Hebrew Watchword and Instructor,* Bernard M. Kaplan expounded on the two great traditions available to Jewish youth. He wrote that

one may be a perfect Jew and a perfect American at the same time. Judaism and Americanism as two lofty and independent ideals, are not only in full harmony with each other . . . both stand for what is lofty, true, and just. Judaism represents the highest conceptions of religion and morality. Americanism, on the other hand, represents the highest conceptions of republican and constitutional government. . . . It should be the ambition of every American Jewish youth to be true and loyal to both ideals. The sublime effort to realize both of these lofty ideals must needs conduce to perfect *manhood,* nobility of character, and genuine patriotism.[8]

Kaplan's lapse into an association of his prescription for dual loyalties with manhood illustrates the obstacles faced by Jewish girls, whose maturity into womanhood would bring them neither full American citizenship nor full participation in traditional Jewish ritual life. Even when the audience or subject of discussion was all female, male prerogatives of citizenship took center stage. Commenting on girls' education, Henry Herzberg wrote, "Every educational cause should provide certain studies which should be the basis of instruction in the ethics of the home, leading to the progress of *womanhood,* and the morals of the state, tending to the maturity of *manhood;* for do not the state and the home compose the vitals of society?"[9] Herzberg might have rhetorically equated the state and the home, but by relegating women to the home and viewing their moral education as a process culminating in mature male contributions to the civil polity, he encapsulated once again the problematic American Jewish citizenship to which girls as well as boys were supposed to aspire.

Still, educating girls was widely perceived as a measure necessary to prevent disintegration and disaffection within American Jewry.[10] Many Jews in America watched in dismay as the traditional male, public bonds of synagogue life dissipated and women moved into the forefront as keepers of tradition. Whether advocating rapid acculturation or fearing radical assimilation, American Jews projected their desires onto girls and fixed upon religious education as an important means of reshaping American Judaism.

Religious education thus became an issue for virtually every strand of American Judaism. Its development meant that the classroom could mediate between ethnicity and acculturation by offering a way to be ethnically and religiously committed while maintaining American identity. Girls as well as boys would have to be included in the grand communal effort to synthesize American and Jewish identity through religious education. If Judaism were to make religious education part of its development in America, then the issue of girls' religious education would have to be formally addressed. Where should it take place? Who should the teachers and students be? When should it happen? How old should the students be? How should Judaism be taught? What would justify departures from tradition? There were few easy or automatic answers to the questions religious education for Jewish girls raised. Some of the solutions changed over time as options expanded and student populations waxed and waned. What remained consistent in the discussion was careful communal consideration of the ways in which gender might provide a bridge to American values or a departure from traditional Jewish values. Exploring the debates over Jewish girls' religious education is a valuable way to trace the centrality of gender to the evolution of American Judaism.

Family Life and Jewish Education

When thinking about providing religious training to their daughters, the first issue parents had to grapple with was the innovation of moving Jewish education outside the circle of family. In America, it seemed, parents might best fulfill their responsibilities by turning over their traditional roles to teachers outside the home. In some ways the movement of religious education from homes to schools and from parents to teachers demonstrated the gradual but definite move toward professionalization that characterized both Jewish and American life during the second half of the nineteenth century. It also reflected, particularly after mass Jewish migration began during the 1880s, the probability that immigrant parents might not be the best equipped people to teach children when the established community demanded that Jewish education also be American education. In other ways, formal Jewish schooling was not so jarring a development. After all, religion was supposed to be practiced both inside and outside the home and therefore could be learned and should be experienced in a variety of settings.

Contradictions abounded, however, as questions about where to provide religious education and who should provide it echoed even bigger questions about what role religion would play in American Jewish life. The irony was that many of the reforms common in American Jewish practice across the denominations tended to compartmentalize religion into something primarily practiced at home just as religious education was leaving the home. At the same time American and Jewish rhetoric both elevated women's domesticity and roles in the home, the synagogue increasingly became the logical place for most religious expression once ritual observance decreased for many American Jews. Another irony was that the synagogue, the public religious space that did continue to exist outside the home, had traditionally been the major religious focus for men. From the mid-nineteenth century on, girls often learned about Judaism in synagogue spaces, despite the fact that those spaces typically excluded them from full participation. It is hardly surprising that many of these American Jewish girls grew up to value and even demand participation in public Jewish life, when their childhood religious education had located them in the public space of the synagogue.

Conventions of gender helped address some, though not all, of these issues. An emphasis on home and family for Jewish girls provided a link between Jewish traditions and American ideals, even when girls' religious education took place entirely outside the home. In practice, however, few girls found the line between religious education in school and at home impermeable. Shared rituals and observances led to family solidarity and increased a sense of Jewishness in the household. This training through home-based ritual observances and home-centered religious sensibilities was common to American Jewish girls from a wide range of social and religious backgrounds. Especially before the early twentieth-century campaign to institutionalize all Jewish girls' religious education in formal classes and organized schools, girls were as likely to receive informal religious training inside the home as formal training outside it. To some degree, mimetic religious education in the home echoed centuries of Jewish girls' traditional instruction in the rituals and observances most closely associated with women, such as kashrut, family purity, and Sabbath or holiday observances. In America, growing awareness of the need for mothers to take their daughters in hand if there was to be any hope of religious continuity made daughters' home-based religious training a more conscious and identifiable part of Jewish girls' education.

Karla Goldman has argued that nineteenth-century Jewish women moved into the synagogue as home-based ritual fell into disfavor among the rapidly growing number of nonorthodox Jews in America and as men chose professional life over synagogue activity. It is clear that women did carve out a new role for themselves in the synagogue, to the extent that late nineteenth-century rabbis complained about the gross feminization of their congregations. By 1916, contributors to a symposium on "Women and the Synagogue" felt women's Jewish education to be especially urgent because without it women would be hard pressed to explain their increased presence in the synagogue.[11] However, it is less clear that increased prominence in the synagogue necessarily meant abandonment of the home as Jewish space.[12]

Most families, even those who had forsaken nearly all the traditional forms of ritual, still identified their homes and families as Jewish. Formal rituals like conducting Passover Seders and lighting Chanukah candles were associated with the home and practiced by a large majority of American Jews. Families living in areas without large Jewish communities were often even more likely to cling to certain home-based rituals, as a reminder of a religious affiliation they could not necessarily enact on a regular basis. Jewish girls growing up in families that retained however slight a sense of distinctive identity were exposed to a religious sensibility that also served an educational purpose.[13]

Mothers and fathers both played roles in educating their Jewish families. There was widespread communal agreement that mothers should take charge of their daughters' religious training. Mother-daughter relationships were the primary justification for American Jewish press support for girls' Jewish education. The 1867 columns of *Jewish Messenger* stated emphatically that "it behooves us to . . . employ all our energies to see to it that our daughters retain their national characteristic. And this can best be reflected by the religious example of their mothers." Without such maternal role models, the article went on to warn, the "fair daughters of Heaven" could not expect "to become, in the course of time, good Jewish mothers to their offspring."[14] In his popular weekly column in *American Hebrew*, New York's Hebrew Orphan Asylum superintendent Dr. Herman Baar overlooked no occasion to remind Jewish mothers of their important responsibilities. He repeatedly issued "an urgent appeal to the mothers of Israel, requesting them that they, in their homes and families, as in bygone days should lend their influence and power, their help and fostering care to the strengthening of our religion."[15] Baar considered maternal influence an even more powerful strategy than the establishment of Jewish schools or an increase in synagogue attendance.

Mothers were supposed to be the primary teachers of all their young children and their older daughters but were criticized for not knowing enough to fulfill their appointed roles. Clearly religious education outside the home was necessary, if only to prepare Jewish women for religious education inside the home. Publications designed especially for the Jewish girls and women who were assigned the responsibility of sustaining cultural and religious traditions began to appear during the second half of the nineteenth century. A series of prayer books designed explicitly for Jewish girls and women provided one kind of religious education. The first English language prayer books for American Jewish women were generally translations from the German. The publisher of an early example, *Ruchamah: Devotional Exercises for the Daughters of Israel,* stated bluntly in 1852 that "in the absence of any Hebrew educational institution for females in this country; and under the consequent impossibility of their receiving adequate instruction in the Hebrew language, or in their religious duties; a work that should at once satisfy their hearts and minds, would be a most valuable boon to them."[16]

Like similar books over the next several decades, *Ruchamah* included prayers for daily private worship, for religious activities associated with women, for holidays, and even for entering synagogues for public worship. Nearly all these prayer books included at least a reference, if not an entire prayer, to women who were more religious than their husbands and therefore responsible for the spiritual well-being of the entire household. Such women were encouraged to ask God to

> grant me firmness of mind, that I succumb not to the temptation of his example: grant me meekness of temper, that my unavoidable resistance to his authority may be mild and kindly, and such as beseemeth her who fears thee, Lord, and observes thy commandments.[17]

If a nineteenth-century woman was supposed to perch atop the pedestal of idealized domesticity, she would indeed need God's help to remain pious and submissive in the face of a husband's irreligious ways. By 1912, the compiler of *Yohale Sarah: Containing Religious Duties of the Daughters of Israel and Moral Helps* assumed that many of his readers enjoyed at least a limited religious education, and he urged them to put their knowledge into action at home.[18]

American Jewish girls worried less about their mothers' preparation for their roles as religious models, generally regarding them as central to their religious education. Traditional ritual observance might or might not be at the heart of that religious instruction. Gertrude Mandelbaum's mother sat at the Passover Seder and explained the ceremony to all the children.[19] Where actual mothers were unavailable or unwilling to accept responsibility for their daughters' religious education, substitutes sometimes stepped in. Irma Levy learned Bible stories from her maternal grandmother, who urged her to resist her immediate family's strong assimilationist tendencies and cling to her religious identity. Irma felt she and her grandmother were the only members of the family with "a passionate Jewish consciousness."[20] Jewish organizations, too, took for granted the importance of maternal training and attempted to provide it in institutional settings when necessary. As a resident of the Chicago Home for Jewish Orphans in 1907, Fannie Goldman noticed the active role of the superintendent's wife in lighting Sabbath candles, presiding over liturgical services, and blessing the children. The replication of Jewish family life through weekly Sabbath observance that included a communal meal, collective prayer, Jewish stories, and personal time with the superintendent and his wife demonstrated the importance attached to the home as the religious epicenter.[21]

Aspects of family rituals centered around holidays also made them significant parts of Jewish girls' religious education, a point not lost on the girls themselves. Helen Jacobus wrote of the impact of her girlhood experiences in Richmond on her religious sensibilities, recalling, "We lit our candles on Friday night, and my mother blessed them with the ancient blessing of the women of Israel. My father read the Sabbath eve service, and we all touched the cup of wine to our lips. Our neighbors thought it beautiful."[22] Blanche Wolf Kohn remembered the "air of festivity" attached to her own youthful Sabbaths, commenting that Saturdays had been days of rest and pleasure, when "there was a feeling of relaxation and of difference" and when "people who were lucky enough to have families knew they would have a chance to see each other and discuss the doings of the last few days."[23]

Although mothers and daughters were understood to have a special bond, in some homes fathers took responsibility for daughters' Jewish education. In Philadelphia during the early 1900s, Leah Dvorah Orenstein's

Blanche Wolf, age 19, 1905. A native of
Philadelphia, Blanche graduated from Bryn
Mawr College. *Courtesy of the Philadelphia
Jewish Archives Center.*

father used family meals as an opportunity to test his children's knowledge, pointing to items on the table and asking Leah Dvorah to name
them in Hebrew. Though the family spoke Yiddish at home, during "Sabbath and holidays we were forbidden to speak Yiddish, instead we spoke
Hebrew, the holy language (Lushen Kodesh) because the Sabbath and our
holidays were holy." Leah Dvorah's father was also the one who made the
decision that it was time for her to learn the daily prayers, although he

left the actual teaching to Leah Dvorah's mother.[24] Bessie Newburger grew up in a far less traditionally observant household, yet her father still made sure she received a thorough education about Judaism, feeling that "although we might not subscribe to its rituals, it was a great religion and heritage and one that we should know and be proud of."[25]

Many of the fathers most devoted to their daughters' Jewish education were themselves religious educators. Libbie Levin attended the Moses Montefiore Hebrew School her father headed in Chicago. After she graduated, her father enrolled her in a private Talmud class so that she could continue her Jewish education.[26] Pauline Hirsch's father also oversaw her Jewish education beyond graduation from religious school, requiring her to review a page of Talmud with him before she could go on Friday evening walks with suitors.[27] Talmud was not a typical subject for Jewish girls to study in even the most progressive schools, and both Libbie and Pauline's ability to study it reflected their fathers' commitment to educating their daughters thoroughly.

The pattern of fathers' encouragement of their daughters' religious studies appeared most often in the families of teachers, scholars, and rabbis like the Levins. Learned men with no sons on whom they could bestow their erudition were particularly likely to focus on their daughters' religious education. Many of the exceptionally knowledgeable Jewish women of the late nineteenth and early twentieth centuries grew up in families such as these, Henrietta Szold being perhaps the best example. Rabbi Benjamin Szold taught his oldest daughter as intensively as he could have a son. At the turn of the century, Henrietta was renowned among the leaders of the American Jewish community for her erudition. Interestingly, none of Henrietta's sisters received the same level of training from their father, though all had a better Jewish education than most of their contemporaries. Rebekah Bettelheim also attributed her Jewish education to her father. Rabbi Aaron Bettelheim, who occupied pulpits all over the United States during the late 1800s, shared his friend Benjamin Szold's conviction that girls should be religiously educated. An oldest daughter like Henrietta, Rebekah, too, was treated in educational terms like the oldest son and reaped the benefits of her father's Jewish scholarship.[28]

Despite the interest and concern of some Jewish parents with the formal Jewish education of their daughters, the importance of structured education remained a hard sell to many parents, who continued to believe that home-based, experiential Jewish training was sufficient. Alexander

Dushkin, an administrator and teacher in New York, described the frustrating situation confronting Jewish educators attempting to reach more girls.

> Tradition confined the education of Jewish girls to the home. A knowledge of the customs and laws applying to the life of the family, familiarity with Jewish folk lore and folk song, and training as virtuous, industrious, and loyal wives and mothers—these were the standards of female education among the Jews for many centuries. Of school learning there was none for the Jewish girl.[29]

Ingrained habits were difficult to combat, especially when Jewish education in America suffered from a notorious lack of the funds that might have facilitated better outreach to Jewish girls and their parents. In the presence of limiting traditions and the absence of enlightened attitudes about girls' religious education, Henrietta Szold warned, "the Jewish girl's Jewish education is no better taken care of in a land of golden opportunities than in a crowded Jewry of the East, where at least she lives an intense Jewish life, with its manifold educational influences."[30] It seemed obvious to many community leaders and a growing number of parents that girls' Jewish education was too important to be left to the home. By the late nineteenth century, the time was ripe to approach girls' Jewish education in a more systematic way than had previously been the case in America.

The Development of Religious Schooling for Girls

Jews in America began to support their daughters' Jewish education as both the natural consequence of the gradual movement toward equalizing boys' and girls' education more generally and as an attempt to preserve religious traditions they feared would be lost in their new environments. However, through the beginning of the twentieth century, girls' Jewish education was seriously hampered by the overall lack of organization and consistency. A chaotic mixture of congregational schools, private teachers, philanthropic institutions, and community organizations offered wildly disparate educational experiences to Jewish students.

The Jewish immigrants of the mid-nineteenth century often sent their children, girls and boys, to schools conducted in the basement or vestry rooms of their synagogues rather than public elementary schools. In doing so, they were adopting the Catholic model of education. As minorities in Protestant America, both Jews and Catholics had to prioritize their interests. Most, though not all, nineteenth-century Catholic immigrants opted for separate parochial schools. The heavily Protestant and typically missionary nature of most public schools was unacceptable to them. At first, many nineteenth-century Jewish immigrants agreed. Some felt that the social environment of public schools was hostile to Jewish children, and others felt that the educational environment of public schools was hostile to Judaism. As a result, they preferred to establish separate Jewish schools, where religion would not be relegated to a supplementary subject and where their children would learn among other young members of their own communities.

Most of the Jewish schools of the mid-nineteenth century were associated with German-speaking synagogue communities. Though public schooling had already been linked to American citizenship for decades, the influx of non-English-speaking immigrants into the United States during the mid-nineteenth century altered the relationship of children, schooling, and ethnicity at least temporarily. Jewish families who opted for German-speaking schools were not unusual in this context, as other families did much the same in many places with large German populations, such as Chicago, Cincinnati, and Milwaukee.[31] These schools taught both secular and religious subjects, although the latter were generally confined to holiday rituals, liturgical Hebrew, and possibly Bible lessons. Emily Fechheimer went to elementary school at her Cincinnati synagogue, along with many other of the congregants' children. Her

> schoolhouse was in the annex of the synagogue which most all of the children of the members of the congregation attended. We were taught English and Hebrew. The *Chumish* I could not understand, and told my beloved father I could not see why it was taught us and please to have the teachers do away with it. As he was president of the congregation then, he brought it before the board, who quite agreed with me, and I was very happy after it was removed from our studies.[32]

These schools were exclusively for Jewish children, and the curriculum was precariously balanced between religious and secular subjects. During the 1860s, Hannah Greenebaum and Lizzie Spiegel both attended the Zion School at Chicago's Zion Temple, where the rabbi taught German and Hebrew and two other teachers taught secular subjects. When the Zion School closed in 1867, the students moved on to public schools.[33]

The ease with which the textual study of the *Chumish,* or Pentateuch, was banished from the lessons or with which the students moved into public schools reflects the priorities of the parents. Religion per se was not necessarily the major motivation for these Jewish schools. As denominationalism began to grow in the United States and the differences among modes and levels of observance intensified, it became very difficult for explicit religious instruction to remain the primary justification even for Jewish schools associated with particular synagogues. In expanding midwestern cities like Chicago, as well as more established ones like Cincinnati, the growth of public education at midcentury reflected the diverse student population by gradually downplaying (though never entirely eliminating) the Protestant character of the schools. While many Catholic parents continued to choose parochial schools, growing numbers of Jewish parents began to send their children to local public schools. They looked for other formats for religious education, now seen as supplementary rather than central by most Jewish parents. In the contest between Jewish and American identity that school choice signified, American identity was winning by the 1870s.

Parents searching for other models of religious education could turn to several supplementary alternatives to Jewish schools. Beginning in the antebellum period, a different sort of Jewish education had developed in Philadelphia.[34] Founded in 1838 by Rebecca Gratz and the Hebrew Ladies' Benevolent Society, the Hebrew Sunday School Society provided religious education to Jewish children in an early effort to stem a tide of assimilation that had already washed over the Philadelphia Jewish elite.[35] The Sunday schools in Philadelphia were coeducational from the start, and as communities all over the United States began to emulate the system of supplementary religious school on Saturdays or Sundays, they also adopted the coeducational mode.[36] Early Sabbath schools were generally associated with specific congregations, although, as was the case with Philadelphia's Hebrew Sunday School Society, there were communally administered ones as well. Gratz, Isaac Leeser, and Simha Peixotto, the leaders of the original movement, prepared textbooks and instructional materials that became standard issue in Sunday schools, or Sabbath schools, around the country.[37]

Maud Nathan attributed her religious interests to the Sabbath school she and her brother went to in New York on Sundays during the 1870s.

Maud, whose mother prayed with her in English and in Hebrew every evening, was "taught the history and principles of our religion and . . . to read Hebrew. All this training in Jewish ritual, Jewish principles, and Jewish traditions has formed the background of my spiritual life."[38] Amy Steinhart learned enough Bible history and Hebrew to read prayers at the congregational Sabbath school she attended in 1880s and 1890s San Francisco.[39] The inherently supplementary nature of Sabbath schools suited the majority of American Jews, who preferred not to be defined primarily by their religion. As a result, they became quite widespread. By 1888, cities with small Jewish populations as far flung as Galveston, Texas, boasted Sabbath schools.[40] As public school became the educational environment of choice for nearly all American Jewish families toward the end of the nineteenth century, Jewish day schools often converted into Sabbath schools. The Hebrew Education Society of Philadelphia, chartered by the legislature of Pennsylvania as an all-day school, held out until 1878 but then transformed itself into a supplementary school barely distinguishable from the Hebrew Sunday School Society's networks of Sabbath schools.[41]

Despite their popularity, Sabbath schools met withering criticism. To many critics, the Bible stories and ethics around which the curricula typically centered seemed too universal and not Jewish enough. Henry Austryn Wolfson, a student and later a prominent scholar at Harvard with an interest in Jewish education, called Sabbath schools "a form of religious education more successfully carried out by Presbyterians than by reform Jews."[42] Sabbath school teachers, who were frequently untrained volunteers, were accused by other educators of ignorance and lack of professionalism. A heated debate at the Jewish Chautauqua Society's Second Summer Assembly in 1898 condemned the use of prizes and other "incentives" in Sabbath schools as outright bribes which served no educational purpose.[43] The vague content of some Sabbath school lessons affected the students negatively. Hortense Moses grew up thinking her Baltimore Sabbath school "a dreaded duty and a bore, and attendance at the synagogue a meaningless method of discipline, a necessary accompaniment to the boredom of the religious school regime."[44] Sabbath schools may have been frequent providers of Jewish education to girls, but their effectiveness was uncertain.

Wolfson's critique of Sabbath schools stemmed from his role as a teacher in a different network of Jewish schools, the Talmud Torahs. At the Cambridge Hebrew School where he taught while a student at Harvard, students attended classes every afternoon after public school sessions ended.[45] While Talmud Torahs resembled Sabbath schools in their inherently supplementary nature, they differed dramatically in the frequency of their classes and the rigor of their curriculum. Talmud Torahs appeared several decades after the Jewish Sabbath school movement began. They owed their development in part to the revival of interest in Jewish learning among a cadre of influential American-born Jews centered in Philadelphia and New York.[46] Talmud Torahs also grew in number and size in response to the immigrants arriving in America after 1880, many of whom were determined to provide their children with a more intensive Jewish education than was available in even the best Sabbath schools.[47]

A comparison between Baltimore's Hebrew Religious School Association and Hebrew Education Society illustrates the differences between the two systems of Jewish education. Whereas the Sabbath schools of the former required English as a prerequisite for entrance and teachers spoke only English in the weekly classes, the Talmud Torahs of the latter defined themselves as schools for Hebrew education. By the opening years of the twentieth century, many Jewish educators in Talmud Torahs had embraced Zionism. While Jewish nationalism was not necessarily a part of the Jewish immigrant mindset, many families preferred a Hebraic curriculum, which at least was rooted in a holy language, to the vapid religious instruction in English offered by most Sabbath schools.[48] The Talmud Torah classes of the Hebrew Educational Society met daily for two hours after school, in addition to Sunday classes and Sabbath services. Older students, whose religious education was virtually ignored by the Sabbath school movement, met daily in the early evenings.[49]

The curriculum of the Hebrew Education Society, which progressed from "sufficient knowledge of the Hebrew language" to "the simpler narrative portions of the Pentateuch" to the "more and more difficult poetry of the later prophets" to "the poets and philosophers of the Middle Ages," assumed a commitment to years of daily classes in language, liturgy, and history. The Hebrew Education Society of Baltimore saw itself as "a model to others who are as deeply concerned as we with the solution of the problem of Jewish education."[50] Jewish communities around the country adopted similar methods and developed networks of Talmud Torahs in their own cities. In Portland, Oregon, attendance at Talmud Torah was a part of daily routine for many Jewish children. "We would go to school, come home from school, go to Hebrew School and come home from Hebrew School, from Monday through Thursday, never on Fridays, and again on Sunday," Frieda Gass wrote of her busy schedule in Portland.[51] Jewish students all over the United States shared these educational experiences at Talmud Torahs.

Frieda's religious schooling at a Talmud Torah included the coeducation common to Sabbath schools and Talmud Torahs alike. With few exceptions, Talmud Torahs followed Sabbath schools by adopting the coeducational practice prevalent in the public schools they were designed to supplement. The possible distractions of coeducational religious classes were dismissed in comparison to the benefits of having

> both sexes represented. Politeness, and a consideration for feminine thought are thus practically drawn forth from the young men, while the young women find their minds stimulated and broadened by the expression of masculine thought. If the subjects studied in class are made sufficiently interesting, no inattention or frivolity need be feared.[52]

In small communities coeducation was necessary to ensure large enough classes, but large communities also made coeducation standard practice.[53] In response to Chicago's Montefiore Talmud Torah's appeal for funds in 1886, local businessman Lazarus Silverman donated one hundred dollars on the condition that girls be accepted along with boys. He believed strongly that girls' religious education was vital to the future of American Jewry.[54] American children, most Jewish parents believed, should learn in coeducational settings, no matter what the subject matter of their education.

In addition to synagogues and religious school associations, the important Jewish community institutions found in urban areas where large concentrations of American Jews lived also provided religious education. Some of these institutions offered classroom space to Sabbath schools and Talmud Torahs, as did the Hebrew Industrial School in Boston and the Chicago Hebrew Institute, but some also provided their own religious instruction.[55] Girls who could not afford regular Sabbath school or Talmud Torah tuition were offered free religious education at the Jewish Educational Alliance in Baltimore.[56] Immigrant girls in Chicago could take religious classes at the Jewish Manual Training School. These classes were financed by the Reform Sinai Temple and taught by locally prominent Rabbi Bernhard Felsenthal's daughter Julia.[57]

Many of these providers of Jewish education had motives beyond providing religious training. The Hebrew Free School Association in New York made no effort to disguise its goal of rapid Americanization and explicitly modeled its combined religious and industrial schools on the missionizing work of the Protestant Children's Aid Society.[58] In 1891, a representative of the Hebrew Free School Association declared in reference to the immigrant children sought as students:

> Our efforts are not restricted to the imparting of religious instruction, but extend to the inculcation of doctrines calculated to make our pupils, and through them their families, desirable and useful members of the community, instead of perpetuating the mental and physical depravity into which generations of oppression and persecution have forced them and from which they have escaped to claim protection and enlightenment at our hands.[59]

Since the established Jewish community acknowledged no contradiction between Jewish and American identity, it seemed not only natural but also necessary for religious schools to educate for both.

The complicated motives of many Jewish educators, thinly disguised at best, aimed to use religious education as the vehicle for ensuring the "adjustment" of immigrant children to their new lives as Americans. This additional set of expectations represented a change from the goals of earlier American Jewish education, a change set into motion by mass migration beginning during the 1880s. Whereas mid- to late nineteenth-century educators had seen religious education as the salvation of a small religious community acculturating all too rapidly or as a means of ensuring continuity, some turn-of-the-century educators considered religious education a way to promote discontinuity between presumably hopeless Jewish parents and potentially salvageable Jewish children. Educators saw immigrant parents' desires to give their children a religious education as an opportunity to "rear American citizens out of these legacied children of Russia and Austria," stressing the importance of fostering in them "appreciation for the best in American institutions and American principle."[60] For instance, convincing children and through them their parents to speak English rather than Yiddish at home became an important part of the Jewish educational establishment's agenda. At the closing exercises of the Hebrew Education Society of Philadelphia in 1904, speaker Cyrus

Hebrew Education Society Council, 1919. By 1919, the children of the eastern European Jewish immigrants who attended the religious and vocational classes offered by Philadelphia's Hebrew Education Society had demanded and received a say in their own education. *Courtesy of the Philadelphia Jewish Archives Center.*

Sulzberger addressed the students about the importance of using English to study religion, asking them "to use their influence to bring about the abolition of jargon in a land where English is the vernacular."[61] Teaching Judaism was clearly not the only goal of the religious schools.

In this context, girls' religious education became a convenient entree into the more important goal of moral indoctrination and training for respectability. The Columbia Religious and Industrial School for Jewish Girls focused on these gendered concerns. Originally founded in New York just after 1900 to counteract Christian mission schools, the Columbia Religious and Industrial School offered Hebrew, Biblical history, singing, sewing, and dressmaking. The school, "ever mindful of the importance of daily religious instruction," employed students from the newly reorganized Jewish Theological Seminary in the hope that Jewish education would "rescue our girls from the evil influences of the streets" and, together with industrial training, "furnish a home center that will develop respectable, religious, and industrious Jewish women." The lessons in Jewish history and liturgy were "so taught and explained as to leave with these young women lasting impressions of a pure Jewish life." Both for their own sake and the sake of their benevolent patrons, the girls who attended the school were drafted into an Alumnae Club so that the school could keep in touch with graduates during "their young woman-hood, that subtle period of life when girls develop the best or the worst instincts of their future."[62] These thinly veiled concerns about sexuality infused the programs and rhetoric of the Columbia Religious and Indus-trial School. Though the administrators and teachers were no doubt sin-cerely interested in the success, happiness, and religious devotion of their students, their preoccupation with Jewish girls' morality was the primary rationale behind every aspect of the school program.

The Content of Religious Education

These concerns with Americanization, morality, and domesticity natu-rally affected the content of girls' religious education. However, despite the shared assumptions of most religious schools that their main task was to teach girls about their religious traditions and moral behavior, other goals diverged. An array of different programs and activities resulted. Much like the curriculum in public schools through the late 1800s, the curriculum in Jewish religious schools varied widely.

The limited time devoted to religious education often meant that the goals of Jewish educators exceeded any possible outcome. As one exam-ple, recent high school graduate Jennie Mannheimer was required to teach Bible, Scriptures, history, and Hebrew to her class at the Rockdale Avenue Sabbath School in Cincinnati in 1890. Each student attended the Sabbath school on Sundays from 9:00 to 11:35 a.m., taking four thirty-five minute classes with one fifteen-minute break. The class work was or-ganized along the lines of a catechism, although the students were also ex-pected to familiarize themselves in a rudimentary way with Biblical texts.[63] Though Jennie prepared diligently for each week, the quality of her students' religious education necessarily suffered from such brief classroom time.

Some supplementary religious schools were more successful than oth-ers in structuring a limited amount of classroom time to the best possible advantage. An 1892 visitor to Temple Emanu-El's Sabbath school in New York was pleasantly surprised by the students' familiarity with Jewish history and post-Biblical Jewish literature. He found the girls' knowledge particularly unexpected and impressive, remarking

> how pleasing and how beautiful to see young girls of thirteen or fourteen take a lively and lasting interest in the Hebrew poets of the Middle Ages, and thus feel more strongly that the Jews of all these centuries are essentially the same in spirit and that we have but one faith.[64]

The Reform synagogue's instructional emphasis on Hebrew literacy was especially striking, given the fact that by 1892, the American Reform movement had decreased the amount of Hebrew used in synagogue services. As a cultural legacy, however, Hebrew was evidently seen as important enough to be a part of girls' Jewish education. Other schools continued to include German in the curriculum to accommodate the second, third, and fourth generation daughters of German-speaking Jewish immigrants. At the Anshe Emeth school in Philadelphia, Carrie Amram was graded weekly in German as well as Hebrew, Bible, and translation. This school monitored the students carefully by recording days absent, demerit marks, and weekly rank in classes ranging from twenty to twenty-five students. Carrie learned enough at Anshe Emeth to prepare her for studies at Gratz College, a Philadelphia institution of higher Jewish education, after she graduated from high school.[65]

Private schools were better able to control their curricula and to connect Jewish education with religious practice. The Kohut College Preparatory School for Girls, which served as both a boarding and a day school for girls in New York, held religious services for boarders on Friday nights and required students to attend synagogue services with prominent communal activist Rebekah Bettelheim Kohut on Saturday mornings.[66] The school, which opened with one hundred pupils attracted by the sterling reputation of the Kohut name, offered a dual secular and religious curriculum. Rebekah Kohut took pride in the religious environment of the school and personally oversaw her students' development into knowledgeable, practicing Jews.

> To communicate my own religious enthusiasm to my pupils was my aim, and I did not count my work well done, unless, in addition to knowledge of the Bible and ceremonial observance, I instilled into them certain

moral and ethical standards which would strengthen them for the future. And so I tried to make religion so significant and beautiful and stimulating to the imagination that the young girls whose lives had been entrusted to me might be stirred to the soul.[67]

Kohut believed the combination of secular and religious learning and observance the most effective means of promoting Jewish continuity, especially among women. However, the success of Kohut's school was short-lived due to financial problems. Not many parents sustained an interest in full-day Jewish schools. The benefit of such school programs was rarely acknowledged until the development of dual curriculum day schools several generations later.

At the opposite end of the spectrum from the traditionally religious Kohut College Preparatory School for Girls, secular Yiddish schools divorced Jewish literacy from religious practice completely, concentrating on the cultural and ethical aspects of Judaism. The Yiddish schools explicitly set out to create an American Jewish population informed about its dual heritage. Describing the National Radical Schools in 1916, one proponent wrote, "While the rising Jewish generation should as a matter of course grow up as good American citizens, part and parcel of the great American nation, the Jewish children should not at the same time be strangers to the Jewish people throughout the world."[68] In Chicago in 1916, the National-Radical Yiddish School held classes three times a week for students between the ages of seven and fifteen. The course work included Yiddish language and literature, Jewish history, folk songs, and guided discussions of Jewish and general social problems. The two highest grades learned some Hebrew. In an effort to placate both the most traditional and the most radical constituencies of the school, Jewish legends and Bible stories were incorporated into the curriculum, but they were taught out of order so as not to be confused with Jewish history.[69]

The gap between Rebekah Kohut's school and the National-Radical Yiddish School demonstrates how little coordination of religious curricula there was. While all the Sabbath Schools of the Hebrew Sunday School Society in Philadelphia might attempt to teach their students the same material regardless of which school they attended, congregational Sabbath schools, Talmud Torahs, and secular Yiddish schools in the same city, let alone other cities, developed their own programs independently. Due to the difficulty of providing comprehensive Jewish education in weekly Sabbath school classes or even more frequent Talmud Torah classes, the administrators of many religious schools left the content of the classes to the discretion of the individual teachers and made no attempt to standardize curricula. In New York, the Educational Alliance's Annual Report of 1902, which included detailed descriptions of other courses' content, merely said of the Department of Hebrew and Religion that "the aim of the work is to impart a knowledge of Hebrew language and the Bible; to train the pupils in the fundamental principles underlying the Jewish religion and ethics, and so to make a beginning in the study of Jewish literature."[70] Little direction was given to teachers as to what they should cover in class.

To some extent, the dearth of direction represented a feeling shared by the community at large through the turn of the century that as religious schools were only designed to supplement religious life as lived in Jewish homes by Jewish families, the actual content of the classes was of minor importance. The combination of declining ritual observance in many, if not most, American Jewish homes, and a push for the modernization of Jewish education eventually led to greater concern with classroom practice in religious schools. Many Jewish educators were dismayed that religious school curricula had to be so basic as to include, as Jennie Buffenstein's Denver Bible class did in 1900, explanations of the Jewish calendar, descriptions of the contents of the Pentateuch, and justifications for the observance of major holidays.[71] Having to teach these foundational elements of Judaism, which had in a perhaps mythical past been the province of Jewish families, seemed clear proof that "the religious life in Israel has lost much of its former fervor and intensity."[72] If religious education were to complement secular education in form and content, clearly something had to be done.

Samson Benderly and the Modernization of Jewish Education

Standardization of religious education did not begin until a large philanthropic gift funded a comprehensive study of Jewish education in New York in 1909. The study surveyed the current systems of religious instruction and Americanization programs, recognized the range of curricular offerings in religious schools, organized the most successful teachers, publicized the problem of religious education in the community at large, and supported the operation of model schools to test structural and instructional educational innovation.[73] When Samson Benderly left his position at the Hebrew Education Society of Baltimore to head the new Bureau of Jewish Education (BJE) of the *Kehillah,* New York's experiment in Jewish communal organization, he was confronted with the tangle of religious schools, disparate curricula, unprofessional teachers, and communal resistance identified by the 1909 survey.[74] The time was ripe for the modern religious educational system he worked to put into place in New York through the BJE. Though Benderly was successful in establishing networks of Jewish schools that served girls as well as boys, adolescents as well as children, and teachers as well as students, the percentage of all New York Jewish children who attended any sort of religious school remained relatively small.[75] Benderly also found it difficult to export his ideas to other cities, as only the very largest communities could effectively centralize and professionalize religious education to the same extent as New York. In spite of these limitations, Benderly's program was a watershed in American Jewish education and exerted a powerful influence visible in religious schooling throughout the United States.

Starting with his experiences as a Jewish educator in Baltimore during the late 1890s and early 1900s, Benderly had tried to realize his plans for a thoroughly modern religious education. Unlike many other Jewish educators, he started from the premise that "religious schools in America need and should not replicate religious schools in Europe."[76] He began with minor, seemingly superficial innovations such as requiring the teachers to be neatly dressed, putting flower pots in every classroom, and insisting on child-centered classes.[77] In these ways he incorporated elements of American progressive education into religious schooling. Eventually, he articulated a fully developed vision of a system of religious education. His approach to Jewish education rested on what his student and colleague Alexander Dushkin called "a social-engineering approach through the 'leverage' of community responsibility and programming, and a social psychological approach placing Jewish teaching within the total education of the American Jew for worthy citizenship."[78] Borrowing heavily from the developing progressive educational theory of the early 1900s, Benderly set out to establish communal commitment for Jewish education within the context of a democratic framework and pluralist society.[79]

In 1903, Benderly had explained his goals to the Sixth Zionist Congress. First, he emphasized, Jewish education in America was compatible with public education and should be structured as a supplementary means of counteracting the undesirable effects of purely secular schooling. Second, Jewish education should be self-supporting through tuition and free itself of the bonds and stigma of charitable support. Third, religious educational systems should be communal, completely distinct from congregational Sabbath schools or private *cheders*, both of which Benderly "doomed to oblivion, at least in this country." Communal religious education, run by a "well-organized, properly-trained, and fully-informed staff of salaried, responsible teachers, guided by an able superintendent," would replicate the better parts of public education in religious education. Fourth, women should constitute a significant part of the teaching staff, a development that would improve the quality of Jewish home life as well as Jewish education. Fifth, the curriculum should be organized to cover a "period of twelve years, with an average of four periods a week, each lasting about one hour and a half" and including Hebrew language, Jewish literature, Jewish history, and Jewish religion. "Detailed ceremonial celebrations of all holidays" and student religious services at the schools would bring to life the lessons learned in classrooms. Finally, the religious schools should develop a close and mutual relationship to American institutions for professional Jewish education, sharing personnel, ideas, and communal support.[80]

As head of the BJE in New York, Benderly was ideally placed to oversee the "establishment of a large number of communal self-supporting schools in harmonious correspondence with American life."[81] He formed a group of trainees, including Alexander Dushkin, Isaac Berkson, Libbie Suchoff, Emanuel Gamoran, Mamie Goldsmith, and Rebecca Aaronson.[82] These "Benderly Boys," as even the women were known, combined Jewish traditionalism and cultural Zionism to embody the possibilities of communal support for Jewish education. In addition to gathering around him this talented group of educators, many of whom were concurrently pursing graduate degrees at Columbia with such luminaries as John Dewey and Edward Thorndike, Benderly also convinced pillars of the New York Jewish community to support his endeavors.[83] Judah Magnes, the head of the *Kehillah*, Israel Friedlander, a professor at the Jewish Theological Seminary, and Jacob Schiff, a major financier and philanthropist, all worked to expand the BJE's programs. The most traditionally observant community leaders were initially suspicious of a centralized system of Jewish education that might weaken ritual observance. However, they, too came to see that "order, methods, and decorum do not mean the destruction of Orthodox Judaism but the reverse."[84] As a sign of his faith in the new system, for instance, businessman and philanthropist Harry Fischel agreed to affiliate the Orthodox Uptown Talmud Torah with the BJE.[85]

One of Fischel's primary motivations for taking such a step was that affiliation with the BJE would facilitate the establishment of classes for girls at the Uptown Talmud Torah.[86] Benderly's success at widening the female student base in all kinds of Jewish schools was the most immediately visible of his accomplishments. After expanding and adjusting existing teaching staff and curricula, the BJE opened new schools especially for girls "because owing to the traditional neglect of the education of Jewish girls, it was considered of particular importance to emphasize their education."[87] All three of the model schools operated by the BJE were for girls. These schools, known as Hebrew Preparatory Schools, served more than 1,100 students between eleven and fifteen years old at three different locations in New York. The girls' schools offered Hebrew language, Bible, modern Hebrew literature, Jewish history, and Jewish activities in music, arts and crafts, dance, and drama.[88] As Judah Magnes, head of the *Kehillah,* put it,

> these Preparatory Schools will, in the course of time, not only give an education to many Jewish girls now absolutely neglected, but will also furnish us with Jewish women teachers who will devote themselves particularly to the Jewish education of the thousands of Jewish immigrant girls who, strangely and sadly enough, are now almost entirely without religious and moral instruction.[89]

The BJE sponsored both regular religious school classes for girls and intensive teacher training courses. With the cooperation of Mordecai Kaplan at the Teachers Institute of the Jewish Theological Seminary, a particularly demanding year-long course was offered to young women between the ages of seventeen and twenty-one who had a high school education and some knowledge of Hebrew. These students were expected to continue studying once they began to teach.[90] Convinced that at least half of the future teaching staff in religious schools should be women, Benderly worked energetically with adolescent girls. He was particularly proud of the Association of Jewish High School Girls and considered such organizations important as much for their role in promoting religious education as a career as in enriching the Jewish content of girls' lives more generally.[91]

The difficulty of obtaining a teaching job after attending normal school in the highly politicized public school system in New York worked in Jewish education's favor, as many girls were convinced to enter Jewish education by guarantees of immediate job placement. Girls' families and the Jewish community at large were persuaded by the broader benefits cited for girls' advanced Jewish education.

> If the Public School suffer from over-feminization, our schools . . . suffer from over-masculinization. What a fund of love and devotion to Judaism lies dormant in the breast of the Jewish woman, and how little we have taken advantage of it. How much more stability would the Jewish home have if, out of every fifty Jewish mothers, one had once been a Jewish teacher, and twenty others had received a Jewish education.[92]

It was axiomatic to the Benderly group that "the Jewish teacher, besides being an educated man or woman, must possess a Jewish education."[93]

Adolescent Jewish Girls and Religious Training

One of Benderly's greatest influences on the American Jewish community was his commitment to religious education for adolescents, which reflected the Benderly group's professional engagement with the early twentieth-century social science literature on the teenage years as a distinctive stage of life. As Alexander Dushkin, Rebecca Aaronson, Emanuel Gamoran, and others studied education and psychology at Columbia, they could not fail to be affected by the discussions of adolescence current during the 1910s. With awareness of adolescence came a variety of new educational philosophies and methods aimed specifically at adolescents. Jewish education incorporated much of the new thinking, particularly as the campaign to maintain teenagers' interest in Jewish learning beyond confirmation accelerated. Critics questioned Sabbath schools and other systems of religious education that abandoned Jewish students just as they entered what might be the most critical stages of their lives for determining Jewish affiliation and identity.

As one of the first educators to focus on Jewish adolescents in general and Jewish teenage girls in particular, Henrietta Szold feared the consequences of secular education outpacing religious education. While she firmly approved of the large numbers of Jewish girls graduating from high school by 1900, she warned that "the salvation of Jewish girls as Jewesses and, for the present at least, as fine specimens of womanhood depends upon a proper alignment of their Jewish education with their secular education."[94] Benderly agreed. He urged the American Jewish community to consider the truth that "the years between fourteen and twenty have no less an important bearing upon the development of the pupil's character than childhood."[95] Szold and Benderly worked to convince parents and their daughters that extended religious education was at least as valuable as prolonged secular education both for the development of individual girls and the welfare of the community at large.

There were factors working both for and against the idea of adolescent religious education. In its favor was the growing number of adolescents attending high school. While many children of Jewish immigrant families still could not afford to stay out of the workforce once they finished elementary school, high school graduation became a realistic goal for growing numbers of them. Just as Jewish parents had typically looked for some kind of religious instruction to complement their children's education in the free public schools, so were they more willing to consider the importance of continuing religious education once continuing secular education was in place, at least as an ideal. Working against Jewish education for adolescence was the weight of tradition. In even the most traditional European communities, only the exceptional male students remained in religious schools past bar mitzvah age. Once boys were thirteen, they were men according to religious law and therefore presumably old enough to work as men, too. Given the expectation that they would learn what they needed to know at home, almost no one was concerned about girls' adolescent religious instruction.

In America, however, things were different. Once more Jewish children were staying in school longer, extended religious education seemed less foreign an idea. Once Sabbath schools and Talmud Torahs around the country established the principle of formal Jewish education for girls, there was no reason to consider their adolescent religious training any less important than that of boys. As a pilot program, the BJE selected five hundred Jewish girls attending New York public high schools and offered them weekly classes in Hebrew, Bible, prayers, Jewish history, Jewish customs, and Jewish music. Benderly reported "the genuine change . . . becoming manifest in these girls," whose "enthusiasm for things Jewish" affected "even indifferent parents, nay, even antagonistic parents."[96]

Other solutions to the problem of curtailed adolescent religious education were also proposed. Henry Pereira Mendes, rabbi of New York's Spanish and Portuguese Synagogue, suggested that a better solution than extended schooling in the classroom might be to ask "you ladies and mothers and sisters" to encourage "those youths and maidens from seventeen to twenty to go to their minister to receive the proper instruction." According to Mendes's plan, personalized instruction would end in adulthood with "proper membership in the congregation" rather than a school diploma.[97] Mendes, like Rebekah Kohut and other more traditionally observant Jews in America, was concerned not only with the issue of religious education but also religious practice. Greater exposure to Jewish education should, in this formulation, lead automatically to greater commitment to ritual observance.

Alice Seligsberg, a friend and colleague of Henrietta Szold, believed that forcing adolescent girls to engage in religious study might permanently turn them against religion, whereas freedom of choice would allow those who were interested a chance to share their enthusiasm with like-minded companions while those who were not interested would at least not find their indifference turned into resentment. Dividing Jewish studies into "religious *instruction* or study on the one hand, and religious *education* on the other," Seligsberg suggested that the former be applied to young girls' study of Jewish literature, Bible, Hebrew, and Jewish history, while the latter should encompass teenage girls' "intensifying . . . desire for righteousness, and their nearer approach to an understanding of perfection" through ethical study. Like Mendes, Seligsberg stressed personal relationships among teachers and students. In the context of organizing a "purely religious (not philanthropic or social) society of girls and women, whose Associates would rank according to the number of years of study *voluntarily* given to religious education," she hoped to keep Judaism alive for the adolescent girls, whose souls she envisioned as "lifted up like empty cups, waiting to be filled."[98]

Benderly, Szold, Mendes, and Seligsberg all faced the reality that for those adolescents who did receive religious education, confirmation classes were the most likely substance to fill their empty cups. The development of confirmation as an adolescent rite of passage led to its wide acceptance among American Jewish families across denominations.[99] It seemed logical to many American Jews that fifteen or sixteen was a more appropriate age for religious maturity than twelve or thirteen. The increasing attention paid to adolescence as a stage of life supported the idea of confirmation. Though age and ceremony varied depending on time, place, and rabbinic preference, confirmation marked an important stage in many late nineteenth- and early twentieth-century adolescent Jewish girls' lives no matter what their families practiced at home. Martha Simon was confirmed in Chicago in 1889, despite the fact that the only religious ritual in her childhood home was lighting candles on Chanukah.[100] Adele Jules was confirmed at the Madison Avenue Temple in Baltimore because her parents thought participation in the classes would encourage her to join other temple youth activities.[101] It was difficult for professional Jewish educators to claim that adolescents' religious education should not be focused on confirmation when even families generally uninterested in Jewishness sent their daughters to confirmation classes.

For some girls, confirmation was a deeply moving religious experience. Irma Levy considered her confirmation "the tremendous event of my youth. . . . I felt almost suffocated with wonder and joy at the moment when, before the open ark, my rabbi placed his hands on my head and blessed me. To myself I vowed that my life would forever be dedicated to my people."[102] Blanche Wolf experienced a similar sense of conviction when she stood and "proclaimed my Faith in Judaism and recited the Ten Commandments, just as thousands of children had done before."[103] Decades later Emily Fechheimer still remembered the poem she recited at her Cincinnati confirmation, recalling, "Each child was assigned one and said it aloud. It was a very large class, I think about twenty-eight or thirty children, boys and girls. . . . Each girl confirmant carried a bouquet while walking up the aisle and placed it on the pulpit as an offering."[104] Jewish children participated in similar confirmation ceremonies across the United States from the second half of the nineteenth century forward. By 1900, confirmation was firmly established as the standard highlight of youthful religious experience.

Widespread acceptance of confirmation by American Jews did not make the rite of passage any more palatable to religious educators. Critics of confirmation feared the emptiness of the preparatory classes and the growing social, rather than religious, significance of the ceremonies. As early as the mid-nineteenth century, *Israelite* reported that radical American Jews denounced confirmation as "humbug" and traditional Jews denounced confirmation as a "Gentile custom," although the author of the article pointed out that no suggestions were forthcoming from either side to "tell us of a better mode of proceeding to impress upon the mind of the youth the responsibility of an Israelite."[105]

What concerned the cadre of professional Jewish educators was the idea of teaching toward a test or ceremony rather than toward religious understanding and commitment. The curricula of confirmation classes were no more uniform across the country than other religious education classes were, but in general, the rigid, formalistic nature of education designed as preparation for a particular event was less than inspiring. Most confirmation classes were based on Jewish catechisms. Rabbi Kaufman Kohler's popular *Guide for Instruction in Judaism: A Manual for Schools and Home,* which was issued in several editions, was one example of the Jewish manuals aimed at the confirmation audience.[106] Jennie Buffenstein's 1903 confirmation notebook recorded a series of highly formal, mechanical notes, most likely copied out of a book such as Kohler's or a verbatim transcription of what the teacher said. In answer to a question about the purpose of confirmation, Jennie wrote (or copied), "The object of the ceremony of confirmation is to exhibit before God and man that we have been taught in the tenets of our ancestral faith, and that we are conscious of our duties as Israelites." The constant use of the word "Israelites" as late as 1903 indicates how stilted and stylized confirmation classes often were.[107]

Criticism leveled at confirmation focused on other problems as well. Writing in 1903, Henrietta Szold pronounced confirmation an educational failure.

The confirmation service for girls, in which the principle embodied itself and which was to be the flower of female education, fell far short of fulfilling the hopes it had aroused. Like much of the work attempted by the reformers, it will have to be done over again by another generation. It was sterile, ineffectual. It failed to stimulate the Jewish development of women because it was an assertion of the principle of female education in theory only. In practice it put up with a minimum of superficial knowledge and an apology for Jewish training. With those outside of the reform party, it had the effect of throwing discredit upon the principle of female education.[108]

Szold expressed several concerns about the prevalence of confirmation. Like Benderly and the BJE educators, she believed that American conditions called for more in-depth religious education over a longer period of time than confirmation classes could possibly provide. As a traditionally oriented Jew, she also feared that what was to her the obvious failure of

Confirmation class at Rodeph Shalom, 1916. The Philadelphia congregation's confirmation class included far more girls than boys and was led by a female teacher. *Courtesy of the Philadelphia Jewish Archives Center.*

confirmation to increase the religious commitment or observance of adolescent American Jews would compromise larger efforts to target girls for Jewish education.

Confirmation's role as a social marker for Jewish girls also fell subject to heavy criticism. In 1908, Philadelphia's *Jewish Exponent* confirmation notices consisted of invitations to open houses in honor of the occasion rather than religious or even ceremonial reports. Announcements like "Mr. and Mrs. G. Bonnlem, of 5012 Greene Street, Germantown, will be at home Sunday, June 7, after 8 P.M., in honor of the confirmation of their daughter RENA" had replaced earlier reproductions of actual confirmation programs.[109] The printed program itself for the confirmation held at Philadelphia's Congregation Rodeph Shalom in 1919 devoted a quarter of its space to listing the addresses and "at home" times of the confirmants.[110] While in other ways the program resembled those of previous years with its selection of benedictions, speeches, and floral offerings, the emphasis on the social nature of what was meant to be a religious event called into question the purpose and efficacy of confirmation, particularly for girls, for whom confirmation was then the only religious rite of passage available. Early developments in the idea of bat mitzvah ceremonies, the first of which was held only a few years later, reflected all these criticisms of confirmation by initially returning the focus to more intensive Jewish education and practice.

Resistance to Religious Education for Jewish Girls

The criticism of the social turn confirmation had taken reflected a larger problem in the religious education of Jewish girls in America. Adolescent girls, especially those from middle-class families, were so busy developing their credentials as Americans that they often had little time left over to focus on their identities as Jews. Whether they liked it or not, whether they gave it much thought or not, they were born Jews and remained Jews. Becoming American and maintaining that all-important social and national identity was not as automatic a process. Second and third generation Jewish girls in America were in some ways the litmus test of their families' success in acculturation. It was a serious obstacle to the growth of religious schooling that for many middle-class girls, Jewish education was just one of the many extracurricular activities necessary to prove their status and that of their families. During the 1890s, Blanche Wolf "had extra German and French lessons after school, to say nothing of music, dancing, and gymnasium classes" in addition to confirmation classes.[111] Sophie Ruskay's mother admonished her uninterested daughter, "You don't want to grow up into an ignoramus, do you? You have to learn to read from the prayer book, to say your night-prayers. . . . More we don't expect." Sophie's mother placated her with a promise that she could go to dancing school next season and buy a few fancy dresses.[112]

The focus on "accomplishment" was a source of great concern for Jewish social critics, who feared that religious education was forced to take a back seat to spiritually insignificant endeavors. A *Jewish Messenger* editorial bemoaned the tendency of parents to invest too little time and money in their daughters' religious development.

> It cannot be said that we do not love our daughters; far otherwise. We expend large sums to enable them to vie with others, in all that the world deems essential to education. For that purpose, we send them to the most fashionable seminaries. We obtain for them the best pianofortes, and see them well drilled in dancing. Now to all this we do not object, if parents have a taste that way; although our experience teaches,

that those very fashionably taught, do not at all times answer expectations formed of them, unless they have been schooled in religion. Hence we contend, that unless parents devote some of their own time, or if that is deemed inconvenient, adapt some plan by which their daughters may become conversant with their religion, its rites, its doctrines, and its promises, their labor has been lost.[113]

This editorial appeared in 1860 but might have been written in any of the succeeding decades as well. Even after Jewish education became far more institutionally and communally organized, teachers were still frustrated by parental apathy. After Anna Goldberg's 1914 plan to start a school for Jewish girls in Chicago was rejected by the community, she wrote with exasperation, "As soon as the need of money was mentioned, the Maxwell Street Yankees of Douglas Park withdrew their children. Money can be had for everything; for music and dancing; but when it comes to Jewish education only excuses are offered. How cheap Judaism has become to many of our parents."[114]

Goldberg's disappointment stemmed from a sense of lost opportunity. She joined other Jewish educators who were astonished by Jewish parents' failure to recognize the critical need for providing religious education to their daughters. Once girls' religious education had been justified as serving a crucial role in developing the future of American Judaism, women were theoretically endowed with an important place in the Jewish community. When parents preferred to expend their resources on middle-class female accomplishments like music and dancing rather than particular Jewish achievements of learning and education, they denied their daughters what could be a unique place in American Jewish life. These "Yankee" parents, much to Goldberg's dismay, placed their understanding of what it took to be an American ahead of their ideas about what it took to be an American Jew. In expressing her frustration with parental short-sightedness, Goldberg and others operated with a very different set of assumptions from the parents whom they criticized for cheapening Judaism by not investing sufficient family and educational resources in it.

Although it was unlikely that centuries of tradition were the major concern for the "Maxwell Street Yankees" who so frustrated Goldberg, a reluctance to overturn long-standing models of educating girls at home for domestic religious roles was still an important reason for resistance to Jewish girls' religious education among some Jews in America. Talmudic injunctions against teaching females the full religious curriculum continued to hold sway in many households. Mothers and fathers alike sometimes refused their daughters' desires to learn more, either because of a lack of resources or a traditional reluctance to teach girls. Parental reluctance to buck tradition seemed to lag behind communal enthusiasm for girls' religious education.

In addition, the focus on Jewish women's motherhood and domesticity as vehicles for religious expression demonstrated the cultural limits on educating Jewish girls. Writers for the American Jewish press advocated religious schooling for girls but with the caveat that too much education might lead girls to press for religious leadership. One commented that holding "the advocates of political power for ladies" up as models of womanhood was inadvisable, as "the gentleness and refinement, the kindness and affectionate tenderness, which are the distinguishing characteristics of woman, that tend to make home beautiful and cast a happy influence over everything at home, are not to be found in these people."[115] Only if religious education were focused on the future cultural roles of girls as wives and mothers would it be acceptable to many elements of the American Jewish community.

By the late nineteenth century, it had become clear that parental indifference to girls' education, rather than theological or even cultural opposition to it, impeded its development. There were rabbinic sources for the dismissal of the need for Jewish girls' education, but these sources became the object of outright derision as "inherited Oriental principles."[116] If considered at all, the rabbinic proscriptions were cited only to be refuted. An 1898 editorial in *American Israelite* pointed to textual sources that Jewish girls historically had enjoyed religious education despite rabbinic proscriptions and named several learned women mentioned in the Talmud. Isaac Mayer Wise, author of the editorial, used this evidence to prove the point that "the neglect and exclusion of the female sex in school and place of worship are not Jewish, they are oriental, adopted from a nation whose women were slaves, which was never the case in Israel." Wise, a major figure in American Reform Judaism, was writing from a particular perspective—he went on to criticize "our orthodox brethren" for continuing to exclude women from full membership in the religious community.[117] Yet his point seemed valid to most of the Jews in America who concerned themselves with religious education at all. Few, if any, American Jewish educators gave much thought to antiquated sources forbidding girls any Jewish education at all. As calls for women's religious education grew stronger and mothers were elevated as the primary inculcators of religious affiliation and sentiment, less and less was heard about dated restrictions on women's Jewish learning. "Inherited Oriental principles" had no place in American Jewish education.

Ironically, Jewish educators found that the traditional lack of emphasis on Jewish girls' education actually made it easier to convince parents of the benefits of modern or experimental methods of religious instruction. Alternative Jewish schools benefited from the more flexible attitudes toward girls' religious education. Zionist schools with Hebrew literary curricula caught on faster with girls because, Alexander Dushkin pointed out, "it was easier to get Jewish parents to permit the teaching of these modern 'fads' to girls than to boys."[118] The Zionist religious schools, which started in America as early as the 1890s, also achieved a measure of popularity with girls because the Zionist movement considered the education of women a necessary and vital part of its agenda.

Secular Yiddish schools also counted more girls than boys as pupils, as even radical parents interested in giving their sons a Jewish education sometimes sent them to more traditional Talmud Torahs or *cheders*. Yiddish literacy was so common among Jewish girls in eastern Europe that a Jewish school with an emphasis on Yiddish seemed a natural choice for immigrant parents, sometimes regardless of their political persuasion.[119] Leah Dvorah Orenstein enjoyed her schooling at the Philadelphia branch of the Workmen's Circle, where the *Yiddishe Folkschule* provided Yiddish classes in Jewish history, literature, grammar, and current events. Her parents had already seen to it that Leah Dvorah was fluent in Yiddish, the language the family spoke at home.[120] Yiddish served as the link between their religious observance at home and their daughter's Jewish education at school, despite the radical orientation of the Workmen's Circle, which might well have stopped them from sending any of Leah Dvorah's brothers there.

For those parents who decided that a more traditional style of Jewish education might be the best way to resist assimilation, religious schooling offered by a variety of communal institutions might be acceptable for girls, but not for boys. Even if their daughters attended religious school at the Educational Alliance, for instance, their sons usually continued to receive religious instruction in small *cheders* and other more traditional settings. Commenting on the "great preponderance of girls in our classes," Educational Alliance superintendent David Blaustein explained in 1898, "that is because the parents think the instruction is good enough for girls but not for boys."[121] Nearly twenty years later, the Educational Alliance was still reporting greater success in its religious school with girls, whose "parents are not so rigid in their requirements, on the old theory that a woman's education was a matter of no great importance to the community."[122]

The numbers of boys and girls enrolled in religious schools reflected these attitudes. In 1890, 56 boys and 119 girls attended religious classes at the Hebrew Free and Industrial School Society of St. Louis. These students, the institutional report noted, not only "obtain[ed] an acquaintance with our sacred literature, but also receive[d] a fundamental knowledge of the language of this country."[123] All those parents who were continuing to send their sons to Yiddish-speaking teachers, the report implied, deprived them of the opportunity to learn English as well as more modern religious instruction. The number of girls still outpaced the number of boys attending the religious schools of the Hebrew Educational Society of Philadelphia in 1909, as Hebrew Schools Nos. 2 and 3 ended the year with combined totals of 24 boys and 91 girls.[124]

These low numbers reflected the fact that the modernization and expansion of Jewish education continued to meet resistance. Even in New York, where the BJE was most influential, in 1921, only 25 percent of 275,000 Jewish children of school age received any form of religious instruction. In successful middle-class neighborhoods, the percentage was even lower. Only 20 percent of the Jewish children in Harlem attended religious schools, and weekly Sabbath schools were once again making serious inroads on daily Talmud Torahs.[125] The incorporation of female teachers into the Jewish schools also proceeded more slowly than Benderly had hoped. In 1918, a majority of Sunday school teachers were women, but only 23 percent of the BJE teachers, who had to meet a far more demanding standard, were women.[126] In addition, as Jonathan Sarna has pointed out, Benderly's commitment to female leadership in Jewish education rarely extended to placing even his own female disciples into administrative positions. This discrepancy between his rhetoric and his actions may have stemmed in part from his belief that his vision of Jewish education would not be taken seriously unless men remained the authorities.[127] While it was indisputably true that, thanks to the BJE, more girls than ever before attended religious school and became Jewish educators, Benderly's dream of a systematic, modern American Jewish education was never quite realized.

The Meaning of Girls' Religious Education
for American Judaism

Benderly may not have realized his vision in full, but the trajectory of turn-of-the-century Jewish education's growth showed that even in locations far from the center of professional Jewish education in New York, children and adolescents were learning as individuals, members of families, and participants in communal activities that Judaism was a viable and vibrant force in America. The choice most Jewish parents made early on that religious instruction should complement rather than replace "American" education helped bolster their larger project of working out American Jewish identity.

The specific purpose of various kinds of programs varied. Clearly, the confirmation training Jennie Buffenstein attended in Denver in 1903 was as different from Amelia Allen's weekly Sabbath school sessions in Philadelphia during the 1860s as it was from the lessons Gertrude Mandelbaum learned at her mother's knee in Chicago before World War I. Yet all these girls, and thousands like them during the late 1800s and early 1900s, could see through religious education of one kind or another that American and Jewish identity need not negate each other. Jennie Buffenstein's confirmation class notebook was one among many other school notebooks in subjects such as botany and civics, all of which she preserved as valuable. Amelia Allen continued her experiences as a student in both public school and Sabbath school as a teacher in both the American and Jewish educational systems. Gertrude Mandelbaum excelled academically and participated enthusiastically in the social life of her heavily Jewish public high school, but she also treasured her mother's religious teachings.[128]

It is important to note that the inherently supplementary nature of most Jewish education in America also had an effect. Especially for those first generation immigrant families who were used to placing Judaism and Jewishness at the center of their lives, relegating religious instruction to an extracurricular activity was potentially threatening to Jewish continuity. But because the very idea of formal religious education, especially for girls, was relatively new, most of these families continued to rely on the home as the locus of Jewish education. They demonstrated their own interest in acculturation by combining traditional modes of religious training within the home with developing American modes of Jewish education in structured environments outside the home. Jewish education did not have to be the sole province of the professionals unless families preferred it that way. This potential tension between home and school, family and teachers as purveyors of Jewish education lasted beyond the early part of the twentieth century, but from 1860 to 1920, when immigration from various parts of Europe was at its highest levels, part of the challenge of acculturation for many Jews in America was striking a balance between Jewish and American identity. One important example of this integration in action was the way in which Jews dealt with holiday observances, accentuating the elements of Jewish holidays that seemed most consonant with American culture, such as freedom on Passover and consumption on Chanukah.[129] Throughout this period, Jewish education became and remained key to the process.[130]

As a communal strategy, then, religious education affected Jewish girls on at least two levels, even if they did not participate in it as individuals. First, Jewish education both reflected and shaped greater participation of women in the religious aspects of American Jewish life. Although gender distinctions were preserved even in the most liberal institutions of Reform Judaism, none of the young denominations were free from the effects of a more democratically, if still selectively, educated laity of boys and girls, men and women. The earliest bat mitzvah ceremonies of the 1920s simultaneously critiqued confirmation as a watered-down Jewish rite of passage and staked a claim that Jewish girls did deserve some rite of passage of their own.[131] Although attempts by Jewish women to pursue rabbinic ordination were still sporadic and unsuccessful, ever-increasing numbers of religiously educated Jewish women began to attend American institutions of higher Jewish learning. Some, such as the students at the Jewish Theological Seminary's Teachers Institute, were training to be educators, but many others wanted to extend their youthful religious education into meaningful adult experiences within American Judaism.[132]

The American Jewish community at large generally supported all these efforts, both for its own internal enrichment and as yet another way to demonstrate that Jewish life was consonant with American life. This was the second of the ways in which Jewish education affected girls, whether or not they had formal religious education of their own. The expansion and development of Jewish education in America during the latter part of the nineteenth and, especially, the early part of the twentieth centuries represented a sustained attempt to develop an organic American Jewish identity. It was not the only attempt; projects such as the Jewish Publication Society of America, for instance, had similar goals.[133] But educators from Rebecca Gratz to Samson Benderly saw in Jewish children the future of Judaism in America. Any educational system that relied only on family-based religious instruction or targeted only the intellectual or economic elites or focused only on boys could not succeed. The structural need in American Jewish life was to bring religious education to as many children, and preferably adolescents as well, as possible. It was clear even to Benderly that no one system, no matter how rational and thorough, could meet the needs and desires of all Jews in America. Yet he, like his predecessor Gratz, recognized that religious education designed specifically for the special needs of Jews in America could and should provide a route toward a knowledgeable, integrated American Jewish identity. Girls could not help but benefit from growing communal commitment to their inclusion in this ideal.

The innovation of formal religious education for girls informed a new relationship of girls and women to the Jewish community that paralleled their experience of expanding social opportunity for American women. The movement of girls' religious education out of the home and into the classroom, the public nature of ceremonies associated with religious education, and the extension of religious education to adolescents all spoke to the growing interest in and acceptance of women's vital role in defining American Jewry. Just as American women more generally gained access to formal channels of economic, social, cultural, and civic power at the turn of the century, Jewish women's stock of religious education greatly improved their ability to demand and participate in similar activities within their own communal institutions. As boys' traditionally rigorous religious education became less prevalent and the number of girls receiving formal religious training increased, the balance of power shifted in an American Jewish community committed to preserving distinction through knowledge, if not always through observance.

While Jewish women had always been perceived as the keepers of home-based observances, they now became associated with the guardianship of all religious principles and traditions worth preserving in an open society that in many ways prescribed success through homogenization. The centrality of gender to the communal project of defining American Judaism affected every Jewish girl's religious upbringing. Assumptions about women's inherent spirituality, the role of women in creating homes at once American and Jewish, and the necessity for training girls to anchor their communities placed the responsibility for producing a particularly American Jewry squarely on the shoulders of women. American

Jewish girls learned in many different types of schools, from many different kinds of teachers, that they held the power to direct the future of the American Jewish community. Though their opportunities were still circumscribed by gender and class, Jewish girls' religious experiences had the capacity to imbue them with a unique influence in their modernizing world. Religious education for girls expanded dramatically because of the strong argument women could make for a religious authenticity and commitment that required education for their own sake. By learning Jewish ritual, literature, and philosophy, girls could understand Jewish history and position themselves in relation to their own community's present and, more broadly, American Jewry's future. Religious education connected Jewish girls to the past, present, and future of the American Jewish community.

5

"Such a World of Pleasure"
Adolescent Jewish Girls and American Youth Culture

On a typical day in New Orleans during the Civil War, six-teen-year-old Clara Solomon rose early to go to the Louisiana Normal School. She dawdled over breakfast and left the house reluctantly, complaining of poor health. She would have much preferred to stay home with her mother. At school, she noticed the dwindling number of students who continued to attend classes in the midst of occupied New Orleans. After a school day spent in lessons on deportment as well as geography, arithmetic, elocution, and literature, Clara walked slowly home with friends, their usual after-school gatherings curtailed by the exigencies of war. When she got home, she discussed her day with her mother, sewed, played the piano, and waited to see if her father would be able to return from his business travels that evening. She accompanied her mother to pay a call on their Jewish neighbors and went home in time for a supper meager by prewar standards. After supper, she settled down to read and do some schoolwork, waiting impatiently for her sister to come upstairs to their room and companionably "book it" with her in their diaries. As she wrote her diary entry for the day, she privately cursed the war and all despicable Yankees. She and her sister washed up, returned to their diaries for a few more lines scribbled before bed, blew out the candles, and went to sleep.[1]

Half a continent and half a century away, eighteen-year-old Emily Frankenstein hopped out of bed early to get started on her day in Chicago during World War I. She joined her father for breakfast and helped pack him up for the day at his medical office. After getting dressed and briefly practicing her piano exercises, she walked to the Kenwood-Loring School, where she and her friends enjoyed a cozy mix of the classes and school activities taken for granted by healthy high school girls. After school, she took the tram downtown with several of her Jewish neighborhood friends who did not attend her exclusive private school. A little while later, she made an excuse to her friends and left to meet her beau Jerry, home on leave from his post as a quartermaster in the American army. When they returned to Emily's house, they stayed outside and spooned on the porch swing until her father came out and suggested that it was time for Jerry to leave. With his departure went all thoughts of the war. Emily had not been home all day and stayed up for a while to read, do homework, and update her diary. Moving quietly around the room she shared with her sister, she prepared for bed in silence and fell asleep almost immediately.[2]

The girlhood experiences of Clara and Emily appeared to differ in many respects. The Civil War affected Clara much more directly than World War I did Emily, especially in terms of the dislocations and straitened financial circumstances of the Solomon family. Clara spent much of her day at home with her family, while Emily spent most of her time with friends outside her house. The schooling Clara received at the Louisiana Normal School in 1861 was considerably less rigorous than the education offered to Emily at her private girls' school in 1918. Clara sewed daily as part of the household economy, whereas if Emily found time to sew at all, she was most likely to knit something as a present for her father or her suitor. Girls in New Orleans during the early 1860s spent a minimum of time walking around by themselves because of both social convention and physical danger in the tightly guarded city. Girls in Chicago during the late 1910s enjoyed more freedom to travel about the city.

Despite the significant gaps between Clara and Emily's experiences, they also shared a great deal. They both kept diaries as a matter of course. Both played the piano and read for pleasure on a daily basis. They both shared bedrooms with their sisters. Though they spent their time with friends differently, both held their friends in great esteem and enjoyed the activities that took place in peer environments. They both had close relationships with their families. Most important, both identified with other girls they knew, and they viewed their various peer activities as means of coming to terms with their places in the world.

On the surface, little of Clara or Emily's daily routine seemed much affected by the fact that they were Jewish. Neither prayed daily, observed the dietary laws of *kashrut*, or attended Jewish schools. Both noted Christmas in their diaries. Yet in countless small but important ways, the fact of their Jewishness affected the very shape of their lives. Clara never attended school on Saturdays because it was the Sabbath. Her family went to great lengths to obtain matzoh for Passover, no easy feat in wartime New Orleans. Whenever family finances allowed, they owned seats in both the men's and women's sections of their synagogue, Dispersed of Judah. Emily attended services at Chicago's Temple Sinai. Her extended family had elaborate Sabbath dinners at her maternal grandmother's house with some regularity. She decorated her bedroom with rugs produced by the Bezalel School of arts and crafts in Jerusalem.[3]

Most significantly of all, Clara and Emily's social circles away from school were primarily Jewish. The neighbors Clara and her mother visited, the group of girls Emily spent time with after school, the eligible young men both thought about—whether in the abstract for Clara or the flesh for Emily—all were Jewish. This was no coincidence. Nothing in their girlhood experiences forced them to socialize exclusively with other Jewish people. In fact, both of them consistently made non-Jewish friends at school. However, the thorny problems of identity and integration for Jewish girls in America stretched across the decades from Clara to Emily and were to a great extent resolved by the American Jewish social world surrounding them. There were times and places where they were in specifically American environments, such as the public high schools most adolescent Jewish girls attended by 1900. There were also times and places where they were in specifically Jewish environments, such as synagogues. Much of the time they moved easily in and out of a variety of turn-of-the-century surroundings. However, they were most often in the company of other American Jewish youth like them who, whether they thought about it or not, faced the same issues of integrating youth culture and Jewish identity in America.

The increasing importance of peers as well as parents in dealing with these issues arose from changes in ideas about adolescence. New space for youth culture emerged during the second half of the nineteenth century and continually widened at the beginning of the twentieth century. More than ever before, adolescents interacted with peers as much as, if not more than, with members of their families. In the United States, expanding educational opportunity and the growing trend toward a stage of life between schooling and marriage left girls and boys with the time and, depending on class, wherewithal to develop a culture of their own, centered on shared social, cultural, and even economic experiences. Gender was also an important factor in the development of youth culture.

Assumptions about differences between men and women exerted considerable influence on the coming of age of boys and girls and resulted in the creation of a separate girl culture within American youth culture. This girl culture was significantly affected by changes in gender ideology. By the end of the nineteenth century, the model American girl was defined by more than earlier ideals of morality and domesticity, although these qualities retained cultural significance. The model American girl was also known for blooming health, independence of spirit, and cultivated taste.[4] She was educated and active, her freedom and autonomy increasing as time went on. Though girl culture changed in response to social metamorphosis during the period from 1860 to 1920, fundamental continuities in the impact of class, gender, and family structure contributed to consistencies in girls' experiences throughout the period.

Adolescent Jewish girls found that their relationship to American girl culture reinforced their feelings of being American. By sharing the activities and experiences of other girls their age, they could identify with American girlhood on every level. Jewish girls from a wide range of backgrounds participated in the evolution of American girl culture in a number of ways. If able to attend high school, they joined their classmates in school activities and class events designed in part to construct a common culture for girls and boys regardless of their individual circumstances of home and family. Whenever financial or family situations allowed, they acquired skills like piano playing and dancing as external manifestations of internal cultivation. They exercised their bodies as well as their minds in pursuit of the good health associated with American girlhood. They read the same books as each other and as other American girls, which helped develop shared literary idioms and ideas about the narratives of their own lives. They joined clubs and societies of peers with similar interests. They participated in evolving systems of dating that provided common experiences for adolescents all over the country while still encompassing a variety of ethnic and religious traditions of courtship. Without abandoning their religiously defined roles as keepers of tradition, they mediated their families' integration into American society by pursuing cultural and social experiences that would link them to their peers and allow them to help construct the meaning of American girlhood.

Of course, there never was a singular "American girlhood." Despite the growing viability of youth culture as the focus of American adolescence, the effects of various distinguishing factors differentiated the experiences of white American youth. While growing numbers of American teenagers received some sort of secondary schooling, boys were still far more likely to go to work before finishing, and girls were more likely to graduate from high school. Changes in educational theory and practice led to increasingly differentiated curricula so that even when girls and boys attended the same schools, by the early twentieth century, they might well have taken different classes.[5] The social activities that brought girls and boys together in environments and spaces other than school exposed class divisions, as adolescent leisure was a marker of some teenagers' freedom from family economic responsibility. The dictates of class and work cut across gender lines but left various groups of adolescent boys and girls with different sets of social and cultural options dependent on time and money. Both work and school gradually moved adolescents into groups of people close to their own age. Regardless of class, some families were more reluctant than others to allow their daughters to spend more time with peers than parents and siblings. Immigrant families especially struggled with finding a balance. Immigrant children and adolescents could see that their interactions with peers would provide a path toward acculturation. Immigrant parents could also see this, but they were torn between wanting their children to integrate and wanting them to stay close to family and tradition.

The relationship between Jewish girls' family structures and experiences of American girl culture was especially affected by class. Whereas the family was typically a social and cultural unit for middle-class Jewish girls, the family was often an economic unit for working-class and recent immigrant Jewish girls. Middle-class families took trips together, attended concerts together, and supported their daughters' social and affective ties to peers as part of family strategies of acculturation. In working-class families where each member left home every day for a different kind of daily experience, family solidarity coalesced around economic success and was threatened by daughters' involvement in an external girl culture. If working-class or recent immigrant girls wished to become American, they did so at the risk of distancing themselves from their families in ways that middle-class girls did not need to worry about as much. Immigrant and working-class girls found idealized American girlhood more difficult to realize but generally held themselves to the standard nonetheless. They, too, were exposed to the model through education, work, and popular culture. By adapting their dress, directing their reading, and adopting some of the manners of the model American girl, they could not only become part of a significant cultural trend but also elevate their own families' status by achieving social integration. As a result, middle-class girlhood became the ideal, if not the reality, across class lines.

Hovering over all the other factors shaping Jewish girls' involvement with youth culture was religious identity, which in some form remained an important part of most of their lives and set them apart in some ways from their non-Jewish counterparts. In general, American Jewry wanted Jewish girls to resemble other American girls without forsaking all sense of religious or ethnic distinction. General assumptions that American girlhood encompassed high standards of morality, if not any specific religiosity, provided Jewish girls with the means to achieve a kind of synchronicity. Though pressures to be American girls as well as Jewish girls had the potential to become problematic for adolescents in search of identities, in practice the conflict was relatively minimal. So many of the behaviors and values of American girlhood and traditional Jewish girlhood were similar that conflict was far more likely to arise as a result of class issues or family structure.

Consequently, very few girls sacrificed their Jewish identity in their efforts to achieve recognition as Americans. The fluid boundaries of "Americanness," which expanded at the turn of the century—however reluctantly—in reaction to mass immigration and increased urbanization, allowed Jews in America to retain religious distinction as part of their conceptions of self. Most Jewish girls accepted their Jewishness and many took great pride in it, but few chose to be defined by it. By virtue of their age, they were part of a group of people just beginning to be recognized as a distinct social category. In many cases, their primary allegiance was to youth culture rather than religious culture. However, they rarely had to make such a stark choice. It was not only possible but also desirable for Jewish girls to participate in the American youth culture of the moment without ever turning away from their Jewish identities.

Socializing at School

The growth of secondary education encouraged the emergence of a youth culture of leisure, as adolescents who spent significant time with each other at school were likely to develop similar interests as a result of their proximity and shared experiences. Both middle- and working-class adolescents prioritized leisure activities enjoyed with their peers. Social critics concerned about coeducation in high schools acknowledged that "the social relations have been of far greater benefit than the intellectual."[6] In many American Jewish communities, the coeducational activities of Jewish youth were popular not only for their own sake but also as a sort of preparatory pool of suitable (i.e., Jewish) spouses. While peer groups had always socialized to some extent, the growing recognition of adolescence as a life stage qualitatively different from childhood or adulthood supported the development of social activities associated largely with teenagers.[7] Schools provided the setting for girls and boys to spend most of their free time with their peers rather than their families.

Because schools provided both the time and the space for the construction and expression of girl culture, middle-class girls who stayed in school longer had an easier time approaching the American component of their identity. Immigrant girls, who were likely to work during adolescence and find education in community institutions, found that economic circumstances removed them from the opportunities offered by regular schools. Like schools, work did function as a focus of acculturation for Jewish girls. However, the heavily ethnic nature of the work environments in which most immigrant girls tended to find themselves made the process slower for them.[8]

For middle-class girls, social life connected with schools took many forms. Singing in glee clubs, attending school banquets and events, going to dances, working on school newspapers, and meeting school friends for theater outings and sleigh rides were only some of Jewish girls' leisure activities. While a few of these ventures were inaccessible for immigrant or working-class girls, some became an important part of their lives as well. Those girls who spent most of their days at work rather than in school created groups of their own among coworkers and still spent much of their time with peers rather than family.[9] It was harder for working girls to find the time to participate in a debate club or go to a museum, but they managed to spend significant amounts of time with their friends outside work. As popular culture and consumption became more central to adolescence, both class and gender lines blurred enough to allow the emergence of a broadly observed youth culture.

Adolescent Jewish girls who did attend high school could take advantage of the range of activities available there. Edna Ferber associated her time at Ryan High School in Appleton, Wisconsin, around 1900 with "four years of the most exhilarating and heartening fun."

It was, for us, a clubhouse, a forum, a social center, playground, a second house. We danced, flirted, played tennis there; learned to think and speak on our feet, learned a sense of honor and fair play, learned, in the best sense of the word, freedom of thought and conduct. . . . We sprawled on the grass and talked; we had dates in the cool shade of the side porch, we rehearsed school plays, practised for contests.[10]

Jewish girls all over the country participated in the construction of school and community culture through school activities. One student at Omaha's Central High

was the first Jewish girl, and I think the first girl, ever to have been editor-in-chief of the *Register*, the high school paper. There was some bias. Mother wasn't so sure that she even wanted to let me run. She didn't want me to be hurt. I assured her that if I didn't get elected I would not be hurt. I won. I was the first girl to become editor-in-chief of the *Register*.[11]

She did not allow her gender or her religious identity to stand in the way of her desire to play a role in her school culture.

Youth culture developed in both private and public schools. The closed nature of the private schools could lead to a strong attachment to school history, while the newness of the public schools during the late 1800s could lead to a strong sense of creating school traditions. The private school Marya Mannes attended in New York had always required the girls to take four years of Latin and perform a play in Latin during their senior year. As the title character in her class's much anticipated production of *Ulysses*, Marya ensured her own immortality at the school by nearly wounding the director when she shot an arrow toward the wings.[12] The scrapbook Rhona Kuder kept during her senior year reflected her passion for the spirit and activities of Western Female High School in Baltimore. With pages devoted to dances, class trips, classes, teachers, classmates, student officers, and school songs, Rhona described such seminal events as the junior-senior banquet and her class's meeting with President Taft at the White House in loving detail. As the banquet ended, she wrote, "the City College Orchestra played 'Home Sweet Home' and away we went, tired and happy but above all, blessing our dear old 'High' which brought us such a world of pleasure."[13]

High school provided Jewish girls with all kinds of educational and social experiences. Sarah Jackson, who was only able to graduate from Brooklyn's Manual Training High School due to the efforts of her older siblings, took full advantage of the activities she acknowledged as privileges. She joined the dramatics society and served as an editor on the school paper. She also formed part of a group that studied the economic problems of the period, a group that "had to overcome the opposition of the Chairman of the History Department, who thought we were wild-eyed radicals."[14] Bella Cohen, who came to America as a toddler, used the experience as editor of her high school magazine to launch a career in journalism.[15] At Western Female High School in Baltimore, Rhona Kuder learned about student government and parliamentary procedure as treasurer of her class, although she found the position so time-consuming that she had to resign from the orchestra.[16]

As Rhona discovered, school activities could be a wearying business for even the most energetic adolescent. As an eighteen-year-old living at home while attending the University of Maine, Ann Green kept a diary oriented primarily around her busy social life. During the first two exhausting weeks of 1922, Ann went to two dances, a Chanukah program, a concert, and a basketball game. She was invited out to dinner and to a party, went out to lunch with school friends, and turned down another dance invitation. Even after her social calendar was rudely interrupted by the resumption of classes the third week in January, her complaints about studying all day and the rigors of Spanish and English courses were frequently punctuated with excited comments about tryouts for the girls' mandolin club and dramatic society.[17] College was no less social for her than high school had been. She had learned valuable lessons about how to participate in youth culture.

Like Ann, some girls found the social aspects of school distracting. Some even found it threatening to the more important activities of making life decisions. Conflict between educational and social goals was a constant presence in Jennie Franklin's adolescence, reflecting the expectation that her school experiences would encompass both. She lamented, "I am anxious, crazy to learn but at the same time want to go out and have a good time."[18] Jennie's worries stemmed at least in part from her feeling that her academic accomplishments would not constitute real achievement unless she also succeeded in the social realm of youth culture. In Seattle, Bella Weretnikow experienced similar conflict and also perceived herself as socially awkward. After attending a school entertainment in 1896, she commented wistfully in her diary:

> Enjoyed it very much. But somehow I never feel happy among a crowd of people Whether it is envy at their accomplishments or seeming free-ness from care, I know not. Hope, courage, and happiness are to be found only in the society of good books.[19]

Like Jennie, Bella tried to keep her eye on her academic goals, but she, too, was deeply concerned about her apparent social failures. Girlhood was a time for social as well as academic accomplishment, and schools were supposed to provide the best environment for both.

One reward for the hustle and bustle of Jewish girls' academic and so-cial calendars was their integration into larger communities. In Worces-ter, Massachusetts, Minnie Goldstein discovered that her stellar school career as captain of the girls' debating team, staff member of the school magazine, secretary of the Pythagorean Club for math lovers, and presi-dent of the Botany Research Club connected her in tangible ways to the larger community. With the help of a prize from the Worcester College Club, she was able to continue her education at Boston University.[20] Rose Zetzer, who kept a penny savings book and organized Red Cross committees at Eastern High School in Baltimore during World War I, was similarly recognized as a valuable member of a broader civic com-munity. She received a War Work Campaign Certificate, lauding her as a "Victory Girl" who helped "provide comfort and cheer for an American fighter."[21]

School graduations gave Jewish girls further opportunities to display publicly their commitments to their peers and their communities. By join-ing other students from a variety of backgrounds in commencement cer-emonies that served as rites of passage, they consolidated their participa-tion in youth culture. At Henrietta Szold's graduation from Western Fe-male High School in 1877, for example, she delivered an address entitled "Our Public Schools" and received one of the coveted Peabody medals awarded by Western to the highest ranking students.[22] Her award and her choice of topic demonstrated her integration into her school community and the appreciation she felt for the inclusive educational system embod-ied in American high schools. Certain features of Henrietta's graduation remained standard at commencement ceremonies over the next several decades. A mixture of student orations, musical performances, and class

Rose Zetzer, age 14, 1918. This photograph shows Rose just before she entered Baltimore's Eastern Female High School. It is possible that she was wearing either her confirmation or eighth grade graduation dress. *Courtesy of the Jewish Museum of Maryland, JMM 1998.86.40.*

readings and songs characterized Class Day at the Kenwood-Loring School in 1918 as much as Western Female High School in 1877.

Emily Frankenstein's graduation from the small private school in Chicago was an important event not only in her own life but in her family's history as well. Wearing a pink organdy dress trimmed with roses and scallops, she joined her Kenwood-Loring classmates in the front of the school auditorium, their proud parents seated behind them. The graduation program reflected both school spirit and the heightened patriotism engendered by World War I, as the student body sang the school song and the whole audience joined in "The Star Spangled Banner,"

"Keep the Home Fires Burning," the "Marseilles," "My Country 'Tis of Thee," and "Stars and Stripes Forever." Though she was glad her family and some of her parents' friends came to recognize her accomplishment, Emily chose to spend the rest of her graduation evening at a school dance with her boyfriend Jerry, away from her family. Graduation was not only a mark of educational attainment for her but also a sign of her enlarged freedom to choose where to go and what to do. In acknowledgment of her newfound autonomy, her parents did not object to Emily's decision not to have a family party and even held their peace about Jerry, whom they did not think a suitable beau for their daughter. In the course of that one graduation day, Emily affirmed her position as an educated American young woman whose adolescence had gradually moved her away from her family and toward her peers. Dressed as an American girl, surrounded by Jewish friends from similar middle-class backgrounds, accompanied by a young Jewish man on leave from the United States army, Emily danced the night away in a contented fusion of cultures and sensibilities.[23]

Emily managed to integrate her American Jewish identity into her adolescent experiences, but not everyone coped as successfully as she did. During the late nineteenth and early twentieth centuries, adolescent Jewish girls had to add their religious and ethnic affiliation to the mix of peer identification and school culture. It was not always easy. Edna Ferber was an enthusiastic member of the debating society at her beloved high school, but she and her friend Esther were torn every week between their participation in the synagogue choir and the high school debating society.

> Friday night's service held an agony of suspense for Esther and me. . . . Would Dr. Gerechter have a sermon or would he not? A sermon meant being hideously late. . . . There was the final hymn to be sung. . . . Having galloped through the hymn we clapped the books shut, bowed our impatient heads for the benediction. . . . We turned and fled down the temple steps with a clatter of heels and sped toward the Ryan High School, temple of learning.[24]

Edna found it difficult to balance her commitments as a member of both her Jewish and school communities. For her the challenge was all the greater because her family was not ritually observant. Her parents had no objections to Edna spending Saturdays at the high school instead of observing the Sabbath more traditionally, but they did expect her to attend synagogue on Friday nights, which Edna found difficult to understand. As her experience made clear, Jewish identity remained visible in America despite the expansion of peer socialization.

The Feminine Graces

Because gender conventions played such an important role in structuring youth culture and integration, certain feminine accomplishments as well as school and social events facilitated Jewish girls' experiences with American girlhood. By pursuing some aspects of a generalized American girlhood at home, Jewish girls also involved their families in their goals. In some cases, their parents' desires shaped their girlhood. Acquiring particular skills, such as proficiency in music or dancing, helped Jewish girls become or at least appear more like other American girls. Knowing how to dance was a prerequisite for one of the most important social interactions young men and women could share. Knowing how to play the piano exhibited culture and facilitated social dancing. Playing the piano also demonstrated the kind of cultural achievement Jewish families often aspired to. Girls who could play the piano and dance elevated the entire family's social status.

Learning to play the piano was a pursuit common to middle-class American girls of all backgrounds, and Jewish girls were no exception. Viewing music lessons as a visible sign of refinement and, in the case of families originally from Germany, as a transatlantic expression of *Bildung*, Jewish families in America were deeply involved with what one historian has called the "female romance with the piano."[25] As Lottie Strogoff, who grew up in Vermont, explained her own early introduction to the piano:

At the age of ten years old or so, a little girl usually began taking piano lessons. Maybe some mothers started their little girls a year or two younger, but never any older. In any case, piano lessons she had to take, for they really were a must. It made no difference if the young lady in question were musical or not, whether she had any love for music or not, that didn't enter into it at all. If her parents had a piano or not made no difference either. She simply had to take piano lessons the same as she had to go to school.[26]

In fact, playing the piano and going to school served similar functions in middle-class Jewish households. Both activities displayed the financial comfort that allowed girls time for education and culture as well as providing experiences common to American girlhood in general.

Many Jewish girls took piano lessons for granted. They were as natural a part of their routine as homework. Rosa Feinberg in the 1860s, Jennie Franklin in the 1890s, and Emily Frankenstein in the 1910s all wrote regularly in their diaries about playing the piano.[27] Elise Stern and Helen Arnstein's mothers both insisted that their daughters conform to the expectations of the turn-of-the-century San Francisco Jewish community and learn to play.[28] The girls had little say in the matter. Helen Arnstein and her sister practiced "for hours and hours" but were not "especially talented or eager."[29]

Music became a ruling passion for a few Jewish girls who were both talented and eager. Hannah Greenebaum practiced three hours a day and left high school at fifteen to devote more time to her music. After Setty Swartz graduated third in her class from Hughes High School in Cincinnati in 1886, she went abroad to pursue a more serious study of music.[30] A few girls even parlayed their musical talents into careers. Gertrude Englander attended a conservatory after leaving school in Cincinnati and spent decades as a successful international pianist and music teacher.[31] For Gertrude, the routine lessons of middle-class girls were the catalyst for a very different sort of life than most of her peers.

Such success as Gertrude achieved was rare, but its possibility and the class status associated with girls' musical endeavors made piano playing a presence in the lives of immigrant Jewish girls as well. Whenever they could, working-class families were willing to make sacrifices to support the personal and family benefits that might accrue from their daughters' feminine accomplishments. Although Rose Cohn's Colorado music teacher "would rap my knuckles with a ruler from time to time when I made mistakes, which was often," Rose's mother was committed to the idea that playing the piano would help make her daughters American girls.[32]

Owning and playing a piano were so widely understood as external signs of success in acculturation that immigrant and working-class families also brought pianos into their homes as soon as they could afford to do so.[33] After feeling ashamed while paying a social call that she could neither play the piano nor sing, Bella Weretnikow convinced her mother that she should buy a piano in order to be more like other girls. Shortly thereafter, Bella gave up part of a precious day of studying for University of Washington entrance examinations to buy a piano at an auction, but she returned empty-handed.[34] Social and cultural expectations that sixteen-year-old Bella should learn to play the piano could not outweigh financial considerations, even in her reasonably successful immigrant household. Those immigrant girls who did play the piano were aware of their music lessons' positions as bridges to American girlhood. When Louise Berliawsky took piano lessons in Rockland, Maine, she was "very self-conscious and very aware of the difference in environments" between her own home and the home of her "fancy teacher."[35] Her weekly trip to the piano teacher's home was a journey in social and cultural space as well as physical distance. By joining hundreds of thousands of other American girls in learning to play the piano, she also helped set her family on the road to social integration.

Whether piano lessons served the cause of personal interest, gender expectations, or social mobility, they also came under fire as a waste of time. A pseudonymous letter to *Israelite* complained in 1875 that

> if one half the time was spent in mental improvement, that is wasted in trying to learn the piano (which so very many have not the least talent for), how fit a mate it would make a girl for many an intelligent man, who inwardly laughs at the badly played waltz or polka.[36]

Though expressions of distaste for the nature of girls' piano lessons had no appreciable effect on their popularity, cynical comments continued to appear.

A dialogue entitled "Bombshells into the Pianos," published in the Jewish children's religious periodical *Sabbath Visitor* in 1883, noted that as modern conditions made much of women's former household labor obsolete, "the women have no longer plenty to do in managing the income and turning it to the best advantage." When asked what they should do with their apparently copious free time, the fictional speaker offered no constructive suggestions but rejected the "useless pretension" of widespread music lessons, arguing that "our women especially suffer through this toying, which deceives them with a kind of busy idleness: strumming on the piano shouldn't count as work." He wished

> that a barricade could be made with a million pianos, and that it could be shot at with bombshells. Every girl of the educated classes loses half

her youth playing the piano. . . . I believe that among ten thousand women there is one who can execute a piece of music with intelligence and taste. But what kind of result is this for so many thousands of hours? And is that a proper expenditure of time that nine thousand nine hundred and ninety-nine should toil at a thing for which have neither taste nor vocation?

The speaker's cry for "Bombshells into pianos!" may have represented a growing concern with the content of girls' education but did little to dissuade families from their conviction that almost no matter what else she did, the well-brought up, demonstrably cultured American Jewish girl played the piano.[37]

Piano lessons led naturally to another favorite pastime of Jewish girls, dancing. While not quite as ubiquitous as piano lessons, dancing school was also a common feature of girls' adolescence. From Maud Nathan in 1870s New York to Florence Klein in 1890s Chicago to Hannah London in 1910s Boston, Jewish girls learned dancing and the social graces that supposedly accompanied it.[38] Dorothy Kuhn wrote proudly to her father that her musical skill had progressed to the point that she played the piano when her friends visited so that they could dance. This application of her piano lessons was much more important to her than the cultivation of music appreciation per se. Sophie Ruskay's mother convinced her to take piano lessons by promising her that dancing school would be next. Eventually, Sophie spent all her Saturday afternoons with her cousins at Brook's Dancing School in New York. They learned dances ranging from the waltz to the Highland Fling and, equally importantly, also practiced partnering the boys they would later accompany to dances and soirees.[39] Thirteen-year-old Sophia Heller had similar experiences in Milwaukee, where during the winter of 1861 she went to Saturday evening dancing classes with her mother and brother at Mr. Vesie's dancing school. These classes were an intergenerational activity for the Hellers, Bohemian immigrants who considered dancing a skill necessary for their family projects of acculturation and upward mobility.[40]

Dancing school was not only for middle-class Jewish girls. Hilda Satt, who arrived in Chicago in 1892 at the age of ten, learned to dance at Hull House. Jewish communal institutions often offered dancing instruction as a supervised form of recreation for working-class and immigrant youth.[41] The Educational Alliance in New York sponsored large dances to make sure that dancing took place among well-matched adolescents in a suit-

able environment rather than more heterogeneous, less-supervised neighborhood dance halls.

Even in single-sex high schools, dances were important extracurricular
activities. High school senior Rose Zetzer saved dance cards signed by
other girls who served as each other's partners in the absence of boys.[42]
Rhona Kuder devoted a whole page of her 1912 scrapbook to describing
the Halloween dance held in the gymnasium of her public high school for
girls.[43] As enjoyable schoolgirl diversions in their own right and as preparation for more socially significant encounters as marriageable young
women, dances combined feminine graces with social exposure to become common features of Jewish girls' participation in youth culture.

Dancing was also an important point of departure into social interaction with peers, especially Jewish male peers. While visiting a Catskills resort on what amounted to a husband-hunting trip in 1877, Amelia and
Fannie Allen attended dances especially to look for eligible Jewish bach-
elors.[44] They used their well-rehearsed feminine graces to demonstrate
their desirability as American wives while also restricting themselves to a
pool of Jewish men. As far as Fannie and Amelia were concerned, any potential husband must be able to match their own combination of American girlhood experiences and strong Jewish identity. Ann Green, whose
crowded college social life in early 1920s Maine included frequent
dances, made a point of mentioning in her diary that she and her escort
were often the only Jewish couple in attendance.[45] Even when finding a
marriage partner was not the immediate motivation for attending a
dance, Jewish girls like Ann still tended to prefer Jewish escorts.

Just as dancing skills were necessary but not sufficient attributes for
American Jewish girls' potential marriage partners, in some cases neither
was Jewish identity alone. The Allen sisters' trip to the Catskills was unsuccessful in part because neither sister wanted to leave an urban environment. Amelia wrote after a country dance, "I felt as if my hands
wanted a good washing after having danced with those great country
chaps. These are citified airs I suppose, but I firmly believe I would never
do for a farmer's wife."[46] She had purposely attended a dance for young
Jewish men and women, but she perceived herself as too sophisticated for
the Jewish men she met there. Two generations later, dancing continued
to be a popular pastime for Jewish youth. Emily Frankenstein's clandestine outings with the beau her parents disapproved of often ended in
dancing at one of Chicago's Jewish clubs. In order to avoid discovery,
Emily and Jerry frequented the dances held at eastern European Jewish

clubs, which they could be sure her parents would not dream of enter-ing.[47] In their case the objection was one of class and ethnicity. Emily's parents took it for granted that their American Jewish daughter should learn how to dance and play the piano, but they had no intention of see-ing these feminine charms go to waste on someone who was not of their middle-class status and had not even been born in the United States. It is telling that in Chicago, as in other cities, the "downtown" Jewish clubs held dances just as the "uptown" Jewish clubs did. Dancing played a significant role in youth culture and social integration into American life for all parts of the Jewish community. Like other elements of American Jewish girl culture, girls found that it both shaped and was shaped by the intersection of their Jewish identity with their American identity.

Physical Culture and the American Jewish Girl

Another aspect of youth culture that shaped adolescent Jewish girls' ex-periences was physical culture. In addition to the traditional feminine ac-complishments of music and dance, turn-of-the-century girls were also expected to maintain a certain level of healthiness. Educators began to pay attention to the absence of physical education in the schools, while child savers and labor reformers began to focus part of their rhetoric on the poor health of working girls. Soundness of body as well as mind be-came an important feature of American girlhood during the last decades of the nineteenth century, in contrast to the frailty and nervousness asso-ciated with older models of womanhood.[48]

The growing presence of physical culture in formal school curricula at the turn of the century reflected this development. Regular classes in cal-isthenics, physiology, and hygiene gradually made their way into girls' schools. Baltimore's public schools added physical culture to elementary school curricula in 1898, although Western Female High School, which had a large Jewish population, did not institute formal, twice weekly physical education classes until 1912. Due in part to the years of ground-work laid by women advocates of physical culture, the activities caught on quickly. A basketball team formed immediately, and at a Western High School Physical Training Exhibition in 1912, junior and seniors displayed their athletic prowess with demonstrations of dumbbells, folk dances, rings, ropes, bars, marching, and free exercises. By 1920, public schools typically had entire departments of physical training. Rose Zetzer's Class

Day exercises at Baltimore's Eastern Female High School included a program by the Gymnasium department as well as the Chemistry, Latin, and English departments.[49]

There were several rationales for increasing attention to girls' physical well-being. In a letter published in the alumnae column of Baltimore's Eastern High School newspaper, an 1894 graduate reminded the current girls of Eastern High that physical education was aimed at the "most glorious and soul-satisfying career of all," motherhood.

> Through your gym work you are building up sound bodies and healthy minds, and, I hope, are learning to be "good sports." What child does not appreciate a mother who is a good sport—one who will not lie to him or cheat him, who will keep her promises to him, who will play the game "fair"?[50]

Though the end of the nineteenth century and beginning of the twentieth century saw great changes in the conception of well-trained bodies and minds, for many, the new American girl, mobile and healthy as never before, was still largely in training as a wife and mother.

Preparation for motherhood remained a strong justification for girls' physical culture, but by the 1910s, exercise was increasingly associated with weight control and body image as well. Writing home to her parents about summer camp in 1917, Marie Lowenstein described her days full of physical activity and assured her mother that despite the unflattering picture she was sending home, "I am *not* any stouter. That's the costume."[51] The fact that Marie felt it necessary to assure her mother that she had not gained weight reflected a growing female concern with body image during the early twentieth century. American culture increasingly considered physical condition as the exterior representation of spiritual well-being, and girls, in particular, were deluged with pressures to maintain their appearance of fitness as a reflection of moral fortitude.[52]

Heralding good health and bodily strength as emblematic of modern women, Jewish writers and communal leaders joined the movement to position physical culture as a desideratum of girls' adolescent experiences. Periodicals like *American Jewess* encouraged Jewish girls to adopt this model of American girlhood. *American Jewess* editorialized about the "New Woman" and recommended nutrition, exercise, and fashion strategies to mothers and daughters concerned about their relationships to modernizing girl culture. Articles about successful Jewish girls profiled young women who were educated, well-dressed, spiritually inclined, and healthy examples of American Jewish girlhood.[53]

Discussions of the education and training of Jewish girls resounded with calls for physical culture, which included "a knowledge of the laws of health" as well as proper exercise and nutrition.[54] "J," an anonymous contributor to *Jewish Messenger* in 1890, insisted that Jewish girls required physical training whether they were rich or poor, as wealthier girls' health suffered from the "enervating effect of ease, luxury," while poorer girls found that "prolonged, strained, hard work" adversely affected their health. "In both cases," she continued

> the results would be better, the end more easily and successfully achieved, the amount of force and ability for something still better increased with each additional physical beauty, if but a part of this time, from early childhood on, be given to physical training of some kind, a physical training that includes free, unrestrained exercise of mind and body together.[55]

The connection "J" made between mind and body appeared frequently in rationales for physical training. Another correspondent cautioned that "while Jewish girls continue to have hour-glass figures, they will never possess more than pint-cup brains."[56] These writers were convinced that strength of mind and body were interrelated. For many writers and their readers, physical culture entailed mental education as well as bodily training and dress reform and was a harbinger of the new womanhood they wished Jewish girls to emulate.

Many Jewish girls needed little encouragement to convince them to exercise their bodies. They exulted in their physical prowess. Gertrude Mandelbaum relished her position as center on the girls' basketball team at Marshall High School in Chicago and liked nothing better than to dash around the court clad in the "white Middy Blouses with black ties, Black cotton Bloomers which reached to our knees, black cotton stocking and white Gym shoes with laces" that made up her uniform. Jennie Franklin contentedly remarked to her diary that she was considered an exceptionally strong swimmer.[57]

All kinds of physical activity attracted girls. During the 1860s, Emily and Rosa Fechheimer enjoyed using gymnastic equipment, especially vaults, rings, and poles. In 1878, Amelia Allen wrote excitedly in her diary, "Last week made my debut as a 'skatist' at the Rink. Enjoyed the

Young Women's Hebrew Association calisthenics class, ca. 1915. By hanging American flags in the gym, the New York institution lost no opportunity to remind the girls of their opportunities and obligations as American girls. *Courtesy of the 92nd Street YM-YWHA Archives.*

fun thoroughly. Think that by practice I may become learned in the art."[58] A generation later Bella Weretnikow caused a mild scandal by donning split skirts and riding a bicycle to and from the University of Washington during the late 1890s. During the early 1920s, Dorothy Peck grew closer to her father as a result of the ice skating and horseback riding lessons he gave her.[59]

When family and school could not support Jewish girls' physical activity, institutions stepped in. Institutions ranging from settlement houses to clubs inscribed some form of physical culture into their programs for girls in an effort to produce healthy, active American Jewish girls.[60] Major community institutions like the Educational Alliance in New York and the Chicago Hebrew Institute offered gymnasium facilities and calisthenics to girls on a regular basis, though less frequently than to boys. From their early days, the Hebrew Technical School for Girls and Clara de Hirsch Home for Working Girls encouraged physical training and open air exercise. Believing that "the physical standard of the Russian Hebrews is far below that of any other large class of immigrants," the girls' vocational schools stressed immigrants' fitness as a means of bringing them up to American standards of health as well as increasing their wage-earning potential. The Settlement House in Milwaukee sponsored an indoor pool with long daily hours to accommodate working women and men.[61]

Physical activity thus brought Jewish girls personal pleasure as well as helping them adhere to cultural standards for American girlhood. If they were to be as active as they needed to be to go to school, socialize, help out around the house, work, and participate in Jewish community life, they would need to be in good health. When they actually or conveniently lapsed into illness, as Amelia and Fannie Allen in the 1870s were wont to do, they might have been excused from unpleasant tasks but also missed out on enjoyable opportunities.[62] By 1900, hardly any adolescent girls used poor health as an excuse. Ann Green took for granted her ability to observe the fast of Yom Kippur in 1922 because she knew that she was in such good shape.[63] For American Jewish girls, physical culture was both an end in itself and a means to the goal of joining the ranks of modern American women renowned for their good health and stout constitution.

Reading and the Construction of Culture

Modern American girls gravitated toward intellectual exercise as much as physical activity. Cultural standards for American girlhood could also be expressed in more private ways than social dancing or athleticism, though all were potentially subversive of traditional gender conventions. Reading was a critical, if usually less public, step along Jewish girls' path toward becoming American. Sharing books and literature with their non-Jewish counterparts helped them develop a literary idiom that affected and was affected by girls' common pleasures and hopes for the future. From learning to read in English, a first step for immigrant girls, to learning about literature, an important step for girls who explicitly set out to acquire cultivated taste, reading was a critical component of American girl culture. Reading became a daily part of girls' lives across virtually every distinction of class, family structure, or background. Though many adolescents in America were omnivorous readers who devoured books in no particular order, they still developed definite preferences and opinions about the material they read. With family encouragement and collective participation, reading became a means of Americanization that at least temporarily closed an all-too-common generation gap, especially in immigrant families. Reading served as a highly enjoyable educational process as well, both for girls who wanted to learn more than they did at school and for girls who were forced to rely upon books rather than formal schooling for their own education.

Reading also served as a gateway into communities. Girls were already used to the idea that the people around them identified themselves with larger groups by choosing to read about them or read the same material as they did. The turn-of-the-century American Jewish press, for instance, offered passports into various segments of the Jewish community in America. Subscribing to a periodical published in German for liberal Jews made one kind of statement about identity, subscribing to a Yiddish newspaper for socialist Jews another, and subscribing to an English weekly for immigrants intent on rapid acculturation still another. Making decisions about the kinds of things they read placed Jewish girls in the position of choosing their own communities, of American readers, of American girls, of Jewish adolescents, of supporters of Western culture.

No matter what else they did, Jewish girls spent time reading almost daily. In 1860s New York, nineteen-year-old Bertha Wehle noted in her diary that she was slowly making progress through Victor Hugo's *Les Miserables,* one of the several tasks she had assigned herself in her quest to become a better-educated teacher.[64] Florentine Scholle spent her adolescence in San Francisco and New York reading works by William Makepeace Thackeray, Charles Dickens, Sir Walter Scott, and James Fenimore Cooper. For a literature class she took after graduating from high school in 1881, she familiarized herself with John Milton and William Shakespeare and even peeked at the *Decameron* on the sly.[65] The books Florentine read in the 1880s were standard fare for girls at the turn of the century. Helen Arnstein referred to George Eliot, Dickens, and Thackeray as "all the things that were read at the time."[66] Books for a younger audience such as *Black Beauty, A Little Princess, The Little Lame Prince,* and Hans Christian Andersen's fairy tales were also popular for decades.[67]

The popularity of certain books was reinforced by the place of honor accorded them by libraries and librarians. Once past the fairy tale stage, Sophie Ruskay relied on a friendly New York librarian to lead her to Louisa May Alcott and began to look down upon friends who still read children's books. Later the librarian also gave Sophie books by Dickens and Cooper, "happily unaware of the generous number of pages that I hurriedly skimmed—pages of description, long, arid stretches that interrupted the more exciting and romantic narrative."[68] The library was an especially important source of books for girls who lived in small towns or poor families. Rose Cohn loved to go to her school library in Colorado, where she "gobbled up every book on those shelves—Elsie Dinsmore, the Rollo Boys, Kipling, Dickens, Thackeray—anything printed was for me."[69] On Saturdays in turn-of-the-century Omaha, whole Jewish families spent the afternoon in the public library.[70] Theirs was a ritual of education and acculturation rather than religion.

Jewish girls who kept diaries sometimes tracked their reading habits and pleasures, either as they finished books or in one long list at the end of the diary. Amelia Allen preferred the latter format, recording thirty-nine books and authors in the back of her 1877 diary. She may well have read more than thirty-nine books during the course of the year, as the scope of the books she listed suggests that she had wide-ranging literary interests. In 1877, Amelia read everything from Alcott's *Rose in Bloom* to *Illustrated Library of Travel—Central Asia* to Jane Austen's *Pride and Prejudice* to William Dean Howells's *Counterfeit Presentment*. She read poetry and essays as well as fiction.[71] Jennie Franklin had similarly eclectic taste, although she either did not condescend to read "lightweight" authors such as Alcott or chose not to write them down in the list at the end of her 1890 diary. Unlike Amelia, Jennie almost exclusively recorded big books like Eliot's *Felix Holt* or Helen Hunt Jackson's *Ramona,* with the occasional Shakespearean play for balance.[72] The practice of listing books in diaries remained common for a long time, although by 1923 Ann Green recorded only fourteen books, a number insignificant beside the seventy-eight movies she saw that year.[73]

The centrality of books and reading to girls is most clearly evident for those who dedicated separate journals as reading logs. After receiving a blank journal stamped "Books I Have Read" for her fifteenth birthday in 1901, Helen Jacobus kept a detailed record of her reading for almost three years. The entries each occupied two pages. The left-hand page included the title, author, publisher, date completed, and literary category; the right-hand page included comments and quotations. Between January 1 and December 20, 1901, Helen wrote entries for at least fifty books and probably read more. The dates she recorded indicate that at times she was apparently taking less than three days to read long novels like *David Copperfield.* Like Amelia Allen, Helen was not embarrassed by her enjoyment of so-called children's literature and equitably accorded Alice Caldwell Regan Rice's *Mrs. Wiggs and the Cabbage Patch* the same amount of space as any other book.[74]

Helen's love of books did not mean she was an uncritical reader. After finishing *Elizabeth and the German Garden* by Mary Elizabeth Beauchamp Russell, she remarked, "I sympathize with Elizabeth with her aesthetic tastes, but I certainly cannot agree with her in thinking that duty to her husband and children is second only to her books and flowers." She liked novels with strong female characters and wrote in despair of Dickens, "If only he wouldn't make his women either fools or dolls!" She was even more disgusted with *The Rubaiyat of Omar Khayyam,* which she dismissed by commenting, "His philosophy is simply repulsive. His beliefs, or rather his unbelief, takes away much of the pleasure found in the real greatness of the poem." Helen also saw her own adolescent trials reflected in the travails of literary characters, writing in 1901, "Never have I felt such affinity for any character in fiction as I have with Maggie Tulliver. The characters in this book are not mere puppets, but one feels, loves, and grieves with them as living men and women. *Mill on the Floss* ranks among the first of the books I love."[75]

Helen was not alone in stating her opinion about her reading. Plowing her way through Shakespeare's collected works in 1896, Bella Weretnikow found *Pericles* decidedly inferior to *Hamlet* and *The Mer-chant of Venice,* although she maintained that "the bible and Shakespeare are my favorite books."[76] As a child and adolescent in the Midwest, Edna Ferber exulted in "undirected, haphazard" reading of everything from *Punch* magazine to Mary Mapes Dodge's children's tale *Hans Brinker and the Silver Skates* but was proud to state "that I loathed the Elsie Dinsmore books and found the lachrymose Elsie a bloody bore."[77] Presaging her developing literary taste, sixteen-year-old Marie Syrkin read Milton's *Prometheus Bound* and informed her diary in 1915 that "there is something soul satisfying in the sonorous flow of language of the ancients that I find entirely lacking in modern literature."[78] These girls not only enjoyed reading for its own sake but also took command of the books they read. They used reading as an incubator for ideas and opinions of their own.

They also read as a way to stay close to their families. Most Jewish parents encouraged reading, both for its educational value and as a marker of the leisure time afforded the privileged. With limited juvenile literature available in the 1870s and 1880s, Sara Liebenstein and her sister proceeded directly from *St. Nicholas Magazine* to weighty tomes by Edward Bulwer-Lytton. Their parents encouraged them to read good books, and their mother was particularly eager that they should absorb as much knowledge as possible by reading.[79] For Frieda and Belle Fligelman in Montana during the 1890s, reading was an important indoor activity for a frequently snowbound family. Frieda preferred "very good classic things" but also read Alcott and the Elsie Dinsmore books along with her sister. The two girls both cried over the Elsie Dinsmore books, prompting their mother to hide them whenever they brought them home from the library. The Fligelman family's bookshelves were filled with books of history, political philosophy, geography, and literature. Belle and Frieda's parents turned reading into a group project, a way of spending time together and enhancing their family's closeness. Belle loved their frequent family reading sessions.

> When we were on Dearborn Avenue we had kerosene lamps at night. Mother would mend stockings on one side of the lamp, in their bedroom, and my father would sit on a chair on the other side, with Frieda and me, and read aloud to us. [He read] aloud *Alice in Wonderland,* singing "Soup of the Day, Beautiful Soup," giving it all he had. *Les Misérables,* with tears running down his lean cheeks while he read where the bishop told Jean Valjean and the police officer that the silver candlesticks were not stolen from him. No, they were a gift from him to Jean Valjean. *Black Beauty, King Lear* and that terrible Regan. All books he felt we ought to read.[80]

For the Fligelman family as for others, good literature and other forms of reading were visible signs of and enablers of Americanization. While growing up in an immigrant Jewish agricultural colony in New Jersey, Bluma Bayuk shared her intense "love affair with the written word" with her mother, bringing home the "wondrous tales of *Snow White, Cinderella,* or *Black Beauty.*" Bluma believed the "headiest excitement of learning was our introduction into the world of books. What a smorgasbord of literary feasts awaited the accomplished reader!" In a generational role reversal, she encouraged her father to teach her mother to read and write to fulfill her mother's desire to learn American ways.[81] Sometimes specific books captured the American ideal for large groups of girls. Louisa May Alcott's books, for instance, provided immigrant Jewish girls with a model for becoming American and adopting middle-class family life. In different times and places, Mary Antin, Rose Gollup, and Elizabeth Stern were all inspired by *Little Women* to try to be American girls.[82] When immigrant families did not conform to the American standards set out in Alcott or other domestic fiction, the gap between ideal and reality caused some immigrant girls great anguish. By living vicariously thorough fictional figures, Bella Cohen could dismiss her Lower East Side environment as a temporary trial that would surely lead to the kind of triumph that always awaited her literary heroines.[83]

Equally important for the ability of reading to aid Americanization was its power as a more broadly construed source of education. Bella Weretnikow tried to supplement her schoolwork with independent reading but had so many assignments that she could not "afford to read so much outside text books," even though she like "reading outside much better." Despite time constraints, she still bought three volumes of George Eliot just because she thought they would be good additions to her library. Five days later she purchased a few more books at a secondhand store, including a history of the Jews.[84] A generation later, Marie Syrkin also read outside school as a way to educate herself. When she finished *The Kreutzer Sonata* in 1915, she decided to next "study Marx, to attain at least a fair portion of the world's knowledge."[85] Depending on her schooling would not result in the kind of learning she wanted. By making choices about what to read and setting goals for their reading, these girls took control of their own education.

Reading was also a kind of continuous education for girls who had already completed their formal schooling. Louise Waterman, who learned little besides a smattering of languages and decorative arts at an academy in New York, turned to reading after her mother died in 1890, as a way to honor her mother's reverence for learning.[86] Amused by seventeen-year-old Gertrude Edelstein's ignorance despite her high school education, her boyfriend Lew Berg accused her of not using her mind and brought her books to read. During the late 1910s, they read H. G. Wells, Kipling, and Voltaire together and even dabbled in Beatrice and Sidney Webb's writings.[87] When Minnie Publicker graduated from her Philadelphia high school in 1917, she could not turn to her immigrant family or a sympathetic beau for the kind of culture she desired, so she turned to reading instead.

> I was very busy reading my books. I got my little sophistication in those days by reading what I did. I read almost all of Tolstoy and Balzac. I was a very ardent reader and I literally lived at that library in the Parkway. . . . all those authors that I read gave me something—they taught me something that Mother and Dad could never have.[88]

The books and authors so beloved by American Jewish girls brought them benefits beyond the pleasure of reading.

Significant as reading was for girls who attended or had finished high school, it was all the more vital for girls whose family and financial circumstances made extended education an impossibility. In an effort to increase her literacy and improve her mind as well as share time with her mother, Rose Schneiderman read Bible stories in Yiddish to her mother, who could only read the Hebrew prayer book. She also read more current books and news aloud, including a Yiddish serialization of Emile Zola's *J'accuse*. Lacking any guidance, Rose saved her pennies to buy English dime novels but read hardly any of the classics.[89] Rose Gollup asked a librarian at the Educational Alliance in New York for help and proceeded along the common path from *Little Women* to Shakespeare. She explicitly read to learn and find out about new ideas and was proud to read Cherneshefsky's *What Is to Be Done? or The Vital Question* in English translation.[90] Like Rose, Lucy Fox was first exposed to radical ideology through reading. After arriving in the United States at age nine, she immediately went to work in a cigar factory in Chicago, eventually taking English and citizenship classes at Hull House at night. Her radical friends at work encouraged her to read Edward Bellamy's *Looking Backward,* Grant Allen's *The Woman Who Did,* and William Morris's *News From Nowhere.* She studied these texts "as my grandfathers Reb Chaim and Avrom Boruch had studied the Bible," and she became a committed anarchist by the time she turned fifteen in 1899.[91] Lucy, like other adolescent readers, internalized what she read. The cumulative effect of reading the same books as their non-Jewish counterparts was the construction of a shared culture and idiom. Through a kind of literary osmosis, reading served as a basis for American girlhood that was as accessible to Jewish girls as to any other readers.

Unlike other aspects of American girl culture such as school activities and social dances, reading did not appear to be much affected by Jewishness. If Jewish girls could enjoy the sanctimonious Christian sentiment preached by the Elsie Dinsmore books or the radicalism of *What Is to Be Done?* then their religious identity was clearly not impeding their "smorgasbord of literary feasts." In fact, the opposite may have been true, as their Jewishness expanded rather than limited their reading. It seems likely that Rose Gollup and Lucy Fox were first inspired to read anarchist literature by their mostly Jewish coworkers. More to the point, Jewish girls read books on Jewish subjects that their non-Jewish contemporaries were probably not encountering. Florentine Scholle and Sophie Ruskay both considered nineteenth-century author Grace Aguilar's Jewish-themed writings among their favorite works of literature. Sophie read and reread Aguilar's novel *The Vale of Cedars,* crying every time over the persecution of the Jews depicted in the book.[92] Despite her affection for *The Mill on the Floss* and Maggie Tulliver, Helen Jacobus was less satisfied with George Eliot's *Daniel Deronda,* which she felt "gave an untrue picture of Jewish life."[93] Adolescent Jewish girls' reading practices reflected the ways in which they synthesized American and Jewish culture. They read the same things as their American peers but also read things tied to their religious and ethnic identities.

Peer Socialization in Societies and Clubs

Adolescent Jewish girls parlayed their reading interests into participation in activities of other kinds, joining literary societies, forming reading clubs, and publishing anthologies or newspapers. Like other young women, they consciously set out to enhance the cultural levels of their communities—often, in their case, the American cultural levels of their Jewish communities. It was not that Jewish girls never joined literary societies or clubs outside their Jewish communities. Eighteen-year-old Hannah Greenebaum was only too pleased to become the first Jewish member of the prestigious Chicago Women's Club in 1876.[94] However, Hannah was acceptable to the Chicago Women's Club not only on her own merits but also because her family was financially well-off and widely perceived to be thoroughly American and integrated into the Chicago elite. Genteel and often unacknowledged exclusion combined with attachment to Jewish community to steer most Jewish girls into the direction of Jewish clubs and societies even when, as in Hannah's case, they did also belong to non-Jewish social organizations. During World War I, Emily Frankenstein still joined the club middle-class Jewish girls in Chicago were expected to join, despite facing far fewer social barriers than Hannah Greenebaum had two generations earlier.[95] Throughout the period between the 1860s and 1910s, a great deal of Jewish girls' peer socialization took place in a Jewish environment.

Girls' membership in Jewish groups gave them one set of tools to fashion for themselves a life both American and Jewish. Within the Jewish community, there were social organizations to meet every girl's interests.

Hannah Greenbaum, age 20, 1878. This studio photograph, taken in Chicago on the occasion of Hannah's engagement to Henry Solomon, represents Hannah's transition from girlhood to womanhood as she prepared to marry. *Courtesy of the Chicago Jewish Archives.*

Sarah Cohen walked from Boston's West End to the Civic Service House in the North End for Zionist youth meetings during the 1910s.[96] Adele Jules belonged to Job's Daughters, a group in Baltimore for Jewish girls whose fathers were Masons.[97] Large or small, based on mutual interests or geographical proximity, clubs provided girls with social spaces whose boundaries they participated in defining. Not all were serious or intellectual endeavors. Girls joined less weighty clubs as well. Dorothy Kuhn, for instance, belonged to a group of Jewish girls that met on Sunday afternoons with the goal of accidentally on purpose running into a group of boys and spontaneously taking joy rides or having parties.[98]

As the daughter of native-born parents, Dorothy probably took her American identity for granted but still gravitated toward Jewish peers. Immigrant girls found even greater value in clubs where they could meet other girls from similar backgrounds with similar concerns and also share experiences they would never have at home. When in 1905 Celia Stanetsky joined a club for immigrant Jewish girls, she considered it more important than school for helping her become an American girl. In fact, she and the other fifteen girls who came together at the North End Union settlement house in Boston were almost all active in the club for much longer than they could afford to stay in school. Celia and her peers called themselves the Jerusalem Stars, explaining that "we thought of Jerusalem because we were all Jewish girls and 'stars' because we were all bright and wide awake." Over a period of years, the Jerusalem Stars learned to sew, listened to their club leader read them poetry, studied art, gave stereopticon lectures of their imaginary travels, and eventually raised enough money to go to Washington, D.C. as a group.

> We roamed about the White House, wide-eyed with excitement and joy from our wonderful experience. This was a great opportunity for us girls of immigrant parents, and many of us foreign-born. We sang "My Country 'Tis of Thee," "The Star Spangled Banner" and "America the Beautiful" with extreme fervor and devotion, proclaiming our love for our country with all our hearts and souls.[99]

Celia's beloved club provided its members with ample opportunity to explore and construct their identities as Americans and Jews. Sewing, reading, and ultimately traveling to the nation's capital were all effective ways for the Jerusalem Stars to learn and practice what was expected of them as American girls, and the Jewish environment of the club demonstrated in practice that there was no reason not to meet this expectation as Jewish girls.

The popularity of the Saturday Evening Girls (SEG) in Boston was another example of the synthesis of cultures clubs made possible. Originally begun in 1899 as a library-based story hour for immigrant Jewish and Italian working girls, the SEG rapidly expanded into a cluster of clubs for girls of all ages. By 1914, the literary programs included folk lore for fourth graders; myths and legends for fifth and sixth graders; poems with stories for seventh graders; Iliad, Odyssey, and King Arthur legends for eighth graders; English literature stories for high school freshmen and sophomores; travel stories for high school juniors; poetry appreciation for high school seniors; and current events and other programs for the working girls on either Friday or Saturday evenings.[100] A devoted group of volunteer librarians, teachers, and philanthropists dedicated hours each week to overseeing the cultural and literary development of immigrant girls, who could not rely on their own homes for such training. The SEG evolved into a Boston institution, eventually moving into its own building and spinning off the Paul Revere Pottery as a sort of in-house crafts training program for particularly artistic or dextrous girls.[101]

Americanization through literary activity was a major—and explicit—goal of the SEG. In an address given at the dedication of a new building in 1914 and reprinted in the *S.E.G News,* the speaker credited the SEG with giving the members "many varied and unusual experiences for girls of our stations." She continued:

> We have throughout the process of American assimilation, retained our originality and racial traditions, and helped to maintain and to prosper the integrity of our homes. We have as individuals had no easy lives. Most of us were started out with nothing, and it has been too difficult to acquire something; but the way has been pleasant, and to-day, we find ourselves grown from foreign little girls into American young women.[102]

Especially for immigrant girls who could not stay in school, the SEG was an important and enjoyable site of educational activity. By faithfully attending the talks and programs, immigrant girls could make up for at least part of their lost school education. They could also support each other's quest to become American by achieving a kind of cultural literacy that, once obtained, might also affect their families.

As with the SEG clubs, adolescent literary activities were a critical part of adaptation to American society and participation in girl culture. In 1909, a group of girls living at the Jewish Foster Home in Philadelphia started a Girls' Literary Society. Even if their families could not provide American Jewish homes, they wanted to be sure they could behave as their peers did. At a typical meeting, the program opened with a song sung by all the members and then continued with readings, recitations, and songs by individual girls, followed by a group session of riddles and jokes. Mindful of their home at a Jewish institution, they also incorporated religious themes into the programs. In December of 1909, for instance, Lena Berkowitz presented an essay on Chanukah as her contribution. A program combining self-conscious exploration of literature with a discussion of Jewish holiday origins and observances was a typical example of the synthesis created by Jewish girls' participation in youth culture.[103]

The Girls' Literary Society did not confine itself to strictly literary pursuits as it integrated Jewish interests and American girl culture. Having chosen blue and white as club colors, voted to limit the club to fifteen girls, and decided to preserve all *Jewish Exponent*'s references to their meetings, the Girls' Literary Society proceeded to stage debates on topics of current interest. The November 21, 1909, debate on woman suffrage was favorably received by the teachers of the Jewish Foster Home, who acted as judges. The minutes recorded that "the facts were strong on both sides but after much discussion the judges decided that the affirmative side produced the strongest arguments." The solemn tone of the minutes reflected the members' concern with running their club as a proper American club should be run. Each week the girls who belonged to the Girls' Literary Society pored over Cushing's *Manual* to learn the intricacies of parliamentary procedure.[104]

As first generation Jews in America, the members of the Girls' Literary Society recognized that learning to conduct their adolescent club would help prepare them for the adult world of clubs and societies that awaited them as they grew older. If women were supposed to transmit culture, then Jewish girls needed to train for their roles as transmitters. In 1899, a group of Jewish girls in Minneapolis formed the Clara de Hirsch Club, named after the world-renowned philanthropist who regularly contributed to Jewish girls' causes. Five years later, the girls' club commemorated its anniversary in the *Clara de Hirsche Journal,* the "official organ" of the club. With amusement, member Jessie B. Cohn recalled "the little maids of five years ago, with their frocks scarcely reaching their shoe tops and their hair hanging in glorious braids down their backs" who had founded the literary group. By 1904, the "queer little compositions, recitations, and original stories which somehow would take the form of a fairy tale" had given way to the literary production of "full fledged young ladies" entirely conversant not only with the intricacies of parliamentary law but also with the literary graces and social conventions expected of young women in America. The Jewish nature of the group in no way impeded its American style or substance.[105]

The immigrant and working-class Jewish girls of the SEG, Jewish Foster Home's Girls' Literary Society, the Clara de Hirsche Club, and others used literary societies as American-born and middle-class Jewish girls had long known they could be used, as organizations that would both preserve Jewish identity and promote American identity. In Chicago during the 1870s, it had seemed natural for Jennie Rosenfeld and other second-generation children of the original Jewish settlers to start a literary society.

> Well, we started our experiment in culture, by meeting in the vestry rooms of Sinai Temple. . . . The young men took part in the programs by spouting Shakespeare. We didn't know much about plays, but we knew Shakespeare wrote good ones, & unless you could quote some passage from his works, you were just an ignoramus. So we had the great bard, tons & tons of him, until some original soul suggested a club paper. That was a stroke of genius or originality, of daring, and we all fell for it.[106]

Jennie and her friend Bella Adler collaborated on the newspaper for the fledgling Zion Literary Society.[107] Though the paper lasted for only one issue, the literary society became a cultural institution for Chicago's middle-class Jewish youth. Born ten years after Jennie Rosenfeld, Sara Liebenstein also went to meetings of the Zion Literary Society.

> At each meeting recitations and essays, written by the members, were read for the edification and criticism of the audience. Humor was welcome, but the general tone was very serious, and the young people, who came from every quarter of the city, could match wits and acquaint themselves with the issues of the day.[108]

Sponsoring an annual Purim masquerade in addition to recitations, lectures, and theatricals, the Zion Literary Society retained a Jewish identity nobody thought incongruent with an interest in American literary culture.

By the time Jennie Franklin went to high school in Chicago during the late 1880s and early 1890s, there were several Jewish literary groups in the city. Jennie preferred the Hebrew Literary Society, which met every Friday night for debate and reviews. Members of the Hebrew Literary Society did not shy away from controversial topics, debating, for instance, the question of whether "the intellect and faculties of the darker races [are] essentially inferior to those of white."[109] After graduating from high school, Jennie continued to bring together her Jewish social world with her American cultural interests by joining the Philomathians. The Philomathians was a new Chicago Jewish literary society, composed of fifteen women above the age of eighteen and fifteen men above the age of twenty-one. Aiming "to promote mental development," the literary society met every other Sunday morning for good conversation. When the Philomathians disbanded in 1895, its unstated purpose had also been fulfilled, as several of the original Jewish Philomathians were married to each other.[110] Mutual interests in literary activities and American culture brought young Jewish men and women together in the most suitable of environments, a triumph for the acculturating American Jewish community of Chicago.

Courtship, Dating, and Sexuality

Coeducational literary societies served purposes beyond intellectual stimulation. They functioned as intermediate spaces between school social life and adult social life. One of their other major roles was that of informal matchmaker, bringing together young Jewish women and men. Regardless of background, most Jews in America probably would have agreed that the most important like-minded people adolescent Jewish girls could meet were the male counterparts who would eventually become their beaus and husbands. To facilitate these meetings, communities went out of their way to provide opportunities for Jewish girls and boys to interact. Although, in general, Jewish girls participated fully in contemporary youth culture, their experiences with courtship and dating revealed the limits of their social integration. Adolescent Jewish girls had non-Jewish classmates, coworkers, and friends, but they almost never dated them, let alone married them. The intermarriage rate was less than 2 percent in 1910 and did not even reach 3 percent until the 1940s.[111] Dating was one of the only ways in which Jewish girls were at all restricted by religious tradition. Few considered this restriction a negative one, given their typically solid sense of Jewish identity. There were other factors to be considered in courtship and marriage, such as class, education, or ethnic background, but Jewishness was sine qua non.

For the most part, girls in urban areas with large Jewish populations had little trouble developing a Jewish social life. In San Francisco during the 1890s, Amy Steinhart took for granted the entirely Jewish social circles she moved in.

> We had a pretty well separated social life. We went to parties given by Jewish people with very few exceptions. . . . We just took it for granted. And I think there was a little bit of feeling about people who broke away from Jewish friendships.[112]

Even Helen Arnstein's parents, who identified as Jewish but practiced no religion at all, joined the Jewish social club in San Francisco to make sure their daughters would meet—and eventually marry—young Jewish men.[113] Lucille Eichengreen's parents vacationed in Interlaken, a popular Jewish resort on Lake Michigan, specifically for the purpose of keeping their daughter as surrounded by appropriate Jewish boys during the summer as she was during the school year in Chicago.[114]

Despite individual, family, and communal support, not everybody succeeded in the social realm. Girls in less-populated areas had more trouble participating in a Jewish social life. In the rural South during the early 1860s, Eliza Moses lived far away from any remotely acceptable Jewish young men other than her cousin Albert. She and Albert, perhaps inevitably, fell in love, but they kept their romance a secret because they knew their parents would think they were too young. After Albert was killed in a Civil War battle, Eliza mourned not only for the loss of her love but also for the loss of her future. She could not imagine where she would find another Jewish man to love now that "God, who knows and does all things for the best, has seen fit to deprive me of my greatest treasure."[115] She never considered for a moment the possibility of looking for a non-Jewish mate, nor would her parents have allowed such a move. Very few parents wanted their daughters to refrain completely from courtship. Virtually none would have denied them the chance for marriage, but most prioritized Jewish tradition. Jewish girls were hardly alone in limiting the circle of potential suitors. They would not have been acceptable social escorts, let alone spouses, for a significant number of American Christians, either. By maintaining a primarily Jewish social life, girls could both demonstrate their commitment to Jewish identity and continuity and, incidentally, avoid the stigma of exclusion.

Eliza's geographic and social isolation led to her trouble in finding an acceptable beau and eventually husband, but there were other reasons Jewish girls found it difficult to preserve Jewish traditions while also acclimating to modernizing American standards of love and marriage. Fannie and Amelia Allen both spent miserable years trying to move from girlhood to adulthood by making a proper match. Fannie complained to her diary in 1875 that "Amelia and I are just the age to enjoy fun, but the young men now-a-days seem to prefer wealth and the foolishness of flirting." Serious-minded young women of very modest means, Amelia and Fannie were frustrated in their searches for appropriate Jewish husbands. "I am longing and longing for the one thing I suppose all girls wish for at my age," Amelia wrote.[116] Fannie prayed, "If I only could have somebody to love me all in all and a baby of my own to bring up, I am afraid one part of my life will be dead if I do not have that."[117]

Because Jewish tradition placed such importance on marriage and family, American Jewish communities made efforts to provide venues for young men and women to meet, mingle, and, hopefully, marry. Difficulties such as those Fannie and Amelia faced hurt their families and community as well as themselves and were to be prevented whenever possible. In addition to literary societies and clubs, communities sponsored picnics, lectures, dances, and other social events as a means of bringing Jewish couples together. Everyone involved understood that a fifteen-year-old girl might not marry the seventeen-year-old boy with whom she shared a dance or two at a Purim ball, but the event allowed her to meet and spend time with a Jewish peer group that would function as a de facto marriage pool for her within a few years. The presence of adults as well as peers at many of these functions underlined the Jewish social life that girls could expect to continue as adults.

Whole communities sometimes got involved in these activities, especially in smaller towns. During the 1880s in Mississippi, Clara Lowenburg and her friends looked forward to the annual Sunday school picnic on the first warm Sunday in May largely because of the social opportunities the outing afforded.

> All the Temple congregation went as well as the Sunday School children and the teachers. Every family prepared huge baskets of lunch. Wagons for the children started from our house at eight o'clock so as not to disturb the Episcopal church goers near the Temple on Sunday. The children were up and ready at dawn and such an exciting day as we all had, such romantic wanderings in the woods, and buggy drives unchaperoned, during the day or driving home in the evenings.[118]

It is likely that all the Jews in Natchez already knew each other, but an event such as this one, which offered something to those of all ages, provided both an example of the importance of Jewish community and family life and the opportunity for young men and women to move closer to achieving it.

Those buggy rides Clara recalled so fondly demonstrated the mix of tradition and modernization present in Jewish girls' social encounters. The all-Jewish cast of characters was traditional, but the unchaperoned scenes of "romantic wanderings" were not. Within the framework of Jewish community, the heterosocial practices of Jewish girls and boys changed dramatically during the latter part of the nineteenth century and early twentieth century. As for other American youth, nineteenth-century patterns of supervised courtship in a family setting gradually shifted to public group activities and mixed peer group interactions. By the twentieth century, courtship had become significantly more private in all senses of the word, and by the 1910s, dating no longer led directly to marriage as courtship had in the past. These changes were never linear in nature. Mixed peer group interactions like literary societies and clubs did not just disappear as dating became more common, and plenty of marriage-minded courtship continued well into the twentieth century. However, girls and their families had to work out how best to deal with the social options of modern youth relative to Jewish tradition. While few Jewish families in America adhered to the letter of a religious law that actually prohibited men and women from being alone with each other, they still had to balance respect for tradition with commitment to integration into the modern American world.

Parents often remained involved with their daughters' social lives in an effort to make sure they fulfilled both sets of expectations. They tried to continue exerting at least a limited amount of control as romantic relationships moved outside the safety of the family parlor. Helen Arnstein's father, who during the late 1890s allowed his two daughters to go out with young men only if they went together, encouraged them to receive callers in an upstairs sitting room primarily so that he could keep an eye on them.

> We had a big clock in the hall and once when a young man was visiting—both my sister and I had to receive together—the clock registered ten strokes and we all heard the ten strokes downstairs. Then all of a sudden—it seemed a very short time—it struck eleven. The young man said, "Oh, I'm overstaying my welcome. Time goes so quickly here," or some polite statement of that kind. Afterwards, we caught a glimpse of my father running upstairs in his short nightgown and he said, "He was staying too long!" He was very strict about our lives.[119]

American girls across the country, regardless of background, dealt with similar situations. Other than the critical emphasis on socializing with and eventually marrying Jewish men, Jewish girls' courtship experiences differed little from those of their same-class counterparts.[120]

Whatever their parents' feelings on the subject, Jewish girls often made their own decisions about how to adapt to the changing options available to them. Some simply enjoyed the opportunities that came their way. It felt natural to them to spend time with their peers rather than their parents. On a summer's day in 1862, Bertha Wehle accompanied her brother Theodor and several of his friends on a daylong tramp into the countryside close to New York City.

> Yesterday, Saturday, we made an excursion which was as near to my ideal of such a day as possible. . . . How can I describe this happy, happy day. I know not why I experienced such pleasure. We played gracehoops, ten pins, danced, blind man's buff, ran races, talked. Such lovely air! What a sweet delightful secluded spot! They were so very agreeable. So attentive to our slightest wants. What a difference there is in the society of some persons compared with others. I don't know—is it the country air that somehow elevates me above myself; that makes me feel better and happier when I am alone with nature, and nature's own great God?[121]

Despite not observing the Sabbath in the traditional sense, Bertha did find the outing spiritual as well as social. However, the delightfully "agreeable" and "attentive" young men were the highlight of the day for her.

During the 1860s, outings like the one Bertha and Theodor enjoyed so much typified the ways in which peer socialization was moving out of the parental parlor while still maintaining a fairly public nature. As the nineteenth century drew to a close, an element of privacy increasingly characterized potentially romantic interactions. A whole new advice literature appeared to help young people manage their own social lives.[122] Prescriptions about appropriate gender roles and courting practices shaped many Jewish adolescents' experiences. As advice manuals recommended, both Lizzie Black and Rosa Wachtel gave their suitors their photographs so that their beaus could carry them around in their pockets, ready to show their love at the slightest provocation. They also wrote love letters. After reading a letter from Lizzie, daughter of an established Jewish family in Milwaukee, her fiancé Simon Kander responded:

> My own dear darling Lizzie: It is not half past one o'clock PM and your dear letter I just received. I cannot describe the thrill of pleasure with which I read it over and over again. My dear love, how I would like to be with you this evening. It seems an awful long time since I saw you. Your picture is a solace. I have had it in my hand gazing upon it a good deal today. I just read your sweet letter again. You cannot imagine with what happiness I read over that letter. . . . With love to your folks, and love and many kisses to you, dear darling, I remain affectionately, your devoted lover, Simon.[123]

There is no reason to doubt Simon and Lizzie's emotions. However, both the content and the form of this 1881 letter clearly represent the shifting conventions of young love, American style. Every advice manual on the market suggested referring to photographs, kisses, and repeated readings of lovers' correspondence.[124]

In Cincinnati, Rosa Wachtel received love letters from her suitor that explicitly expressed regret for not measuring up to established standards for such missives. Martin Marks apologized in his June 10, 1890, letter, "I suppose you know by this time that I am not an expert love letter writer. I tried to get a book and copy one but there is none in town."[125] He was worried about living up to the appropriate standard without access to an example. Reading his letters at home in Cincinnati, Rosa probably did not mind any lack of conventional form, as Martin's declarations of love superseded any formulas. The day after his apologetic letter, composed on the roads he traveled as a salesman, he wrote her:

> I don't think there has been a moment since I left you that you have not been in my thoughts—isn't it remarkable that so small a person can fill so large a space. I always knew that Cupid cut some very queer pranks—but I never gave the God of Love credit for one tenth of the influence that I now know he wields. I've read love stories and thought they were overdrawn—I was mistaken, they fall short of the mark. . . . I am not satisfied with this letter there is not enough Love in it—if every word was Love it would not express the fullness of my Love for you—I never knew how far short words fail of expression— until I tried to write you a Love letter—I think if I had my arms around you for a few minutes and looked into your eyes I would become inspired and almost grow eloquent in telling of the great love I bear you.[126]

Martin may have been apologetic about his form but probably had no need to defend the heartfelt emotional content of his letters to his eager correspondent.

Martin's concern with the form as well as the content of his billet-doux demonstrated the penetration of American courtship ritual and culture into the Jewish community. As in this letter, the content of most of Rosa and Martin's correspondence was secular in nature. They took each other's Jewishness for granted and made only offhand references to religious practice or tradition. Although Jewish identity helped bring them together—Martin met Rosa when he was traveling through Cincinnati and looking for a family with which to spend the Sabbath—it was background rather than foreground for their relationship. Though intensely personal, his letters were self-conscious performances of the new romantic ideals forming around courtship and marriage at the turn of the century. Within the bounds of the Jewish tradition that helped shape their meeting and their world, Rosa and Martin interacted according to the evolving standards of modernizing relationships.

The encounter between tradition and modernity in courtship and dating also influenced Jewish girls' feelings about sexuality within their relationships. Changing standards of the acceptability of physical contact played a role, as did individual girls' personal inclinations. During the

1880s, for instance, after a large dance attended by young people from miles around, Clara Lowenburg and her friends returned home

> In a wagon filled with hay and drawn by mules. . . . The woods in the hills were very dense and beautiful and driving home in the daybreak was a beautiful experience, all tired and relaxed and cozy in the hay with our lovers all snuggled up against us and an excused arm supporting us, watching the day break and hearing the birds sing.

Other than dancing, only this kind of physical contact was acceptable in Clara's world. At eighteen, she "had never kissed any man except on birthdays and in some of the many kissing games we played at parties." For Clara's generation, at least, the fashionable custom "to hold a lady's arm or elbow crossing the street or going up and down steps . . . was really the only excuse a man had to touch his lady or give her an admiring squeeze or loving pat."[127] Even the party games Clara seemed to enjoy were not universally acceptable to Jewish girls and their families. In 1890, Jennie Franklin dismissively wrote of a group of her peers that her opinion of them was "not very high since they indulge in that shameful practice of kissing games."[128]

Although they reacted differently to it, both Clara and Jennie were encountering the shift in the parameters of acceptable physical contact. While mid- to late nineteenth-century public peer socializing did not allow a great deal of time or space for physical contact, late nineteenth- and early twentieth-century peer interaction away from parents provided much more leeway. By the early 1900s, adolescent girls and boys often spent time alone rather than in groups and had significantly more time and space to experiment if they chose to do so.

Like other turn-of-the-century American girls, Jewish girls found that the physicality of male-female relationships was a subject rarely discussed. Edna Ferber could not recall "one word of decent enlightenment that was ever said or revealed to me on the subject of sex."[129] Even during the late 1910s, Minnie Publicker still went to her wedding night without once having discussed sex with her mother. Whatever she knew she had learned through books, which she did not find the most practical or helpful of sources.[130]

In the absence of sustained help from their parents in these matters, adolescent girls often were left to work out their feelings on their own. Although she perhaps overdramatized her feelings in her 1915 diary, sixteen-year-old Marie Syrkin was very ambivalent about her budding physical desires. She was the daughter of parents who considered themselves enlightened and modern and would probably have talked openly with her about sexuality, but she still "often wonder[ed] whether my nature is an exceptionally ardent one, whether I have been deprived of the natural share of maidenly modesty which is every young girl's portion." She dreamed about kissing Weinstein, the current object of her affections, "a long, tortuous, passionate kiss, one mad embrace." After "sparing no pains to make myself as pleasing to the eye as modesty permit," she was gratified when Weinstein seemed to notice. She worried that her spring passion would compromise her schoolwork, writing in her diary, "I am horrified at my sensuality. I, the purely intellectual, I desire to experience the sweet sensation of a chaste embrace and soulfelt kiss. How disgraceful!" When Weinstein sat next to her in the school library, she was inspired to write "several Byronian couplets," but, she wryly observed, he ruined the mood when he blew his nose in "a decidedly unpoetic fashion."[131]

Marie admitted that her "poetic imagination" led her to claim emotions she did not actually feel. She was torn between her conception of herself as a girl of traditional "maidenly modesty" and as a dramatic figure who by rights should "become afflicted with a 'grande passion'" which would "serve to vary the monotony of daily existence and give fuel to my emotions." In reality, her relationship with Weinstein was conducted on a prosaic plane. She asked him to write in her autograph album at the end of the term but almost certainly never told him of his pride of place in her diary. Still, the language and emotion Marie used is telling of the shrouds of secrecy and even shame wrapped around adolescent girls' sexuality.[132]

Emily Frankenstein also found physicality and sensuality a disturbing—if initially enjoyable—part of her long romantic relationship with Jerry in Chicago. Unlike Marie's one-sided and half-invented infatuation with Weinstein, Emily and Jerry's relationship was mutual. Emily had many occasions to set and stretch boundaries. Social mores had changed significantly since Clara Lowenburg's day, and Emily spent many hours of temptation alone with Jerry in both public and private settings. During one of his furloughs in 1918, they nestled in the dark on the porch swing in front of the Frankensteins' house and discussed the implications of Jerry's interest in Christian Science for their future. They finally agreed that his interest was primarily spiritual rather than theological, as was

Emily's attachment to Judaism. They sat in their accustomed position, her head on his shoulder, his arm around her, but Emily gradually let him stretch out with his head in her lap, a request she had denied him in the past. She was a little surprised at herself and confided to her diary that night:

> I could hardly believe it was I sitting on the swing—with Jerry's head in my lap—and I looked down and saw his body clad in khaki—I sort of sighed—but said, "No one ever taught me what to do," as I ran my hand through his hair and patted his cheek.[133]

After this interlude she referred far more often in her diary to touching and kissing Jerry until their relationship became increasingly troubled. Though she did not admit it even in the privacy of her diary, Emily's first, possibly unconscious, reaction to their problems was to distance herself from Jerry physically. She made sure they went on more double dates and tried not to be alone with him as often as before, decreasing the possibility of physical encounters of any kind.

The less convinced Emily was that she and Jerry would actually marry as originally planned, the less willing she was to engage in any kind of sexual behavior with him. Her decisions reflected the ambivalent social mores of the day, which increasingly allowed even "nice girls" to touch their dates but only within limits. Engaged couples had considerably more leeway, and sociological studies such as those carried out by physician Clelia Duel Mosher demonstrated that they often took advantage of it.[134] However, as Emily withdrew from Jerry, she began to resent his insistence on intimacies with which she was no longer comfortable. What started as an effect of her growing doubts about her relationship eventually became a cause for not continuing that relationship into marriage.

Even though by Emily's day it was widely accepted that adolescent dating did not lead directly to marriage as courtship once had, marriage was still very much on Jewish girls' minds. If that had not been the case, they might have been more likely to spend time with non-Jewish young men, but since they virtually all were committed to the idea of marrying only Jewish men, they also dated only Jewish men. With endogamy as a given, there were, of course, other factors involved with Jewish girls' decisions about whom to date and ultimately to marry. Some of these factors were also connected to Jewish identity. For instance, Mary Upsico, a seventeen-year-old eastern European immigrant living in Des Moines in 1886, was so committed to living a Jewish family and community life that, caught "between faith and love," she broke her engagement with a Jewish man who refused to leave Deadwood, South Dakota, for a town with a Jewish community.[135] Marriage, for her, was also about family life, and she believed that both needed to be infused with the kind of Jewishness only a sizable community could provide.

Other factors were not necessarily connected to Jewish identity per se, although they did have to do with the conflict between tradition and modernity. Jewish girls wanted a say in what their marriages would be like, regardless of religious and social traditions. Once Rosa Wachtel and Martin Marks became engaged in 1890 and began to plan their wedding, they continued to communicate via letters about everything from living arrangements to the balance of power between spouses. Martin assured Rosa that he disagreed with her father's old-fashioned opinion that wives must obey their husbands.

I don't believe that way—I believe that a wife is every way the equal of her husband and for complete happiness there must be complete equality between husband and wife. I don't believe in a submissive wife— when you become my wife I want you to become my partner—not a silent partner but my equal partner with all that that implies.[136]

Despite his previous concern with preserving the formalities in his letters, he seemed far less interested in bowing to the gender conventions of marriage so prevalent in American society and Jewish tradition. Rosa and Martin imagined themselves as pioneers of the coming century, in which marriage would become a match of equals. While Rosa did tend their home and children after they married, Martin never failed to discuss all his business concerns with her in order to make the best decisions for their family. The emerging model of romantic marriage enveloped Martin and Rosa's lives together as an American Jewish couple committed to both tradition and modernization in their lives and loves.

There were other hurdles for Jewish couples. As for young people all over the country, a number of factors played a major role in courtship, dating, and marriage. Because marriage was presumed to be the social destiny for all men and women, it was important for young women and men to spend their time with peers who were their equals so that, when the time came, they could make appropriate matches. It is clear how this worked within the Jewish community in terms of segregated social life, but Jewish identity alone was not enough of a qualification. Class, ethnicity, and religious observance mattered, too.

Clara Lowenburg's experiences during the 1880s typified the process by which even the most resistant Jewish girls came to the realization that similarities in background were important qualities of social peers. Clara faced sustained parental opposition to her adolescent sweetheart, Hymie Jacobs, who came from one of the first eastern European immigrant families to settle in Mississippi. The Lowenburgs joined the rest of the community in collecting money for the immigrants who came to live among them but maintained a social distance whenever possible. Hymie and his brother Aaron ran a small country store, another mark against them in a milieu, where educated Jewish girls were expected to marry professionals or big businessmen. Clara cared about Hymie, who "thought I ought to promise to wait for him until he had made enough money to marry me." However, her father "didn't approve of him and thought it an impossible match for me, who had had every advantage of education and he had scarcely been educated at all."[137]

Clara and Hymie both understood the barriers to their relationship, although Hymie continued to press his suit. Not until Abe Moses began to court Clara seriously was she confronted with the necessity of making a choice. Abe, thirteen years her senior and a successful banker, was an attractive option, "neat and well-dressed, interested in the things I liked and did, and had great civic pride, and was liked by everybody." Abe was also a man with financial prospects. He made his intentions clear by inviting her to see his properties in the country in his buggy. That Abe had properties to show her was an important part of his attractiveness as a suitor to Clara's family. The Jacobs family was understandably bitter about their inability to compete. Hymie's brother said Clara was divided "'between capital and labor.'" Clara still loved to spend time with Hymie, but she "didn't like his family who were still Pollacks to my German born father" and decided "I would never be satisfied with Hymie for a life's companion." Clara eventually combined real affection with social acceptability to marry Abe, the man who could fulfill both personal and communal expectations.[138]

Clara was somewhat more candid than Emily Frankenstein was decades later about the prejudices she eventually realized she shared with her family. Emily's parents criticized Jerry's spotty education and lack of definite plans for the future, but their major objection was his eastern European origin. For an upper middle-class, thoroughly Americanized Jewish family of German descent, the possibility of a daughter's marriage to an immigrant, no matter how charismatic, was deeply disturbing. During Jerry's period of World War I military service, the Frankensteins confined themselves largely to silent, if obvious, disapproval. However, once Emily graduated from high school and Jerry was demobilized, the danger became more immediate. In March 1919, Emily was forbidden to see Jerry again. Her mother took her to Baltimore, Annapolis, and Washington, D.C., on an extended round of family visits characterized by social gatherings populated by more appropriate suitors.[139]

Upon returning to Chicago, Emily clandestinely continued to meet Jerry. They made plans for their shared future and Emily began to wear his ring on a chain around her neck, but the combination of her parents' unyielding disapproval and the persistence of Albert Chapsky, her would-be suitor and the son of a middle-class German Jewish family in Minneapolis, took its toll. After Albert unsuccessfully proposed to Emily over Thanksgiving, she began to grow disaffected with Jerry. She

> still continued to meet Jerry—but somehow I couldn't feel happy to the degree when I was with him. His grammar—oh—what a shame. I tried to correct his mistakes but it was hard work. He was very enthusiastic about his advertising work—but I couldn't get him to study advertising theoretically. Albert had given me a list of books he was reading on advertising—I got some of the books from the public library & read them diligently & took profuse, exact notes. I begged Jerry to read the same books but he wouldn't.

Jerry's poor grammar and lack of ambition, not to mention different class background, suffered in comparison to Albert's growing charms. Turning Albert down again in March 1920, Emily realized that she "was falling desperately in love with him" and began to withdraw from Jerry. In May 1920, she saw Jerry for the last time to return his ring, letters, and gifts. A few days later she accepted Albert's renewed proposal and decided to write a separate diary about her life with him.[140]

The Significance of Jewish Girls' Participation in American Girl Culture

The new life Emily envisioned for herself and Albert would not be so different from her old one. Far from rejecting tradition or her parents' lives, she chose to embrace them. She was not even willing to marry within her faith but outside her social circle, especially a religious doubter like Jerry, who posed a double threat to her class status and her Jewish values. Her Jewishness, shaped by her class, education, and family background, played a critical role in her life decisions, even though Emily did not think of herself as particularly religious. For Emily, as for other American Jewish girls, Jewish identity mattered. For Emily, as for other American Jewish girls and ultimately the American Jewish community in all its variety, it was not only possible but also positive to combine elements of Jewish tradition with elements of American modernization.

It is telling that everyone involved in both Clara and Emily's choices of husbands was Jewish. Participating in the modernization of courtship, dating, and sexuality was no threat to the American Jewish community, as long as young Jewish people remained true to tradition in their choice of partners. Though Clara and Emily's decisions about their futures were heavily influenced by the expectations of their families and the conventions of their communities, they still took their power to make these decisions for granted. Their freedom to choose beaus and husbands was largely a product of acculturation into an increasingly individualist American society, although Jewish law had always required the consent of both parties to a marriage. Most Jewish girls freely chose to seek out Jewish men with similar backgrounds and sensibilities to their own as the basis for establishing integrated American Jewish homes.

Jewish girls joined their non-Jewish counterparts in a process of peer socialization and by so doing placed themselves in relation to changing American standards of gender, youth, and coming of age. At the same time, the fundamental continuities of girl culture over a long period as well as the similarities between ideas about American and Jewish girlhood made it easy for them to adopt these standards without wreaking havoc on religiously informed cultural continuities within American Judaism. Their successful construction of an identity as American girls that would not require the abandonment of all Jewish religious culture reflected the struggle of their families and communities for integration into American society. Consistent with their dual roles as keepers of tradition and agents of acculturation, adolescent Jewish girls made a smooth transition into contemporary youth culture by transforming it into something that moved them toward acculturation without requiring the relinquishment of religious sensibilities. Their development into American girls helped set the standard for the much sought after development of an American Jewish community.

Conclusion

Nothing demonstrates so clearly the complicated route adolescent Jewish girls took toward adulthood and individuality than the ways in which they embraced American youth culture yet balanced their participation with a measure of traditionalism. Playing the piano, reading Shakespeare, and joining the school glee club offered only indirect threats of acculturation to the Jewish values of most girls, especially those exposed to religious education that explicitly encouraged a melding of Jewish and American identity. Girls adhered to no narrow ideological line, nor did they march along a one-way street, moving ever closer to modernity and further from tradition. Their complex, individual identities were far more likely to evolve from a series of intersections in a spiral course where tradition and modernity merged and diverged. The continuing importance of religious identity in their lives, however observed, both inhibited and encouraged their uneven progress toward a destination never final, as Americanness and Jewishness challenged and changed each other.

The later lives of adolescent diarists Fannie Allen of Philadelphia and Bella Weretnikow of Seattle illustrate the complexity of coming of age on the twisting paths traveled by Jewish girls in late nineteenth- and early twentieth-century America. As she grew older, Fannie found her youthful ambitions to do something extraordinary with her life fade. She confessed to her diary in 1875, "Strange to say, notwithstanding all my former ambition to be something great, I would now be contented to be a wife and mother, which, now that I am wiser, seem to be what I was intended for."[1] Fannie's ambitions may have faded, but they never disappeared entirely. After spending well over a decade frustrated and unhappy as a consequence of her persistently single state, in 1887, she finally married Moses de Ford at the age of thirty-two. With the encouragement of her husband, a student at Jefferson Medical College, she entered the Women's Medical

College of Pennsylvania. After they completed their training, they opened a practice together and campaigned for better hygiene conditions while raising three children. Fannie also became a supporter of woman suffrage.

In some ways Fannie's commitment to service resembled that of her grandmother Anna Marks Allen, who with her husband Lewis had brought up seven children while she was heavily involved with the Female Hebrew Benevolent Society and the Philadelphia Jewish Foster Home and Orphan Asylum. In other ways Fannie's combination of domestic and professional life inspired a generation of suffragists, including her own daughter, Miriam Allen de Ford. Though her secular career modernized the call to service that her grandmother had heeded within the Jewish community, her role as wife and mother and her devotion to Judaism maintained important elements of traditionalism in her life as well. Fannie indeed became "something great": an accomplished woman whose adolescent wavering between tradition and modernity was ultimately resolved, not by a choice of one over the other, but by a sustained commitment to both.[2]

Just as the context of women's educational, professional, and family options had changed over the decades between Fannie Allen de Ford and her grandmother, they also changed within individual's lives. Bella Weretnikow spent most of her adolescence furiously studying, determined to pursue the education she was sure would make her life as an American girl and woman nothing like her illiterate immigrant mother's life. Her mother supported her in this ambition, even at the risk of alienating Bella's father and stepfather, both of whom preferred a more traditional future for their daughter. Though she decided early on to study law, Bella had some reservations about going into a field so unusual for women at the dawn of the twentieth century. She decided not to go into prosecution, "as that [was] too masculine" and therefore too unconventional even for her own comfort.[3] After graduating from the University of Washington, Bella did attend law school, passing the bar in 1901. To celebrate, she and her classmates dined out on the local delicacy of oysters, a meal flagrantly transgressive of the Jewish laws of kashrut. One of the first women and first Jews to become an attorney in the far West, Bella certainly seemed to have achieved her goal of utterly rejecting her mother's traditional identity for her own modern one.

Bella began a successful practice in Seattle and was featured in an *American Israelite* story that elicited a congratulatory message from another lawyer, a Lewis Rosenbaum from Nashville who was interested in relocating to Seattle. After reading Bella's recommendation and paying a visit, Louis, his mother, and his siblings all made the move across the country. Not long thereafter, Bella wrote in her unpublished memoirs, "the career somehow lost most of its glamour, and finally I decided to give it all up and get married, just like other girls did—as my father had advised me many years ago."[4] She and Lewis were married for more than fifty years. They had three children, two of them daughters who eventually attended Sarah Lawrence College. At no point in her memoirs did Bella express any regret about the choice she made. As she settled down to domestic life, she might have resembled her mother in some ways, but the education and class privileges that her particular history had brought her ensured her a very different life. In this sense, Bella's adolescent ambitions were realized as a consequence of modernization that affected even traditional lifestyles and roles for women.

Tradition and modernity may have been on either end of a continuum along which adolescent Jewish girls developed individual identities, but as Fannie and Bella's life stories reveal, they also affected each other. The extraordinary group consciousness that the American Jewish community maintained long past the first decades of the twentieth century owed something to the role Jewishness played as a mediating factor. This group consciousness was not merely the result of prejudice or other negative pressures. Jewishness offered something valuable and precious even to Jews living, almost for the first time, in an environment where they actually had the choice of whether or not to honor their religious heritage by identifying with it. The subjective experiences of adolescent Jewish girls, who found religious and national identity were each capacious enough to mesh in their individual identities, paralleled the collective experiences of American Jewry. When modernization called for moving away from the kind of community Jewish traditions prized so heavily, Jewish girls, like American Jewry as a whole, tended to reject it in favor of religious heritage or ethnic culture. When traditionalism seemed to require insulation from assimilation, Jewish girls, like American Jewry as a whole, chose acculturation instead, working hard to adapt an ancient heritage to contemporary times. Though some effort was required, it seemed worthwhile to try to blend the old and the new.

The story of Jewish girls, as individuals and as representatives of American Jewry during the last decades of the nineteenth century and first decades of the twentieth century, is an important part of the Jewish encounter with other cultures and societies. Modernization's emphasis on individualism posed particular challenges to Jews accustomed to the safety and identity provided them by community. For so long, in so many places and times, Jews had been identified first by their Jewishness that it came as a shock—and became the central issue of modern Judaism—when the modern condition brought with it a greater fluidity of identity. The special freedom promised by the United States, a freedom sought after by all Jewish immigrants to America, may have made the American case unique in one sense, but in many ways the American Jewish experience was but one more episode of the saga of modern Jewish history. The generational conflicts, gendered process of acculturation, and rising prominence of Jewish youth in the United States were paralleled in Jewish communities worldwide. While America may have offered girls and women greater opportunity, the common struggles of Jewish youth all over the Western world at the turn of the century suggest the ways in which American Jewish girls' experience reflected and predicted modern Jewish history.

The cycle of balancing conflict between modernization and tradition found in adolescent Jewish girls' lives has been repeated again and again in American history as well as Jewish history. Every new group that has come to the United States has had to adapt in some way to a new culture and environment. As in the Jewish immigrant communities of both the nineteenth and the twentieth centuries, children have often made the transition more quickly and successfully than adults. Religions brought to the United States, like Judaism, have often been redefined in an open American society that theoretically disapproves of religious or ethnic restraint or particularism. Gender, class, and race have also been important components of the process of acclimation to modernity. Twentieth-century American history has seen repeated instances of this process, not only within the Jewish community but also across other ethnic immigrant groups or racially distinct groups or mobile class groups.

The continuous encounter of tradition and modernity so central to the story of adolescent Jewish girls makes them effective representatives of important themes of contemporary American history. As girls, their experiences reflected the interaction of modernization and gender. As adolescents, they benefited from the growing importance of youth in modern society. As Jews, their attempts to balance the heritage of the past with the demands of the future embodied the challenge of modern Judaism. Their continuing affinity for tradition disrupts any attempt to perceive a linear progression toward modernization. Even in their own time, turn-of-the-century adolescent girls were recognized as significant arbiters of the encounter between Jewishness and Americanness. In historical perspective, their significance is even greater, as the experiences of adolescent Jewish girls in America are critical to the understanding of the fluid, ambivalent, and interactive encounter of tradition and modernity.

Notes

ABBREVIATIONS

American Jewish Archives (AJA)
American Jewish Historical Society (AJHS)
Center for Advanced Judaic Studies Library, University of Pennsylvania (CAJSL)
Chicago Historical Society (CHS)
Chicago Jewish Archives (CJA)
Jewish Museum of Maryland (JMM)
Maryland Historical Society (MHS)
New York Public Library (NYPL)
Philadelphia Jewish Archives Center (PJAC)
Rutgers University Manuscripts and Special Collections (RU)
92nd Street Young Men's/Women's Hebrew Association (YM/WHA)

NOTES TO THE INTRODUCTION

1. Rachel Rosalie Phillips diary, unprocessed collection, AJA. Rachel Rosalie Phillips was the daughter of a distinguished Jewish family with colonial roots in New York and Philadelphia. She spent several months during the Civil War with her uncle Adolphus Solomons in Washington, D.C., who as liquor purveyor to the Union army moved in elite social circles. It is not clear from the diary how old she was in 1864. However, as she was proposed to during her extended visit, it can probably be assumed she was at least fifteen years old. She was not yet married in 1866, at the time she wrote one of the random entries for that year.
2. Brumberg, *The Body Project*, and Hunter, *How Young Ladies Became Girls*.
3. Prell, *Fighting to Become American*.
4. Weinberg, *The World of Our Mothers*, and Glenn, *Daughters of the Shtetl*.
5. For an introduction to these issues, see Conway, *When Memory Speaks*.
6. For a discussion of Jewish girls and diaries in a slightly later time period, see Brumberg, "The 'Me of Me,'" in Antler, ed., *Talking Back*. In this article and in *The Body Project*, the generally accepted idea that keeping a diary is a mark of literacy and leisure associated with class privilege leads Brumberg to surmise that few, if any, Jewish girls wrote diaries until the fortunes of American Jewry rose during the early twentieth century. This assumption overlooks the sizable population of middle-class Jews already living in America prior to 1900, whose class and cultural inclinations led Jewish girls to keeping diaries much as their non-Jewish counterparts did.
7. Jennie Franklin Purvin (1873–1958) was the daughter of Henry B. and Hannah Mayer Franklin. She was born and educated in Chicago. She married Moses L. Purvin in 1899 and had two daughters. She became active in a variety of Chicago civic causes, including a successful campaign to clean up the city's beaches. She was also active in the National Council of Jewish Women and the early Jewish camping movement.
8. January 21, 1864, Rachel Rosalie Phillips diary, unprocessed collection, AJA; Emily Frankenstein diary, Emily Frankenstein Papers, CHS; Jennie Franklin diary, Jennie Franklin Purvin Papers, MS 502, AJA; Amelia Allen diary, ACC 1603, PJAC; Ann Green diary, Robison Family Papers, P-678, AJHS; Marie Syrkin diary, Marie Syrkin Papers, MS 615, AJA; Mathilde Kohn diary, SC-6391, AJA. Amelia Allen (b. 1856) was the daughter of Lewis Marks and Miriam Arnold Allen, both from Philadelphia Jewish families associated for decades with

241

| *Notes to the Introduction*

congregation Mikveh Israel. She taught in the Philadelphia public schools and became active in
the Hebrew Sunday School Association founded by Rebecca Gratz. She was among the founders
of the Young Women's Union and took charge of its kindergarten and Household School in
1886. Ann Eleanor Green Robison (1904–1995) was born in Russia but immigrated with her
family to Maine as a young child. She graduated from the University of Maine and spent decades
as a journalist, educator, and philanthropist. She married Adolph Robison in 1927. Marie Syrkin
(1899–1989) was the daughter of Nachman and Bassya Ossnos Syrkin. She came to the United
States with her family as a nine-year-old. Her father was a prominent Zionist and her mother
was also an activist. She began to write at an early age and later became a well-known literary
scholar and Zionist, becoming one of the first professors at Brandeis University. She married
three times, finally settling down with poet Charles Reznikoff in 1930. Emily Louise Frankenstein (b. 1899) was the daughter of American-born Jews of German descent. Her father, Victor
Frankenstein, was a doctor and prominent member of the established Jewish community in
Chicago. She grew up in Chicago and graduated from the Kenwood Loring School in 1918. She
took classes at the University of Chicago. Mathilde Kohn immigrated to the United States from
Czechoslovakia in 1866 as an adolescent after her father's death. She and her mother Antonie
and her sister lived with several relatives in North and South Carolina.

9. See Smith-Rosenberg, "The Female World of Love and Ritual"; Hunter, "Inscribing the Self
in the Heart of the Family: Diaries and Girlhood in Late-Victorian America"; Blodgett, *Centuries
of Female Days*; Franklin, *Private Pages*; Lensink, "Expanding the Boundaries of Criticism"; and
Hoffman and Culley, eds., *Women's Personal Narratives.*

10. See Ulrich's comments on the "dailiness, the exhaustive, repetitious dailiness" in *A Midwife's Tale*, 9.

11. Davis, "Women's Frontier Diaries"; Franklin, *Private Pages;* Blodgett, *Centuries of Female
Days.*

12. May 1, 1861, Eliza Moses diary, transcribed extracts from the journals of Eliza M. Moses
and Albert Moses Luria, edited by Stanford E. Moses, SC-8504, AJA. Few journal entries were
transcribed; Stanford Moses seems to have heavily edited the diary.

13. April 3, 1862, Bertha Wehle diary, SC-12789, AJA. The AJA holds a transcribed and
probably heavily edited version of the diary prepared by Bertha's sons Walter and George Naumberg. Bertha Wehle (1843–1897) was the daughter of a well-to-do New York Jewish family. She
graduated from high school and became a teacher, continuing to take classes at Cooper Union.
She married Elkan Naumberg in 1866.

14. April 14, May 7, 1875, April 20, 1876, Fannie Allen diary, ACC 1602, PJAC. Frances
(Fannie) Allen de Ford (1855–1937), daughter of Lewis Marks and Miriam Arnold Allen, was
Amelia Allen's sister. She was less involved in the Philadelphia Jewish community than Amelia
and, at the urging of future husband Moses de Ford, she eventually went to medical school. She
both graduated and married in 1887. She and her husband campaigned for improved public
health in Philadelphia, and she also supported woman suffrage. They had three children.

15. April 3, 1915, Marie Syrkin diary, AJA.

16. January 5, 1862, Eliza Moses diary, AJA.

17. Bella Weretnikow diary, Bella Weretnikow Rosenbaum Papers, MS 179, AJA. Bella
Weretnikow Rosenbaum (b. 1880) was the daughter of eastern European immigrants, who settled first in Winnipeg and then moved to Seattle in 1893. After her parents divorced, her father
Zachariah moved to Portland, Oregon. Bella graduated from the University of Washington and
then attended the law school there.

18. February 23, 1868, Rosa Feinberg diary, Seidenfeld-Liebenstein Family Papers, Coll. 167,
CJA. Rosa Feinberg Liebenstein (1851–1936) was the daughter of wealthy German Jewish immigrants, who returned to Germany at frequent intervals. She married Charles Liebenstein.

19. October 31, 1866, Mathilde Kohn diary, AJA. Unlike the other diaries used as sources in
this book, Mathilde's diary was originally written in German. The AJA holds the German original and an unattributed partial translation.

20. April 10, 1915, Marie Syrkin diary, AJA.

21. Ashkenazi, ed., *The Civil War Diary of Clara Solomon*, 67. Clara Solomon Lilienthal
Lawrence (1844–1907) was the daughter of Solomon P. and Emma Solomon Solomon. She grew
up in New Orleans and was a student at the Louisiana Normal School during the Civil War occupation of New Orleans. In 1865, she married Julius Lilienthal, who died two years later, and in
1872, she married her deceased husband's non-Jewish doctor, George Lawrence.

22. Emily Frankenstein, Chicago, to Victor Frankenstein, Chicago, undated letter, Emily

Frankenstein Papers, CHS. The letter is written in markedly more childish handwriting than the diary Emily began in 1918, suggesting that she had already been keeping a diary for some time before she started what appears to be the only one that survived.

23. For a discussion of the meaning and use of diaries by other adolescent girls, particularly middle-class Protestants, see Hunter, "Inscribing the Self in the Heart of the Family"; Brumberg, *The Body Project*; and Roberts, "Telling 'Truth Truly.'"

24. April 13, 1915, Marie Syrkin diary, AJA.

NOTES TO CHAPTER I

1. See "Our Girls" and subsequent articles in *American Israelite,* January and February 1875, and "The Religious Education of Our Females" and subsequent articles in *Jewish Messenger,* June 1867.

2. *Jewish Messenger,* March 7, 1890.

3. Julia Richman (1855–1912), a graduate of the Normal College in New York, was the daughter of Moses and Theresa Melis Richman, well-off Jewish immigrants from Prague. She was a public school teacher and eventually the first female district superintendent in New York City. She organized the Young Women's Hebrew Association and later was heavily involved with the Educational Alliance and the National Council of Jewish Women. Although she was very active in various immigrant aid programs, her support for radical Americanization made her a somewhat controversial figure in the Jewish community. Martha Morton (1865–1925), daughter of Joseph and Amelia Marks Allen, was also a graduate of New York's Normal College. She began writing at an early age but was forced to use a male pseudonym to get her plays produced until she had made a name for herself. She was denied membership to the American Dramatists Club because she was a woman. Morton made a fortune during her long career as a playwright. Her participation in the *Jewish Messenger* symposium was somewhat unusual for her, as she was not much involved with Jewish causes. She married Hermann Conheim in 1897.

4. Ella Jacobs, daughter of Rabbi George Jacobs, grew up in Philadelphia during the last quarter of the nineteenth century. She was a graduate of the Girls' Normal School in Philadelphia, a teacher in both secular and religious schools, and eventually the principal of a Philadelphia public school. She was a founder of the Young Women's Union and later an active member of the Jewish Chautauqua Society and National Council of Jewish Women. Fannie Binswanger Hoffman (1862–1949) was a contemporary of Jacobs. Daughter of Rabbi Isidor and Sophie Elizabeth Polock Binswanger, she was born in Philadelphia but traveled widely and was educated in both the United States and Europe. She was active at Mikveh Israel and in the National Council of Jewish Women. She was the moving force behind the 1885 founding of the Young Women's Union in Philadelphia, which provided education, recreation, and services for Jewish women and children. She married Charles I. Hoffman and had five children.

5. *Jewish Messenger,* March 14, 1890.

6. *Jewish Messenger,* March 7, 1890. Annie Nathan Meyer (1867–1951) was the daughter of Robert Weeks and Annie Augusta Florance Nathan. She came from a distinguished Sephardic family with colonial roots. She married Alfred Meyer in 1887 only after extracting his promise to support her writing. They had one daughter. An advocate for women's higher education and improved work conditions, she was among the founders of Barnard College in 1889 but was also a staunch antisuffragist.

7. *Jewish Messenger,* March 7, 14, 21, 1890.

8. *Jewish Messenger,* March 7, 14, 1890.

9. *Jewish Messenger,* March 21, 1890. Minnie (Miriam) Dessau Louis (1841–1922) was the daughter of Abraham and Fanny Zachariah Dessau. She was raised in a small Jewish community in Georgia but later attended the Packer Collegiate Institute in Brooklyn. She married Adolph H. Louis in 1866 and launched a career of writing and social service. She founded what became the Hebrew Technical School for Girls in New York. She was also involved with the Hebrew Free School kindergarten and the Mount Sinai Training School for Nurses and active in the Jewish Chautauqua Society and National Council of Jewish Women.

10. *Jewish Messenger,* March 21, 28, 1890.

11. *Jewish Messenger,* March 7, 14, 21, 1890. Italics in the original.

12. Jennie Franklin diary, 1890, Jennie Franklin Purvin Papers, Box 2278e, MS 502, AJA.

13. March 31–April 4, April 29, January 17, April 18, March 16, 1890, Jennie Franklin diary, AJA.

14. October 6, December 2, 1890, Jennie Franklin diary, AJA.

15. May 25, September 24, 15, 1890, Jennie Franklin diary, AJA.

16. January 11, February 8, September 7, 1890, Jennie Franklin diary, AJA.

17. November 19, 1890, Jennie Franklin diary, AJA.

18. July 13, October 2, September 10, July 9, 15, 18, 20, August 21, 1890, Jennie Franklin diary, AJA.

19. August 29, 23, October 26, 1890, Jennie Franklin diary, AJA.

20. This brief summary is based on DeLuzio, "'New Girls for Old,'" especially chapter 1. See also Demos and Demos, "Adolescence in Historical Perspective"; Bakan, "Adolescence in America"; Modell, Furstenberg, and Hershberg, "Social Change and Transitions to Adulthood in Historical Perspective"; and Hawes, "The Strange History of Female Adolescence in the United States."

21. For examples of early, generally male-centered work on adolescence in America, see Kett, *Rites of Passage,* and Demos, *Past, Present, and Personal.* Graff's more recent study, *Conflicting Paths,* allots to girls only the "female path" divided into traditional, transitional, and emerging "subpaths."

22. Major studies of female juvenile delinquency include Alexander, *The Girl Problem,* and Odem, *Delinquent Daughters.* There are exceptions to this focus. See, for example, Green, "The 'Boy Problem' and the 'Woman Question.'"

23. Several edited collections bring together this literature. See Hiner and Hawes, eds., *Growing Up in America: Children in Historical Perspective*; Graff, ed., *Growing Up in America: Historical Experiences*; West and Petrik, eds., *Small Worlds*; Elder, Modell, and Parke, eds., *Children in Time and Place*; and Austin and Willard, eds., *Generations of Youth.*

24. These ideas have entered popular historical discourse as well. See Hine, *The Rise and Fall of the American Teenager,* and Palladino, *Teenagers.*

25. Sorin, *Tradition Transformed,* 27.

26. For general overviews of this period, see Sorin, *Tradition Transformed*; Diner, *A Time for Gathering*; and Sorin, *A Time for Building.*

27. The five-volume history of American Jewry published by Johns Hopkins University Press in 1992 exemplifies the newer approach, which is best explicated in Diner, *A Time for Gathering.*

28. No summary can do justice to the sophistication of Paula E. Hyman's arguments in *Gender and Assimilation in Modern Jewish History.*

29. Sarna, *A Great Awakening.*

30. Goldman, *Beyond the Synagogue Gallery.*

31. The classic work is Meyer, *Response to Modernity.*

32. See Silverstein, *Alternatives to Assimilation.*

33. For more on *tekhines,* see Weissler, *Voices of the Matriarchs.*

34. Hurst, *Anatomy of Me,* 47–48, 64. Fannie's search may have been lifelong, as indicated by the title of her memoir. Fannie Hurst (1889–1968) was born in St. Louis. She was the daughter of Samuel and Rose Koppel Hurst, middle-class Jewish parents who were both American-born themselves. She graduated from Washington University and married musician Jacques Danielson in 1915. Fannie began writing at an early age and became one of the best-known and best-paid American female novelists and screenwriters of the 1920s. She was also active in New Deal politics and various relief efforts for Jews in Europe.

35. March 28, April 1, 1915, Marie Syrkin diary, AJA.

36. August 28, 1862, Bertha Wehle diary, AJA.

37. June 12, 1896, Bella Weretnikow diary, AJA.

38. Simon, *A Wider World,* 9. Kate Simon (1912–1990) was the daughter of David and Lonia Babicz Simon. She arrived in the United States with her family as a toddler. She grew up in the heavily immigrant Bronx neighborhood she later immortalized in *Bronx Primitive* and attended New York public schools and Hunter College. Her personal life was marked by tragedy, as her first husband, her daughter, and her younger sister all died of brain tumors. She wrote a well-received series of travel books and three memoirs.

39. Nathan, *Once upon a Time and Today,* 30–31. Maud Nathan (1862–1946), daughter of Robert Weeks and Annie Augusta Florance, was Annie Nathan Meyer's sister. She was educated in New York and Green Bay, Wisconsin, and married her cousin Frederick Nathan in 1880. Their only daughter died as a child. She was very active in the New York Consumer's League and General Federation of Women's Clubs. She was also visible in the Jewish community, becoming the first woman speaker at congregation Shearith Israel in New York. Unlike her sister, Maud was a staunch suffragist.

40. See Prell, "The Dilemma of Women's Equality in the History of Reform Judaism."

41. Clara Lowenburg Moses, "My Memories," 48, 1939, SC-8499, AJA. Clara Lowenburg Moses (1865–1951) was the daughter of Isaac and Ophielia Mayer Lowenburg, German immigrants to the United States. Her mother died when she was six years old, and her father remarried. She grew up in Natchez, Mississippi, where there was a small, tightly knit Jewish community. She attended school in both Natchez and Germany. In 1890, she married Adolph Moses, who committed suicide in 1899, and in later life she became a Christian Scientist.

42. May 25, June 4, 1882, Birdie Stein diary, Friedenwald Family Papers, 1984.23, JMM. Birdie Stein Friedenwald (1866–1942) was born in Baltimore's middle-class, traditional Jewish community. She attended public high school there and in 1892 married Dr. Henry Friedenwald, son of one of the most prominent Jewish families in Baltimore.

43. July 8, 1862, Eliza Moses diary, AJA.

44. May 20, September 8, December 31, 1875, April 5, August 17, 1876, Fannie Allen diary, PJAC.

45. On the Sabbath schools and the network of benevolent associations founded in Philadelphia by Rebecca Gratz, see Ashton, *Rebecca Gratz*. Rebecca Gratz (1781–1869) was the daughter of Michael and Miriam Simon Gratz. The Gratz family was prominent in the Philadelphia Jewish community that had colonial and Sephardic roots. She was heavily involved with numerous organizations, including the Female Association for the Relief of Women and Children in Reduced Circumstances, the Philadelphia Orphan Asylum, the Female Hebrew Benevolent Society, the Hebrew Sunday School Society, and the Jewish Foster Home. She also raised six nieces and nephews. Rebecca Gratz's charitable and educational work made her a legendary figure during her own lifetime within both the Jewish and civic communities of Philadelphia.

46. For more on the Sunday School system in Philadelphia, see chapter 4, "'A Perfect Jew and a Perfect American': The Religious Education of Jewish Girls." Amelia and Fannie Allen's family attended the renowned Mikveh Israel, a synagogue that retained traditional ritual and liturgy long after most of its congregants turned away from strict observance in their homes. January 1, February 20, April 14, May 13, February 5, September 27, 1876, June 18, 1878, Amelia Allen diary, PJAC.

47. April 8, 1862, Bertha Wehle diary, AJA.

48. Polacheck, *I Came a Stranger,* xiii. Hilda Satt Polacheck (1882–1967) came to the United States as a young child when her parents Louis and Dena Satt immigrated from eastern Europe. She and her siblings attended Chicago's Jewish Training School. Although Hilda went to work in a knitting factory at age thirteen, she was drawn into the social service networks of Hull House and developed a relationship with Jane Addams, who encouraged her to write and even helped arrange a semester of study at the University of Chicago.

49. Klein, *A Passion for Sharing,* 24. Marion Rosenwald (b. 1902) was the daughter of Julius and Augusta Nusbaum Rosenwald. Her father was a Sears-Roebuck magnate. She grew up in Chicago.

50. Rothman, *The Haas Sisters of Franklin Street,* 70–71.

51. Helen Arnstein Salz, oral history, 2, AJA. Helen Arnstein Salz (b. 1883) was the daughter of Ludwig and Mercedes Mandelbaum Arnstein. She grew up in San Francisco's heavily acculturated Jewish community during the 1880s and 1890s. Her wealthy parents gave their children a somewhat eclectic education but also encouraged their individual talents, including Helen's gift for poetry and other writing. She married Ansley Salz in 1911.

52. Hart, *The Pleasure Is Mine,* 19. Sara Liebenstein Hart (b. 1869) was born in Chicago, one of Henry and Theresa Liebenstein's seven children. Her mother was traditionally observant, but none of her children followed in her footsteps. Sara attended both public and private schools. She was later involved with organizing the Juvenile Court of Chicago. She married Adam Wald in 1888 and moved to Louisiana, later returning to Chicago and marrying Harry Hart.

53. Ferber, *A Peculiar Treasure,* 42–43. Edna Ferber (1885–1968), daughter of Jacob and Julia Neumann Ferber, was born in Kalamazoo, Michigan, and lived with her family in small, often anti-Semitic towns throughout the Midwest. As a child she wanted to be an actor but at seventeen went to work as a journalist instead to help support her family. She slowly made a name for herself as a writer, and after moving to New York in 1912, she became part of the Algonquin Round Table. She became one of the most popular novelists and screenwriters in America, winning a Pulitzer Prize in 1925 for *So Big.*

54. Jennie Rosenfeld Gerstley, "Reminisces," 141–145, Box 2072, AJA. Jennie Rosenfeld Gerstley (1859–1937) was born in Chicago to German Jewish immigrants. Her father died when

she was relatively young, but her mother was determined to provide Jennie with the opportunities of any other middle-class Jewish girl. She was among the first girls in Chicago to graduate public high school, and she also attended normal school and taught for a few years before marrying Henry M. Gerstley. She served as a delegate to the Biennial Meeting of the Federation of Women's Clubs in 1914.

55. April 27, 1918, Emily Frankenstein diary, CHS.

56. April 27, 1918, Emily Frankenstein diary, CHS.

57. April 27, 1918, Emily Frankenstein diary, CHS.

58. January 3, 1878, Amelia Allen diary, PJAC.

59. April 8, 1875, Fannie Allen diary, PJAC.

60. Ruskay, *Horsecars and Cobblestones* (New York: A.S. Barnes, 1948), 186–187. Sophie was one of the earliest Jewish girls to attend what later became Hunter College, a popular institution of higher learning among Jewish girls in New York. See Markowitz, *My Daughter the Teacher.*

61. October 15, October 14, October 8, October 13, 1862, Bertha Wehle diary, AJA.

62. Ashkenazi, *The Civil War Diary of Clara Solomon,* 25, 48, 196, 216, 67, 388, 421, 385.

63. June 12, January 7, January 22, January 8, February 21, March 10, 1896, Bella Weretnikow diary, AJA.

64. January 30, March 6, April 19, September 2, June 12, 1896, Bella Weretnikow diary, AJA.

65. Hurst, *Anatomy of Me,* 54, 75–77. See also Brandimarte, "Fannie Hurst."

66. April 7, April 6, April 23, 1915, Marie Syrkin diary, AJA.

67. May 6, April 1, April 12, May 9, 1915, Marie Syrkin diary, AJA.

68. Levy, *920 O'Farrell Street,* 95–96. Harriet Lane Levy was born to Polish immigrants in San Francisco. She attended public schools there and was one of the first Jewish girls to attend the University of California at Berkeley.

69. April 30, June 4, June 7, 1918, Emily Frankenstein diary, CHS.

70. April 8, October 6, 1862, Bertha Wehle diary, AJA.

71. Berg, *Molly and Me,* 55. Ironically, Gertrude's professional persona on the radio as Molly Goldberg probably echoed the experiences of her mother, Diana (Dinah) Edelstein, in many ways. Gertrude Edelstein Berg (1899–1966), daughter of Jacob and Diana Edelstein, was born in New York but also grew up in the Catskills resort her family helped run. She graduated from public high school and took writing courses at Columbia. She married Lewis Berg in 1919 and had two children. Gertrude impressed NBC executives with her idea for a series about a Jewish family, and *The Rise of the Goldbergs* aired almost continuously on the radio from 1929 to 1945 and then on television from 1949 through 1954. The Goldbergs were an upwardly mobile Jewish family whose experiences helped set the framework for all situation comedies. In her role as writer, producer, and star, Gertrude was one of the most powerful women in the entertainment industry.

72. June 8, 1896, Bella Weretnikow diary, AJA. Bella's love and admiration for her mother are clear throughout her diary. She was especially appreciative of her mother's support for her educational aspirations.

73. Klein, *A Passion for Sharing,* 21. Edith Rosenwald (1895–1980) was the daughter of Sears, Roebuck magnate Julius Rosenwald and his wife Augusta. After marrying Edgar Stern, she moved to New Orleans and continued her father's legacy of educational philanthropy, founding numerous schools and contributing to the development of Dillard University. She was also involved in civic education and voter registration. Adele Rosenwald was her sister.

74. Hart, *The Pleasure Is Mine,* 16–17.

75. Adler, *A House Is Not a Home,* 15. Polly Adler (1900–1962), daughter of Morris and Gertrude Koval Adler, was born in eastern Europe and came to the United States alone as a thirteen-year-old girl. When World War I broke out and prevented her father from continuing to support her, her schooling was cut short and she had to go to work. At seventeen, she was raped by the factory foreman and had an abortion, after which she moved away from her American relatives and eventually was drawn into the underworld of Prohibition. After her first arrest for running a house of prostitution in 1922, Polly attempted to start a legitimate business, but it failed and she spent much of the rest of her career as a prominent and glamorous madam, who somehow always managed to avoid arrest. She retired in 1943 and finished high school and began college.

76. Regina Katz Sharlip, "Memoirs of Galicia," SC-217, PJAC. Regina Katz Sharlip was the daughter of Hersh and Toba Fuchs Katz. She was one of five siblings. The whole family immi-

grated to Philadelphia when she was a child. She graduated from William Penn High School in Philadelphia.

77. Rebecca J. Gradwohl, "The Jewess in San Francisco," *American Jewess,* October 1896. Natalie Seeling, Amelia Levinson, and Adele Solomons were all doctors practicing in San Francisco. Adele Solomons was the daughter of Gershom Mendes Seixas and Hannah Marks Solomons. She was a graduate of Hahnemann Medical College.

78. "The American Jewess and an American Jewess," undated, unidentified draft of an article, Folder 2, Box 2, George Kohut Papers, MS 381, AJA. Internal evidence suggests that the article was prepared for *Opinion.* Rebekah Bettelheim Kohut (1864–1951) was the daughter of Rabbi Albert and Henrietta Weintraub Bettelheim. She was a young child when her family immigrated to the United States. She grew up in Richmond, Virginia, and then in San Francisco, where she graduated from high school and attended the University of California. In 1887, she married Rabbi Alexander Kohut, a contemporary of her father who shared a commitment to traditional Jewish religion. She had eight stepchildren but no children of her own. Rebekah was active in the New York Women's Health Protective Association and the sisterhood at her husband's congregation, Central Synagogue. After her husband's death in 1894, she increased her involvement in such organizations as the National Council of Jewish Women, the Young Women's Hebrew Association, and the World Congress of Jewish Women. She started a school for girls, edited a newspaper for Jewish children, and worked on issues of women's employment during World War I. She wrote two memoirs and was one of the most well-known Jewish women in America for the first half of the twentieth century.

79. *Sabbath Visitor,* June 5, 1891.

80. *Sabbath-School Visitor,* April 1874.

81. A. S. Isaacs, New York, to Henrietta Szold, Baltimore, 31 October 1879, Box 1, Folder 4, MS 38, Henrietta Szold Papers, JMM. Henrietta Szold (1860–1945) was born in Baltimore, the oldest daughter of Rabbi Benjamin and Sophie Szold. Her family was traditionally observant, and her father supplemented her public school education with lessons in German, Hebrew, and religious texts. She became a teacher after graduating from high school and established one of the first night schools for immigrants in the United States. She also began to make a name for herself in the American Jewish community as a writer and translator, becoming a key member of the new Jewish Publication Society in 1888 and playing an important role in many of JPS's major publications. After her father died, she moved to New York with her mother and studied at the Jewish Theological Seminary, although she never intended to be a rabbi. She was among the first Zionists in America and visited Palestine in 1909, returning to found Hadassah, the women's Zionist organization. In 1920, Henrietta moved to Palestine to supervise Hadassah's medical operations. The World Zionist Congress appointed her to its Palestine executive board in 1927, and her efforts in the fields of public health, education, and social work made a lasting contribution to the national infrastructure. During the 1930s, Henrietta was instrumental in making Youth Aliyah into an organization which saved thousands of Jewish children from the Holocaust by bringing them to Palestine. She stayed in Palestine during World War II and died there as an icon of both Zionism and Jewish women worldwide.

82. Mrs. Maurice C. Benjamin, "Private Schools for Jewesses," *American Hebrew,* March 19, 1912.

83. *American Hebrew,* April 14, 1916.

84. *American Jewess,* January 1898.

85. "When a Man Wants a Wife," unidentified, undated clipping reprinted from the *Pittsburg Gazette,* pasted into Jennie Franklin diary, AJA.

86. Rosa Fassel Sonneschein (1847–1932) was born in Austria and well educated there. In 1864, she married Solomon Sonneschein, a Reform rabbi who occupied pulpits in Europe and America. The Sonnescheins moved to St. Louis in 1869 and stayed there for more than twenty years. Rosa was active in the Jewish community, founding a Jewish women's literary society and several choral groups. She began to write for Jewish periodicals during the 1880s and also served as a correspondent for the German press. The Sonnescheins had four children and a stormy marriage that finally ended in divorce in 1893. Rosa put her writing skills to use as a journalist and founded *American Jewess* in 1895 as a magazine for American Jewish women. *American Jewess* was not a financial success and only appeared for four years, but during that time it was influential and reflected Rosa's advocacy for Zionism, religious observance, and expansion of American Jewish women's roles.

87. Rabbi David Philipson, "The Ideal Jewess," *American Jewess,* March 1897.

88. Minnie D. Louis, "Educational Work among Jewish Girls," *American Hebrew,* July 22, 1898; "The New America, and American Jewish Women: A Symposium," *American Hebrew,* September 26, 1919.

89. "The New America, and American Jewish Women: A Symposium," *American Hebrew,* September 26, 1919. Carrie Obendorfer Simon (1872–1961) was the daughter of Leo and Mary Wise Obendorfer. She grew up in Cincinnati and was a graduate of the Cincinnati Conservatory of Music. She was an active member of the National Council of Jewish Women as a young woman. She married Hebrew Union College rabbinical student Abram Simon in 1896 and had two sons. She later turned her attention to synagogue affairs and in 1913 founded the National Federation of Temple Sisterhoods to promote Jewish social service and the home.

NOTES TO CHAPTER 2

1. Jennie Rosenfeld Gerstley, "Reminisces," 59, 1931–1934, Box 2072, AJA.

2. Important contributions to the large literature on the emergence of secondary education in the United States include Cremin, *American Education*; Krug, *The Shaping of the American High School*; Raubinger et al., *The Development of Secondary Education*; and Reese, *The Origins of the American High School*. Other than tracing the development of coeducation, very little of the historiography deals with gender and secondary education in any sustained way.

3. For examples of contemporary sources (unconsciously) revealing the basic conservatism of secondary education throughout this period, even among authors pushing for expansion of educational opportunity, see Kelly, *Little Citizens*; Department of Education, City of New York, Division of Research and Reference, *The School and the Immigrant*; Finney, *The American Public School*; and Blake et al., *The Education of the Modern Girl*. Relevant secondary studies include Katz, *The Irony of Early School Reform*; Graham, *Community and Class in American Education, 1865–1918*; Bowles and Gintis, *Schooling in Capitalist America*; and Katznelson and Weir, *Schooling for All*. Much of this secondary literature is so critical of the conservative agendas of American schools that it often overlooks the identifiable benefits that even a "tainted" secondary education afforded virtually all students irrespective of class, race, or gender.

4. On the expansion of secondary education and the development of youth culture in high schools, see Modell, "Dating Becomes the Way of American Youth"; Graebner, "Outlawing Teenage Populism"; and Ueda, *Avenues to Adulthood*.

5. On education and adolescence in the United States, see Kantor and Tyack, eds., *Work, Youth, and Schooling*; Modell, Furstenberg, and Hershberg, "Social Change and Transitions to Adulthood in Historical Perspective"; and Troen, "The Discovery of the Adolescent by American Educational Reformers, 1900–1920."

6. Coser, Anker, and Perrin, *Women of Courage*; Ewen, *Immigrant Women in the Land of Dollars*; and Friedman-Kasaba, *Memories of Migration* all explore the relationship between education and work in Jewish immigrant women's lives.

7. For elaboration of the ways in which gender ideology shaped women's work and education, see Clifford, "Marry, Stitch, Die, or Do Worse."

8. Contemporary literature grappled with these issues. See Meyer, ed., *Woman's Work in America*; Allinson, *The Public Schools and Women in Office Service*; and Goodsell, *The Education of Women*. For discussions of the ways in which these issues played out in vocational education for girls, see Carter and Prus, "The Labor Market and the American High School Girl," and Crowder, "The Lux School."

9. Jastrow, *Looking Back,* 97. Marie Grunfeld Jastrow (1898–1991) was born in Poland and lived in Serbia before immigrating to the United States at age ten with her parents, Julius and Johanna Deutsch Grunfeld. She grew up in the Yorkville district of Manhattan. Marie wrote all her life, although her first book was not published until she was eighty-two years old. She married Abraham Jastrow in 1921 and had two children.

10. Henrietta Moscowitz Voorsanger autobiography, 8–9, Box 3, Elkan C. and Henrietta Voorsanger Papers, MS 256, AJA. Anna Moscowitz Kross (1891–1979) was born in Russia and immigrated to the United States as a toddler with her parents Maier and Esther Drazen Moscowitz. She attended Columbia University after graduating from high school and at nineteen years old in 1910 became the first female graduate of New York University's law school. Her legal career focused on working women and juveniles' concerns. In 1933, she became the first woman appointed as a judge in the city magistrates court. She later became the commissioner of corrections for New York City. She married Isidor Kross in 1917 and had two children.

11. June 12, 1918, Emily Frankenstein diary, Emily Frankenstein Papers, CHS.
12. Beckerman, *Not So Long Ago,* 54, 66–67. Emma Beckerman (b. 1898) was born in Austria, moved to Hanover as a toddler, and then immigrated to the United States with her family in 1904. She grew up in New York. After graduating from elementary school in 1912, she attended the Hebrew Technical School for Girls. She went to work at age fifteen as an office girl.
13. Meckler, *Papa Was a Farmer,* 189–195, 245–248, 256, 260–264, 269. Brenda Weisberg Meckler (b. 1900) was the daughter of parents who immigrated to Boston in 1904 and then decided to farm near Cincinnati. She graduated from high school and a special summer normal course and became a teacher.
14. Henrietta Moscowitz Voorsanger autobiography, 13–14, AJA.
15. Ruth Sapinsky, "The Jewish College Girl," quoted in Marcus, ed., *The American Jewish Woman,* 705.
16. Fannie quoted in Rosenbaum and Segerjeds, eds., *Our Story,* 62–63.
17. Simon, *A Wider World,* 7–8.
18. "The Education of a Young Woman of Family, ca. 1881," in Marcus, ed., *The American Jewish Woman,* 338. Florentine Scholle Sutro (1864–1939) grew up in San Francisco and New York but also lived in Germany for a few years. In 1878, she joined Felix Adler's Sabbath school class for the children of members of the new Ethical Culture Society. She graduated from a kindergarten teacher training course.
19. Hartman, *I Gave My Heart,* 25–26. May Weisser Hartman (b. 1900) was the daughter of Jacob and Fannie Weisser. Sixth of eight children, she was born in the United States and grew up in New York. She married Gustav Hartman.
20. Gertrude Mandelbaum Ades, "Family History," 13, 1992, CHS. Gertrude Mandelbaum Ades (b. 1907) was the daughter of Isaac and Sarah Funk Mandelbaum. She grew up in Chicago and graduated from John Marshall High School in 1925. She took classes at the Art Institute of Chicago during her senior year in high school.
21. Minnie Seltzer Schechter, "Memoirs: Three-Quarters of a Century of Life in Philadelphia," 1981, 3, SC 239, PJAC. Minnie Seltzer Schechter (b. 1900) immigrated to Philadelphia with her family in 1903. She finished two years at Camden High School and then went to work as a stenographer.
22. For elaboration of this point, see Weinberg, "Jewish Mothers and Immigrant Daughters."
23. Annual Office Report for Year 1921–1922, Scholarship Association for Jewish Children, 3, Box 2278m, Jennie Franklin Purvin Papers, MS 502, AJA.
24. Weinberg, "Longing to Learn."
25. Jennie Jackson, "Memoirs," 29, 98–101, 1972, Asher Library, Spertus Museum of Judaica, Chicago. Betty (b. 1883), Edith (b. 1885), Jennie (b. 1889), and Sarah (b. 1895) Jackson were four of the six children of Moses Dillon and Rebecca Silberstein Jackson. They grew up in New York. Betty graduated from Girls' High School and the Teacher's Training School in Brooklyn. Sarah graduated from the Manual Training High School and then the Brooklyn Public Library Training School.
26. Antin, *The Promised Land,* 200–201. Mary Antin (1881–1949) was the daughter of Israel Pinchus and Esther Weltman Antin. She was born in Polotsk and immigrated to Boston with her family in 1894. She quickly made her way through the Boston schools and graduated from Girls' Latin School, an education that was partly financed by the publication of her book *From Plotzk to Boston* in 1899. She married non-Jewish geologist Amadeus William Grabau in 1901 and studied at both Barnard and Columbia Teachers College. They had one daughter but separated by 1919. She wrote both *The Promised Land* and *They Who Knock at Our Gates* (1914) as proimmigration works and lectured widely on the subject. She was less well-known during the latter part of her life, except as a proponent of anthroposophy.
27. Cohen, *Out of the Shadow,* 194. Rose Gollup Cohen (1880–1925) was the daughter of Abraham and Annie Gollup. By 1893, her whole family had immigrated to the United States. She went to work immediately and soon became involved in union activity in the garment industry. She also worked at several institutions for immigrant children and became Leonora O'Reilly's assistant at the Manhattan Trade School for Girls. She attended classes at the Educational Alliance and the Rand School and became something of a celebrity in 1918, when she published *Out of the Shadow,* one of the first immigrant autobiographies. She married Joseph Cohen and had one daughter. She suffered from poor health all her life and died at age forty-five.
28. Allan Davis, "The Work of the Educational Alliance," 9, 1910, Educational Alliance

Papers, MS-JCC.E.28, AJHS. For more on the Educational Alliance, see chapter 3, this volume, and Bellow, *The Educational Alliance.*

29. Carlin and Carlin, *Just So You Know,* 16. Sara Carlin (b. 1893) grew up in Chicago. She left school at age fifteen.

30. If Margaret had blatantly overstepped her bounds, it is unlikely that the Solis family would have recommended her to their Jewish neighbors, the Mitchells, or that the Mitchells would have retained her for several years as they did. November 20, December 11, 1864, October 19, November 17, 1865, Margaret Quandril Clark Griffis diary, RU.

31. Warburg, *Reminiscences of a Long Life,* 79. Frieda Schiff Warburg (1876–1958) was the daughter of Jacob and Therese Loeb Schiff, members of the highest echelon of the elite German-Jewish community in New York at the turn of the century. She married Felix Warburg in 1895 and had five children. She had a long and active philanthropic career, with special interests in Jewish and children's causes. See Chernow, *The Warburgs,* for more on the social milieu of the Loeb and Schiff families.

32. Emily Fechheimer Seasongood, "Childhood Home in Cincinnati," in Marcus, ed., *Memoirs of American Jews, 1775–1865,* 66. Emily Fechheimer Seasongood (1851–1941) was the daughter of Marcus and Nannie Fechheimer, Bavarian immigrants. She grew up in Cincinnati. She was confirmed by Isaac Mayer Wise at the Lodge Street Synagogue in 1864. She married Alfred Seasongood in 1871.

33. Clara Lowenburg Moses, "My Memories," 1939, SC-8499, AJA.

34. Solomon, *Fabric of My Life,* 25. Hannah Greenebaum Solomon (1858–1942), daughter of Michael and Sarah Spiegel Greenebaum, was born in a wealthy Chicago family devoted to classical Reform Judaism. She attended but did not graduate from public high school and was a serious student of music. In 1879, she married Henry Solomon. They had three children. Her family's social status and commitment to charitable causes made her the logical choice to chair the Jewish Women's Committee during the Chicago World's Fair of 1893, out of which emerged the National Council of Jewish Women. Hannah became the NCJW's first president. In that role she was involved in many causes, including religious education, immigrant aid, and social services for women. She was also among the first women to speak from synagogue pulpits. Even after stepping down from the NCJW presidency, she remained involved with a variety of reform movements, including suffrage and international women's issues.

35. Hannah Greenebaum's brother Henry, who knew the Bloomfield family from Chicago, helped finance Fannie's initial forays abroad. Sigmund Zeisler, "Fannie Bloomfield Zeisler," Fannie Bloomfield Zeisler Papers, MS 587, AJA. Fannie Bloomfield Zeisler (1863–1927), daughter of Salomon and Bertha Jaeger Blumenfeld, was born in Austria and moved with her family to Appleton, Wisconsin, as a small child. After her family moved to Chicago, she graduated from Chicago's Dearborn School of Music as the only Jewish girl in her class and then studied music in Europe. Launching a very successful career as a concert pianist and teacher, her popularity peaked in the late 1890s but continued for several decades.

36. Clara Lowenburg Moses, "My Memories," 60, 62, 56, 66, AJA.

37. Presumably, her mother also wrote to her daughter, but only her father's letters have been preserved. Jacob G. Joseph, Buffalo, to Beatrice Joseph, Paris, 3 September, 17 October 1913, Box 1, Folder 1, Beatrice J. Hammond Papers, MS 291, AJA. Beatrice Joseph Foreman Monheimer Hammond (b. 1896) was the daughter of Jacob G. and Blanche Block Joseph. She grew up in Buffalo, New York. After graduating from Buffalo Seminary, she studied in Europe for a year, living with her aunt Julia in Paris. She married Gerhardt Foreman in 1916. After divorcing him, she later married Henry Monheimer and then Leonard Hammond.

38. Helen Arnstein Salz, oral history, 7–8, AJA.

39. Henrietta Szold, "Our Public Schools," quoted in Becker, ed., *Western High School Past and Present,* 49–50. See also Wraga, *Democracy's High School.*

40. For a more optimistic view of American education and a strong critique of the early revisionist literature cited above, see Ravitch, *The Revisionists Revised.* Ravitch, along with many of the other contributors to the conversation about the history of education, has modified her views to an extent, leading to a more nuanced historical approach to American education that characterizes it as neither evil nor perfect.

41. Burstall, *The Education of Girls in the United States,* 1–5.

42. Tyack, ed., *Turning Points in American Educational History,* 396.

43. This small group of exceptional women is clearly not a scientific sample, but the fact that the overwhelming majority of them graduated from high school represents the degree to which

secondary education had already been accepted by the Jewish community during the 1870s and 1880s, when most of them went to school. "Biographical Sketches of Communal Workers," *The American Jewish Year Book,* 5666/1905–1906 (Philadelphia: Jewish Publication Society of America, 1905), 32–118.

44. Cremin, *American Education,* 545.

45. For more on the social significance of expanding education, see Graham, *Community and Class in American Education;* Ravitch and Goodenow, eds., *Educating an Urban People;* and Tyack, *The One Best System.* More sharply critical views include Angus and Mirel, *The Failed Promise of the American High School;* Spring, *Education and the Rise of the Corporate State;* and Thelin, "Left Outs and Left Overs."

46. Cross, ed., *The Educated Woman in America,* presents some of the seminal writings on the subject. For more on this tradition, see Cott, ed., *History of Women in the United States;* Schwager, "Educating Women in America"; Stock, *Better Than Rubies;* and Woody, *A History of Women's Education in the United States.*

47. Burstall, *The Education of Girls in the United States,* 196.

48. Burstall, *The Education of Girls in the United States,* 75, 46.

49. Hurst, *Anatomy of Me,* 42. See also Brandimarte, "Fannie Hurst."

50. Mildred Blum Lowenthal, "About Me, My Family, My World—1898–1981," 1981, SC-1141, AJA. Mildred Blum Lowenthal (b. 1898) was the daughter of Richard and Mary Blum. She grew up in Milwaukee and Chicago. She went to Sabbath school at Sinai Temple in Chicago. She attended the University of Chicago High School and then the Benjamin Dean School in New York.

51. Carmen Kahn Freudenthal, "The First 82 Years of My Life," 7, AJA. Carmen Sylva Henrietta Kahn Freudenthal (b. 1898) grew up in Sedalia, Missouri. Her family went for prolonged visits to European relatives every year. She attended Sedalia High School and then graduated from Hosmer Hall in St. Louis in 1916. She started college at Washington University but graduated from Smith College in 1920. She worked as a social worker and encyclopedia saleswoman. She married Louis E. Freudenthal in 1932 and moved to New Mexico.

52. Elise Stern Haas, oral history, 21, 1972, SC-4430, AJA. Elise Stern Haas (b. 1893) was the daughter of Sigmund and Rosalie Meyer Stern. She grew up in San Franciso, where she attended Miss West's and Miss Murison's schools. She married Walter Haas in 1914.

53. Helen Arnstein Salz, oral history, 8, AJA.

54. Amy Steinhart Braden, oral history, 34, 1965, SC-1294, AJA. Amy Steinhart Braden (1879–1978) grew up in San Francisco. She went to Sabbath school and attended Madame Ziska's school. She graduated from the University of California, Berkeley, in 1900 and became a social worker. She married H. Robert Braden in 1924.

55. Simon, *The Biography of Alice B. Toklas.* Alice Babette Toklas (1877–1967) was the daughter of Ferdinand and Emma Levinsky Toklas. She went to Miss Lake's school in San Francisco and attended the University of Seattle. She was a talented enough musician to consider becoming a concert pianist. Her life was permanently changed when in 1907 she met Gertrude Stein in Paris. They lived together until Stein's death. After Stein's death, Toklas became an author in her own right, publishing several cookbooks and a memoir.

56. Clara Lowenburg Moses, "My Memories," 50, AJA.

57. Gertrude Hess Elkus memoir, 6, Elkus Family Collection, P-686, AJHS. Gertrude Hess Elkus (b. 1873) was the daughter of Joseph and Selma Hess. She grew up in a wealthy New York Jewish family and attended Miss Brackett's school. She married Abram Elkus.

58. Leonora F. Levy's school composition, December 1864, Amy Hart Stewart Papers, SC-12013, AJA.

59. Sulzberger, *Iphigene,* 44, 40–42. Iphigene Ochs Sulzberger (1892–1990) was the daughter of Adolph Ochs and granddaughter of the prominent Reform Rabbi Isaac Mayer Wise. She grew up in New York, where her father's position as owner and publisher of the *New York Times* assured the family of power and prestige. She attended Dr. Julius Sachs's school and the Benjamin Dean School. After graduating from Barnard, she married Arthur Sulzberger and had four children. She was president of the New York Parks Association and a trustee of the *New York Times,* Barnard College, Hebrew Union College-Jewish Institute of Religion, and Cedar Knolls School for Girls.

60. "A Statement of the Theory of Education in the United States of America as Approved by Many Leading Educators," 1874, in Tyack, ed., *Turning Points in American Educational History,* 325.

61. Kerr quoted in Hartman, *A History of the Western High School in Seven Decades, 1844–1913*, 54. Hartman taught at Western for fifty-three years.
62. W. R. Garrett, "The Future High School," 1891, in Tyack, ed., *Turning Points in American Educational History*, 388.
63. Burstall, *The Education of Girls in the United States*, 173.
64. For an example of such hand-wringing, see Charles W. Eliot, "The Gap between the Elementary Schools and the Colleges," 1890, in Tyack, ed., *Turning Points in American Educational History*, 373.
65. Alice Marks's composition book, 1882–1883, Box 2, Alice Davis Menken Papers, P-23, AJHS. Alice Davis Marks Menken (1870–1936) was the daughter of Michael and Miriam Davis Marks. She was descended from several prominent Sephardic families and a member of the DAR. She helped establish the Shearith Israel Sisterhood in New York and became active in juvenile delinquency work, founding the Jewish Board of Guardians and the Jewish Big Sister movement. She wrote several books about women's social welfare. She married Mortimer Menken in 1893 and had one son.
66. Hurst, *Anatomy of Me*, 46.
67. Meckler, *Papa Was a Farmer*, 241.
68. Registration Records, 1899, McKinley High School Registers, Box 2, Series IIC, McKinley High School Records, CHS.
69. Graduation Records, McKinley High School Registers, Box 1, Series IIA, McKinley High School Records, CHS.
70. Schloff, *"And Prairie Dogs Weren't Kosher."*
71. Burstall, *The Education of Girls in the United States*, 193.
72. Hartman, *A History of the Western High School in Seven Decades*, 38; Becker, ed., *Western High School Past and Present*, 183.
73. Gertrude Mandelbaum Ades, "Family History," 7, CHS.
74. Counts, *The Selective Character of American Secondary Education*, 141.
75. Henrietta Moscowitz Voorsanger autobiography, 8, AJA.
76. Lena Meyerson quoted in Rosenbaum and O'Connor-Segerjeds, eds., *Our Story*, 60–61.
77. Minnie D. Louis, "The Industrial Education of Jewish Girls," *Hebrew Standard*, April 5, 1907.
78. See Baum, "What Made Yetta Work?" 32–38, and Hyman, "East European Jewish Women in an Age of Transition, 1880–1930."
79. Leah Dvorah Orenstein, "Leah's Legacy," 51–52, 56, PJAC. Leah Dvorah Orenstein (b. 1913) was the daughter of Yitzhak and Doba Orenstein. She was one of seven siblings. The family immigrated from Russia to the United States in 1920.
80. Cohen, *Out of the Shadow*, 251.
81. Cohen, *Out of the Shadow*, 246.
82. Adler, *A House Is Not a Home*, 17.
83. On women and work, see Kessler-Harris, *Out to Work*.
84. Julia Richman, "Training Home-Makers," *American Hebrew*, September 2, 1898. For more on Richman's troubled relationship with the immigrant Jewish community, see Berrol, "Julia Richman and the German Jewish Establishment."
85. Goldie Bamber, Boston, to Trustees of the Baron de Hirsch Fund, New York, January 1902, reporting on the Hebrew Industrial School of Boston, Box 24, Baron de Hirsch Papers, I-80, AJHS.
86. Report of the Baron de Hirsch Agricultural and Industrial School, January 15, 1899, 5, Box 126, Baron de Hirsch Fund Papers, I-80, AJHS.
87. Quoted in Schloff, *"And Prairie Dogs Weren't Kosher,"* 135–136.
88. Quoted in Becker, ed., *Western High School Past and Present*, 136.
89. *Jewish Messenger*, March 7, 1890.
90. Carmen Kahn Freudenthal, "The First 82 Years of My Life," 7, 1980, SC-3727, AJA.
91. Henrietta Szold, "The Education of the Jewish Girl," *Jewish Comment*, June 12, 1903.
92. *Jewish Messenger*, March 21, 1890.
93. *Jewish Messenger*, March 14, 1890.
94. See, for example, Green, "The 'Boy Problem' and the 'Woman Question.'"
95. Mary A. Livermore, "What Shall We Do with Our Daughters?" quoted in Woody, *A History of Women's Education in the United States*, 65–66.
96. Cremin, *American Education*, 645.

97. "Cardinal Principles of Secondary Education," 1918, in Tyack, ed., *Turning Points in American Educational History,* 396.

98. Finney, *The American Public School,* 195–196.

99. Sylvia Hirsch Lehman Stone, oral history, 8, 1982, SC-12048, AJA. Sylvia Hirsch Lehman Stone (1902–1984) was the daughter of Emil and Cora Altmayer Hirsch. She grew up in San Francisco and graduated from Lowell High School and the University of California, Berkeley. She married Lucien (Mike) Lehmann in 1926 and, following his death, she married her adolescent sweetheart, Dan Stone, Sr., in 1959.

100. Minnie Seltzer Schechter, "Memoirs: Three-Quarters of a Century of Life in Philadelphia," 2–3, 1981, SC-239, PJAC.

101. Setty Swartz's report cards, Box 4, Folder 5, Setty Swartz Kuhn Papers, MS 173, AJA. Setty Swartz Kuhn (b. 1868) was the daughter of Joseph Louis and Caroline Stix Swartz. She grew up in Cincinnati, where she was confirmed by Isaac Mayer Wise at age thirteen. She graduated Hughes High School in 1886 and then went to the Cincinnati College of Music and took Bible classes at Hebrew Union College. She married Simon Kuhn in 1893. A founder of the University School in Cincinnati, she was also involved in the Better Housing League and fundraising for the Palestine Orchestra.

102. Prior to 1900, course work differed little for boys and girls attending coeducational schools. Curriculum lists, 1886–1890, West Division High School Registers, Box 1, Series IB, West Division High School Records, CHS; Curriculum lists, 1899–1903, McKinley High School Registers, Box 1, Series IIB, McKinley High School Records, CHS. See Cremin, *American Education,* 546ff.

103. David E. Weglien quoted in Becker, ed., *Western High School Past and Present,* 114.

104. In general, college preparatory courses were traditionally academic with a special emphasis on languages, while scientific courses emphasized mathematics and science instead of languages, and general courses provided broad academic offerings for students whose formal education would end with high school. Counts, *The Selective Character of American Secondary Education,* 55–56, 69, 59.

105. Hartman, *A History of the Western High School in Seven Decades,* 48, 58, 65; Becker, ed., *Western High School Past and Present,* 33, 57, 64, 66, 69–71, 75–76. Students' report cards bear out these changes. See, for example, Birdie Stein, Western Female High School report cards, Friedenwald Family Papers, 1984.23, JMM; Mabel Kraus, Western High School report cards, Box 1, Folder 12, MS 3, Kraus Family Papers, JMM.

106. Becker, ed., *Western High School Past and Present,* 55, 63–64, 82.

107. John and Evelyn Dewey presented the classic statement of progressive education in *Schools of Tomorrow* (New York: Dutton, 1915). Cremin's *The Transformation of the School* traces these educational developments as they appeared both before and after "progressive education" was labeled as such.

108. For more on the inclusion of vocational training within the rubric of secondary education, see Gillette, *Vocational Education,* and Herick et al., *The Sixth Yearbook of the National Society for the Scientific Study of Education: Part I: Vocational Studies for College Entrance.* Relevant secondary literature includes Kantor, "Choosing a Vocation"; Lazerson and Grubb, eds., *American Education and Vocationalism*; Reese, *Power and the Promise of School Reform*; and Zelizer, *Pricing the Priceless Child.*

109. Curriculum Lists, 1908, Chicago English High and Manual Training School Register, Box 3, Series IIIE, Crane Technical High School Records, CHS; Research files related to article on Lucy Flower School, Nancy Green Papers, CHS. The boys' school was renamed the Crane Technical High School.

110. Tyack and Hansot provide the basic narrative of coeducation in *Learning Together.* Studies of the effects of vocationalism on coeducation include Biklen, "The Progressive Education Movement and the Question of Women"; Graves, *Girls' Schooling during the Progressive Era*; Powers, *The "Girl Question" in Education*; and Rury, *Education and Women's Work.*

111. For a contemporary discussion, see Marvin, *Commercial Education in Secondary Schools.*

112. Allinson, *The Public Schools and Women in Office Service,* 25, 12.

113. Counts, *The Selective Character of American Secondary Education,* 111.

114. In continuing to value a broad education, parents, teachers, and students drew on nineteenth-century traditions of liberal education. As one representative expression of the older traditions, see Orton, ed., *The Liberal Education of Women.*

115. George Howland, *Thirty-Fourth Annual Report of the Board of Education of the City of Chicago, 1887–1888,* 81, filed in Nancy Green Papers, CHS.

116. Henry Leipziger, "Some Tendencies of Modern Education," Proceedings of the Twelfth Summer Assembly, 1910, 122–123, Jewish Chautauqua Society Papers, MS-NAT.J185, AJHS.

117. Goldstein, *A Pioneer Woman,* 12. Bertha Markowitz Goldstein (b. 1895) was the daughter of Morris and Dora Rosenberg Markowitz. The family moved to New York in 1899, but Bertha lived with her grandparents and graduated from high school in Burlington, Vermont. She graduated from Hunter College in 1915 and became heavily involved with the Zionist group Pioneer Women.

118. Rose Zetzer, scrapbook, 1921, Box 1, Folder 14, MS 86, Rose Zetzer Collection, JMM. Rose Zetzer (b. 1904) was the daughter of Jacob and Baila Hendler Zetzer. She grew up in Baltimore, where she graduated from Eastern Female High School in 1921. In 1925, she became the first woman to be admitted to the Maryland Bar Association. She was also a member of Hadassah and the National Woman's Party.

119. Woody, *A History of Women's Education in the United States,* v. 2, 229. Woody, like most other educational historians since his book first came out in 1929, framed virtually all of his discussion of coeducation around the issue of coeducational colleges and universities rather than high schools. See Graves, *Girls' Schooling during the Progressive Era,* for a recent exception.

120. Nathan, *Once upon a Time and Today,* 40–41.

121. Hart, *The Pleasure Is Mine,* 20.

122. Nathan, *Once upon a Time and Today,* 42.

123. Finney, *The American Public School,* 182.

124. Undated news clipping about the graduation exercises of South Division High School's senior class, 1891, Box 2278f, Folder "Education," Jennie Franklin Purvin Papers, MS 502, AJA.

125. For more on G. Stanley Hall's theories as related to girls' adolescent education, see Goodsell, *The Education of Women;* Grinder, "The Concept of Adolescence in the Genetic Psychology of G. Stanley Hall"; and Rury, "Vocationalism for Home and Work."

126. Quoted in Burstall, *The Education of Girls in the United States,* 164.

127. J. E. Armstrong described this experiment in "Limited Segregation," *School Review* 14 (Jan.–Dec. 1906): 726–738.

128. Quoted in Hartman, *A History of the Western High School in Seven Decades,* 80.

129. The essays in Blake et al., *The Education of the Modern Girl,* demonstrate how inevitable was the application of adult gender ascriptions to adolescents. Also underlining the separate status of girls' education and work were vocational manuals for girls, such as Laselle and Wiley, *Vocations for Girls;* Wanger, *What Girls Can Do;* and Weaver, *Profitable Vocations for Girls.*

130. Morris, comp., *History and Records of the Class of 1885, Chicago West Division High School,* CHS. Esther Friend Falkenau (b. 1867) grew up in Chicago. She was confirmed by Bernhard Felsenthal at Zion Temple in 1881 and graduated from West Division High School in 1885. She married Harry Falkenau in 1893. Carrie Hershman (b. 1868) grew up in Chicago. She graduated from West Division High School in 1885 and married Isaac Guthmann in 1892.

131. Lizzie Black Kander, "Then and Now," written for her high school reunion in 1902, Lizzie Black Kander Papers, Microfilm reels 1400–1401, AJA. Lizzie Black Kander (1858–1940) was the daughter of John and Mary Pereles Black. She grew up in Milwaukee and graduated from Milwaukee High School in 1878. She married Simon Kander in 1881. Involved in the Milwaukee Jewish Mission, she served as president of "The Settlement" and presided over its most famous project, *The Settlement Cook Book,* which went through numerous printings after its initial 1903 publication. She supported vocational education for women and served on the Milwaukee school board.

132. September 6, 1876, Fannie Allen diary, ACC 1602, PJAC; Ella Jacobs's autograph book, 1876–1889, SC 223, PJAC. Anna Allen was Amelia and Fannie Allen's younger sister.

133. Burstall, *The Education of Girls in the United States,* 71.

134. Nathan, *Once upon a Time and Today,* 44–45.

135. Helen Arnstein Salz, oral history, 22, AJA.

136. Leaphart, ed., "Montana Episodes," 90. Belle Fligelman Winestine (1891–1985) was the daughter of Herman and Minnie Fligelman, who immigrated from Romania to Helena, Montana, in 1889. Belle and Frieda were raised by their father and their stepmother, Getty Vogelman. Like her older sister, Belle was determined to go to college. She graduated from the University of

Wisconsin and worked as a journalist and woman suffrage activist. She served as Congress-woman Jeanette Rankin's legislative assistant and remained politically active for decades, successfully running for the Montana Senate in 1932. She married Norman Winestine and had three children.

137. At tuition-free City College and Hunter College in New York, Jewish student representation was significantly higher. By 1920, Jewish students comprised 78.7 percent of the student body at City College and 38.7 percent of the student body at Hunter. The large discrepancy between the male and female percentages reflects the continuing reluctance of parents to send their daughters to college. "Professional Tendencies among Jewish Schools in Colleges, Universities, and Professional Schools," *The American Jewish Year Book* 5681/1920–1921 (Philadelphia: Jewish Publication Society of America, 1920), 383–393.

138. For more on this relationship, see Bledstein, *The Culture of Professionalism*; Cremin, *American Education*; and Fass, *The Damned and the Beautiful*.

139. These statistics, which refer to white students only, are drawn from the Commissioner of Education's annual reports. Burstall, *The Education of Girls in the United States*, 196.

140. "Professional Tendencies among Jewish Students in Colleges, Universities, and Professional Schools," *The American Jewish Year Book* 5681/1920–1921 (Philadelphia: Jewish Publication Society of America, 1920), 383–393.

141. Bertha Szold's certificate of proficiency, signed by Ada E. Adams, 1891, L88.11.359, JMM. Many years later an article about Bertha Szold recounted the story. *Baltimore Evening Sun*, December 21, 1953, photocopy in Oheb Shalom Collection, L88.11.59, JMM. Bertha Szold Levin (1874–1958) was the daughter of Rabbi Benjamin and Sophie Schaar Szold and Henrietta Szold's younger sister. She grew up in Baltimore, where she graduated from Western Female High School and attended the Misses Adams' school before graduating from Bryn Mawr in 1894. She married Louis H. Levin in 1901 and had five children. A teacher before her marriage, she eventually became the first woman appointed to the Baltimore City school board. She worked on Baltimore's *Jewish Comment* and was also active in Hadassah, the women's Zionist organization founded by her sister.

142. Sulzberger, *Iphigene*, 67–68.

143. National Education Association, *Report of the Committee of Ten on Secondary School Studies*, 51–53. This interpretation of the report follows Krug, *The Shaping of the American High School*, 39ff.

144. The history of women's education has focused on higher education to the near exclusion of secondary education. See, for example, Frankfort, *Collegiate Women*; Gordon, *Gender and Higher Education in the Progressive Era*; Graham, "Expansion and Exclusion"; Newcomer, *A Century of Higher Education for American Women*; and Solomon, *In the Company of Educated Women*.

145. Jennie Mannheimer, "Higher Education for Women," address read at the Oratorical Exercises of the University of Cincinnati, reprinted in *Sabbath Visitor*, May 29, 1891. Jennie Mannheimer (1870–1943) grew up in Cincinnati, where she was confirmed in 1885 and graduated from Hughes High School in 1888. She attended the University of Cincinnati. Her mother, Louise Mannheimer, wrote about child care and mothering. Jennie became a drama coach and oratory instructor. She was director of the School of Expression at the Cincinnati College of Music and eventually opened the Jane Manner Drama Studio.

146. The American Jewish press tended to support women's higher education, albeit cautiously. See, for example, *American Hebrew*, November 20, 1891.

147. Lizzie Spiegel Barbe, *Memoirs* (n.p., n.d.), Spiegel Family Papers, Coll. 78, CJA. Lizzie Theresa Spiegel Barbe (1856–1943) was the daughter of Marcus and Caroline Frances Hamlin Spiegel. Her mother was a convert from Quakerism. After her father's death during Civil War military service, the family moved to Chicago, where she was confirmed at Zion Temple by Bernhard Felsenthal. She attended both private and public schools in Chicago but did not graduate from high school. She became very active in the Chicago section of the National Council of Jewish Women.

148. Henrietta Szold, Baltimore, to John F. Goucher, Baltimore, undated, Box 1, Folder 1, MS 38, Henrietta Szold Papers, JMM. The Alumnae Association was founded by the Class of 1897 in 1899, and Henrietta Szold was the first president. Hartman, *A History of the Western High School in Seven Decades*, 67.

149. On "college girl" fiction see Inness, "'It Is Pluck but Is It Sense?'"

150. "What the American College Means to the Jewess," *American Hebrew*, June 26, 1914.

151. Sylvia Hirsch Lehman Stone, oral history, 16, 19, AJA.

152. *Sunday Jewish Courier,* November 14, 1920, quoted in Marcus, ed., *The American Jewish Woman,* 628–629.

NOTES TO CHAPTER 3

1. Cohen, *Out of the Shadow,* 127, 198.

2. More recent historiography rejects the "German versus Russian" model, but there is no denying the presence of serious communal divides. For an example of the older model, see Sorin, "Mutual Contempt, Mutual Benefit."

3. For overview discussions of this dynamic among immigrant groups other than Jews, see Bodnar, *The Transplanted;* Dinnerstein, Nichols, and Reimers, *Natives and Strangers;* and Perlmann, *Ethnic Differences.*

4. Minnie D. Louis, "Educational Work among Jewish Girls," *American Hebrew,* July 22, 1898.

5. For more on this strategy, see Carlson, *The Quest for Conformity,* and Weiss, ed., *American Education and the European Immigrant.*

6. In big cities with large immigrant populations like Chicago and New York, extremely crowded school districts meant that children were not even guaranteed regular elementary education. See Berrol, "Immigrant Children at School, 1880–1940," and Brumberg, *Going to America, Going to School.*

7. The importance of education is apparent in the histories of Jewish communities in America. See, for example, Cutler, *The Jews of Chicago;* Berrol, *East Side/East End;* Goren, *New York's Jews and the Quest for Community;* Sarna and Smith, eds., *The Jews of Boston;* and Friedman, ed., *When Philadelphia Was the Capital of Jewish America.*

8. Polacheck, *I Came a Stranger,* 37–39. It should be noted, however, that Hilda enjoyed the education provided by the school and insisted that she never felt patronized in any way.

9. Letter reporting 1894 activities of the Philadelphia Committee of the Baron de Hirsch Fund, 5 February 1895, Box 15, Volume I 11/94–4/99, Baron de Hirsch Fund Papers, I-80, AJHS.

10. Berrol, "Julia Richman and the German Jewish Establishment"; Berrol, *Julia Richman,* 44–46.

11. Circulation list of the Associated Jewish Press, reproduced in *Jewish Directory of Chicago,* 1884, CHS.

12. For more on the Jewish press, see Park's contemporary account, *The Immigrant Press and Its Control.* See also Goren, "The Jewish Press," and Howe, *World of Our Fathers.*

13. Specialized studies include Baader, "From the 'Priestess of the Home' to 'The Rabbi's Brilliant Daughter'"; Loth, "The *American Jewess*"; and Seller, "Women Journalists and the Women's Page of the *Jewish Daily Forward.*"

14. Rabbi David Philipson, "The Ideal Jewess," *American Jewess* 4 (March 1897): 257–262.

15. Rosa Sonneschein, "The Woman Who Talks," *American Jewess* 1 (August 1895): 260; *American Jewess* 1 (April 1895): 39.

16. In 1884, *Sabbath Visitor* had a circulation of 5,500 households. Circulation list of the Associated Jewish Press, reprinted in *Jewish Directory of Chicago,* 1884, CHS. It is likely that issues were passed around among friends and family, so that the readership was even wider than the circulation numbers indicate. Little has been published on Jewish children's periodicals, but several Hebrew Union College term papers have studied them. For example, see Baskin, "The Image of Women in the *Sabbath Visitor*"; Cohn, "*The Sabbath Visitor,* A Child's Paper"; and Heneson, "The Image of Women in *Young Israel* and *The Sabbath Visitor* during the Years 1876 and 1877."

17. Rose Lenore Cohn Brown, "The Story of the Years in Colorado from 1890–1903," 40, 1971, SC-1435, AJA. Rose Lenore Cohn grew up in Carbondale, Colorado, and later married Abraham L. Brown.

18. *Sabbath Visitor,* March 16, 1883.

19. Flora Rothschild, Greenville, to *Sabbath-School Visitor,* Cincinnati, 30 December 1874. The publication changed names slightly several times but was called *Sabbath Visitor* for most of its run.

20. "Beruria, the Wife of Rabbi Meir," *Sabbath-School Visitor,* April 1874.

21. Seller, "Women Journalists and the Women's Page of the *Jewish Daily Forward.*"

22. Metzker, ed., *A Bintel Brief*, 70–71, 55–56.

23. Bella Cauman, "Zionism," *S.E.G. News*, March 13, 1915; Sadie Guttentag, "Education of Women," *S.E.G. News*, December 11, 1915, in bound volume of *S.E.G. News* issues, 1914–1917, AJHS.

24. Pearl Frank, "Education," *The Club Scroll* 1 (June 1923), monthly publication of Baltimore's Synagogue House, 1994.112.10, JMM.

25. *Alliance Review* 2 (January 1902): 311–312, Box 2, Educational Alliance Papers, MS-JC.E28, AJHS. Rose Lisner Sommerfeld (d. 1927) had been the supervisor of Baltimore's Russian evening school and then organized the Daughters of Israel Home for Working Girls in Baltimore. She was a charter member of the National Council of Jewish Women. From 1889 to 1924, she served as the Resident Directress of the Clara de Hirsch Home for Working Girls in New York. Belle Lindner Israels Moskowitz (1877–1933) was the daughter of Isidor and Esther Freyer Lindner, immigrants from East Prussia. She grew up in New York and attended public schools and Columbia University's Teachers College. In 1900, she began working at the Educational Alliance, where she organized entertainments and exhibits until she married Charles Henry Israels in 1903. They had three children. After her marriage, she worked with the National Council of Jewish Women and the United Hebrew Charities and wrote for *The Survey*. When her husband died in 1911, Belle went to work in the Labor Department of a garment industry manufacturers association and then became an industry consultant. She married social worker Henry Moskowitz in 1914. She helped elect Al Smith as governor and became his major political advisor.

26. For more on the S.E.G. see Larson, "The Saturday Evening Girls."

27. Rebecca G. Heiman, "Library Clubhouse Report, 1916–1917," *S.E.G. News*, June 9, 1917, in bound volume of *S.E.G. News* issues, 1914–1917, AJHS.

28. Mrs. Isidor (Ida) Straus, "The Recreation Room for Girls," *Jewish Charity* 4 (January 1905): 117–119. Ida Straus was married to one of the Straus brothers of Macy's Department store fame and fortune. She and her husband were active philanthropists and achieved immortality when they died together on the *Titanic* in 1912.

29. Notes on the Louisa M. Alcott Club, Louisa M. Alcott Club Papers, I-210, AJHS.

30. For a history of the Educational Alliance, see Bellow, *The Educational Alliance*, and Howe, *World of Our Fathers*. On the Chicago Hebrew Institute, see Philip L. Seman, "A People's Institute," undated *Jewish Charities* article pasted in scrapbook, Box 1, Philip L. Seman Papers, MS 578, AJA. Seman was the superintendent of the Chicago Hebrew Institute. For the Young Women's Union, see *The History of the Young Women's Union of Philadelphia, 1885–1910*, and Rose, "World of Our Mothers."

31. Announcement of Courses, 1900–1901, 11, Educational Alliance Papers, MS-JCC.E28, AJHS.

32. David Blaustein, New York, to A. S. Solomons for the Baron de Hirsch Fund, New York, 17 May 1900, Box 27, Folder "NY Edu Alliance," Baron de Hirsch Fund Papers, I-80, AJHS.

33. Annual Report, 1895, 11–12, Educational Alliance Papers, MS-JCC.E28, AJHS.

34. Samuel Greenbaum, "Report of Committee on Women's Work," printed in Annual Report, 1895, 39–42, Educational Alliance Papers, MS-JCC.E28, AJHS.

35. David Blaustein, "From Oppression to Freedom," copy of an article published in *Charities*, April 4, 1903, Box 2, Folder 7, Paul Abelson Papers, MS 4, AJA.

36. Annual Report, 1902, 40, Educational Alliance Papers, MS-JCC.E28, AJHS.

37. Annual Report, 1902, 28–29, Educational Alliance Papers, MS-JCC.E28, AJHS.

38. Announcement of Courses, 1900–1901, 29, Educational Alliance Papers, MS-JCC.E28, AJHS.

39. William H. Maxwell, "Address," printed in Annual Report, 1902, 43, Educational Alliance Papers, MS-JCC.E28, AJHS.

40. William H. Maxwell, "Address," printed in Annual Report, 1902, 42, 44, Educational Alliance Papers, MS-JCC.E28, AJHS.

41. Annual Report, 1902, 19, Educational Alliance Papers, MS-JCC.E28, AJHS.

42. Mrs. Morris Loeb, Report of the President of the Women's Auxiliary Society to the Educational Alliance, printed in Annual Report, 1907–1908, 87, Educational Alliance Papers, MS-JCC.E28, AJHS.

43. William H. Maxwell, "Address," printed in Annual Report, 1902, 44, Educational Alliance Papers, MS-JCC.E28, AJHS.

44. Philip L. Seman, "What Does Our Educational Department Do?" *Chicago Hebrew Institute Observer*, February 1914.

258 | Notes to Chapter 3

45. An article in *Jewish Messenger*, May 2, 1890, describes the activities of the Jewish Training School, as does Polacheck in *I Came a Stranger*.

46. Mrs. Julius (Goldie) Stone, Chicago, to H. L. Sabsovitch for the Baron de Hirsch Fund, New York, 7 July 1910, Box 24, Folder "Chicago Heb Institute," Baron de Hirsch Fund Papers, I-80, AJHS.

47. Constitution of the Chicago Hebrew Institute, quoted in Report of the Chicago Hebrew Institute, 1919, 9, Council of Jewish Federation and Welfare Funds Papers, I-69, AJHS.

48. Report of the Chicago Hebrew Institute, 1919, 28, Council of Jewish Federation and Welfare Funds Papers, I-69, AJHS. See also "Our Educational Activities," *Chicago Hebrew Institute Observer*, February 1915.

49. Report of the Chicago Hebrew Institute, 1919, 28, Council of Jewish Federation and Welfare Fund Papers, I-69, AJHS. Philip L. Seman also elaborated on this broader understanding of Americanization in "An Interpretation of Americanization," *The Reform Advocate*, October 19, 1918.

50. Report of the Chicago Hebrew Institute, 1919, 2, 4, 10, 13–14, Council of Jewish Federation and Welfare Funds Papers, I-69, AJHS; Philip L. Seman, "Progress of Some Current Institute Activities," *Chicago Hebrew Institute Observer*, August 1914. See also Gems, "The Rise of Sport at a Jewish Settlement House."

51. Report of the Chicago Hebrew Institute, 1919, 18, Council of Jewish Federation and Welfare Funds Papers, I-69, AJHS.

52. Report of the Chicago Hebrew Institute, 1919, 22–26, Council of Jewish Federation and Welfare Funds Papers, I-69, AJHS.

53. Joseph Kahn and Joseph J. Klein, "Preliminary Outline of Report on the Educational Activities, Current and Proposed, of the Young Women's Hebrew Association," Box 1, Folder 64, Young Women's Hebrew Association Records, YM/WHA.

54. Joseph Kahn and Joseph J. Klein, "Preliminary Outline of Report on the Educational Activities, Current and Proposed, of the Young Women's Hebrew Association," Box 1, Folder 64, YM/WHA.

55. Superintendent's Report, July 1, 1907, Box 2, Folder 9, YM/WHA.

56. Class Committee minutes, December 5, 1916, Box 1, Folder 58, YM/WHA.

57. Class Committee minutes, December 5, 1916, Box 1, Folder 58; Superintendent's Report, November 1917, Box 2, Folder 15, YM/WHA.

58. Superintendent's Report, September 1, 1907, Box 2, Folder 9; Annual Report, 1922, Box 2, Folder 16, YM/WHA.

59. Superintendent's Report, September 1, 1907, Box 2, Folder 9, YM/WHA.

60. Annual Report, 1923, Box 2, Folder 17, YM/WHA.

61. For a general history of the Young Women's Union, see Rose, "World of Our Mothers."

62. For an overview comparison to non-Jewish women's involvement in settlement house activity, see Carson, *Settlement Folk*, and Jane Addams's writings on the subject, including "The Subjective Necessity for Social Settlements," in Addams et al., *Philanthropy and Social Progress*.

63. The number of married women on the board gradually increased as the original founders married but wished to remain involved with the YWU. A core group married late or never and continued to work with the YWU for decades. See the board member lists in *The History of the Young Women's Union of Philadelphia, 1885–1910*.

64. Bodek, "'Making Do,'" 156. *History of the Young Women's Union of Philadelphia, 1885–1910* is the single best source of information on YWU programs. Mary Cohen (1854–1911) was the daughter of Henry and Mathilda Samuel Cohen. She grew up in Philadelphia, where she attended the Misses Lymans' school. She became a prolific writer who contributed frequently to the American Jewish press. Active in Philadelphia's Jewish community, she became the superintendent of the Hebrew Sunday School Society. Katherine Cohen (1859–1914) was Mary Cohen's sister. She attended the Chestnut Street Seminary and studied art in Philadelphia and New York. She also spent time studying in Europe and developed a career as a sculptor. Involved in the Jewish community as well, she illustrated books for Jewish children and headed the choir at Philadelphia's Mikveh Israel. Several of her sculpture commissions were for Jewish institutions such as Gratz College. Alice Jastrow was the daughter of prominent Philadelphia rabbi Marcus Jastrow.

65. Quoted in Rose, "World of Our Mothers," 101. Mary and Katherine Cohen, Amelia Allen, Alice Jastrow, and Ella Jacobs were all the daughters of well-known, established Jewish

families in Philadelphia. Most of them were in their early twenties when they founded the YWU with Fanny Binswanger.

66. Hebrew Education Society, Annual Report, 1888, 21–22, Box 1, Folder 1, Hebrew Education Society of Philadelphia Records, MS 59, PJAC. Annie Jastrow was Alice's sister and the daughter of Rabbi Marcus Jastrow.

67. *The History of the Young Women's Union of Philadelphia, 1885–1910*; Evelyn Bodek, "'Making Do,'" 157.

68. See Hartogensis, "The Russian Night School of Baltimore," and Levin, "Henrietta Szold and the Russian Immigrant School."

69. *Jewish Comment*, September 27, 1901.

70. Schneiderman with Goldthwaite, *All for One*, 39. Rose Schneiderman (1992–1972) was the daughter of Samuel and Deborah Rothman Schneiderman. Her family immigrated to the United States from Poland when she was eight years old, and she entered the paid work force five years later. Trained as a cap maker, Schneiderman forged a lifelong commitment to trade unionism, socialism, and feminism on the shop floor. She was a highly successful organizer in the New York Women's Trade Union League and the International Ladies' Garment Workers Union as well as the suffrage movement. Franklin D. Roosevelt later appointed her to the National Labor Advisory Board.

71. David Blaustein, "The Inherent Cultural Forces of the Lower East Side," *Jewish Comment*, December 4, 1903.

72. Stone, *My Caravan of Years*, 90–91. Goldie Tuvin Stone (b. 1874) was born Olga Tuvin in Ploksch, Russia. She immigrated at age fifteen and lived with relatives in New York. She later moved to Chicago and became very active in helping Jewish immigrants there. She married Julius Stone.

73. Unidentified newspaper article, December 1910, clipping in Box 1, Folder 5, Esther Weinshenker Natkin Papers, Coll. 150, CJA.

74. Excerpt of John Foster Carr, "Guide to the United States for the Jewish Immigrant," reprinted in *Jewish Comment*, August 30, 1912.

75. Goldie Prelutsky Covan's memoirs, 1914–1916, translated from the Yiddish, Coll. 125–056, CJA. Goldie Prelutsky Covan (1901–1979) was the daughter of Todra and Bassie Lea Prelutsky. She was born in eastern Europe and immigrated to Chicago at age thirteen in 1914. She wrote her memoirs soon after arriving because she wanted to keep a record of her life and the problems caused by immigration. In 1924, she married Morris Covan.

76. Kriesberg, *Hard Soil, Tough Roots*, 150. Bessie Turnonsky Kriesberg was Rose Turnonsky's daughter.

77. Hebrew Education Society, Annual Report, 1912, 10, Box 1, Folder 1, Hebrew Education Society of Philadelphia Records, MS 59, PJAC.

78. O'Brien, *English for Foreigners*, 1909, quoted in Tyack, ed., *Turning Points in American Educational History*, 240.

79. O'Brien, *English for Foreigners*, 1909, quoted in Tyack, ed., *Turning Points in American Educational History*, 239–240.

80. Friedman, *A Memoir* (Chicago: privately printed), 3–4, Asher Library, Spertus Museum of Judaica, Chicago. Ruth Labes Friedman was Rose Schachter Labes's daughter.

81. Joseph Kahn and Joseph J. Klein, "Preliminary Outline of Report on the Educational Activities, Current and Proposed, of the Young Women's Hebrew Association," Box 1, Folder 64, YM/WHA; Report of the Chicago Hebrew Institute, 1919, 27, Council of Jewish Federations and Welfare Funds Papers, I-69, AJHS.

82. Counts, *The Selective Character of American Secondary Education*, 109.

83. David Blaustein, "From Oppression to Freedom," copy of an article published in *Charities*, April 4, 1903, Box 2, Folder 7, Paul Abelson Papers, MS 4, AJA.

84. Italics in the original. Mathilde Schechter, "Annual Report of the President," 1907, 9, Columbia Religious and Industrial School for Girls Papers, I-24, AJHS. Mathilde Roth Schechter (1857–1924) was born and orphaned in Germany, where she attended local schools and the Breslau Teacher's Seminary. She taught in Germany for several years and then went to study at Queens College in England, where she met and married world-renowned scholar Solomon Schechter in 1887. They had three children. In 1902, the Schechters moved to New York so Solomon could take up his new appointment as president of the Jewish Theological Seminary. Mathilde presided over a home that welcomed Jewish scholars and activists. She was

also involved with Jewish communal work, establishing the Columbia Religious and Industrial School for Girls and founding the Women's League of the United Synagogue of America.

85. Spewack, *Streets*, 66. Bella Cohen Spewack (1899–1990) was born in Romania and came to New York as a toddler after her parents divorced. Her mother remarried in 1911 but was soon abandoned by her new husband. Fanny managed to keep her daughter out of the workforce long enough for Bella to graduate from public high school and begin her career as a journalist. In 1922, Bella married fellow writer Sam Spewack. Together they launched a highly successful career as lyricists, librettists, and screenwriters, collaborating on such classics as *Kiss Me Kate*. They rarely wrote about Jewish topics but remained involved in the community, contributing time and money to various Jewish causes.

86. Fanny Goldstein, editorial, *S.E.G. News* January 8, 1916, in bound volume of *S.E.G. News* issues, 1914–1917, AJHS.

87. Henrietta Szold, "The Education of the Jewish Girl," *Jewish Comment*, June 12, 1903.

88. Bella Weretnikow Rosenbaum, "My Life," Bella Weretnikow Rosenbaum Papers, MS 179, AJA.

89. Sadie American for the National Council of Jewish Women, New York, open letter to National Council of Jewish Women members, 25 September 1913, Ida Davis Papers, SC-2685, AJA. Sadie American (1862–1944) was the only child of Oscar and Amelia Smith American. She grew up in Chicago and graduated from high school there. In 1893, she became a founding member of the National Council of Jewish Women, which she then represented in the United States and abroad for decades. She was also active in the Illinois Consumers' League in Chicago and Jewish social service in New York.

90. Bella Weretnikow Rosenbaum, "My Life," AJA.

91. Lillian Herstein, transcript of oral history, 1970–1971, Chicago Sinai Congregation Oral History Project, Coll. 240, CJA. Ethel Lillian Herstein (1886–1983) was the daughter of Wolf and Ciipe Belle Herstein, who emigrated from Lithuania to Chicago shortly after the Civil War. Her father died when she was twelve and her mother ran a bookstore. She was the only one of her siblings to finish high school, and she graduated from Northwestern University in 1907. As a high school teacher, she became active in her union and eventually served on the executive board of the Chicago Teachers Union. She worked with the Women's Trade Union League and as a union organizer in several industries. She was also involved with the Jewish Labor Committee, Hadassah, and the National Council of Jewish Women.

92. Gertrude Mandelbaum Ades, "Family History," 7–8, 1992, CHS.

93. During this period, the American Jewish community adopted the definition of an orphan as a child without one or both parents. See Friedman, *These Are Our Children*, and Bogen, *The Luckiest of Orphans*.

94. *The Chicago Jewish Community Blue Book*, 15–16.

95. *American Israelite*, July 25, 1873.

96. S. M. Fleischman, "Education of the Orphan," Proceedings of the Second Summer Assembly, 28, Jewish Chautauqua Society Papers, MS-NAT.J185, AJHS.

97. Goldstein, *The Home on Gorham Street and the Voices of Its Children*, 51–55; Zmora, *Orphanages Reconsidered*, 20, 41, 109–110, 153.

98. Leopold Deutelbam, *Tender Memories* (Chicago: n.p., 1937), 40, 18–19.

99. This argument is developed at length in Zmora, *Orphanages Reconsidered*, 93–97, 99–100, 105–110, 124–125.

100. Zmora, *Orphanages Reconsidered*, 162–163.

101. London, *A Girl from Boston*, 45–46. Hannah London (b. 1894) grew up in Boston. She attended Girls' High and graduated from Radcliffe before becoming the Girls' Club supervisor at Hecht House.

102. Copy of *Baltimore Sun* article on Daughters in Israel, July 1895, Vertical File—Daughters in Israel, JMM.

103. *The Chicago Jewish Community Blue Book*, 94.

104. Oscar Leonard, "A Truly Jewish Home for Girls," *Jewish Charities* 6 (December 1915): 75–76.

105. Daughters in Israel Annual Report, 1912, Vertical File—Daughters in Israel, JMM; Rachel Frank Skutch, "Report of Chairman of Trade Training," 1913, Vertical File—Daughters in Israel, JMM. For an extended treatment of the Clara de Hirsch Home for Working Girls in New York, see my article "Jewish Women and Vocational Education in New York City, 1885–

1925," chapter 4 of my dissertation, "'A Fair Portion of the World's Knowledge,'" and Sinkoff, "Educating for 'Proper' Jewish Womanhood."

106. Dora Weil, Superintendent's Report, 1915, Vertical File—Daughters in Israel, JMM.

107. Regina Weinberg, Superintendent's Report, 1920, Vertical File—Daughters in Israel, JMM.

108. Regina Weinberg, Superintendent's Report, 1920, Vertical File—Daughters in Israel, JMM.

109. Miriam K. Arnold, "Industrial Home for Jewish Girls of Philadelphia, PA," in *Proceedings of the Council of Jewish Women, Fifth Triennial Convention, Cincinnati, Ohio, December the First to the Eighth, 1908,* 206.

110. *The Chicago Jewish Community Blue Book,* 94.

111. "The Problem of the Immigrant Girl," *American Hebrew,* August 5, 1910; Baron de Hirsch Fund, New York, to Jewish Colonization Association, Paris, 17 May 1912, Box 16, Baron de Hirsch Fund Papers, I-80, AJHS; Carrie Wise, New York, to Jewish Colonization Association, Paris, 23 May 1912, Box 16, Baron de Hirsch Fund Papers, I-80, AJHS.

112. Sadie American, New York, to Jewish Colonization Association, Paris, 20 September 1910, Box 16, Baron de Hirsch Fund Papers, I-80, AJHS; Sadie American, "Address," *Jewish International Conference on the Suppression of the Traffic in Girls and Women,* 64–67.

113. Dorm Committee Reports, 1914, June 4, 1916, Box 3, Folder 6, YM/WHA.

114. Dorm Committee Minutes, 1914, Box 3, Folder 6; June 1916, Box 3, Folder 6; December 1917, Box 3, Folder 6; March 1919, Box 1, Folder 60, YM/WHA.

115. Lerner, *In Retrospect,* 63–66.

116. Class Committee minutes, December 5, 1916, Box 1, Folder 58, YM/WHA.

117. Annual Report, 1905, 8, Box 1, Folder 1, Hebrew Education Society of Philadelphia Records, MS 59, PJAC.

118. Clara de Hirsch Home Board minutes, April 24, 1898, Box 1, Folder 1, Clara de Hirsch Home for Working Girls Records, YM/WHA; *The History of the Young Women's Union of Philadelphia, 1885–1910.*

119. Superintendent's Report, July 1, 1907, Box 2, Folder 9, YM/WHA; program for the entertainment given by the alumnae club of the Columbia Religious and Industrial School at the Hebrew Technical School for Girls, March 29, 1908, Columbia Religious and Industrial School for Girls Papers, I-24, AJHS. For extended treatment of the Hebrew Technical School for Girls, an important New York institution, see my article, "Jewish Women and Vocational Education in New York City, 1880–1925"; chapter 4 in my dissertation, "'A Fair Portion of the World's Knowledge'"; and Joselit, *Aspiring Women.*

120. Stone, *My Caravan of Years,* 92.

NOTES TO CHAPTER 4

1. January 1, May 13, February 5, 1876, Amelia Allen diary, ACC 1603, PJAC.

2. April 18, 1875, Fannie Allen diary, ACC 1602, PJAC.

3. Historians of the Jewish experience in America have made brief references to the innovation of coeducational religious schooling and inclusion of girls in some community programs, but no comprehensive history exists. For example, the following studies all discuss Jewish education without paying much attention to the opportunities and limitations girls faced: Bloom, "History of Jewish Education in Baltimore"; Gartner, ed. *Jewish Education in the United States*; King, "Jewish Education in Philadelphia"; Korey, "The History of Jewish Education in Chicago"; Litov, "The History of Jewish Education in Washington, D.C., 1852–1970"; Pilch, ed., *A History of Jewish Education in America*; Reimer, "Passionate Visions in Contest"; Todes, "The History of Jewish Education in Philadelphia, 1782–1873." The comprehensive bibliography edited by Drachler, *A Bibliography of Jewish Education in the United States,* has remarkably few entries on girls' Jewish education. For a rare exception, albeit one that focuses on an earlier period, see Ashton's work, particularly *Rebecca Gratz.*

4. For a useful, though not always rigorous, overview of girls' religious education, see Zolty, *"And All Your Children Shall Be Learned."*

5. For more on the early girls' schools, see Hyman, *Gender and Assimilation in Modern Jewish History,* especially chapters 2 and 4.

6. Mrs. Harry Sternberger, "Jewish Womanhood: Its Power and Opportunity," *American Hebrew,* August 22, 1919.

7. Minnie D. Louis, quoted in *Jewish Messenger*, March 21, 1890.

8. Emphasis added. Bernard M. Kaplan, "Judaism and Americanism," *The Hebrew Watchword and Instructor* (February 1898): 3–4.

9. Emphasis added. Henry Herzberg, "The Scope of Education," Proceedings of the Second Summer Assembly, 28, 1898, Jewish Chautauqua Society Papers, MS-NAT.J185, AJHS.

10. For a discussion of the ways in which turn-of-the-century American Jewry as a whole viewed women as potential saviors of Judaism, see Sarna, *A Great Awakening*, 18–27.

11. Women and the Synagogue: A Symposium," *American Hebrew*, April 14, 1916.

12. Women and the Synagogue: A Symposium," *American Hebrew*, April 14, 1916.

13. Goldman contends that "the inability of the American Jewish community to create institutions strong enough to frame a vital and observant Jewish domestic life," in combination with American Jewry's desire to bring Judaism in line with other American religions, profoundly weakened women's traditional religious domesticity. This argument oversimplifies the extent to which Jewish women's religious domesticity and the Jewish family both functioned as institutions in and of themselves. While some religious rituals may have been abandoned by many American Jews, the relationship between public and private Judaism was not a zero-sum game. The pervasive rhetoric about Jewish women's religious domesticity persisted in sermons, the press, and private writings long after women had secured a more prominent place in the synagogue. Nineteenth-century American Jewish girls may have grown accustomed to practicing their Judaism within the space of the synagogue, but they also experienced Judaism within the home and generally expected religious domesticity to be a part of their future lives. *Beyond the Synagogue Gallery*, especially 33–37.

14. *Jewish Messenger*, June 21, 1867.

15. Dr. Herman Baar, "The Martyr-Mother," *American Hebrew*, December 23, 1887.

16. Raphall, comp. and trans., *Ruchamah*.

17. "Exercise for a Wife Who is Married to an Irreligious Husband," in Raphall, comp. and trans., *Ruchamah*, 131–132. For another example, see Mayer, trans., *Hours of Devotion*.

18. Hirschowitz, comp., *Yohale Sarah*.

19. Gertrude Mandelbaum Ades, "Family History," 7, 1992, CHS.

20. Lindheim, *Parallel Quest*, 7. Irma Levy Lindheim (1886–1978) was the daughter of Robert and Mathilda Morgenstern Levy. She was born into a New York Jewish family with German roots. She attended Dr. Julius Sachs's School for Girls, an elite institution for Jewish girls, but her family celebrated no Jewish holidays and gave Irma virtually no religious education. In 1907, she married Norvin Lindheim. They had five children. Shortly after her marriage, she became an ardent Zionist under Henrietta Szold's influence. She succeeded Szold as president of Hadassah and nearly completed the rabbinical training at the Jewish Institute of Religion. Irma moved to a kibbutz in Palestine in 1933 and spent the rest of her long life fundraising for various Zionist and Jewish causes.

21. Deutelbaum, *Tender Memories*, 14–17.

22. Apte, *Heart of a Wife*, ed. Rosenbaum, 90–91. Helen Jacobus Apte (1886–1946) was the daughter of Joseph and Alice Selig Jacobus, German immigrants. She grew up in Richmond and Atlanta. Due to poor health, she never finished high school. She married Day Apte in 1909 and had one daughter.

23. Blanche Wolf Kohn, "Keep the Sabbath Day Holy: A Plea to Mothers and Daughters," speech transcript, 1939, Blanche Wolf Kohn Papers, ACC 2406, PJAC. Blanche Wolf Kohn (1886–1983) grew up in Philadelphia. She attended the William Penn Charter School and graduated from Bryn Mawr in 1905. Active in both the Jewish and general Philadelphia worlds of social service, she founded the Settlement Music School in 1908. She married Isidor Kohn.

24. Leah Dvorah Orenstein, "Leah's Legacy," 7–8, 1987, ACC 1547, PJAC.

25. Bessie Newburger Rothschild memoir, 37, ACC 1638, PJAC. Bessie Newburger Rothschild (b. 1897) was the daughter of Samuel Meade and Helen Gutman Newburger. Her family moved to New York in 1908 when her father obtained a seat on the New York Stock Exchange. She went to Sabbath school and was confirmed at Temple Emanuel when she was thirteen years old. She attended the Alcuin School and then went to Barnard.

26. Braverman, *Libbie*, 6.

27. Pauline Hirsch Milch quoted in Selavan, *My Voice Was Heard*, 62–63.

28. On Szold's girlhood and education, see especially Dash, *Summoned to Jerusalem*; Fineman, *Woman of Valor*; Levin, *The Szolds of Lombard Street*; and Lowenthal, *Henrietta Szold*. On Kohut's girlhood and education, see especially Antler, *The Journey Home*.

29. Dushkin, *Jewish Education in New York City,* 240.

30. Henrietta Szold, "The Education of the Jewish Girl," *Jewish Comment,* June 12, 1903.

31. See McAfee, *Religion, Race, and Reconstruction.*

32. *Chumish* is a Hebrew word for the Pentateuch. Emily Fechheimer Seasongood, "Childhood Home in Cincinnati," in Marcus, ed., *Memoirs of American Jews,* 61.

33. Solomon, *Fabric of My Life,* 24; Barbe, *Memoirs.*

34. See Ashton, *Rebecca Gratz.*

35. For the history of the Philadelphia Jewish community, see Friedman, ed., *Jewish Life in Philadelphia, 1840–1920,* and Friedman, ed., *When Philadelphia Was the Capital of Jewish America.*

36. In so doing they followed the example of American public schooling. For a comprehensive history, see Tyack and Hansot, *Learning Together.*

37. Irene M. Gross, "The Hebrew Sunday School Society," Box 4, Folder 18, Hebrew Sunday School Society Records, MSS 6, PJAC. See also Ashton, *Rebecca Gratz,* and Rosenbloom, "Rebecca Gratz and the Jewish Sunday School Movement in Philadelphia." Simha Peixotto worked with Gratz in many women's groups. She and her sister, Rachel Peixotto Pyke, ran a private school in their home and brought their pedagogic experience to the nascent Hebrew Sunday School Society. Simha Pexiotto also prepared Jewish Foster Home boys for their bar mitzvahs.

38. "Maud Nathan: Sephardic Aristocrat, ca. 1867," in Marcus, ed., *The American Jewish Woman,* 269–271.

39. "San Francisco's Jewish Women: Assorted Models, 1890s," in Marcus, ed., *The American Jewish Woman,* 361.

40. *Galveston Daily News,* November 6, 1888, photocopied clipping in Levi Charles and Leonora R. Harby, SC-4526, AJA.

41. Korn et al., *75 Years of Continuity and Change.* See also Todes, "The History of Jewish Education in Philadelphia."

42. Henry Austryn Wolfson quoted in "The American Jewess and an American Jewess," reprint of an article from *Opinion,* n.d., Rebekah Kohut Papers, Box 2, MS 381, AJA.

43. Proceedings of the Second Summer Assembly, 45–47, 1898, Jewish Chautauqua Society Papers, MS-NAT.J185, AJHS.

44. Hortense Moses, "What Does Zionism Mean to Me," typescript speech, undated, Box 1, Folder 17, MS 51, Jacob Moses Papers, JMM.

45. Steinfeld, *My Mother's Daughter,* 8–9. Dorothy Peck Steinfeld was one of Wolfson's students. She attended the Cambridge Hebrew School every day after school for five years.

46. For more on this revival, see Sarna, *A Great Awakening.*

47. Reimer, "Passionate Visions in Contest" provides a clear picture of the distinctions between the two types of religious school systems in his Boston case study.

48. Sarna points out that the Hebraists' success in focusing Jewish education around Hebrew education eventually led to the schools being known as Hebrew schools rather than Talmud Torahs. Sarna, "American Jewish Education in Historical Perspective," 17. See also Mintz, ed., *Hebrew in America.*

49. Baltimore Hebrew School Association Records, 1998.157.1, JMM; Bloom, "History of Jewish Education in Baltimore."

50. Harry Friedenwald, "The Hebrew Education Society," *Jewish Comment,* January 1, 1904.

51. Frieda Gass Cohen, quoted in Libo and Howe, *We Lived There Too.* Frieda Gass Cohen's family immigrated to New York in 1909 and then went to Portland in 1911. She attended a Talmud Torah and also spent time at the Neighborhood House.

52. Stimulus (pseudonym for Mary M. Cohen), "Bible Classes in Our Sunday Schools," *American Hebrew,* November 14, 1882. A reprint of this article is in Mary Cohen's scrapbook, Box 4, Charles J. and Mary M. Cohen Collection, MS 3, CAJSL.

53. A picture of Ida Davis's 1916 Talmud Torah class in Duluth shows both boys and girls, in fairly equal numbers. Ida Davis Collection, SC-2685, AJA.

54. Korey, "A History of Jewish Education in Chicago," 76.

55. Report of the Hebrew Industrial School of Boston to the Baron de Hirsch Fund, January 1897, Box 24, Baron de Hirsch Fund Papers, I-80, AJHS; detailed report about Chicago Hebrew Institute with recommendations for improvement, 1919, Council of Jewish Federations and Welfare Funds Papers, I-69, AJHS.

56. Kellman, "Dr. Samson Benderly," 31.

57. Hart, *The Pleasure Is Mine,* 75.

58. Berrol, "Julia Richman's Work in New York," 40–41.

59. Report of the Hebrew Free School Association, *American Hebrew,* December 11, 1891.

60. Proceedings of the Second Summer Assembly, 1898, 31, Jewish Chautauqua Society Papers, MS-NAT.J185, AJHS.

61. Annual Report, 1905,16, Box 1, Folder 1, Hebrew Education Society of Philadelphia Records, MS 59, PJAC.

62. Annual Reports, 1907, 1910, 1911, The Columbia Religious and Industrial School for Jewish Girls, Columbia Religious and Industrial School for Jewish Girls Papers, I-24, AJHS.

63. 1890 materials on teaching at the Rockdale Avenue Sabbath School, Box 1, Folder 2, Jennie Mannheimer Papers, MS 259, AJA.

64. Visit to the Sunday School," *American Hebrew,* February 26, 1892.

65. Report of Attendance, Deportment, and Recitations of Carrie Amram for 12 Weeks beginning February 3, 1884, Julius and Carrie Amram Greenstone Papers, ACC 777, PJAC. Carrie Amram Greenstone (1871–1914) was the daughter of Werner D. and Ester Amram. She grew up in Philadelphia, where she attended Sabbath school at Anshe Emeth. She was a member of the first graduating class of Gratz College in 1901. She married Philadelphia rabbi Julius Greenstone in 1902.

66. For more about Kohut's commitment to women's education and philanthropy, see Antler, *The Journey Home,* and Rogow, *Gone to Another Meeting.* See also Kohut's memoirs, *My Portion* and *More Yesterdays.*

67. Quoted in "Rebekah Kohut, An Exemplar of the New Independent Woman, 1899," in Marcus, ed., *The American Jewish Woman,* 481–483.

68. A. Glanz, "The National Radical Schools," *American Hebrew,* June 16, 1916.

69. Krug, "History of the Yiddish Schools in Chicago."

70. Annual Report, 1902, 30–31, Educational Alliance Papers, MS-JCC.E28, AJHS.

71. Bible Notebook, 1900, Jennie Buffenstein Collection, Coll. 125–038, CJA.

72. Herman Baar, "The Martyr-Mother," *American Hebrew,* December 23, 1887.

73. Kaplan and Cronson, "First Community Survey of Jewish Education in New York City, 1909."

74. Benderly, *Aims and Activities of the Bureau of Education of the Jewish Community (Kehillah) of New York City* (New York: n.p., 1912), 6–7. The *Kehillah* was the short-lived organized Jewish community structure in New York. See Goren, *New York's Jews and the Quest for Community.* Samson Benderly (1876–1944) was one of the most important and influential Jewish educators in the United States. Educated in Palestine, he came to Baltimore to study medicine at Johns Hopkins University but was permanently sidetracked by a passionate devotion to Jewish education. See Mamie G. Gamoran, "The Story of Samson Benderly," n.d., SC-854, AJA, and Winter, *Jewish Education in a Pluralist Society.*

75. In 1911, only 41,404 out of 200,000 Jewish children in New York were estimated to attend some kind of religious school. Julius H. Greenstone, "Jewish Education in the United States," *The American Jewish Year Book* 5675/1914–1915 (Philadelphia: Jewish Publication Society of America, 1914).

76. Isaac Fein, "Early Jewish Education in Baltimore," 5, Vertical File—Education, JMM.

77. Isaac Fein, "Early Jewish Education in Baltimore," 5, Vertical File—Education, JMM.

78. Dushkin, *Living Bridges,* 9.

79. For more on this philosophy, see Kronish, "John Dewey and Horace M. Kallen on Cultural Pluralism"; Kronish, "John Dewey's Influence on Jewish Educators"; Winter, *Jewish Education in a Pluralist Society;* and Sarna, "American Jewish Education in Historical Perspective."

80. Benderly, "The Jewish Educational Problem," *Jewish Comment,* March 22, 1912.

81. Benderly, "The Jewish Educational Problem."

82. Alexander Dushkin (1890–1976) was born in Poland and came to the United States as a child. He was interested in Jewish education from a young age and earned a doctorate at Columbia University. During a long career in Jewish communal life, he was active in the BJE, Hebrew University, and Camp Modin, one of the first Jewish camps in America. Libbie Suchoff (1891–1970) was born in Minsk and immigrated to the United States with her family as a child. She attended New York public schools and Hunter College. As a public school teacher with a master's degree from Columbia, she was exactly the kind of educator Benderly was looking for. He asked her to head programs for adolescent Jewish girls. Libbie married Isaac Berkson in 1919. The Berksons and Alexander and Julia Dushkin were also involved in the early Jewish summer camp movement. Mamie Goldsmith (1900–1984) was educated in the New York public schools and

earned a degree from the Teachers Institute of the Jewish Theological Seminary, which worked closely with Benderly in producing professionally trained Jewish educators. She was involved with the Association of Jewish High School Girls as part of her work with the BJE. Mamie married Emanuel Gamoran in 1922. She was particularly concerned with girls' religious education, writing a confirmation service for them that was widely used in the United States. Rebecca Aaronson (1894–1975) was born in Baltimore and educated at Teachers College and the School for Jewish Communal Work in New York. She worked with Benderly to run a teacher training school for Jewish girls under the aegis of the BJE. She married Rabbi Barnett Brickner. Rebecca remained committed to Jewish education for herself and others throughout her life. In 1925, she conducted a synagogue service in Cleveland, and just before she turned 80, she earned an M.A. in Hebrew from the Cleveland College of Jewish Studies.

83. Dushkin, *Living Bridges,* 10; Kronish, "John Dewey's Influence on Jewish Educators," 419.

84. "The Progress of Jewish Education in New York," *Jewish Comment,* March 22, 1912.

85. "The Progress of Jewish Education in New York."

86. Gurock, *When Harlem Was Jewish,* 107.

87. Dushkin, *Jewish Education in New York City,* 107.

88. Benderly, *Aims and Activities,* 36–37; Dushkin, *Living Bridges,* 11–12, 17.

89. Judah Magnes, New York, to Eugene S. Benjamin, 16 January 1912, Box 29, Folder—NY Kehillah, Baron de Hirsch Fund Papers, I-80, AJHS.

90. Benderly, *Aims and Activities,* 25.

91. "Interesting High School Girls in Judaism," *American Hebrew,* January 2, 1914.

92. Benderly, *Aims and Activities,* 24–25.

93. Benderly, *Aims and Activities,* 18.

94. Szold, "The Education of the Jewish Girl."

95. Benderly, "The Jewish Educational Problem."

96. Samson Benderly, "For the Education of Jewish Girls," *American Hebrew,* January 2, 1914.

97. Henry Pereira Mendes, "Response to the Report of the National Committee on Religious School Work," in *Report of the Sisterhood of the Spanish and Portuguese Synagogue in the City of New York,* 212.

98. Alice L. Seligsberg, "Concerning the Religious Education of Jewesses," *American Hebrew,* March 29, 1912. Alice Seligsberg (1873–1940) was the daughter of Louis and Lillian Wolff Seligsberg. She grew up in New York and was one of the first graduates of Barnard. A close friend and colleague of Henrietta Szold, she was a social worker with a special interest in girls' problems. From 1913 to 1918, she directed Fellowship House, an agency in New York which provided social activities, personal counseling, and employment services to girls who left Jewish orphanages. She joined the original Hadassah study group and became a fervent Zionist, devoting herself to fostering girls' love of Judaism in both America and Palestine.

99. Jewish confirmation ceremonies dated from the early nineteenth century in Europe and included girls almost from their inception, but they did not become common in the United States until the 1850s. Goldman, *Beyond the Synagogue Gallery,* 27.

100. Siskin, *Martha W. Newman, 1876–1980.* Martha Washington Simon Newman (1876–1980) was the daughter of Leopold and Henrietta Mayer Simon. She grew up in Chicago, where she was confirmed by Emil Hirsch at age thirteen. She attended South Division High School for one year and later graduated from the kindergarten course at the Armour Institute of Technology. After marrying Marc Newman in 1902, she organized the kindergarten at the Maxwell Street Settlement and taught at the Madison School.

101. Adele Jules Kronsberg, "Memories of West Baltimore," 1984, 1984.54.4, JMM. Adele Augusta Jules (b. 1909) was the daughter of Samuel and Flora Goldstone Jules. She grew up in Baltimore, where she went to Western Female High School and then graduated in Forest Park High School's first graduating class in 1926. She was confirmed at the Madison Avenue Temple. After high school, she attended Brewbaker's Business School.

102. Lindheim, *Parallel Quest.*

103. Blanche Wolf Kohn, "Keep the Sabbath Day Holy: A Plea to Mothers and Daughters."

104. Emily Fechheimer Seasongood, "Childhood Home in Cincinnati," 71.

105. "Religious Instruction," *The Israelite,* June 21, 1856.

106. Kohler, *Guide for Instruction in Judaism,* 9.

107. Confirmation Class Notebook, 1903, Jennie Buffenstein Collection, Coll. 125-038, CJA.

108. Szold, "The Education of the Jewish Girl."

109. *Jewish Exponent*, June 5, 1908.

110. "Festival of Confirmation, Shabuouth 5679—June 4, 1919," Box 1, Folder 13, Gerstley-Loeb Family Papers, MSS 45, PJAC.

111. Blanche Wolf Kohn, "Keep the Sabbath Day Holy."

112. Ruskay, *Horsecars and Cobblestones*, 18–19.

113. "Religious Education for the Daughters of Israel," *Jewish Messenger*, October 19, 1860.

114. Quoted in Korey, "The History of Jewish Education in Chicago," 79.

115. *Israelite*, January 8, February 12, 1875.

116. "We Need a Female College," *Israelite*, January 8, 1858.

117. *American Israelite*, March 24, 1898. The contents of the editorial make it clear that Isaac Wise wrote it. He refers to his first pulpit in Albany, New York, where he experimented with some of the synagogue changes he would continue to advocate.

118. Dushkin, *Jewish Education in New York City*, 83.

119. Dushkin, *Jewish Education in New York City*, 95.

120. Leah Dvorah Orenstein, "Leah's Legacy," 52.

121. "Views of the Superintendent, Mr. David Blaustein."

122. Annual Report, 1916, 46, Educational Alliance Papers, MS-JCC.E28, AJHS.

123. Report of the Hebrew Free and Industrial School Society of St. Louis to the Central Committee of the Baron de Hirsch Fund, December 17, 1890, Box 218, Baron de Hirsch Fund Papers, I-80, AJHS.

124. Annual Report, 1909, 16, Box 1, Folder 1, Hebrew Education Society of Philadelphia Records, MS 59, PJAC.

125. "To Provide Every Child with Religious Education," *American Hebrew*, May 27, 1921. In comparison, close to 80 percent of Jewish children in London were estimated to attend some kind of religious school. Greenstone, "Jewish Education in the United States."

126. Dushkin, *Jewish Education in New York City*, 276–277.

127. Sarna, "American Jewish Education in Historical Perspective," 14–15 and personal communication, October 29, 2000.

128. Jennie Buffenstein's school notebooks, CJA; Amelia Allen diary, PJAC; Gertrude Mandelbaum Ades, "Family History," CHS.

129. For an extensive treatment of this issue, see Heinze, *Adapting to Abundance*.

130. For examples of how this push for integration of American Jewish identity worked in other arenas, see Joselit, *The Wonders of America*.

131. For more on the development of bat mitzvah, see the entries by Hyman in Hyman and Moore, eds., *Jewish Women in America*, 126–128, and by Steinberg and Klapper in Forman-Brunell, ed., *Girlhood in America*, 68–70. As Hyman notes, there is surprisingly little scholarly historical discussion of bat mitzvah.

132. Nadell, *Women Who Would Be Rabbis*, deals with these women and the issues their attendance raised at Hebrew Union College, the Jewish Theological Seminary, and the Jewish Institute of Religion. Antler, *The Journey Home*, also profiles some of these women, whose motives ranged from desire to edit her father's life work (Henrietta Szold) to attaining ordination (Martha Neumark and Helen Levinthal) to intense self-education (Irma Levy).

133. See Sarna, *A Centennial History of the Jewish Publication Society*.

NOTES TO CHAPTER 5

1. Drawn from Ashkenazi, ed., *The Civil War Diary of Clara Solomon*.

2. Drawn from Emily Frankenstein diary, Emily Frankenstein Papers, CHS.

3. See Ashkenazi, 4, 412 (June 19, 1862), 295 (March 20, 1862), 326 (April 12, 1862) and January 19, 1919, April 30, December 25, 1918, Emily Frankenstein diary.

4. See Cogan, *All-American Girl*. Cogan suggests that the "real womanhood" of educated, healthy, independent American women was available throughout the nineteenth century as an alternative to the piety, purity, submissiveness, and domesticity of the "true womanhood" Welter has described. By the turn of the century, "real womanhood" had superseded "true womanhood" as the cultural ideal. For the traditional perspective on model American womanhood during the nineteenth century, see Welter, *Dimity Convictions*.

5. For representative contemporary accounts of this phenomenon, see Briggs, *Girls and Education*, and Orton, ed., *The Liberal Education of Women*. The most relevant secondary sources

are Cogan, *All-American Girl*; Cremin, *American Education*; Kantor and Tyack, eds., *Work, Youth, and Schooling*; and Rury, *Education and Women's Work*.

6. J. E. Armstrong, "Limited Segregation," *School Review* 4 (Jan.–Dec. 1906), 726.

7. See Nelson and Vallone, eds., *The Girl's Own*; Inness, ed., *Delinquents and Debutantes*; Formanek-Brunell, *Made to Play House*; and Searles and Mickish, "'A Thoroughbred Girl.'"

8. The material in this chapter focuses largely, though not exclusively, on middle-class girls. For more on immigrant and working-class girls' leisure, see chapter 3, this volume. More general studies of immigrant women also deal tangentially with some of the issues raised in this chapter. See Ewen, *Immigrant Women in the Land of Dollars*; Friedman-Kasaba, *Memories of Migration*; Weatherford, *Foreign and Female*; Weinberg, *The World of Our Mothers*.

9. For explorations of girls' youth culture at work, see Glenn, *Daughters of the Shtetl*; Meyerowitz, *Women Adrift*; and Peiss, *Cheap Amusements*.

10. Ferber, *A Peculiar Treasure*, 84.

11. Quoted in Rosenbaum and O'Connor-Segerjeds, *Our Story*, 53–54.

12. Mannes, *Out of My Time*, 36–37. Marya Mannes (b. 1909) grew up in New York and graduated from the Veltin School in 1923.

13. Rhona E. Kuder, scrapbook, 1912, 1995.100.1, JMM. Rhona Kuder (b. 1895) grew up in Baltimore and graduated from Western Female High School in 1912.

14. Sarah quoted in Jennie Jackson, "Memoirs," 98–101, 1972, Asher Library, Spertus Institute of Judaica, Chicago.

15. Spewack, *Streets*, xi.

16. Rhona E. Kuder, scrapbook, 1912, 1995.100.1, JMM.

17. January 1, January 12, April 12, April 13, October 2, May 12, 1922, Ann Green diary, Robison Family Papers, P-678, AJHS.

18. November 26, 1890, Jennie Franklin diary, Jennie Franklin Purvin Papers, MS 502, AJA.

19. January 17, 1896, Bella Weretnikow diary, Bella Weretnikow Rosenbaum Papers, MS 179, AJA.

20. Rose S. Klein, biography of Minnie Goldstein Levenson, 2, 1987, SC-6819, AJA. Minnie Goldstein Levenson (b. 1905) was the daughter of Abraham and Rose Rafer Goldstein. She was born in Europe, but the whole family had immigrated to Worcester, Massachusetts, by 1912. After graduating from high school, she attended Boston University.

21. Rose Zetzer, scrapbook, 1921, Box 1, Folder 14, MS 86, Rose Zetzer Collection, JMM.

22. Western Female High School commencement program, June 28, 1877, Box 2, Folder 38, MS 38, Henrietta Szold Papers, JMM.

23. June 7, 1918, Emily Frankenstein diary, CHS.

24. Ferber, *A Peculiar Treasure*, 75–76.

25. *Bildung* is the German term for bourgeois cultivation and education. Kaplan points out that in Germany, as in America, women's piano playing was a visible sign of culture that appeared in rural and working-class homes as well as urban, middle-class homes. See Kaplan, *The Making of the Jewish Middle Class*, 121.

26. Strogoff, *The Other America*, 83.

27. Rosa Feinberg diary, Seidenfeld-Leibenstein Family Papers, Coll. 167, CJA; Jennie Franklin diary, AJA; Emily Frankenstein diary, CHS.

28. Elise Stern Haas, oral history, 20, 1972, SC-4430, AJA; Helen Arnstein Salz, oral history, 5, 1975, SC-10726, AJA.

29. Helen Arnstein Salz, oral history, 5.

30. Setty Swartz Kuhn memoir, Box 3, Folder 10, Setty Swartz Kuhn Papers, MS 173, AJA.

31. Scrapbook, 1915–1943, Gertrude Englander Villensky Papers, SC-3225, AJA. Gertrude Englander Villensky grew up in Cincinnati. She studied music at the Cincinnati College of Music and the Baldwin-Wallace Conservatory of Music and became a well-known concert pianist and music teacher.

32. Rose Cohn Brown, "The Story of the Years in Colorado from 1890–1903," 25, 1971, SC-1435, AJA.

33. See Heinze, *Adapting to Abundance*.

34. June 30, August 10, 1896, Bella Weretnikow diary, AJA.

35. Nevelson, *Dawns + Dusks*, 18. Louise Berliawsky Nevelson (1900–1988) was born in Russia to Isaac and Minna Ziesel Smolerank Berliawsky. She was four years old when her family came to the United States and settled in Maine. As traditionally observant Jews who spoke Yiddish at home, the Berliawsky family was fairly isolated in rural New England, but Louise was

certain from a young age that she was an artist. She married Charles Nevelson and moved to New York, where she had a son and spent the 1920s studying at the Art Students League and with private teachers. She gradually built a reputation as an artist, primarily as a sculptor, and her worldwide travels greatly influenced her work. During the 1950s and 1960s, she staged major exhibitions, and during the 1960s and 1970s, she also accepted major commissions. By the time of her death, she was a member of the American Academy and Institute of Arts and Letters and an influential sculptor.

36. Hyacintha, "About Our Girls," *Israelite*, January 8, 1875.

37. "Bombshells into the Pianos," *The Sabbath Visitor*, March 16, 1883.

38. Nathan, *Once upon a Time and Today*, 34–35; Florence Klein, oral history, 1978, CJA; London, *A Girl from Boston*, 14. Florence Klein (b. 1883) grew up in Chicago. She graduated from South Division High School in 1901.

39. Ruskay, *Horsecars and Cobblestones*, 18–19, 113–120.

40. Sophia Heller Goldsmith memoir, 7–8, 1904 and 1918, SC-4069, AJA. Sophia Heller Goldsmith (1848–1929) was the daughter of Bernhard and Sarah Levit Heller. Her family immigrated from Bohemia to the United States when she was an infant. She grew up in Milwaukee in heavily German cultural circles, which impeded her fluency in English. She married Phillip Goldsmith in 1865.

41. Polacheck, *I Came a Stranger*, 76–77. Allan Davis, "The Work of the Educational Alliance," September 16, 1910, Box 2, Educational Alliance Papers, MS-JCC.E28, AJHS.

42. Rose Zetzer, scrapbook, 1921, Box 1, Folder 14, MS 86, Rose Zetzer Collection, JMM.

43. Rhona E. Kuder, scrapbook, 1912, 1995.100.1, JMM.

44. July 25, 1877, Amelia Allen diary, ACC 1603, PJAC.

45. May 12, 1922, Ann Green diary, AJHS.

46. July 25, 1877, Amelia Allen diary, PJAC.

47. Emily Frankenstein diary, CHS.

48. For discussions of physical culture in American women's history, see Brumberg, "'Something Happens to Girls'"; Inness, "'It Is Pluck but Is It Sense?'"; Lancaster, "'I Could Easily Have Been an Acrobat'"; and Spears, *Leading the Way*.

49. Becker, ed., *Western High School Past and Present*, 197; program for Western High School Physical Training Exhibition, April 25, 1912, pasted in Rhona E. Kuder, scrapbook, 1912, 1995.100.1, JMM; program for Eastern High School Class Day, June 10, 1921, pasted in Rose Zetzer, scrapbook, 1921, Box 1, Folder 14, MS 86, Rose Zetzer Collection, JMM.

50. Elizabeth R. Deussen, Baltimore, to Girls of Eastern High, Baltimore, 28 April 1924, published in *The Eastern Echo*, June 1924, 1994.112.12, JMM.

51. Marie Lowenstein, Tripp Lake Camp, Maine, to her mother, Baltimore, 18 August 1917, 1991.127.24a, JMM.

52. For an exploration of the history of girls' body image, see Brumberg, *The Body Project*. Brumberg's earlier book, *Fasting Girls*, provides a complex analysis of the consequences of extreme concern with controlling girls' bodies.

53. Pauline S. Wise, "Successful Business Women," *American Jewess*, May 1895.

54. *Jewish Messenger*, March 21, 1890.

55. *Jewish Messenger*, March 21, 1890.

56. *Jewish Messenger*, March 14, 1890.

57. Gertrude Mandelbaum Ades, "Family History," 21; Sophia Heller Goldsmith memoir, 7–8; Beckerman, *Not So Long Ago*, 67; July 15, 1890, Jennie Franklin diary, AJA.

58. February 24, 1878, Amelia Allen diary, PJAC.

59. Emily Fechheimer Seasongood, "Childhood Home in Cincinnati," in Marcus, ed., *Memoirs of American Jews, 1775–1865*, 60; February 24, March 20, 1878, Amelia Allen diary, PJAC; Helen Arnstein Salz, oral history, 5; Steinfeld, *My Mother's Daughter*, 11–12.

60. See Borish's articles, "'An Interest in Physical Well-Being among the Feminine Membership'"; "'Athletic Activities of Various Kinds'"; and "Jewish American Women, Jewish Organizations, and the Sports, 1880–1940."

61. The Hebrew Technical School's encouragement of physical culture is evident as early as its 1898 curriculum, Box 4, Jewish Foundation for the Education of Women Papers, NYPL, and is explored by Joselit in *Aspiring Women* and "Saving Souls." A similar commitment is evident in the 1900 report of the Clara de Hirsch Home's Training and Education Committee, Box 2, Folder 40, Clara de Hirsch Home for Working Girls Papers, YM/YWHA. "The Clara de Hirsch

Home for Working Girls," *American Jewess,* September 1898; program announcement of The Settlement House, Milwaukee, Lizzie Black Kander Papers, microfilm reels 1400–1401, AJA.

62. See, for example, September 20, 1877, and January 3, 1878, Amelia Allen diary, PJAC.

63. October 2, 1922, Ann Green diary, AJHS.

64. October 14, 1862, Bertha Wehle diary, SC-12789, AJA.

65. "The Education of a Young Woman of Family, ca. 1881," in Marcus, ed., *The American Jewish Woman,* 337–338.

66. Helen Arnstein Salz, oral history, 17.

67. See, for instance, Harriet Stricker Lazarus, "Portrait of a Cincinnati Lady," 14–15, 1981–1993, SC-14057, AJA. Harriet spent her childhood in the 1920s and 1930s reading the books her mother remembered loving as a child herself.

68. Ruskay, *Horsecars and Cobblestones,* 65–66.

69. Rose Cohn Brown, "The Story of the Years in Colorado from 1890–1903," 12.

70. Quoted in Rosenbaum and O'Connor-Segerjeds, *Our Story,* 119.

71. Amelia Allen diary, PJAC.

72. Jennie Franklin diary, AJA.

73. Ann Green diary, AJHS. For more on women and movies, see Rabinovitz, *For the Love of Pleasure.*

74. Apte, *Heart of a Wife,* ed. Rosenbaum. Marcus Rosenbaum, Helen Jacobus Apte's grandson, discusses her reading journal in his notes but did not include the entire text in the book. He did publish large chunks of the reading journal in an appendix. Rosenbaum also notes that Helen burned her adolescent diary. The material in this paragraph is based on her 1902 reading journal, excerpted in *Heart of a Wife,* 198–205.

75. These excerpts are published in Apte, *Heart of a Wife.* The page number in *Heart of a Wife* follows the date from the original reading journal entry. November 6, 1901 (197); April 8, 1903 (206); August 25, 1902 (204); November 1, 1901 (197); December 12, 1901 (198).

76. June 27, January 11, 1896, Bella Weretnikow diary, AJA.

77. Edna Ferber, *A Peculiar Treasure,* 36–37.

78. May 9, 1915, Marie Syrkin diary, Box 2, Folder 9, Marie Syrkin Papers, MS 615, AJA.

79. Hart, *The Pleasure Is Mine,* 17.

80. Leaphart, ed., "Montana Episodes," 87.

81. Purmell and Rovner, *A Farmer's Daughter,* 33–34. Bluma Bayuk Purmell (b. 1888) was the daughter of Moses and Annette Goroshofsky Bayuk. She grew up in the Jewish agricultural community in Alliance, New Jersey, and went to nursing school in Philadelphia.

82. For elaboration of this point, see Sicherman, "Reading *Little Women,*" in Kerber, Kessler-Harris, and Sklar, eds., *U.S. History as Women's History,* 245–266. Elizabeth Levin Stern (1889–1954) was the daughter of Aaron and Sarah Rubenstein Levin. She was born in Poland, and her family immigrated to Pittsburgh when she was a toddler. She attended both the University of Pittsburgh and the New York School of Social Work. In 1911, she married Leon Thomas Stern, and they had two children. A journalist, she also wrote a lightly fictionalized autobiography, *I Am a Woman—and a Jew* under the pseudonym Leah Morton. Her fictional counterpart was more strongly identified with Judaism than Elizabeth Stern, who converted to Quakerism.

83. Spewack, *Streets,* 66.

84. January 9, 10, 11, 16, 1896, Bella Weretnikow diary, AJA.

85. April 12, 1915, Marie Syrkin diary, AJA.

86. Wise, *Legend of Louise,* 10–11. Louise Waterman Wise (1874–1947) was the daughter of Julius and Justine Meyer Waterman, wealthy New York Jews. She attended private school and an Episcopalian Sunday School and at age sixteen began teaching art at settlement houses. In 1899, she met Stephen Wise, a poor, Zionist, activist rabbi of Hungarian background whom her parents could not have disapproved of more strongly. However, they were married in 1900 and began their married life in Portland, Oregon, where they had two children, before moving to New York in 1907. Louise was involved in any number of causes, including visiting nurse associations, adoption agencies, refugee agencies, and Zionism. She was also a translator and an artist. Her daughter Justine Wise Polier became a prominent judge.

87. Berg, *Molly and Me,* 159–160.

88. Minnie Publicker, oral history, 7, 1979, SC-9923, AJA.

89. Schneiderman with Goldthwaite, *All for One,* 39–41.

90. Cohen, *Out of the Shadow,* 252, 279.

91. Lang, *Tomorrow Is Beautiful,* 29. Lucy Fox Robins Lang (1884–1962) was the daughter of Moshe and Surtze Broche Fox. She was born in Kiev, Russia, and her family immigrated to Chicago when she was nine. She went to work immediately and took classes at Hull House at night, with Jane Addams personally intervening so her parents would allow it. Radicalized by her work experiences and reading, she became an anarchist and married fellow anarchist Bob Robins in 1904. They moved to New York, where Lucy worked as a political activist and coordinated campaigns for Emma Goldman, Tom Mooney, and others. In 1918, she met Samuel Gompers and later became his unpaid assistant. After a divorce in the mid-1920s, she married Henry Lang, who stimulated her interest in Zionism. She worked her entire life to support political and labor organizations.

92. "The Education of a Young Woman of Family, ca. 1881," in Marcus, ed., *The American Jewish Woman,* 337–338; Ruskay, *Horsecars and Cobblestones,* 66.

93. Apte, *Heart of a Wife,* December 12, 1901 (198).

94. Solomon, *The Fabric of My Life.*

95. *The Chicago Jewish Community Blue Book* (Chicago: The Sentinel Publishing Company, 1917), 202.

96. Sarah Cohen Levinson reminisces, 2, 1975, SC-6900, AJA. Sarah Cohen Levinson (b. 1897) grew up in Boston. She graduated from Girls' High School in 1914 and Girls' Normal School in 1917 and became a teacher in the Boston public schools.

97. Adele Jules Kronsberg, "Memories of West Baltimore," 1984, 1984.54.4, JMM.

98. Dorothy Kuhn, Cincinnati, to Simon Kuhn, Massachusetts, 25 March 1912, Box 1, Folder 3, Setty Swartz Kuhn Papers, MS 173, AJA.

99. "The Impact of a Settlement House on Impressionable Jewish Girls," in Marcus, ed., *The American Jewish Woman,* 524–525.

100. "L.C.H. Notes," *S.E.G. News,* November 14, 1914, in bound volume of *S.E.G. News* issues, 1914–1917, AJHS.

101. For a complete history of the SEG, see Larson, "The Saturday Evening Girls."

102. The Voice of Appreciation," *S.E.G. News,* December 12, 1914.

103. December 4, 1909, Minutes of the Girls' Literary Society, Jewish Foster Home and Orphan Asylum Papers, Series 1, Association for Jewish Children Records, MS 5, PJAC.

104. November 21, December 12, 1909, Minutes of the Girls' Literary Society, PJAC. On the popularization of parliamentary law, see Doyle, "Rules of Order."

105. Jessie B. Cohn, "United We Stand, Divided We Fall," *Clara de Hirsche Journal* 2 (April 1904): 1–2. Clara de Hirsche Literary Society Papers, I-275, AJHS.

106. Jennie Rosenfeld Gerstley, "Reminisces," 90, 1931–1934, Box 2072, AJA.

107. Jennie Rosenfeld Gerstley, "Reminisces," 91, AJA.

108. Hart, *The Pleasure Is Mine,* 26.

109. February 2, May 9, February 14, 1890, Jennie Franklin diary, AJA.

110. Philomathia record journal, Box 2278L, Folder "Literary Activities—Philomathians," Jennie Franklin Purvin Papers, MS 502, AJA.

111. Sorin, *Tradition Transformed,* 168.

112. Amy Steinhart Braden, quoted in "San Francisco's Jewish Women: Assorted Models, 1890s," in Marcus, ed., *The American Jewish Woman,* 361.

113. Helen Arnstein Salz, oral history, 14.

114. Block and Block, *Memoirs for Our Grandchildren,* 48. Lucille Eichengreen Block (b. 1902) was the daughter of Meyer and Isabella Goodkind Eichengreen. She grew up in Chicago, where she attended the Faulkner School for Girls and was confirmed in 1915. She married Joseph L. Block in 1924.

115. July 8, 1862, Eliza Moses diary, transcribed in extracts from the journals of Eliza M. Moses and Albert Moses Luria, edited by Stanford E. Moses, SC-8504, AJA.

116. May 7, September 8, 1875, Fannie Allen diary, ACC 1602, PJAC; February 5, 1876, Amelia Allen diary, PJAC.

117. April 20, April 5, July 5, August 17, 1876, Fannie Allen diary, PJAC. Fannie did not marry until she was thirty-two years old, and Amelia never married at all.

118. Clara Lowenburg Moses, "My Memories," 68, 1939, SC-8499, AJA.

119. Helen Arnstein Salz, oral history, 15.

120. See Bailey, *From Front Porch to Back Seat,* and Rothman, *Hands and Hearts.*

121. July 20, 1862, Bertha Wehle diary, AJA.

122. See Lystra, *Searching the Heart.*

123. Simon Kander, Monroe, Wisconsin, to Lizzie Black, Milwaukee, 25 January 1881, Lizzie Black Kander papers, microfilm reels 1400–1401, AJA.

124. Lystra, *Searching the Heart,* especially 12–27.

125. Martin Marks, Georgetown, Ohio, to Rosa Wachtel, Cincinnati, 10 June 1890, Wachtel-Marks correspondence, SC-12643, AJA. Rosa clearly treasured these letters, but unfortunately her side of the correspondence has not survived.

126. Martin Marks, Higginsport, Ohio, to Rosa Wachtel, Cincinnati, 11 June 1890.

127. Clara Lowenburg Moses, "My Memories," 68, 99, 83, 78, 80.

128. February 1, 1890, Jennie Franklin diary, AJA.

129. Ferber, *A Peculiar Treasure,* 48–49.

130. Minnie Publicker, transcript of oral history, 12.

131. March 28, March 29, May 23, May 2, April 27, 1915, Marie Syrkin diary, AJA. Marie referred to Weinstein only once by his full name, Aaron Weinstein, and never just as Aaron.

132. April 13, April 27, 1915, Marie Syrkin diary, AJA.

133. June 6, 1918, Emily Frankenstein diary, CHS.

134. For an introduction to the substantial literature on changing standards of sexuality in America, see D'Emilio and Freedman, *Intimate Matters.* In addition to Mosher, see also Davis, *Factors in the Sex Life of Twenty-Two Hundred Women.*

135. Mary Upsico Davidson autobiography, 11–12.

136. Martin Marks, Manchester, Ohio, to Rosa Wachtel, Cincinnati, 12 June 1890, Wachtel-Marks correspondence, AJA.

137. Clara Lowenburg Moses, "My Memories," 68–69.

138. Clara Lowenburg Moses, "My Memories," 99, 80, 99.

139. Undated entry describing the spring of 1919, Emily Frankenstein diary, CHS.

140. Undated 1920 entry, Emily Frankenstein diary, CHS.

NOTES TO THE CONCLUSION

1. October 15, 1875, Fannie Allen diary, ACC 1602, PJAC.

2. Material on Fannie's life is drawn from her diary; "F. A. de Ford Dies: Woman Physician," *New York Times,* January 10, 1937; Whiteman, "Philadelphia's Jewish Neighborhoods"; and Piola, "Frances Allen de Ford." On Anna Marks Allen, see Ashton, "'Souls Have No Sex'" and *Rebecca Gratz*; Friedman, "Founders, Teachers, Mothers, and Wards"; and Eidelman, "Anna Marks Allen."

3. July 16, 1896, Bella Weretnikow diary, Bella Weretnikow Rosenbaum Papers, MS 179, AJA.

4. Bella Weretnikow Rosenbaum, "My Life," 62, Bella Weretnikow Rosenbaum Papers, MS 179, AJA. Material on Bella's life is drawn from her diary and her memoirs at the AJA.

Bibliography

PERIODICALS

American Hebrew
American Israelite
American Jewess
Hebrew Standard
Jewish Charities
Jewish Comment
Jewish Messenger
Maccabæan
New York Times
Reform Advocate
Sabbath School Visitor

MANUSCRIPT COLLECTIONS

Abelson, Paul, Papers, 1892–1954, MS 4, AJA.
Ades, Gertrude Mandelbaum, "Family History," 1992, CHS.
Allen, Fannie, diary, 1875–1884, ACC 1602, PJAC.
Allen, Amelia J., diary, 1876–1878, ACC 1603, PJAC.
American Jewish Women, special topics, nearprint file, Box 1, AJA.
Association for Jewish Children Records, MSS 5, PJAC.
Auerbach, Ella (Mrs. Herman H.), biographical materials, 1919–1969, Miscellaneous File, AJA.
Baltimore Hebrew School Association Minutes, 1868–1871, 1998.157.1, JMM.
Baltimore Recollections, Vertical File, JMM.
Barnard, Florence, high school certificate, 1892, with letter from Rhoda Barnard Sarnat detailing Barnard's biography, 1988, SC-728, AJA.
Baron de Hirsch Fund Papers, I-80, AJHS.
Baumgart, Seraphina, "Seraphina Says," n.d., SC-779, AJA.
Bettman, Iphigene Molony, autobiographical questionnaire, 1964, SC-1004, AJA.
Blake, Marie Martin, Collection, 1893–1896, 1944, MS 1977, MHS.
Bloomfield-Zeisler, Fannie, Papers, MS 587, AJA.
Braden, Amy Steinhart, interview conducted by Edna Tartaul Daniel for the Regional Oral History Office of the Bancroft Library and University of California, Berkeley, 1965, SC-1294, AJA.
Brav, Ruth Englander, "Memoirs of Ruth E. Brav: Mostly Family Recollections by a 20th Century Reform Rebbetzin," n.d., SC-1351, AJA.
Brown Family Papers, P-628, AJHS.
Brown, Rose Lenore Cohn (Mrs. Abraham L.), "The Story of the Years in Colorado from 1890–1903," 1971, SC-1435, AJA.
Buffenstein, Jennie, Collection, school notebooks, 1901–1903, Coll. 125–038, CJA.
Clara de Hirsch Home for Working Girls Collection, Buttenwieser Library, YM/WHA.
Clara de Hirsch Literary Society Papers, I-275, AJHS.
Cohen, Charles J. and Mary M., Collection, MS 3, CAJSL.

Cohen Collection, 1773–1945, MS 251, MHS.
Cohen, Jettie Brenner, "This Is Your Life Jettie Cohen to 1910," by daughter Evelyn Wein, n.d., SC-2270, AJA.
Columbia Religious and Industrial School for Girls Papers, I-24, AJHS.
Cooper, Sarah Silver, biography by grandson David, 1986.3.3, JMM.
Coplan, Kate, Collection, MS 99, Box 1, Folder 3, Box 2, Folder 51, Box 3, Folder 3, JMM.
Council of Jewish Federation and Welfare Funds Papers, I-69, AJHS.
Covan, Goldie Prelutsky, memoir (translated from Yiddish), 1914–1916, Coll. 125-056, CJA.
Crane Technical High School Records, Series III, CHS.
Daughters in Israel, Vertical File, JMM.
Davidson, Cecilia Razovsky, Papers, 1891–1968, P-290, AJHS.
Davidson, Mary, autobiography, 1969–1940, with sequel by Jennie Davidson Levitt, May 1972, SC-2667, AJA.
Davis, Dora Cohen, autobiographical questionnaire, n.d., SC-2679, AJA.
Davis Family Papers, 1926–1932, Box 928, SC-2680, AJA.
Davis, Ida (Mrs. Harry W.), Papers, 1911–1969, SC-2685, AJA.
Dimling, Anna Katherine, scrapbook, 1920–1924, MS 2782, MHS.
Eastern Female High School, commencement program, 1899, 1990.144.1, JMM.
Education—Jewish, Vertical File, JMM.
Education, special topics, nearprint file, Boxes 1–3, AJA.
Educational Alliance Papers, MS-JCC.E28, AJHS.
Elkus Family Collection, P-686, AJHS.
Fels Family Papers, ACC 2384, PJAC.
Frankenstein, Emily, Papers, 1913 (?)-1920, CHS.
Freudenthal, Carmen Kahn (Mrs. L. E.), "The First 82 Years of My Life," 1980, SC-3727, AJA.
Fried, Bertha, biographical information, 1969–1979, SC-3740, AJA.
Friedenwald Family Papers, Birdie Stein diary and Western Female High School report cards, 1984.23, JMM.
Friedman, Ruth Labes, memoir, 1984, Asher Library, Spertus Institute of Jewish Studies.
Friend, Esther, confirmation certificate, 1881, CHS.
Friese, Julia A., report card, 1867–1870, Vertical File, MHS.
Gerstley, Jennie Rosenfeld (Mrs. Henry M.), "Reminisces," 1931–1934, Box 2072, AJA (original at CHS).
Gerstley-Loeb Family Papers, MSS 45, PJAC.
Gold, Rose Bogen, "Good Morning Nurse," n.d., SC-3988, AJA.
Goldman, Sarah Adler, reminisces, SC-4048, AJA.
Goldsmith, Sophia Heller, memoir, 1904 and 1918, SC-4069, AJA.
Goodwin, Julia, memoir of her great-grandmother Julie Kaufman, 992, SC-13790, AJA.
Green, Nancy, research files on Lucy Flower High School, CHS.
Greenberg, Rose, Papers, 1994.112.7–.12, UP 250, JMM.
Greenstone, Julius and Carrie Amram, Papers, 1829–1982, PJAC.
Griffis, Margaret Quandril Clark, diaries, RU.
Haas, Elise Stern, "The Appreciation of Quality." An interview conducted by Harriet Nathan for the Regional Oral History Office of the Bancroft Library and University of California, Berkeley, 1972. SC-4430, AJA.
Hammond, Beatrice Joseph, Papers, MS 291, AJA.
Harby Family Papers, SC-4526, AJA.
Hebrew Education Society of Philadelphia Records, 1834–1952, MS 59, PJAC.
Hebrew Sunday School Society Records, MSS 6, PJAC.
Hebrew Technical School for Girls, Vertical File, JMM.
Hecht, Leonard, Papers, 1874–1945, MS 1308, MHS.
Henschel, Anna, confirmation book, 1885, SC-4932, AJA.
Henschel, Anna and Carrie, confirmation books, 1876 and 1885, SC-4933, AJA.
Herstein, Lillian, transcript of oral history, 1970–1971, Chicago Sinai Congregation Oral History Project, Coll. 240, CJA.
Hirschberg, Nell, autobiographical questionnaire, 1986, SC-5064, AJA.
Jackson, Jennie, memoirs, 1972, CS 71.J234x, Asher Library, Spertus Institute of Jewish Studies.
Jacobs, Ella, autograph book, 1876–1889, SC 223, PJAC.
Jacobus, Dorothy, "Growing Up in Dallas," 1977, SC-5665, AJA.

Jaffe, Ida, confirmation certificate, 1890, SC-10784, AJA.
Jewish Chautauqua Society Papers, MS-NAT.J185, AJHS.
Jewish Directory of Chicago, 1884, CHS.
Jewish Federation of Metropolitan Chicago Collection, Coll. 2, CJA.
Jewish Foundation for Education of Women Collection, Rare Books and Manuscripts Division, NYPL.
Jewish Social Register, Vertical File, JMM.
Kander, Lizzie Black, Papers, 1875–1960, microfilm reels 1400–1401, AJA.
Kaufman, Rachel (Mrs. Jules), biographical interview by Norton B. Stern, 1966, SC-6189, AJA.
Klein, Florence, transcript of oral history, 1978, CJA.
Kohn, Blanche Wolf, Papers, ACC 2406, PJAC.
Kohn Family Papers, Box 1111, AJA.
Kohn, Mathilde, diary and letters, 1866–1868, SC-6391, AJA.
Kohut, Rebekah, Papers, 1896–1951, MS Collection 381 (George Kohut Papers), AJA.
Kraus Family Papers, Mabel Kraus's Western High School report cards, MS 3, Box 1, Folder 12, JMM.
Kronsberg, Adele Jules, Family Collection, 1984.54.4, JMM.
Kuder, Rhona E., scrapbook, 1912, 1995.100.1, JMM.
Kuhn, Setty Swartz, Papers, 1885–1951, MS Collection 173, AJA.
Kulp, Flora, memoir, n.d., SC-13620, AJA.
Kulwin, Muriel Roth, "Yesteryears: When Muriel Was a Little Girl," 1992, SC-13721, AJA.
Kussy, Sarah, Papers, 1869–1956, P-4, AJHS.
Lane, Albert Grannis, history of education in Chicago, 1900–1904, CHS.
Lazarus, Harriet Stricker, "Portrait of a Cincinnati Lady," 1981–1993, SC-14057, AJA.
Lederer, Ephraim and Grace Newhouse, Papers, 1862–1925, ACC 1598, PJAC.
Levenson, Minnie Goldstein, biography by Rose S. Klein, 1987, SC-6819, AJA.
Levin, Nanette Schlichter and Gertrude Levin Saxon Collection, 1994.78, PB 44, JMM.
Levinson, Sarah Cohen, reminisces, 1975, SC-6900, AJA.
Levy, Clairee Rosenbaum, autobiographical questionnaire, 1981, SC-6934, AJA.
Liberles, Lucille, Papers, 1887–1976, MS 17, JMM.
Litman, Ray Frank, Papers, 1864/5–1948, P-46, AJHS.
Louisa May Alcott Club Papers, I-210, AJHS.
Lowenstein, Marie, correspondence, 1917–1921, 1991.127.22–.26, JMM.
Lowenthal, Mildred Blum, "About Me, My Family, My World—1898–1981," 1981, SC-1141, AJA.
Mannheimer, Jennie, Papers, 1890–1943, MS Collection 259, AJA.
Marks, Daisy Glatzer, autobiographical album, SC-7778, AJA.
Marks, Elias, correspondence, 1857, SC-7781, AJA.
Marks, Marguerite Meyer, "Memoirs of My Family," 1984, SC-7796, AJA.
Marshall High School Records, miscellaneous materials, CHS.
McCormick Education Notes, MS 1647, MHS.
McKinley High School Records, Series II A and B, CHS.
Mendel, Rose, reminisces, Cincinnati, OH, 1977, SC-8027, AJA.
Menken, Alice Davis, Papers, 1870–1936, P-23, AJHS.
Meyer, Annie Nathan, Papers, MS 7, AJA.
Miller, Kate B., autobiographical letters, 1941, SC-13647, AJA.
Montor, Martha, correspondence, 1975, SC-8346, AJA.
Morais, Sabato, correspondence, 1881, SC-8370, AJA.
Moses, Clara Lowenburg, "My Memories," 1939, SC-8499, AJA.
Moses, Eliza M., diary, 1861–1862, edited by Stanford E. Moses, SC-8504, AJA.
Moses, Jacob, Papers, MS 51, JMM.
Myers, Josephine, correspondence, 1861, SC-8631, AJA.
National Association of Jewish Social Workers Papers, I-88, AJHS.
Natkin, Esther Weinshenker, Papers, Coll. 150, CJA.
Newman, Pauline, "The Twentieth Century Trade Union Woman: Vehicle for Social Change," interview by Barbara Wertheimer for Program on Women and Work, Institute of Labor and Industrial Relations, University of Michigan and Wayne State University. SC-9071, AJA.
Oheb Shalom Collection, L88, JMM.
Orenstein, Leah Dvorah, "Leah's Legacy," 1987, ACC 1547, PJAC.

Osterman, Rosanna, biographical materials, 1866–1970, SC-9350, AJA.
Phillips, Rachel Rosalie, diary, 1864, unprocessed collection, AJA.
Publicker, Minnie, biographical interview, 1979, SC-9923, AJA.
Purvin, Jennie Franklin, Papers, 1873–1958, MS Collection 502, AJA.
The Quill, magazine of John Marshall High School, 1901–1902, CHS.
Reyher, Rebecca Hourwich, "Search and Struggle for Equality and Independence," interview conducted by Amelia R. Fry and Fern Ingersoll for Regional Oral History Office of the Bancroft Library and University of California, Berkeley, 1977, SC-10103, AJA.
Richman, Julia, biographical materials, SC-10143, AJA.
Robison Family Papers, P-678, AJHS.
Rodgers, Ella G., character book, Vertical File: Education—Galena Female Seminary, MHS.
Rosenbaum, Bella Weretnikow, Papers, 1896–1955, MS 179, AJA.
Rosenberg, Adella, memoirs, SC-230, PJAC.
Rothschild, Bessie Newburger, memoirs, ACC 1638, PJAC.
Salz, Helen Arnstein, "Sketches of an Improbable Ninety Years," interview conducted by Suzanne Riess for the Regional Oral History Office of the Bancroft Library and University of California, Berkeley, 1975, SC-10726, AJA.
Schechter, Minnie Seltzer, "Memoirs: Three-Quarters of a Century of Life in Philadelphia," 1981, SC-239, PJAC.
Schuster, Goldie Jacobs, family history, SC-11060, AJA.
Schwartz, Bessie Halpern, "My Own Story," 1956, SC-11074, AJA.
Seasongood, Emily Fechheimer, autobiography, SC-11128, AJA.
Seasongood, Emily Fechheimer, eightieth birthday book, 1931, SC-11129, AJA.
S.E.G. News, bound volume of 1914–1917 newsletters of the Saturday Evening Girls, Boston, AJHS.
Seidenfeld-Liebenstein Family Papers, Coll. 167, CJA.
Seman, Philip L., Papers, MS 578, AJA.
Sharlip, Regina Katz, "Memoirs of Galicia," SC-217, PJAC.
Slosberg, Mildred, autobiography and family history, 1978–1979, SC-11624, AJA.
Solis-Cohen, Emily, scrapbook, ACC 965, PJAC.
Spiegel Family Papers, Coll. 78, CJA.
Stanfield, Milly, "Looking Back at Ninety," 1991, SC-13977, AJA.
Stern, Amelia Felsenthal, "Aunt Meme's Story," 1967, SC-3414, AJA.
Stewart, Amy Hart, Papers, 1864–1916, SC-12013, AJA.
Stewart, Amy Hart, scrapbook, 1873–1954, SC-12014, AJA.
Stone, Sylvia Levin, "Sylvia L. Stone: Lifelong Volunteer in San Francisco," interview by Eleanor Glaser for Regional Oral History Office of the Bancroft Library and the University of California, Berkeley, 1982, SC-1208, AJA.
Stonehill, Theresa Baer, autobiography and news clippings, 1904–1914, SC-12049, AJA.
Strauss, Helen Graf, autobiographical questionnaire, 1975, SC-12089, AJA.
Sulzberger, Iphigene Ochs, autobiographical questionnaire, 1975, SC-12141; memorial book, 1990, SC-12142, AJA.
Syrkin, Marie, Papers, 1915–1989, MS 615, AJA.
Szold, Bertha, certificates and diplomas, L88.11.359, JMM.
Szold, Henrietta, Collection, 1893–1972, MS 2399, MHS.
Szold, Henrietta, Papers, microfilm reels 386–386G, AJA.
Szold, Henrietta, Papers, 1866–1977, MS 38, JMM.
Villensky, Gertrude Englander, scrapbook, 1915–1943, SC-3225, AJA.
Voorsanger, Henrietta, autobiography, Elkan C. and Henrietta Voorsanger Papers, MS Collection 256, AJA.
Wachtel-Marks Papers, SC-12643, AJA.
Wald, Mina D., correspondence, 1869, SC-12675, AJA.
Wehle, Bertha, diary, excerpts edited by sons Walter and George Naumberg, SC-12789, AJA.
Wendkos, Dora Barenbaum, "Our Voyage to America: 1893," SC-99, PJAC.
West Division High School Records, Series I A and B, CHS.
West End House Papers, I-285, AJHS.
Wohl, Belle Myers, autobiographical questionnaire, 1980, SC-13150, AJA.
Young Men's and Young Women's Hebrew Association of Philadelphia Papers, I-241, AJHS.

Young Women's Hebrew Association Collection, Record Group 5, Buttenwieser Library, YM/WHA.
Zetzer, Rose, Collection, MS 86, JMM.
Zweig, Anna, "My Memoirs," 1968, SC-13424, AJA.

PUBLISHED PRIMARY SOURCES

Addams, Jane, et al. *Philanthropy and Social Progress* (New York: Thomas Y. Crowell, 1893).
Adler, Polly. *A House Is Not a Home* (New York: Rinehart & Company, 1953).
Allinson, May, comp. *The Public Schools and Women in Office Service* (Boston: Women's Educational and Industrial Union, 1914).
Antin, Mary. *The Promised Land* (New York: Penguin Books, 1997).
Apte, Helen Jacobus. *Heart of a Wife: The Diary of a Southern Jewish Woman.* Ed. Marcus D. Rosenbaum (Wilmington, Del., Scholarly Resources, 1998).
Ashkenazi, Elliott, ed. *The Civil War Diary of Clara Solomon: Growing Up in New Orleans, 1861–1862* (Baton Rouge: Louisiana State University Press, 1995).
Becker, Ernest J., ed. *Western High School Past and Present.* Published November, 1944, as part of the Centennial Celebration, Western High School, Baltimore, Maryland (Baltimore: Garamond Press, 1944).
Beckerman, Emma. *Not So Long Ago: A Recollection* (New York: Bloch, 1980).
Benderly, Samson. *Aims and Activities of the Bureau of Education of the Jewish Community (Kehillah) of New York City* (n.p., 1912).
Berg, Gertrude. *Molly and Me* (New York: McGraw-Hill, 1961).
Berkson, Isaac B. "The Community School Center." *The Jewish Teacher* 1 (December 1917): 224–234.
Blake, Mabelle Babcock, et al. *The Education of the Modern Girl* (Freeport, N.Y.: Books for Libraries Press, 1929).
Block, Joseph L., and Lucille E. Block, *Memoirs for Our Grandchildren* (Chicago: privately printed, 1989).
Braverman, Libbie L. *Libbie: Teacher, Counselor, Lecturer, Author, Education Director, Consultant, and What Happens along the Way* (New York: Bloch, 1986).
Briggs, L. B. R. *Girls and Education* (Boston: Houghton Mifflin, 1911).
Burstall, Sara A. *The Education of Girls in the United States* (New York: Macmillan, 1894).
Calisher, Hortense. *Kissing Cousins: A Memory* (New York: Weidenfeld & Nicolson, 1988).
Carlin, Jerome, and Alexander Carlin. *Just So You Know: An Oral History of Leo and Celia Carlin* (n.p., 1991).
The Chicago Jewish Community Blue Book (Chicago: The Sentinel Publishing Company, 1917).
Cohen, Rose Gollup. *Out of the Shadow* (New York: George H. Doran, 1918).
Committee on Religion, New York Section, Council of Jewish Women, comp. *A Book of Prayer for Jewish Girls* (New York: n.p., 1917).
Counts, George S. *The Selective Character of American Secondary Education* (Chicago: University of Chicago Press, 1922).
Course of Studies for Evening Schools (New York: Press of De Leeuw & Oppenheimer, 1895).
Cross, Barbara M., ed. *The Educated Woman in America: Selected Writings of Catherine Beecher, Margaret Fuller, and M. Carey Thomas* (New York: Teachers College Press, 1965).
Davis, Katharine Bement. *Factors in the Sex Life of Twenty-Two Hundred Women* (New York: Harper, 1929).
Department of Education, City of New York, Division of Reference and Research. *The School and the Immigrant* (New York: n.p., 1915).
Deutelbaum, Leopold. *Tender Memories* (Chicago: n.p., 1937).
Dewey, John, and Evelyn Dewey. *Schools of Tomorrow* (New York: Dutton, 1915).
Dushkin, Alexander M. *Jewish Education in New York City* (New York: The Bureau of Jewish Education of New York, 1918).
Dushkin, Alexander M. *Living Bridges: Memoirs of an Educator* (Jerusalem: Keter Publishing House, 1975).
Edelman, Fannie. *The Mirror of Life: The Old Country and the New.* Trans. Samuel Posner (New York: Exposition Press, 1961).

Eliot, Charles W. *A Late Harvest: Miscellaneous Papers Written between Eighty and Ninety* (1924; reprint, Freeport, N.Y.: Books for Libraries Press, 1971).

Eytinge, Rose. *The Memories of Rose Eytinge: Being Recollections of Observations of Men, Women, and Events during Half a Century* (New York: Prentice Hall, 1905).

Ferber, Edna. *A Peculiar Treasure* (New York: Doubleday, Doran & Company, 1939).

Fifty Years Work of the Hebrew Educational Society of Philadelphia, 1848–1898 (Philadelphia: Hebrew Education Society, 1899).

Finney, Ross L. *The American Public School: A Genetic Study of Principles, Practices, and Present Problems* (New York: Macmillan, 1921).

Ford, Gertrude. *81 Sheriff Street* (New York: Frederick Fell Publishers, 1981).

Gamoran, Emanuel. *Changing Conceptions in Jewish Education* (New York: Macmillan, 1925).

Gamoran, Mamie G. "The Story of Samson Benderly." N.d. SC-854, AJA.

Gartner, Lloyd P., ed. *Jewish Education in the United States: A Documentary History* (New York: Teachers College Press, 1969).

Gezari, Temima. "The Role of Art in My Life and in Jewish Education." *Jewish Education* 51 (Fall 1983): 31–36.

Gillette, John M. *Vocational Education* (New York: American Book Company, 1910).

Goldstein, Bert. *A Pioneer Woman: The Memoirs of Bert Goldstein* (Jerusalem: Gefen Publishing House, 1992).

Goodsell, Willystine. *The Education of Women: Its Social Background and Its Problems* (New York: Macmillan, 1923).

Grattan, C. Hartley, ed. *American Ideas about Adult Education, 1710–1951* (New York: Teachers College Press, 1959).

Greenstone, Julius H. "Jewish Education in the United States." In *The American Jewish Year Book 5676/1914–1915* (Philadelphia: Jewish Publication Society of America, 1914), 90–127.

Hapgood, Hutchins. *The Spirit of the Ghetto*. Ed. Moses Rischin (Cambridge, Mass.: Belknap Press, 1967).

Hart, Sara Liebenstein. *The Pleasure Is Mine: An Autobiography* (Chicago: Valentine-Newman, 1947).

Hartman, May. *I Gave My Heart* (New York: Citadel Press, 1960).

Hartman, Pamela A. *A History of the Western High School in Seven Decades, 1844–1913* (Baltimore: Fleet-McGinley Company, 1915).

Henry, Henry A. *A Class Book for Jewish Youth of Both Sexes* (n.p., 1850s?).

Herick, Cheesman A., et al. *The Sixth Yearbook of the National Society for the Scientific Study of Education. Part I: Vocational Studies for College Entrance* (Chicago: University of Chicago Press, 1907).

Herschler, Uri D., ed. *The East European Jewish Experience in America: A Century of Memories, 1882–1982* (Cincinnati: American Jewish Archives, 1982).

Hirschowitz, Abraham E., comp. *Yohale Sarah: Containing Religious Duties of the Daughters of Israel and Moral Helps*. 2nd ed. (New York: n.p., 1912).

The History of the Young Women's Union of Philadelphia, 1885–1910 (n.p., 1910).

Horwich, Bernard. *My First Eighty Years* (Chicago: Angus Books, 1939).

Howe, Julia Ward, ed. *Sex and Education: A Reply to Dr. E. H. Clarke's "Sex in Education"* (Boston: Roberts Brothers, 1874).

Hühner, Leon. *The Jewish Woman in America: An Address Delivered before the Council of Jewish Women* (n.p., 1905).

Hurst, Fannie. *Anatomy of Me: A Wanderer in Search of Herself* (Garden City, N.Y.: Doubleday, 1958).

Hurwitz, Solomon T. H. "The Jewish Parochial School." *The Jewish Teacher* 1 (December 1917): 211–215.

Jastrow, Marie. *Looking Back: The American Dream through Immigrant Eyes* (New York: W. W. Norton, 1986).

Jewish International Conference on the Suppression of the Traffic in Girls and Women, 1910, London, Official Report (London: Wertheimer, Lea & Co., 1910).

Joseph, Samuel K., ed. and trans. Israel Konovitz. "Jewish Education in America at the Beginning of the Twentieth Century." *Jewish Education* 51 (Fall 1983): 3–15.

Kaplan, Mordecai, and Bernard Cronson, "First Community Survey of Jewish Education in New York City, 1909." Reprinted in *Jewish Education* 20 (Summer 1949): 113–116.

Kelly, Myra. *Little Citizens: The Humours of School Life* (New York: Mcclure, Phillips & Co., 1904).

Kimball, Gussie. *Gitele* (New York: Vantage Press, 1960).

Kingsley, Clarence D. "Reasons for Broadening the Basis of College Entrance." In *Eighteenth Annual Report of the Schoolmasters' Association of New York and Vicinity* (n.p.: 1910–1911).

Kohler, Kaufman. *Guide for Instruction in Judaism: A Manual for Schools and Homes.* 2nd ed. (New York: Philip Cowen, 1899).

Kohut, Rebekah. *More Yesterdays: An Autobiography* (New York: Bloch, 1950).

Kohut, Rebekah. *My Portion: An Autobiography* (New York: Thomas Seltzer, 1925).

Kriesberg, Bessie. *Hard Soil, Tough Roots: An Immigrant Woman's Story* (Jericho, N.Y.: Exposition Press, 1973).

Krug, Edward A., ed. *Charles W. Eliot and Popular Education* (New York: Teachers College Press, 1961).

Lang, Lucy Robins. *Tomorrow Is Beautiful* (New York: Macmillan, 1948).

Laselle, Mary A., and Katherine E. Wiley. *Vocations for Girls* (Boston: Houghton Mifflin, 1913).

Lazaron, Morris S. *Religious Services for Jewish Youth* (Baltimore: Meyer & Thalheimer, 1927).

Lazerson, Marvin, and W. Norton Grubb, eds. *American Education and Vocationalism: A Documentary History, 1870–1970* (New York: Teachers College Press, 1974).

Leaphart, Susan, ed. "Montana Episodes: Frieda and Belle Fligelman: A Frontier-City Girlhood in the 1890s." *Montana: The Magazine of Western History* 32 (Summer 1982): 85–92.

Leavitt, F. M., et al. *The Eleventh Yearbook of the National Society for the Study of Education. Part I: Industrial Education: Typical Experiments Described and Interpreted* (Bloomington, Ind.: Public School Publishing Company, 1912).

Lerner, Tillie. *In Retrospect* (New York: Vantage Press, 1982).

Levy, Harriet Lane. *920 O'Farrell Street* (Garden City, N.Y.: Doubleday, 1947).

Lindheim, Irma Levy. *Parallel Quest: A Search of a Person and a People* (New York: Thomas Yoseloff, 1962).

Litman, Simon. *Ray Frank Litman: A Memoir* (New York: American Jewish Historical Society, 1957).

London, Hannah. *A Girl from Boston* (Cambridge, Mass.: Schenkman Publishing, 1980).

Mannes, Marya. *Out of My Time* (Garden City, N.Y.: Doubleday, 1971).

Marcus, Jacob Rader, ed. *The American Jewish Woman: A Documentary History* (New York and Cincinnati: Ktav Publishing House and American Jewish Archives, 1981).

Marcus, Jacob Rader, ed. *Memoirs of American Jews, 1775–1875.* Vol. 3 (Philadelphia: Jewish Publication Society, 1956).

Marvin, Cloyd Heck. *Commercial Education in Secondary Schools* (New York: Holt, 1922).

Mayer, M., trans. *Hours of Devotion: A Book of Prayers and Meditations for the Daughters of Israel.* 5th ed. (New York: Lewine & Rosenbaum, 1886).

Meckler, Brenda Weisberg. *Papa Was a Farmer* (Chapel Hill: Algonquin Books, 1988).

Meites, Hyman L. *History of the Jews of Chicago* (Chicago: Jewish Historical Society of Illinois, 1924).

Metzker, Isaac, ed. *A Bintel Brief: Sixty Years of Letters from the Lower East Side to the Jewish Daily Forward* (New York: Schocken Books, 1971).

Meyer, Annie Nathan. *It's Been Fun: An Autobiography* (New York: Henry Schuman, 1951).

Meyer, Annie Nathan, ed. *Woman's Work in America* (New York: Henry Holt and Company, 1891).

Milner, Lucille. *Education of an American Liberal* (New York: Horizon Press, 1954).

Morris, Ida Tucker, comp. *History and Records of the Class of 1885, Chicago, West Division High School* (Chicago: David Oliphant, 1895).

Morton, Leah [Elisabeth Stern]. *I Am a Woman—and a Jew* (New York: J. H. Sears & Co., 1926).

Nathan, Maud. *Once upon a Time and Today* (New York: G. P. Putnam's Sons, 1933).

Nevelson, Louise. *Dawns + Dusks: Taped Conversations with Diana MacKown* (New York: Charles Scribner's Sons, 1976).

Orton, James, ed. *The Liberal Education of Women: The Demand and the Method: Current Thoughts in America and England* (New York: A. S. Barnes & Company, 1873).

Papers of the Jewish Women's Congress, Held at Chicago, September 4, 5, 6, and 7, 1893 (Philadelphia: JPS, 1894).

Park, Robert E. *The Immigrant Press and Its Control* (New York: Harper & Brothers, 1922).

Pesotta, Rose. *Days of Our Lives* (Boston: Excelsior, 1958).

Picon, Molly, with Jean Bergantini Grillo. *Molly! An Autobiography* (New York: Simon & Schuster, 1980).

Polacheck, Hilda Satt. *I Came a Stranger: The Story of a Hull House Girl* (Urbana: University of Illinois Press, 1989).

Proceedings of the Council of Jewish Women, Fifth Triennial Convention, Cincinnati, Ohio, December the First to the Eighth, 1908.

Proceedings of the Fifth Biennial Session of the National Conference of Jewish Charities, Richmond, 1908 (Baltimore: Kohn and Pollock, 1909).

Proceedings of the First Convention of the National Council of Jewish Women, Held at New York, Nov. 15, 16, 17, 18, and 19, 1896 (Philadelphia: Jewish Publication Society, 1897).

Proceedings of the National Conference of Jewish Social Service at Denver, Colorado, June 7–10, 1925.

Proceedings of the Seventh National Conference of Jewish Charities at Cleveland, Ohio, June 9–12, 1912.

Proceedings of the Sixth National Conference of Jewish Charities at St. Louis, Missouri, 1910 (Baltimore: Kohn & Pollock, 1910).

Proceedings of the Sixth Triennial Convention of the Council of Jewish Women, Philadelphia, Pennsylvania, December 11 to 19, 1911.

"Professional Tendencies among Jewish Students in Colleges, Universities, and Professional Schools." In *The American Jewish Year Book* 5681/1920–1921 (Philadelphia: Jewish Publication Society of America, 1920), 383–393.

Purmell, Bluma Bayuk Rappoport, and Felice Lewis Rovner. *A Farmer's Daughter* (Los Angeles: Hayvenhurst, 1981).

Raphall, M. J., comp. and trans. *Ruchamah: Devotional Exercises for the Daughters of Israel* (New York: L. Joachimssen, 1852).

Report of the Sisterhood of the Spanish and Portuguese Synagogue in the City of New York from November First, Nineteen Hundred and Nine to November First, Nineteen Hundred and Ten (New York: n.p., 1910).

Riis, Jacob. *How the Other Half Lives: Studies among the Tenements of New York* (New York: Charles Scribner's Sons, 1890).

Rikoon, J. Sanford, ed. *Rachel Calof's Story: Jewish Homesteader on the Northern Plains* (Bloomington: Indiana University Press, 1995).

Rosenbaum, Jonathan, and Patricia O'Connor-Segerjeds. *Our Story: Recollections of Omaha's Early Jewish Community, 1885–1925* (Omaha: National Council of Jewish Women, 1981).

Ruskay, Esther Jane. *Necessity of a Jewish Home Background for Jewish Sunday-School Children* (New York: Philip Cowen, 1896).

Ruskay, Sophie. *Horsecars and Cobblestones* (New York: A. S. Barnes, 1948).

Schneiderman, Rose, with Lucy Goldthwaite. *All for One* (New York: P. S. Eriksson, 1967).

Seasongood, Emily. "Childhood Home in Cincinnati." In Jacob Rader Marcus, ed., *Memoirs of American Jews, 1775–1865*. Vol. 3 (Philadelphia: Jewish Publication Society, 1955).

Selavan, Ida Cohen, ed. *My Voice Was Heard* (New York: Ktav Publishing and National Council of Jewish Women, Pittsburgh Section, 1981).

Shoenbrun, Emanuel. *Jewish House Teacher for Men, Women, and Children* (New York: A. H. Rosenberg, 1909).

Simon, Abram. *The Principle of Jewish Education in the Past: Two Essays* (Washington, D.C.: n.p., 1909).

Simon, Kate. *Bronx Primitive: Portraits in a Childhood* (New York: Penguin, 1982).

Simon, Kate. *A Wider World: Portraits in an Adolescence* (New York: Harper & Row, 1986).

Siskin, Edgar E. *Martha W. Newman, 1876–1980: A Tribute* (Chicago: n.p., 1981)

Solomon, Hannah Greenebaum. *Fabric of My Life: The Autobiography of Hannah G. Solomon* (New York: Bloch, 1946).

Solomon, Hannah Greenebaum. *A Sheaf of Leaves* (Chicago: privately printed, 1911).

Spewack, Bella. *Streets: A Memoir of the Lower East Side* (New York: Feminist Press, 1995).

Steinfeld, Dorothy Peck. *My Mother's Daughter: A Memoir* (New York: Bloch, 1990).

Stokes, Rose Pastor. *"I Belong to the Working Class": The Unfinished Autobiography of Rose*

Pastor Stokes. Ed. Herbert Shapiro and David L. Sterling (Athens: University of Georgia Press, 1992).
Stone, Goldie. *My Caravan of Years: An Autobiography* (New York: Bloch, 1946).
Strogoff, Lottie P. *The Other America: A Story of Life in Vermont at the Turn of the Century* (Mount Vernon, N.Y.: Dvora Press, 1970).
Sulzberger, Iphigene Ochs. *Iphigene: Memoirs of Iphigene Ochs Sulzberger of the New York Times Family* (New York: Dodd, Mead, & Company, 1981).
Tucker, Sophie. *Some of These Days: The Autobiography of Sophie Tucker* (Garden City, N.Y.: Doubleday, Doran & Company, 1945).
Unterman, Isaac. *Jewish Youth in America* (Philadelphia: Federal Press, 1941).
Wanger, Ruth. *What Girls Can Do* (New York: Henry Holt and Company, 1926).
Warburg, Frieda Schiff. *Reminiscences of a Long Life* (New York: privately printed, 1956).
Weaver, Eli W. *Profitable Vocations for Girls* (New York: A. S. Barnes, 1915).
Wise, James Waterman. *Legend of Louise: The Life Story of Mrs. Stephen Wise* (New York: Jewish Opinion Publishing Corporation, 1949).
Woolman, Mary. "Trade Schools and Culture." *Educational Review* 37 (February 1909): 183–187.
Yezierska, Anzia. *Hungry Hearts* (Boston: Houghton Mifflin, 1920).
Yezierska, Anzia. *Red Ribbon on a White Horse* (New York: Charles Scribner's Sons, 1950).
Zeublin, Charles. "The Chicago Ghetto." In *Hull-House Maps and Papers: A Presentation of Nationalities and Wages in a Congested District of Chicago* (New York: Thomas Y. Crowell & Co., 1895), 91–114.

SECONDARY SOURCES

Abrams, Jeanne. "*Unsere Leit* ("Our People"): Anna Hillkowitz and the Development of the East European Jewish Woman Professional in the United States." *American Jewish Archives* 37 (November 1985): 275–290.
Alexander, Ruth M. "'The Only Thing I Wanted Was Freedom': Wayward Girls in New York, 1900–1930." In Elliott West and Paula Petrik, eds., *Small Worlds: Children and Adolescents in America, 1850–1950* (Lawrence: University Press of Kansas, 1992).
Altschuler, Glenn C. *Better Than Second Best: Love and Work in the Life of Helen Magill* (Urbana: University of Illinois Press, 1990).
Angus, David L., and Jeffrey E. Mirel. *The Failed Promise of the American High School, 1890–1995* (New York: Teachers College Press, 1999).
Antler, Joyce. "After College, What? New Graduates and the Family Claim." *American Quarterly* 32 (Fall 1980): 409–434.
Antler, Joyce. *The Journey Home: Jewish Women and the American Century* (New York: The Free Press, 1997).
Ashton, Dianne. "Crossing Boundaries: The Career of Mary M. Cohen." *American Jewish History* 83 (June 1995): 153–176.
Ashton, Dianne. *Rebecca Gratz: Women and Judaism in Antebellum America* (Detroit: Wayne State University Press, 1997).
Ashton, Dianne. "'Souls Have No Sex': Philadelphia Jewish Women and the American Challenge." In Murray Friedman, ed., *When Philadelphia Was the Capital of Jewish America* (Philadelphia: Balch Institute Press, 1993).
Austin, Joe, and Michael Nevin Willard, eds. *Generations of Youth: Youth Cultures and History in Twentieth-Century America* (New York: New York University Press, 1998).
Baader, Maria. "From the 'Priestess of the Home' to 'The Rabbi's Brilliant Daughter': Womanhood, Germanness, and *Bildung* in the *Deborah* and the *(American) Israelite*, 1855–1900." Unpublished paper, 1994, SC-14308, AJA.
Bailey, Beth L. *From Front Porch to Back Seat: Courtship in Twentieth-Century America* (Baltimore: Johns Hopkins University Press, 1988).
Bakan, David. "Adolescence in America: From Ideal to Social Fact." In Robert E. Grinder, ed., *Studies in Adolescence: A Book of Readings in Adolescent Development.* 3rd ed. (New York: Macmillan, 1975).
Balin, Carole B. "Unraveling an American-Jewish Synthesis: Rose Sonneschein's *The American Jewess*, 1895–1899." Unpublished paper, 1986, SC-11771, AJA.

Baltzel, E. Digby, Allen Glicksman, and Jacquelyn Litt. "The Jewish Communities of Philadelphia and Boston: A Tale of Two Cities." In Murray Friedman, ed., *Jewish Life in Philadelphia, 1840–1930* (Philadelphia: ISHI Publications, 1983).

Bannan, Helen M. "Warrior Women: Immigrant Mothers in the Works of Their Daughters." *Women's Studies* 6 (1979): 165–177.

Baskin, Eliot J. "The Image of Women in the *Sabbath Visitor.*" Unpublished paper, 1983, SC-763, AJA.

Baum, Charlotte. "What Made Yetta Work? The Economic Role of Eastern European Jewish Women in the Family." *Response* 18 (Summer 1973): 32–38.

Baum, Charlotte, Paula Hyman, and Sonia Michel. *The Jewish Woman in America* (New York: Dial Press, 1976).

Bayly, Ellen Marks. "Liberal Education in the Gilded Age: Baltimore and the Creation of the Manual Training School." *Maryland Historical Magazine* 74 (September 1979): 238–252.

Beifeld, Martin P. "A Study of the *American Jewess.*" Unpublished paper, 1972, SC-13210, AJA.

Bellow, Adam. *The Educational Alliance: A Centennial Celebration* (New York: Educational Alliance, 1990).

Berlin, Miriam H. "The Education of Women: A Tale of Developing Autonomy and Expanding Choices." *Change* 18 (March/April 1986): 50–53.

Berrol, Selma C. *East Side/East End: Eastern European Jews in London and New York, 1870–1920* (Westport, Conn.: Praeger, 1994).

Berrol, Selma C. "Germans versus Russians: An Update." *American Jewish History* 73 (December 1983): 142–156.

Berrol, Selma C. "Immigrant Children at School, 1880–1940: A Child's Eye View." In Elliott West and Paula Petrik, eds., *Small Worlds: Children and Adolescents in America, 1850–1950* (Lawrence: University Press of Kansas, 1992).

Berrol, Selma C. "Julia Richman and the German Jewish Establishment: Passion, Arrogance, and the Americanization of the *Ostjuden.*" *American Jewish Archives* 38 (November 1986): 137–177.

Berrol, Selma C. *Julia Richman: A Notable Woman* (Philadelphia: Balch Institute Press, 1993).

Berrol, Selma C. "Julia Richman's Work in New York." *American Jewish History* 70 (September 1980): 35–51.

Biklen, Sari Knopp. "The Progressive Education Movement and the Question of Women." *Teachers College Record* 30 (September 1978): 316–335.

Bleiberg, James. "Samson Benderly and Jewish Professionals." Unpublished paper, 1981, SC-1067, AJA.

Blodgett, Harriet. *Centuries of Female Days: Englishwomen's Private Diaries* (New Brunswick, N.J.: Rutgers University Press, 1988).

Bloom, Raymond. "History of Jewish Education in Baltimore during the Nineteenth and Twentieth Centuries." Ph.D. diss., Dropsie University, 1972.

Bodek, Evelyn. "'Making Do': Jewish Women and Philanthropy." In Murray Friedman, ed., *Jewish Life in Philadelphia, 1840–1930* (Philadelphia: ISHI Publications, 1983).

Bodnar, John. *The Transplanted: A History of Immigrants in Urban America* (Bloomington: Indiana University Press, 1985).

Bogen, Hyman. *The Luckiest of Orphans: A History of the Hebrew Orphan Asylum of New York* (Urbana: University of Illinois Press, 1992).

Boris, Eileen. *Home to Work: Motherhood and the Politics of Industrial Homework in the United States* (Cambridge: Cambridge University Press, 1994).

Borish, Linda J. "Athletic Activities of Various Kinds': Physical Health and Sports Programs for American Jewish Women." *Journal of Sport History* 26 (Summer 1999): 240–270.

Borish, Linda J. "'An Interest in Physical Well-Being among the Feminine Membership': Sporting Activities for Women at the Young Men's and Young Women's Hebrew Associations." *American Jewish History* 87 (March 1999): 61–94.

Borish, Linda J. "Jewish American Women, Jewish Organizations, and the Sports, 1880–1940." In Steven A. Riess, ed., *Sports and the American Jew* (Syracuse: Syracuse University Press, 1988).

Bowles, Samuel, and Herbert Gintis. *Schooling in Capitalist America: Educational Reform and the Contradictions of Economic Life* (New York: Basic Books, 1976).

Brandes, Joseph. *Immigrants to Freedom: Jewish Communities in Rural New Jersey since 1882* (Philadelphia: University of Pennsylvania Press, 1971).

Brandimarte, Cynthia Ann. "Fannie Hurst: A Missouri Girl Makes Good." *Missouri Historical Review* 81 (April 1987): 275–295.

Braunstein, Susan L., and Jenna Weissman Joselit. *Getting Comfortable in New York: The American Jewish Home, 1880–1950* (New York: The Jewish Museum, 1990).

Brenzel, Barbara M. "History of 19th Century Women's Education: A Plea for Inclusion of Class, Race, and Ethnicity." Working paper no. 114, Wellesley College Center for Research on Women, 1983.

Brown, Victoria Bissell. "Golden Girls: Female Socialization among the Middle Class of Los Angeles, 1880–1910." In Elliott West and Paula Petrik, eds., *Small Worlds: Children and Adolescents in America, 1850–1950* (Lawrence: University Press of Kansas, 1992).

Brumberg, Joan Jacobs. *The Body Project: An Intimate History of American Girls* (New York: Random House, 1997).

Brumberg, Joan Jacobs. "Chlorotic Girls, 1870–1920: A Historical Perspective on Female Adolescence." *Child Development* 53 (December 1982): 1468–1477.

Brumberg, Joan Jacobs. *Fasting Girls: The History of Anorexia Nervosa* (New York: Plume Books, 1988).

Brumberg, Joan Jacobs. "The 'Me' of Me: Voices of Jewish Girls in Adolescent Diaries of the 1920s and 1950s." In Joyce Antler, ed., *Talking Back: Images of Jewish Women in American Popular Culture* (Hanover, N.H.: Brandeis University Press, 1998).

Brumberg, Joan Jacobs. "'Something Happens to Girls': Menarche and the Emergence of the Modern American Hygienic Imperative." *Journal of the History of Sexuality* 4 (July 1993): 99–127.

Brumberg, Stephan F. *Going to America, Going to School: The Jewish Immigrant Public School Encounter in Turn-of-the-Century America* (New York: Praeger Press, 1986).

Brumberg, Stephan F. "Jewish Higher Education and Efforts to Perpetuate Jewish Continuity in America." *History of Education Quarterly* 29 (Summer 1989): 293–300.

Bullough, William A. *Cities and Schools in the Gilded Age: The Evolution of an Urban Institution* (Port Washington, N.Y.: Kennikat Press, 1974).

Burstein, Janet. "Between Two Worlds: Changing Images of Immigrant Jewish Women." In Joyce Antler, ed., *Talking Back: Images of Jewish Women in American Popular Culture* (Hanover, N.H.: Brandeis University Press, 1998).

Butcher, Patricia Smith. *Education for Equality: Women's Rights Periodicals and Women's Higher Education, 1849–1920* (Westport, Conn.: Greenwood Press, 1989).

Carlson, Robert A. *The Quest for Conformity: Americanization through Education* (New York: John Wiley and Sons, 1975).

Carson, Mina. *Settlement Folk: The Evolution of Social Welfare Ideology in the American Settlement Movement, 1883–1930* (Chicago: University of Chicago Press, 1990).

Carter, Susan B., and Mark Prus. "The Labor Market and the American High School Girl, 1890–1928." *Journal of Economic History* 42 (March 1982): 163–172.

Chernow, Ron. *The Warburgs: The Twentieth-Century Odyssey of a Remarkable Jewish Family* (New York: Random House, 1993).

Clifford, Geraldine J. "Marry, Stitch, Die, or Do Worse: Educating Women for Work." In Harvey Kantor and David B. Tyack, eds., *Work, Youth, and Schooling: Historical Perspectives on Vocationalism in American Education* (Stanford: Stanford University Press, 1982), 223–268.

Cogan, Frances B. *All-American Girl: The Ideal of Real Womanhood in Mid-Nineteenth-Century America* (Athens: University of Georgia Press, 1989).

Cohen, Elizabeth. "On Doing the History of Women's Education." *History of Education Quarterly* 19 (Spring 1979): 151–155.

Cohen, Miriam. "Changing Education Strategies among Immigrant Generations: New York Italians in Comparative Perspective." *Journal of Social History* 15 (Spring 1982): 443–466.

Cohn, Edward L. "*The Sabbath Visitor,* A Child's Paper: A Critique, Description, Evaluation in Light of Modern Techniques of Pedagogy." Unpublished paper, 1961, Box 2270b, AJA.

Conway, Jill Kerr. *When Memory Speaks: Reflections on Autobiography* (New York: Knopf, 1998).

Cornell, Frederic. "A History of the Rand School of Social Science, 1906–1956." Ed.D. diss., Columbia University Teachers College, 1976.

Coser, Rose Laub, Laura S. Anker, and Andrew J. Perrin. *Women of Courage: Jewish and Italian Immigrant Women in New York* (Westport, Conn.: Greenwood Press, 1999).

Cott, Nancy, ed. *History of Women in the United States: Historical Articles on Women's Lives and Activities*. Vol. 12. *Education* (Munich: K. G. Saur, 1993).

Cowan, Neil M., and Ruth Schwartz Cowan. *Our Parents' Lives: The Americanization of Eastern European Jews* (New York: Basic Books, 1989).

Cremin, Lawrence A. *American Education: The Metropolitan Experience, 1876–1980* (New York: Harper & Row, 1988).

Cremin, Lawrence A. *The Genius of American Education* (Pittsburgh: University of Pittsburgh Press, 1965).

Cremin, Lawrence A. *The Transformation of the School: Progressivism in American Education, 1876–1957* (New York: Knopf, 1961).

Crowder, Beth Jersey. "The Lux School: A Little Gem of Education for Women." *California History* 65 (September 1986): 208–212.

Cutler, Irving. *The Jews of Chicago: From Shtetl to Suburb* (Urbana: University of Illinois Press, 1996).

Dash, Joan. *Summoned to Jerusalem: The Life of Henrietta Szold* (New York: Harper & Row, 1979).

Davis, Gayle R. "Women's Frontier Diaries: Writing for Good Reason." *Women's Studies* 14 (1987): 5–14.

DeLuzio, Crista. "'New Girls for Old': Female Adolescence in American Scientific Thought, 1870–1930." Ph.D. diss., Brown University, 1999.

D'Emilio, John, and Estelle Freedman, *Intimate Matters: A History of Sexuality in America* (New York: Harper & Row, 1988).

Demos, John. *Past, Present, and Personal: The Family and Life Course in American History* (New York: Oxford University Press, 1986).

Demos, John, and Virginia Demos. "Adolescence in Historical Perspective." *Journal of Marriage and the Family* 31 (November 1969): 632–638.

Diner, Hasia R. *A Time for Gathering: The Second Migration, 1820–1880* (Baltimore: Johns Hopkins University Press, 1992).

Diner, Hasia R., and Beryl Lieff Benderly. *Her Works Praise Her: A History of Jewish Women in America from Colonial Times to the Present* (New York: Basic Books, 2002).

Dinnerstein, Leonard, Roger L. Nichols, and David M. Reimers. *Natives and Strangers: A Multicultural History of Americans* (New York: Oxford University Press, 1996).

Doyle, Don H. "Rules of Order: Henry Martyn Robert and the Popularization of American Parliamentary Law." *American Quarterly* 32 (Spring 1980): 3–18.

Drucker, Sally Ann. "'It Doesn't Say So in Mother's Prayerbook': Autobiographies in English by Immigrant Jewish Women." *American Jewish History* 74 (Autumn 1989): 55–71.

Ducoff, Bernard. "Seventy Years of Jewish Schooling in New Jersey." *Jewish Education* 51 (Fall 1983): 27–30.

Eidelman, Jay M. "Anna Marks Allen." In Paula E. Hyman and Deborah Dash Moore, eds., *Jewish Women in America: An Historical Encyclopedia* (New York: Routledge, 1997), 35–36.

Eisenberg, Ellen. *Jewish Agricultural Colonies in New Jersey, 1882–1920* (Syracuse: Syracuse University Press, 1995).

Eisenstadt, S. N. "Archetypal Patterns of Youth." In Harvey J. Graff, ed., *Growing Up in America: Historical Experiences* (Detroit: Wayne State University Press, 1987).

Elbert, Sarah. "The Changing Education of American Women." *Current History* 70 (May 1976): 220–223, 233–234.

Elder, Glen H., Jr. "Adolescence in Historical Perspective." In Harvey J. Graff, ed., *Growing Up in America: Historical Experiences* (Detroit: Wayne State University Press, 1987).

Elder, Glen H., Jr., John Modell, and Rosse Parke, eds. *Children in Time and Place: Developmental and Historical Insights* (New York: Cambridge University Press, 1993).

Elwell, Sue Levi. "A Critical Evaluation of *Young Israel: A Monthly Magazine for Young People, 1871–1877*." Unpublished paper, 1984, SC-3190, AJA.

Erenberg, Lewis A. "Everybody's Doin' It: The Pre–World War I Dance Craze, the Castles, and the Modern American Girl." *Feminist Studies* 3 (Fall 1975): 155–170.

Eschbach, Elizabeth Seymour. *The Higher Education of Women in England and America, 1865–1920* (New York: Garland, 1993).

Esslinger, Dean R. "Immigration through the Port of Baltimore." In Mark Stolarik, ed., *Forgotten Doors: The Other Ports of Entry into the United States* (Philadelphia: Balch Institute Press, 1988).

Ewen, Elizabeth. *Immigrant Women in the Land of Dollars: Life and Culture on the Lower East Side, 1890–1925* (New York: Monthly Review Press, 1985).

Faragher, John Mack, and Florence Howe, eds. *Women and Higher Education in American History: Essays from the Mount Holyoke College Sesquicentennial Symposia* (New York: W. W. Norton, 1988).

Fass, Paula S. *The Damned and the Beautiful: American Youth in the 1920s* (New York: Oxford University Press, 1977).

Fass, Paula S. "New Proposals for American Education History." *Journal of Interdisciplinary History* 22 (Winter 1992): 453–464.

Fass, Paula S. *Outside In: Minorities and the Transformation of American Education* (New York: Oxford University Press, 1989).

Fein, Isaac. "Early Jewish Education in Baltimore." Vertical File: Education—Jewish, JMM.

Fineman, Irving. *Woman of Valor: The Life of Henrietta Szold, 1860–1945.* (New York: Simon & Schuster, 1961).

Fitzpatrick, Ellen. *Endless Crusade: Women Social Scientists and Progressive Reform* (New York: Oxford University Press, 1990).

Formanek-Brunell, Miriam. *Made to Play House: Dolls and the Commercialization of American Girlhood, 1830–1930* (New Haven: Yale University Press, 1993).

Fox, Vivian C. "Is Adolescence a Phenomenon of Modern Times?" *Journal of Psychohistory* 5 (Fall 1977): 271–290.

Frankfort, Roberta. *Collegiate Women: Domesticity and Career in Turn-of-the-Century America* (New York: New York University Press, 1977).

Franklin, Penelope. *Private Pages: Diaries of American Women, 1830s–1970s* (New York: Ballantine Books, 1986).

Freedman, Estelle. "Separatism as Strategy: Female Institution Building and American Feminism, 1870–1930." *Feminist Studies* (Fall 1979): 512–529.

Friedman, Murray. "Introduction: The Making of a National Jewish Community." In Murray Friedman, ed., *Jewish Life in Philadelphia, 1840–1930* (Philadelphia: ISHI Publications, 1983).

Friedman, Reena Sigman. "Founders, Teachers, Mothers, and Wards: Women's Roles in American Jewish Orphanages, 1850–1925." *Shofar* 15 (Winter 1997): 21–42.

Friedman, Reena Sigman. *These Are Our Children: Jewish Orphanages in the United States, 1880–1925* (Hanover, N.H.: Brandeis University Press, 1994).

Friedman-Kasaba, Kathie. *Memories of Migration: Gender, Ethnicity, and Work in the Lives of Jewish and Italian Women in New York, 1870–1924* (Albany: SUNY Press, 1996).

Gabaccia, Donna. *From the Other Side: Women, Gender, and Immigrant Life in the United States, 1820–1990* (Bloomington: Indiana University Press, 1994).

Garrison, Dee. "The Tender Technicians: The Feminization of Public Librarianship, 1876–1905." In Mary Hartman and Lois W. Banner, eds., *Clio's Consciousness Raised: New Perspectives on the History of Women* (New York: Harper & Row, 1974).

Gay, Ruth. *Unfinished People: Eastern European Jews Encounter America* (New York: W. W. Norton, 1996).

Gems, Gerald R. "The Rise of Sport at a Jewish Settlement House: The Chicago Hebrew Institute, 1908–1921." In Steven A. Riess, ed., *Sports and the American Jew* (Syracuse: Syracuse University Press, 1998).

Glanz, Rudolf. *The Jewish Woman in America: Two Female Immigrant Generations, 1820–1929.* 2 vols. (New York: Ktav and the National Council of Jewish Women, 1976).

Glenn, Susan A. *Daughters of the Shtetl: Life and Labor in the Immigrant Generation* (Ithaca: Cornell University Press, 1990).

Golab, Caroline. "The Immigrant and the City: Poles, Italians, and Jews in Philadelphia, 1870–1920." In Allen F. Davis and Mark H. Haller, eds., *The Peoples of Philadelphia: A History of Ethnic Groups and Lower-Class Life, 1790–1940* (Philadelphia: Temple University Press, 1973).

Goldin, Claudia. "America's Graduation from High School: The Evolution and Spread of Secondary Schooling in the Twentieth Century." *Journal of Economic History* 58 (June 1998): 345–374.

Goldman, Karla. "The Ambivalence of Reform Judaism: Kaufmann Kohler and the Ideal Jewish Woman." *American Jewish History* 74 (Summer 1990): 477–499.

Goldman, Karla. *Beyond the Synagogue Gallery: Finding a Place for Women in American Judaism* (Cambridge: Harvard University Press, 2000).

Goldstein, Howard. *The Home on Gorham Street and the Voices of Its Children* (Tuscaloosa: University of Alabama Press, 1996).

Goodman, Cary. "(Re)Creating Americans at the Educational Alliance." *Journal of Ethnic Studies* 6 (Winter 1979): 1–28.

Gordon, Lynn D. "Annie Nathan Meyer and Barnard College: Mission and Identity in Women's Higher Education, 1889–1950." *History of Education Quarterly* 26 (Winter 1986): 503–522.

Gordon, Lynn D. "Female Gothic: Writing the History of Women's Colleges." *American Quarterly* 37 (Summer 1985): 299–304.

Gordon, Lynn D. *Gender and Higher Education in the Progressive Era* (New Haven: Yale University Press, 1990).

Gordon, Lynn D. "The Gibson Girl Goes to College: Popular Culture and Women's Higher Education in the Progressive Era." *American Quarterly* 39 (Summer 1987): 211–230.

Goren, Arthur A. "The Jewish Press." In Sally M. Miller, ed., *The Ethnic Press in the United States: A Historical Analysis and Handbook* (New York: Greenwood Press, 1987).

Goren, Arthur A. *New York's Jews and the Quest for Community: The Kehillah Experiment, 1908–1922* (New York: Columbia University Press, 1970).

Gould, Joseph Edward. *The Chautauqua Movement* (New York: SUNY Press, 1961).

Graebner, William. "Outlawing Teenage Populism: The Campaign against Secret Societies in the American High School, 1900–1960." *Journal of American History* 74 (September 1987): 411–435.

Graff, Harvey J. *Conflicting Paths: Growing Up in America* (Cambridge: Harvard University Press, 1995).

Graham, Patricia Albjerg. *Community and Class in American Education, 1865–1918* (New York: John Wiley and Sons, 1974).

Graham, Patricia Albjerg. "Expansion and Exclusion: A History of Women in Higher Education." *Signs* 3 (Summer 1978): 759–773.

Graham, Patricia Albjerg. "So Much to Do: Guides for Historical Research on Women in Higher Education." *Teachers College Record* 76 (February 1975): 421–429.

Graves, Karen. *Girls' Schooling during the Progressive Era: From Female Scholar to Domesticated Citizen* (New York: Garland, 1998).

Green, Carol Hurd. "The 'Boy Problem' and the 'Woman Question.'" *American Quarterly* 43 (December 1991): 661–667.

Green, Harvey. *The Light of the Home: An Intimate View of the Lives of Women in Victorian America* (New York: Pantheon, 1983).

Green, Nancy. "Remembering Lucy Flower Tech: Black Students in an All-Girl School." *Chicago History* 14 (Fall 1985): 46–57.

Greene, Victor. "'Becoming American': The Role of Ethnic Leaders—Swedes, Poles, Italians, Jews." In Melvin G. Holli and Peter d'A. Jones, eds., *The Ethnic Frontier: Essays in the History of Group Survival in Chicago and the Midwest* (Grand Rapids, Mich.: William B. Eerdmans, 1977).

Griffin, Gail B. "Emancipated Spirits: Women's Education and the American Midwest." *Change* 16 (January/February 1984): 32–40.

Grinder, Robert E. "The Concept of Adolescence in the Genetic Psychology of G. Stanley Hall." In Robert E. Grinder, ed., *Studies in Adolescence: A Book of Readings in Adolescent Development.* 3rd ed. (New York: Macmillan, 1975).

Gurock, Jeffrey S. *When Harlem Was Jewish, 1870–1930* (New York: Columbia University Press, 1979).

Haller, John S., Jr. "From Maidenhood to Menopause: Sex Education for Women in Victorian America." *Journal of Popular Culture* 6 (Summer 1972): 49–69.

Hanft, Sheldon. "Mordecai's Female Academy." *American Jewish History* 74 (Autumn 1989): 72–93.

Hansot, Elizabeth, and David B. Tyack. "Gender in American Public Schools: Thinking Institutionally." *Signs* 13 (Summer 1988): 741–760.

Harris, Zevi H. "A Study of Trends in Jewish Education for Girls in New York City." Ph.D. diss., Yeshiva University, 1956.

Hartogenesis, Benjamin. "The Russian Night School of Baltimore." *Publications of the American Jewish Historical Society* 31 (1928): 225–228.
Hawes, Joseph. "The Strange History of Female Adolescence in the United States." *Journal of Psychohistory* 13 (1985): 51–63.
Heinze, Andrew R. *Adapting to Abundance: Jewish Immigrants, Mass Consumption, and the Search for American Identity* (New York: Columbia University Press, 1990).
Heneson, Susie L. "The Image of Women in *Young Israel* and *The Sabbath Visitor* during the Years 1876 and 1877." Unpublished paper, 1988, SC-4907, AJA.
Henriksen, Louise Levitas. *Anzia Yezierska: A Writer's Life* (New Brunswick, N.J.: Rutgers University Press, 1988).
Herbst, Jurgen. *The Once and Future School: Three Hundred and Fifty Years of American Secondary Education* (New York: Routledge, 1996).
Herrick, Mary J. *The Chicago Schools: A Social and Political History* (Beverly Hills, Calif.: Sage Publications, 1971).
Hertzberg, Steven. *Strangers within the Gate City: The Jews of Atlanta, 1845–1915* (Philadelphia: Jewish Publication Society, 1978).
Hine, Thomas. *The Rise and Fall of the American Teenager* (New York: Avon Books, 1999).
Hiner, N. Ray, and Joseph M. Hawes, *Growing Up in America: Children in Historical Perspective* (Urbana: University of Illinois Press, 1985).
Hoffman, Lenore, and Margo Culley, eds. *Women's Personal Narratives: Essays in Criticism and Pedagogy* (New York: The Modern Language Association of America, 1985).
Hogan, David John. *Class and Reform: School and Society in Chicago, 1880–1930* (Philadelphia: University of Pennsylvania Press, 1985).
Horowitz, David. "The Activities of a Cultured Cincinnati Jewess: Setty Swartz Kuhn." Unpublished paper, 1967, AJA.
Horowitz, Helen Lefkowitz. "Does Gender Bend the History of Higher Education?" *American Literary History* 7 (Summer 1995): 344–349.
Howe, Irving. *World of Our Fathers* (New York: Harcourt Brace Jovanovich, 1976).
Hunter, Jane H. *How Young Ladies Became Girls: The Victorian Origins of American Girlhood* (New Haven: Yale University Press, 2003).
Hunter, Jane H. "Inscribing the Self in the Heart of the Family: Diaries and Girlhood in Late-Victorian America." *American Quarterly* 44 (March 1992): 51–81.
Hyman, Paula E. "Bat Mitzvah." Entry in Paula E. Hyman and Deborah Dash Moore, eds., *Jewish Women in America: An Historical Encyclopedia* (New York: Routledge, 1997), 126–128.
Hyman, Paula E. "Culture and Gender: Women in the Immigrant Jewish Community." In David Berger, ed., *The Legacy of Jewish Migration: 1881 and Its Impact* (New York: Brooklyn College, 1983).
Hyman, Paula E. "East European Jewish Women in an Age of Transition, 1880–1930." In Judith R. Baskin, ed., *Jewish Women in Historical Perspective*. 2nd ed. (Detroit: Wayne State University Press, 1999).
Hyman, Paula E. *Gender and Assimilation in Modern Jewish History: The Roles and Representation of Women* (Seattle: University of Washington Press, 1995).
Hyman, Paula E. "Gender and the Immigrant Jewish Experience in the United States." In Judith R. Baskin, ed., *Jewish Women in Historical Perspective*. 2nd ed. (Detroit: Wayne State University Press, 1999).
Hyman, Paula E. "The Modern Jewish Family: Image and Reality." In David Kraemer, ed., *The Jewish Family: Metaphor and Memory* (New York: Oxford University Press, 1989), 179–193.
Hyman, Paula E., and Deborah Dash Moore, eds. *Jewish Women in America: An Historical Encyclopedia* (New York: Routledge, 1997).
Inness, Sherrie A., ed. *Delinquents and Debutantes: Twentieth-Century American Girls' Cultures* (New York: New York University Press, 1998).
Inness, Sherrie A. "'It Is Pluck but Is It Sense?' Athletic Student Culture in Progressive Era Girls' College Fiction." *Journal of Popular Culture* 27 (Summer 1993): 99–123.
Joselit, Jenna Weissman. *Aspiring Women: A History of the Jewish Foundation for Education of Women* (New York: Jewish Foundation for Education of Women, 1996).
Joselit, Jenna Weissman. *New York's Jewish Jews: The Orthodox Community in the Interwar Years* (Bloomington: Indiana University Press, 1990).
Joselit, Jenna Weissman. "Saving Souls: The Vocational Training of American Jewish Women,

1880–1930." In Jeffrey S. Gurock and Marc Lee Raphael, eds., *An Inventory of Promises: Essays in American Jewish History in Honor of Moses Rischin* (Brooklyn, N.Y.: Carlson, 1995).

Joselit, Jenna Weissman. "What Happened to New York's 'Jewish Jews'? Moses Rischin's *The Promised City* Revisited." *American Jewish History* 73 (December 1983): 163–172.

Joselit, Jenna Weissman. *The Wonders of America: Reinventing Jewish Culture, 1880–1950* (New York: Hill & Wang, 1994).

Joseph, Norma Baumel. "Jewish Education for Women: Rabbi Moshe Feinstein's Map of America." *American Jewish History* 83 (June 1995): 205–222.

Joseph, Samuel. *History of the Baron de Hirsch Fund: The Americanization of the Jewish Immigrant* (Philadelphia: Jewish Publication Society, 1935).

Kantor, Harvey. "Choosing a Vocation: The Origins and Transformation of Vocational Guidance in California, 1910–1930." *History of Education Quarterly* 26 (Fall 1986): 351–375.

Kantor, Harvey, and David B. Tyack, eds. *Work, Youth, and Schooling: Historical Perspectives on Vocationalism in American Education* (Stanford: Stanford University Press, 1982).

Kaplan, Marion A. *The Making of the Jewish Middle Class: Women, Family, and Identity in Imperial Germany* (New York: Oxford University Press, 1991).

Karp, Abraham J., ed. *Golden Door to America: The Jewish Immigrant Experience* (New York: Viking Press, 1976).

Kellman, Naomi. "Dr. Samson Benderly." *Generations: Magazine of the Jewish Historical Society of Maryland* 4 (December 1983).

Kendall, Elaine. *"Peculiar Institutions": An Informal History of the Seven Sisters Colleges* (New York: G. P. Putnam's Sons, 1975).

Kerber, Linda K. "A Constitutional Right to Be Treated Like American Ladies: Women and the Obligations of Citizenship." In Linda K. Kerber, Alice Kessler-Harris, and Kathryn Kish Sklar, eds., *U.S. History as Women's History: New Feminist Essays* (Chapel Hill: University of North Carolina Press, 1995).

Kessler-Harris, Alice. "Organizing the Unorganizable: Three Jewish Women and Their Union." In Milton Cantor and Bruce Laurie, eds., *Class, Sex, and the Woman Worker* (Westport, Conn: Greenwood Press, 1977), 144–165.

Kessler-Harris, Alice. *Out to Work: A History of Wage-Earning Women in the United States* (New York: Oxford University Press, 1982).

Kessner, Thomas, and Betty Boyd Caroli. "New Immigrant Women at Work: Italians and Jews in New York City, 1880–1905." *Journal of Ethnic Studies* 5 (February 1978): 19–31.

Kett, Joseph F. *Rites of Passage: Adolescence in America, 1790 to the Present* (New York: Basic Books, 1977).

King, Diane. "Jewish Education in Philadelphia." In Murray Friedman, ed., *Jewish Life in Philadelphia, 1840–1930* (Philadelphia: ISHI Publications, 1983).

Klapper, Melissa R. "'A Fair Portion of the World's Knowledge': Jewish Girls Coming of Age, 1860–1920." Ph.D. diss., Rutgers University, 2001.

Klapper, Melissa R. "Jewish Women and Vocational Education in New York City, 1885–1925." *The American Jewish Archives Journal* 53 (2001): 113–146.

Klapper, Melissa R. "'A Long and Broad Education': Jewish Girls and the Problem of Education in America, 1860–1920." *Journal of American Ethnic History* 22 (Fall 2002): 3–31.

Klein, Gerda Weissman. *A Passion for Sharing: The Life of Edith Rosenwald Stein* (Chappaqua, N.Y.: Rossel Books, 1984).

Korelitz, Seth. "'A Magnificent Piece of Work': The Americanization Work of the National Council of Jewish Women." *American Jewish History* 83 (June 1995): 177–203.

Korey, Harold. "The History of Jewish Education in Chicago." Master's thesis, University of Chicago, 1942.

Korn, Bertram Wallace, et al. *75 Years of Continuity and Change: Our Philadelphia Jewish Community in Perspective.* A supplement of the *Jewish Exponent,* March 12, 1976.

Kornbluh, Joyce L., and Mary Frederickson, eds. *Sisterhood and Solidarity: Worker's Education for Women, 1914–1984* (Philadelphia: Temple University Press, 1984).

Kranzler, Gershon. "Pioneers of a Revolution in Jewish Girls' Education." *Jewish Action* 58 (Winter 5758/1997): 56–59.

Krause, Corinne Azen. *Grandmothers, Mothers, and Daughters: Oral Histories of Three Generations of American Ethnic Women* (Boston: Twayne, 1991).

Krause, Corinne Azen. "Urbanization without Breakdown: Italian, Jewish, and Slavic Immigrant Women in Pittsburgh, 1900–1945." *Journal of Urban History* 4 (May 1978): 291–306.

Kronish, Ronald. "John Dewey and Horace M. Kallen on Cultural Pluralism: Their Impact on Jewish Education." *Jewish Social Studies* 44 (Spring 1982): 135–148.
Kronish, Ronald. "John Dewey's Influence on Jewish Educators: The Case of Alexander M. Dushkin." *Teachers College Record* 83 (Spring 1982): 419–433.
Krug, Edward A. *The Shaping of the American High School* (New York: Harper & Row, 1964).
Krug, Mark M. *History of the Yiddish Schools in Chicago* (n.p., n.d.: Asher Library, Spertus Institute of Jewish Studies).
Kulwin, Clifford M. "The American Jewish Woman as Reflected in Leeser's *Occident,* 1843–1869." Unpublished paper, 1980, SC-6511, AJA.
Kutscher, Carol Bosworth. "The Early Years of Hadassah, 1912–1921." Ph.D. diss., Brandeis University, 1976.
Labaree, David F. *The Making of an American High School: The Credentials Market and the Central High School of Philadelphia, 1838–1939* (New Haven: Yale University Press, 1988).
Lancaster, Jane. "'I Could Easily Have Been an Acrobat': Charlotte Perkins Gilman and the Providence Ladies' Sanitary Gymnasium, 1881–1884." *ATQ* 8 (March 1994): 33–52.
Larson, Katherine Clifford. "The Saturday Evening Girls: A Social Experiment in Class Bridging and Cross Cultural Female Dominion Building in Turn-of-the-Century Boston." Master's thesis, Simmons College, 1995.
Lassonde, Stephen. "Learning and Earning: Schooling, Juvenile Employment, and the Early Life Course in Late Nineteenth-Century New Haven." *Journal of Social History* 29 (Summer 1996): 839–870.
Lawrence, Abigail. "The Columbia Religious and Industrial School for Girls: A Collection in the American Jewish Historical Society." Unpublished paper, 1992, AJHS.
Lensink, Judy Nolte. "Expanding the Boundaries of Criticism: The Diary as Female Autobiography." *Women's Studies* 14 (1987): 39–53.
Lerner, Leigh. "The English Message of *The Yiddishe Tageblatt,* 1914–1928." Unpublished paper, 1989, SC-9899, AJA.
Levin, Alexandra Lee. "Henrietta Szold and the Russian Immigrant Night School." *Maryland Historical Magazine* 57 (March 1962): 1–15.
Levin, Alexandra Lee. *The Szolds of Lombard Street: A Baltimore Family, 1859–1909.* (Philadelphia: Jewish Publication Society, 1960).
Libo, Kenneth, and Irving Howe. *We Lived There Too: In Their Own Words and Pictures—Pioneer Jews and the Westward Movement of America, 1630–1930* (New York: St. Martin's Press, 1984).
Litov, Samuel. "The History of Jewish Education in Washington, D.C., 1852–1970." Master's thesis, Dropsie University, 1973.
Loth, David. "The *American Jewess.*" *Midstream* (February 1985): 43–46.
Lowenstein, Steven M. *Frankfurt on the Hudson: The German-Jewish Community of Washington Heights, 1933–1983, Its Structure and Culture* (Detroit: Wayne State University Press, 1989).
Lowenthal, Marvin. *Henrietta Szold: Life and Letters.* (New York: Viking, 1942).
Lystra, Karen. *Searching the Heart: Women, Men, and Romantic Love in Nineteenth-Century America* (New York: Oxford University Press, 1989).
Markowitz, Ruth Jacknow. *My Daughter the Teacher: Jewish Teachers in the New York City Schools* (New Brunswick, N.J.: Rutgers University Press, 1993).
Marks, Patricia. *Bicycles, Bangs, and Bloomers: The New Woman in the Popular Press* (Lexington: University Press of Kentucky, 1990).
Martin, Theodora Penny. *The Sound of Our Own Voices: Women's Study Clubs, 1860–1910* (Boston: Beacon Press, 1987).
Mayer, Susan. "Amelia Greenwald and Regina Kaplan: Jewish Nursing Pioneers." *Southern Jewish History* 1 (1998): 83–108.
Mazur, Edward. "Jewish Chicago: From Diversity to Community." In Melvin G. Holli and Peter d'A. Jones, eds., *The Ethnic Frontier: Essays in the History of Groups Survival in Chicago and the Midwest* (Grand Rapids, Mich.: William B. Eerdmans, 1977).
Mazur, Edward. *Minyans for a Prairie City: The Politics of Chicago Jewry, 1850–1940* (New York: Garland, 1990).
McCandless, Amy Thompson. "Progressivism and the Higher Education of Southern Women." *North Carolina Historical Review* 70 (July 1993): 302–325.

McClymer, John F. "Gender and the 'American Way of Life': Women in the Americanization Movement." *Journal of American Ethnic History* 10 (Spring 1991): 3–20.

McGovern, James R. "The American Woman's Pre–World War I Freedom in Manners and Morals." *Journal of American History* 55 (September 1968): 315–333.

Meyerowitz, Joanne J. *Women Adrift: Independent Wage-Earners in Chicago, 1880–1930* (Chicago: University of Chicago Press, 1988).

Mintz, Alan, ed. *Hebrew in America: Perspectives and Prospects* (Detroit: Wayne State University Press, 1993).

Model, Suzanne W. "Italian and Jewish Intergenerational Mobility: New York, 1910." *Social Science History* 12 (Spring 1988): 31–48.

Modell, John. "Dating Becomes the Way of American Youth." In Leslie Page Moch and Gary D. Stark, eds., *Essays on the Family and Historical Change* (College Station: Texas A&M University Press, 1983).

Modell, John, Frank F. Furstenberg, and Theodore Hershberg. "Social Change and Transitions to Adulthood in Historical Perspective." *Journal of Family History* 1 (1976): 7–33.

Moore, Deborah Dash. "Jewish Ethnicity and Acculturation in the 1920s: Public Education in New York City." *Jewish Journal of Sociology* 18 (December 1976): 96–104.

Nadell, Pamela S. *Women Who Would Be Rabbis: A History of Women's Ordination, 1889–1985* (Boston: Beacon Press, 1998).

Nadell, Pamela S., and Jonathan D. Sarna, eds. *Women and American Judaism: Historical Perspectives* (Hanover, N.H.: Brandeis University Press, 2001).

Nasaw, David. *Children of the City: At Work and at Play* (Garden City, N.Y.: Anchor/Doubleday, 1985).

Nelson, Claudia, and Lynne Vallone, eds. *The Girl's Own: Cultural Histories of the Anglo-American Girl, 1830–1915* (Athens: University of Georgia Press, 1994).

Neu, Irene. "The Jewish Businesswoman in America." *American Jewish Historical Quarterly* 66 (September 1976): 137–154.

Newcomer, Mabel. *A Century of Higher Education for American Women* (New York: Harper & Brothers, 1959).

Odem, Mary E. *Delinquent Daughters: Protecting and Policing Adolescent Female Sexuality in the United States, 1885–1920* (Chapel Hill: University of North Carolina Press, 1995).

Olneck, Michael, and Marvin Lazerson. "The School Achievement of Immigrant Children, 1900–1930." *History of Education Quarterly* 14 (Winter 1974): 453–482.

Otto, Kersten. "The Image of Women in Isaac Mayer Wise's *Die Deborah* between 1855 and 1874." Master's thesis, University of Cincinnati, 1993.

Palladino, Grace. *Teenagers: An American History* (New York: Basic Books, 1996).

Parr, Jordan M. "Chicago Immigrant Jewry as Reflected in the Chicago Foreign Press Survey." Unpublished paper, 1982, SC-9430, AJA.

Peiss, Kathy. *Cheap Amusements: Working Women and Leisure in Turn-of-the-Century New York* (Philadelphia: Temple University Press, 1986).

Perlmann, Joel. *Ethnic Differences: Schooling and Social Structure among the Irish, Italians, Jews, and Blacks in an American City, 1880–1935* (Cambridge: Cambridge University Press, 1988).

Pilch, Judah, ed., *A History of Jewish Education in America* (New York: National Curriculum Research Institute of the American Association for Jewish Education, 1969).

Piola, Erika. "Frances Allen de Ford." In Paula E. Hyman and Deborah Dash Moore, eds., *Jewish Women in America: An Historical Encyclopedia* (New York: Routledge, 1997), 323–324.

Powers, Jane Bernard. *The "Girl Question" in Education: Vocational Education for Young Women in the Progressive Era* (London: The Falmer Press, 1992).

Pratt, Norma Fain. "Transitions in Judaism: The Jewish American Woman through the 1930s." *American Quarterly* 30 (Winter 1978): 681–702.

Prell, Riv-Ellen. "The Dilemma of Women's Equality in the History of Reform Judaism." *Judaism* 30 (Fall 1981): 418–426.

Prell, Riv-Ellen. *Fighting to Become Americans: Jews, Gender, and the Anxiety of Assimilation* (Boston: Beacon Press, 1999).

Rabinovitz, Lauren. *For the Love of Pleasure: Women, Movies, and Culture in Turn-of-the-Century Chicago* (New Brunswick, N.J.: Rutgers University Press, 1998).

Raubinger, Frederick M., et al. *The Development of Secondary Education* (London: Macmillan, 1969).

Ravitch, Diane, and Ronald K. Goodenow, eds. *Educating an Urban People: The New York City Experience* (New York: Teachers College Press, 1981).

Reimer, Joseph. "Passionate Visions in Contest: On the History of Jewish Education in Boston." In Jonathan Sarna and Ellen Smith, eds., *The Jews of Boston: Essays on the Occasion of the Centenary (1895–1995) of the Combined Jewish Philanthropies of Greater Boston* (Boston: Combined Jewish Philanthropies of Boston, 1995).

Reese, William J. *The Origins of the American High School* (New Haven: Yale University Press, 1995).

Reese, William J. "'Partisans of the Proletariat': The Socialist Working Class and the Milwaukee Schools, 1890–1920." *History of Education Quarterly* 21 (Spring 1981): 3–50.

Reese, William J. *Power and the Promise of School Reform: Grassroots Movements during the Progressive Era* (Boston: Routledge & Kegan Paul, 1986).

Riley, Glenda. "Origins of the Argument for Improved Female Education." *History of Education Quarterly* 9 (Winter 1969): 455–470.

Rischin, Moses. *The Promised City: New York's Jews, 1870–1914* (Cambridge: Harvard University Press, 1962).

Roberts, Catherine Elizabeth. "Telling 'Truth Truly': The Startling Self of Adolescent Girls in Nineteenth-Century New England Diaries." Ed.D. diss., Harvard University, 1999.

Rochlin, Harriet, and Fred Rochlin, *Pioneer Jews: A New Life in the Far West* (Boston: Houghton Mifflin, 1984).

Rodgers, Daniel T. "Socializing Middle-Class Children: Institutions, Fables, and Work Values in Nineteenth-Century America." *Journal of Social History* (Spring 1980): 354–367.

Rogow, Faith. *Gone to Another Meeting: The National Council of Jewish Women, 1893–1993* (Tuscaloosa: University of Alabama Press, 1993).

Rose, Elizabeth. "World of Our Mothers: Jewish Immigrant Women, Families, and Social Workers—A Study of the Case Files of the Young Women's Union of Philadelphia." Submitted in partial fulfillment of the requirements for the Bachelor of Arts degree in History in the External Examination Program, December 1986.

Rosen, Evelyn Bodek. *The Philadelphia Fels, 1880–1920: A Social Portrait* (Madison, N.J.: Fairleigh Dickinson University Press, 2000).

Rosenbloom, Joseph R. "Rebecca Gratz and the Jewish Sunday School Movement in Philadelphia." *Publications of the American Jewish Historical Society* 48 (1958): 71–77.

Rosenthal, Susan M. "A Survey of Jewish Education through American Jewish Periodicals." Unpublished paper, 1985, SC-10409, AJA.

Rosenzweig, Linda W. *The Anchor of My Life: Middle-Class American Mothers and Daughters, 1880–1920* (New York: New York University Press, 1993).

Rosenzweig, Linda W. *Another Self: Middle-Class American Women and Their Friends in the Twentieth Century* (New York: New York University Press, 1999).

Rothman, David J. "Documents in Search of a Historian: Toward a History of Children and Youth in America." In Harvey J. Graff, ed., *Growing Up in America: Historical Experiences* (Detroit: Wayne State University Press, 1987).

Rothman, Ellen K. *Hands and Hearts: A History of Courtship in America* (Cambridge: Harvard University Press, 1987).

Rothman, Frances Brasten. *The Haas Sisters of Franklin Street: A Look Back with Love* (Berkeley, Calif.: Judah L. Magnes Museum, 1979).

Rudavsky, David. "Trends in Jewish School Organization and Enrollment in New York City, 1917–1950." *YIVO Annual of Jewish Social Science* 10 (1955): 45–81.

Rury, John L. "Education in the New Women's History." *Educational Studies* 17 (Spring 1986): 1–15.

Rury, John L. *Education and Women's Work: Female Schooling and the Division of Labor in Urban America, 1870–1930* (Albany: SUNY Press, 1991).

Rury, John L. "Vocationalism for Home and Work: Women's Education in the United States, 1880–1930." *History of Education Quarterly* 24 (Spring 1984): 21–44.

Sarna, Jonathan D. "American Jewish Education in Historical Perspective." *Journal of Jewish Education* 64 (Winter/Spring 1998): 8–21.

Sarna, Jonathan D. *A Centennial History of the Jewish Publication Society* (Philadelphia: Jewish Publication Society, 1989).

Sarna, Jonathan D. *A Great Awakening: The Transformation That Shaped Twentieth Century*

American Judaism and Its Implications for Today (Council for Initiatives in Jewish Education, 1995).

Sarna, Jonathan D. "The Making of an American Jewish Culture." In Murray Friedman, ed., *When Philadelphia Was the Capital of Jewish America* (Philadelphia: Balch Institute Press, 1993).

Schloff, Linda Mack. *"And Prairie Dogs Weren't Kosher": Jewish Women in the Upper Midwest since 1855* (St. Paul: Minnesota Historical Society Press, 1996).

Schreier, Barbara A. *Becoming American Women: Clothing and the Jewish Immigrant Experience, 1880–1920* (Chicago: Chicago Historical Society, 1994).

Schwager, Sally. "Educating Women in America." *Signs* 12 (Winter 1987): 333–372.

Schwartz, Shuly Rubin. "'We Married What We Wanted to Be': The *Rebbetzin* in Twentieth Century America." *American Jewish History* 83 (June 1995): 223–246.

Scott, Anne Firor. "What, Then, Is the American: This New Woman." *Journal of American History* 65 (December 1978): 679–703.

Scult, Mel. "Mordecai Kaplan, the Teachers Institute, and the Foundations of Jewish Education in America." *American Jewish Archives* 38 (April 1986): 57–84.

Searles, Patricia, and Janet Mickish. "'A Thoroughbred Girl': Images of Female Gender Role in Turn-of-the-Century Mass Media." *Women's Studies* 10:3 (1984): 261–281.

Seller, Maxine S. "Beyond the Stereotype: A New Look at the Immigrant Woman, 1880–1924." *Journal of Ethnic Studies* 3 (Spring 1975): 59–71.

Seller, Maxine S. "Boundaries, Bridges, and the History of Education." *History of Education Quarterly* 31 (Summer 1991): 195–206.

Seller, Maxine S. "The Education of the Immigrant Woman, 1900–1935." *Journal of Urban History* 4 (May 1978): 307–330.

Seller, Maxine S. "A History of *Women's Education in the United States*: Thomas Woody's Classic—Sixty Years Later." *History of Education Quarterly* 29 (Spring 1989): 95–107.

Seller, Maxine S. "Women Journalists and the Women's Page of the *Jewish Daily Forward*: A Case Study of Informal Education for Immigrant Women." In Joyce Antler and Sari Knopp Biklen, eds., *Changing Education: Women as Radicals and Conservators* (Albany: SUNY Press, 1990).

Shargel, Baila Round. *Lost Love: The Untold Story of Henrietta Szold* (Philadelphia: Jewish Publication Society, 1997).

Sicherman, Barbara. "Reading *Little Women*: The Many Lives of a Text." In Linda K. Kerber, Alice Kessler-Harris, and Kathryn Kish Sklar, eds., *U.S. History as Women's History: New Feminist Essays* (Chapel Hill: University of North Carolina Press, 1995).

Sicherman, Barbara. "Sense and Sensibility: A Case Study of Women's Reading in Late-Victorian America." In Cathy N. Davidson, ed., *Reading in America: Literature and Social History* (Baltimore: Johns Hopkins University Press, 1989).

Silverstein, Alan. *Alternatives to Assimilation: The Response of Reform Judaism to American Culture, 1840–1930* (Hanover, N.H.: Brandeis University Press, 1994).

Simon, Linda. *The Biography of Alice B. Toklas* (Garden City, N.Y.: Doubleday, 1977).

Sinkoff, Nancy B. "Educating for 'Proper' Jewish Womanhood: A Case Study in Domesticity and Vocational Training, 1897–1926." *American Jewish History* 77 (June 1988): 572–600.

Smith, Judith E. *Family Connections: A History of Italian and Jewish Immigrant Lives in Providence, Rhode Island, 1900–1940* (Albany: SUNY Press, 1985).

Smith-Rosenberg, Caroll, and Charles Rosenberg. "The Female Animal: Medical and Biological Views of Woman and Her Role in Nineteenth-Century America." *Journal of American History* 60 (September 1973): 332–356.

Sochen, June. "Jewish Women as Volunteer Activists." *American Jewish History* 70 (September 1980): 23–34.

Soifer, Myra. "American Jewish Education and Culture, as Reflected in *The Reform Advocate* of Chicago, 1897–1920." Unpublished paper, 1976, SC-11682, AJA.

Solomon, Barbara Miller. *In the Company of Educated Women: A History of Women and Higher Education in America* (New Haven: Yale University Press, 1985).

Sorin, Gerald. "Mutual Contempt, Mutual Benefit: The Strained Encounter between German and Eastern European Jews in America, 1880–1920." *American Jewish History* 81 (September 1978): 34–59.

Sorin, Gerald. *A Time for Building: The Third Migration, 1880–1920* (Baltimore: Johns Hopkins University Press, 1992).

Sorin, Gerald. *Tradition Transformed: The Jewish Experience in America* (Baltimore: Johns Hopkins University Press, 1997).

Sorkin, Sidney. *Bridges to an American City: A Guide to Chicago's Landsmanshaften, 1870 to 1990* (New York: Peter Lang, 1993).

Soviv, Aaron. "Attitudes towards Jewish Life and Education as Reflected in Yiddish and Hebrew Literature in America, 1870–1914." Ph.D. diss., Dropsie College for Hebrew and Cognate Learning, 1957.

Spears, Betty. *Leading the Way: Amy Morris Homans and the Beginnings of Professional Education for Women* (Westport, Conn.: Greenwood Press, 1986).

Spring, Joel H. *Education and the Rise of the Corporate State* (Boston: Beacon Press, 1972).

Stafford, Sandra Berkowitz. "In the Interest of Jewish Women: A Rhetorical Analysis of the *American Jewess.*" Master's thesis, Wake Forest University, 1989.

Stahl, Sheryl F. "Trends in the Process of Americanization in the Autobiographical Works of Mary Antin, Rose Cohen, Elizabeth Hasanovitz, and Elisabeth Stern." Unpublished paper, 1987, AJA.

Stambler, Moses. "The Effect of Compulsory Education and Child Labor Laws on High School Attendance in New York City, 1898–1917." *History of Education Quarterly* 8 (Summer 1968): 189–214.

Steinberg, Bonnie, and Melissa Klapper. "Bat Mitzvah." Entry in Miriam Forman-Brunell, ed., *Girlhood in America: An Encyclopedia* (Santa Barbara, Calif.: ABC-CLIO, 2001), 68–70.

Stern, Norton B. "Six Pioneer Women of San Francisco." *Western States Jewish History* 30 (January 1998): 159–168.

Stock, Phyllis. *Better Than Rubies: A History of Women's Education* (New York: Capricorn Books, 1978).

Tabak, Robert. "Orthodox Judaism in Transition." In Murray Friedman, ed., *Jewish Life in Philadelphia, 1840–1930* (Philadelphia: ISHI Publications, 1983).

Tapia, John E. *Circuit Chautauqua: From Rural Education to Popular Entertainment in Early Twentieth-Century America* (Jefferson, N.C.: McFarland & Co., 1997).

Tentler, Leslie Woodcock. *Wage-Earning Women: Industrial Work and Family Life in the United States, 1900–1930* (New York: Oxford University Press, 1979).

Todes, David Uriah. "The History of Jewish Education in Philadelphia, 1782–1873: From the Erection of the First Synagogue to the Closing of Maimonides College." Ph.D. diss., Dropsie College for Hebrew and Cognate Learning, 1952.

Toll, William. *The Making of an Ethnic Middle Class: Portland Jewry over Four Generations* (Albany: SUNY Press, 1982).

Troen, Selwyn K. "The Discovery of the Adolescent by American Educational Reformers, 1900–1920: An Economic Perspective." In Lawrence Stone, ed., *Schooling and Society: Studies in the History of Education* (Baltimore: John Hopkins University Press, 1976).

Troen, Selwyn K. *The Public and the Schools: Shaping the St. Louis System, 1838–1920* (Columbia: University of Missouri Press, 1975).

Tyack, David B. *The One Best System: A History of American Urban Education* (Cambridge: Harvard University Press, 1974).

Tyack, David B., ed. *Turning Points in American Educational History* (Lexington, Mass.: Xerox College Publishing, 1967).

Tyack, David B., and Elizabeth Hansot. *Learning Together: A History of Coeducation in American Schools* (New Haven and New York: Yale University Press and the Russell Sage Foundation, 1990).

Ueda, Reed. *Avenues to Adulthood: The Origins of the High School and Social Mobility in an American Suburb* (Cambridge: Cambridge University Press, 1987).

Ulrich, Laurel Thatcher. *A Midwife's Tale: The Life of Martha Ballard, Based on Her Diary, 1785–1812* (New York: Vintage Books, 1990).

Umansky, Ellen M. "Spiritual Expressions: Jewish Women's Religious Lives in the Twentieth-Century United States." In Judith R. Baskin, ed., *Jewish Women in Historical Perspective.* 2nd ed. (Detroit: Wayne State University Press, 1999).

Vallone, Lynne. *Disciplines of Virtue: Girls' Culture in the Eighteenth and Nineteenth Centuries* (New Haven: Yale University Press, 1995).

Walkowitz, Daniel J. "The Making of a Feminine Professional Identity: Social Workers in the 1920s." *Journal of American History* 95 (October 1990): 1051–1075.

Weatherford, Doris. *Foreign and Female: Immigrant Women in America, 1840–1930* (New York: Facts on File, 1995).

Weinberg, Sydney Stahl. "Jewish Mothers and Immigrant Daughters: Positive and Negative Role Models." *Journal of American Ethnic History* 6 (Spring 1987): 39–55.

Weinberg, Sydney Stahl. "Longing to Learn: The Education of Jewish Immigrant Women in New York City, 1900–1934." *Journal of American Ethnic History* 8 (Spring 1989): 108–126.

Weinberg, Sydney Stahl. *The World of Our Mothers: The Lives of Jewish Immigrant Women* (Chapel Hill: University of North Carolina Press, 1988).

Weiss, Bernard J., ed. *American Education and the European Immigrant: 1840–1940* (Urbana: University of Illinois Press, 1982).

Weiss, Janice. "Educating for Clerical Work: The Nineteenth-Century Private Commercial School." *Journal of Social History* 14 (Spring 1981): 407–424.

Weissler, Chava. *Voices of the Matriarchs: Listening to the Prayers of Early Modern Jewish Women* (Boston: Beacon Press, 1998).

Welter, Barbara. *Dimity Convictions: The American Woman in the Nineteenth Century* (Athens: Ohio University Press, 1976).

Wenger, Beth W. "Jewish Women and Voluntarism: Beyond the Myth of Enablers." *American Jewish History* 74 (Autumn 1989): 16–36.

West, Elliott. *Growing Up in Twentieth-Century America: A History and Reference Guide* (Westport, Conn.: Greenwood Press, 1996).

Whiteman, Maxwell. "The Fiddlers Rejected: Jewish Immigrant Experience in Philadelphia." In Murray Friedman, ed., *Jewish Life in Philadelphia, 1840–1930* (Philadelphia: ISHI Publications, 1983).

Whiteman, Maxwell. "Philadelphia's Jewish Neighborhoods." In Allen F. Davis and Mark H. Haller, eds., *The Peoples of Philadelphia: A History of Ethnic Groups and Lower-Class Life, 1790–1940* (Philadelphia: Temple University Press, 1973).

Winter, Nathan H. *Jewish Education in a Pluralist Society: Samson Benderly and Jewish Education in the United States* (New York: New York University Press, 1966).

Woody, Thomas. *A History of Women's Education in the United States*. Vols. 1 and 2 (1929; reprint, New York: Octagon Books, 1980).

Wraga, William G. *Democracy's High School: The Comprehensive High School and Educational Reform in the United States* (Lanham, Md.: University Press of America, 1994).

Zelizer, Viviana. *Pricing the Priceless Child: The Changing Social Value of Children* (New York: Basic Books, 1985).

Zmora, Nurith. *Orphanages Reconsidered: Child Care Institutions in Progressive Era Baltimore* (Philadelphia: Temple University Press, 1994).

Zolty, Shoshana Pantel. *"And All Your Children Shall Be Learned": Women and the Study of Torah in Jewish Law and History* (Northvale, N.J.: Jason Aronson, 1993).

Zschoche, Sue. "Dr. Clarke Revisited: Science, True Womanhood, and Female Collegiate Education." *History of Education Quarterly* 29 (Winter 1989): 545–569.

Index

About the Author

Melissa R. Klapper is Assistant Professor of History at Rowan University in Glassboro, New Jersey.